THE STRANGE RIDE OF
RUDYARD KIPLING

THE STRANGE RIDE OF
RUDYARD KIPLING

His Life and Works

ANGUS WILSON

Secker & Warburg
London

First published in England 1977 by
Martin Secker & Warburg Limited
14 Carlisle Street, London W1V 6NN

SBN: 436 57516 7

Filmset in "Monophoto" Times 10 on 12 pt and
printed in Great Britain by
Richard Clay (The Chaucer Press), Ltd,
Bungay, Suffolk

For Patrick Woodcock
on whom I rely so much

CONTENTS

LIST OF ILLUSTRATIONS viii
ACNOWLEDGEMENTS xi

1 PARADISE AND THE FALL
    Bombay 1
    Ancestry 7
    Parents 11
    Southsea 17
    After Southsea 35

2 RETURN ON DUTY TO PARADISE
    Kipling's India 59
    Kipling in India, 1882–1889 97
    Kim and the Stories 122

3 VANITY FAIR
    Coming to the Fair 134
    At the Fair 138
    Land Without Hedges 170

4 UNDER-REHEARSED FOR ARMAGEDDON
    A first-class dress parade (The Boer War) 198

5 FOLLY AND MISRULE:
  ENGLAND 1902–1914 232

6 HEALING, HOME AND HISTORY 260

7 ARMAGEDDON AND AFTER
    The Great War 296
    The Post-War Years 318

REFERENCES 344
INDEX 353

LIST OF ILLUSTRATIONS

1 Kipling's parents
2 An example of Lockwood Kipling's work in Bombay
3 Victoria Memorial, Bombay
4 Drawings of Kipling by his Study 5 friend, G. C. Beresford
5 Illustrated letter from Kipling to Mrs Tavenor Perry (Mater)
6 Kipling at United Services College
7 The dining room at Uncle Ned Burne-Jones's house in Fulham Road
8 Comic drawing by Uncle Ned Burne-Jones
9 Rudyard Kipling and his father
10 Rudyard Kipling in Bombay
11 Trix Kipling
12 The Kiplings' house in Lahore, drawn by Lockwood Kipling
13 A prospect of modern Simla
14 On the banks of the Ganges
15 The railway bridge over the Ganges at Benares
16, 17 The two Viceregal Lodges at Simla
18 Boys by the gun, Zam-Zammah, outside the Museum at Lahore
19 Northbank, the Simla house where Kipling stayed
20 Professor and Mrs Hill at Belvedere House, Allahabad
21 Drawings by Rudyard Kipling of Professor and Mrs Hill
22 The Blue Room at Belvedere House
23 Mrs Hill
24 Lurgan's house in Simla
25 The New Gaiety Theatre in the Mall, Simla
26 La Martinière School, Lucknow
27 A name carved on the steps of La Martinière
28, 29 The Mall, Simla, as it is today
30 Chitor, the ruined city of Rajasthan
31 A milestone on the Grand Trunk Road

32 The job printing works of the Pioneer Press at Allahabad
33 Covers of Kipling first editions
34 A Royal Academy version of Mowgli
35 "A Sylvan God" by Arthur Wardle
36 "The Land of Nod" by Charles Sims
37 Caroline Balestier
38 Caroline Balestier before her marriage tö Kipling in 1892
39 Sketches of the three Kipling children by Sir Edward Burne-Jones
40 The three Kipling children in London, 1898
41 Kipling by Shepheard
42 Architect's drawing of Naulakha, the house designed for the Kiplings in 1892
43 Kipling clearing rubbish away from his new well
44 Main Street, Brattleboro, Vermont
45 Kipling's study at Naulakha
46 Kipling in his study at Naulakha
47 Sketches by John Lockwood Kipling made at Lakewood, New Jersey
48 A view of the Strand in the 1890s
49 Nellie Farren
50 Portrait of Rudyard Kipling by Lady Granby
51 An early Cook's poster
52 "Norwegian cock-fighting" on the *Norman Castle*
53 Rudyard Kipling telling one of the *Just So Stories* aboard ship
54 Flying-fish wings taken by Rudyard Kipling
55 Cecil Rhodes leaving Cape Town
56 Dr Jameson in the prison at Pretoria
57 "The Absent-Minded Beggar"
58 The CIVs in the Guildhall on their return from South Africa, 1900
59 The Woolsack: the house at the Cape given to the Kiplings by Cecil Rhodes
60 Eventide, Driefontein, South Africa
61 Kipling with war correspondents at Glovers Island
62 Frontispiece of the printed version of Kipling's speech at Middlesex Hospital, 1908
63 Cartoon of Rudyard Kipling after his last political outburst before the War
64 Ulster Day, September 1912
65 Caricature of Kipling by Max Beerbohm
66 Cartoon in the *Canadian Courier*, 1907
67 Rudyard Kipling in his first motor car, a Locomobile "Steamer"

68   Indian cavalry attacking under fire near Cambrai, November 1917
69   Wounded Indian troops in the Pavilion at Brighton
70   John Kipling in the Irish Guards
71   Kipling with American officers during World War I
72   "Despatches – Is He Mentioned?" by Edgar Bundy
73   "The Avenger" by Frank Dicksee
74   Cartoon in the *Graphic*, 1912
75   Vlamertinghe Military Cemetery, 1918
76   Kipling signing autographs after his installation as Rector of St Andrew's University
77   Mr and Mrs Rudyard Kipling at the wedding of their daughter Elsie to Captain G. Bainbridge
78   Rudyard Kipling in Jamaica in 1930
79   Rudyard Kipling's drawing of Jamaica, 1930
80   Kipling at Vernet-les-Bains, 1911
81   Fairlawne, Tonbridge, 1928, with Victor Cazalet, Hugh Walpole, Elizabeth Russell and Mrs Cazalet
82   Rudyard Kipling at a garden party at Bateman's in 1936
83   Bateman's
84   The desk in Kipling's study at Bateman's
85   Mr and Mrs Rudyard Kipling at Nice

ACKNOWLEDGEMENTS

I acknowledge most gratefully the permission granted to me by the Executors of the Estate of the late Mrs Elsie Bambridge to quote from unpublished sources, and from the same Executors and Macmillan of London and Basingstoke, and Eyre Methuen Ltd, and Doubleday Inc., New York, to quote from published sources. I must thank Mr Michael Horniman of A. P. Watt & Son (agents of the Kipling Estate) for being so helpful.

I am greatly indebted to Charles Carrington. Like every other writer on Kipling, I owe much to his biography. I have also been fortunate enough to have the opportunity of talking to him about Kipling's life, and about his own researches. He has generously made available to me his transcripts of Caroline Kipling's diaries, the entries in which cover the whole of the Kiplings' married life.

To Helen, Lady Hardinge, I am particularly grateful for giving me so much of her time to talking about her close friendship with the Kipling family. Another Kipling friend, Jane Hard (née Stanley) gave me an invaluable picture of the holidays that she and her sister spent as girls at Burwash. She showed me a home-made motion picture which did a great deal to bring to life Kipling and his wife. She has generously allowed me to quote from the unpublished memoirs of her grandmother, Julia Taufflieb, one of the Kiplings' oldest and closest friends. The late Lord Baldwin kindly answered all my questions; I am, of course, like others, in debt to his book, *The Macdonald Sisters*. Sir Ralph Anstruther, Guy Strutt, and Somerset de Chair all talked to me most interestingly about their memories of Kipling. I am indebted to Kipling's goddaughter, Comtesse d'Harcourt, for allowing me to spend a whole day in Kipling's Rottingdean home, The Elms Mr James Craig, whose work on Kipling's father, Lockwood, has added greatly to our information, was generous enough to talk with me about the subject and to allow me to read all his unpublished work.

Acknowledgements

Mr S. W. Alexander answered my queries about Kipling's relations with Beaverbrook most helpfully. Mrs Sutherland, the Curator of Bateman's, made my visits there both rewarding and enjoyable. Elspeth, Countess Baldwin of Bewdley, Mrs Meryl Macdonald Bendle, Miss Betty Macdonald, Lord Montagu of Beaulieu, his archivist, Mr Bartlett, and the Librarian of the National Motor Museum, Mr Georgano, Major Cyril Wilson, Miss Gisela Lebzelter of St Antony's College, Oxford, Dr Rupert Snell of the School of Oriental and African Studies, the Secretary of the Beefsteak Club, and the Librarian of the Athenaeum, all replied most usefully to my enquiries.

Three of my friends gave me most valuable information: Sir Terence Rattigan, Sir Steven Runciman, and Mr Anthony Hobson; my friend Marghanita Laski discussed his poetry with me most illuminatingly and allowed me to listen to her recordings. My colleagues in the History Faculty of the University of East Anglia, Dr Paul Kennedy and Dr Richard Shannon, were most stimulating in discussion about the political aspects of Kipling's life. For information about the Woolsack and Kipling in Capetown I am most grateful to Mrs Philip Garrett. Many people helped me in India and Pakistan: in Bombay, Mr Foy Nissen, and the Deputy Principal of the Jeejeebhoy School of Art; in Allahabad, Mr M. M. Das, Mr Arvind Mehrotra, Mr Alok Rai; in Simla, Mr H. K. Mittoo, the Director of Public Relations of Himachal Pradesh; staff and students of the English Faculty at the University in Simla; in Lucknow, the Bursar of La Martinière School (the original of Kim's school); in Lahore, Dr Shamsul Islam and Mr Mehmud Elahi Rao.

I am, of course, in great debt to the *Kipling Journal* and to its editor, Mr Lancelyn Green, whose book *Kipling and the Children* proved so valuable.

For permission to read and reproduce unpublished material, for answering my questions, and for the helpfulness of the Librarians and their staffs, I must offer my grateful thanks to the following libraries: the Bodleian Library, Oxford; Houghton Library, Harvard University, Cambridge, Mass. (in particular I wish to thank Mr William Bond); Huntington Library, San Marino, California (in particular I wish to thank Mr William Ingoldsby); the Imperial War Museum Library, London; the India Office Library, London; Kipling's library at Bateman's (where Mr R. W. King was so helpful); the Library of Congress, Washington DC (may I thank, in particular, Mr William Matheson); the Library of New College, Oxford (where Mrs Sandra Feneley was very helpful); New York City Public Library

Acknowledgements

(Dr Lola Szladits was most kind and helpful); the Pierpont Morgan Library (where I owe much to the assistance of Mr Herbert Cahoon); Princeton University Library, New Jersey (my particular thanks are due to Mr R. M. Ludwig); Rhodes House Library, Oxford; Texas University Library (may I thank Mr David Farmer of the Humanities Research Center); Toronto Central Library; the Library of the Victoria and Albert Museum. Finally, as usual, I have to say thank you to the staff and my former colleagues of the British Library, Bloomsbury, and the Newspaper Library, Colindale, and the staff of the London Library, for their unfailing courtesy and helpfulness.

I am most grateful to the authors, their executors and publishers for permission to quote from the following: L. S. Amery, *My Political Life* (Hutchinson Publishing Group Ltd); A. W. Baldwin, *The Macdonald Sisters*, and *My Father* (Peter Davies Ltd and George Allen and Unwin Ltd); Lord Birkenhead's speech to the Royal Society of Literature (Royal Society of Literature); J. B. Booth, *The Days We Knew* (Werner Laurie Ltd); Jorge Luis Borges, *Dr Brodie's Report* (Allen Lane and E. P. Dutton & Co. Inc.); Charles Carrington, *Rudyard Kipling* (Macmillan & Co and A. P. Watt and Son); Janet Dunbar, *J. M. Barrie* (Wm. Collins & Co Ltd); L. C. Dunsterville, *Stalky's Reminiscences* (Jonathan Cape Ltd); Mrs A. M. Fleming and W. A. Ramsay, articles in *Chambers Journal* (W. & R. Chambers Ltd); Rupert Grayson, *Voyage Not Completed* (Macmillan & Co. and A. M. Heath & Co.); Rupert Hart-Davis, *Hugh Walpole* (Macmillan & Co); W. D. Howells, *Life in Letters* (Doubleday Inc.); Coulson Kernahan, *Nothing Quite Like Kipling Has Happened Before* (Epworth Press/Methodist Publishing House – the book is out of print); Dennis Kincaid, *British Social Life in India* (G. Routledge and Sons/Routledge Kegan Paul Ltd); Lord Lugard, *The Years of Adventure* (Wm Collins & Co. Ltd); Lady Emily Lutyens, *A Blessed Girl* (Hart-Davis/Granada Publishing Ltd); Florence Macdonald in *The Methodist Times* (*The Methodist Recorder*); John Marlowe, *Milner: Apostle of Empire* (Hamish Hamilton Ltd); Colonel S. M. Moens, *The Story of a Village* (John Beal & Son); Gilbert Murray, *An Unfinished Autobiography* (George Allen and Unwin Ltd and the Oxford University Press); George Seaver, *Francis Younghusband* (John Murray Ltd); quotations from sale catalogues (Sotheby Parke Bernet & Co.); Angela Thirkell, *Three Houses* (Oxford University Press); Frederic van de Water, *Rudyard Kipling's Vermont Feud* (Countryman Press, Taftsville, Vermont, USA); Arthur Waugh, *One Man's Road* (Chapman and Hall Ltd); Evelyn Wrench, *Alfred Lord Milner* (David Higham Associates).

Acknowledgements

I have endeavoured to trace, without success, the copyright owner of Walter Roper-Lawrence's *The India We Served* (1928); the publishers, Messrs Cassell & Co., inform me that their archives were destroyed in the War.

It was kind of Sir Christopher Cockerell to allow me to quote from a letter to *The Times* by his father.

If by some unfortunate mischance I have failed to seek permission and acknowledge where I should have done so, I hope those at loss will accept my apologies.

Much of the post-war literary critical work on Kipling is of a high order. I have seldom cited particular critics, but Kipling scholars will, I think, recognise my familiarity with this work.

Finally I must add that, as always, I owe most to my friend Tony Garrett for good counsel, support, typing from execrable handwriting, and listening to interminable talk of Kipling as he did before to interminable talk of Dickens.

1 PARADISE AND THE FALL

Bombay

> Mother of Cities to me,
> But I was born in her gate,
> Between the palms and the sea
> Where the world and steamers wait
>
> . . . .
>
> Her power is over mine
> And mine I hold at her hands.
>
> "To the City of Bombay", 1894[1]

Rudyard Kipling was a man who, throughout his life, worshipped and respected (a rare combination) children and their imaginings. He took part in children's games, as many witnesses make clear, not, as so many adults do, in order to impose his own shapes, but to follow and to learn as well as to contribute. He would very happily leave adult company to play with children even in his sixties. Perhaps that is not so unusual. Rarer, surely, was his love, as a boy in his teens, of watching the play of babies. It is not surprising, therefore, that the first two or three pages of his underestimated autobiography, *Something of Myself*, in which he invokes his memories of Bombay where he was born on 30 December 1865 and lived until he was six years old, should give us a clue to the elusive magic which lies at the heart of most of his best work.

That magic, I think, came from the incorporation into adult stories and parables of two of the principal shapes which are to be found in the imaginative world of children. The first is that transformation of a small space into a whole world which comes from the intense absorption of a child. The second is the map-making of hazards and delights

1

which converts a child's smallest journey into a wondrous exploration. One or another of these two imaginative charts is present in a considerable number of Kipling's best stories without the reader usually being aware of the source of the enchantment. In the Indian stories the small place turned into a whole world is there as early as his brilliant horror allegory of British rule in the cannibalistic sand pit of "The Strange Ride of Morrowbie Jukes" (written when he was not yet twenty). And it continues to dominate many of the best Indian stories – the lightning-lit picnic place of "False Dawn", the conjured house of Suddhoo from whose tricks no one will escape in the end; the cramped and hidden cowbyre in "Beyond the Pale" which is to change from a theatre of delight into a theatre of terror; the suicide's bungalow room of "Thrown Away"; the doom-laden but idyllic house of that most sheerly beautiful of all Kipling's stories, "Without Benefit of Clergy"; the seedy room in which the archetypal loafer, Jellaludin McIntosh, in "To Be Filed for Reference", is decaying away; the bungalow that sees the horrors of "The End of the Passage"; and that other bungalow where Imray's body lies mouldering in the roof. All these stories, like so much of his early work, have an atmosphere, a sense of place that is far stronger than the events or the people; and that atmosphere, when analysed, proceeds from the making of a small confined area into a total world of play. So powerful was the impression of one sandbank of a great Indian river upon Kipling's imagination that it dominates two of his best stories, first as the scene of Findlayson's dream of the Gods in "The Bridge Builders"; and then as the meeting place of the horrible predators – the crocodile, the jackal and the adjutant stork – in "The Undertakers". The power of many of the *Soldiers Three* stories comes from the sense of the trio's confinement to the Mian Mir barracks and their even more desperate off-duty confinement to aimless shooting on the scruffy scrubland banks of the Ravi. The Parnesius stories of the Roman Legion at the Wall in *Puck of Pook's Hill* gain much of their strength from a similar confinement in space. Surely the two finest of the Mowgli stories have their centres in the ruins of Cold Lairs, either above ground with the hypnotised monkeys or beneath the ruins with the evil old blind cobra of "The King's Ankus". The mill dam and the hive provide the most powerful scenes of his fables. Confined in a lighthouse near Timor, Dowse goes mad with his vision of "streaks" in the Indian ocean. Two men are confined to one small area of hedging for the drama of "The Friendly Brook". From her poky cottage room, Mrs Ashcroft weaves her magic power over the fate of her lover lost yet held, Harry Mockler. There is no more terrible play in a back yard than that of Mary Postgate as she disregards the dying German's cries.

The children's journeys are less usual but perhaps even more powerful. The greatest of all, of course, is Kim's which confines the whole of North India from Lahore down to Benares and from Benares up to the Himalayas to a child's vision, and enlarges that child's vision until the delights and mishaps of his journey make Kim into a man. But Mowgli's world too is strung as much upon journeys – with the Bandar-log through the trees, stampeding Shere Khan with the buffalo, outpacing and outwitting the terrible invading waves of the red dogs – as it is upon the reducing of the whole universe to one place of play – the wolves' cave, playing on the rock with Baloo and Bagheera, or resting within the coils of Kaa, the python. From a well-charted play-place of wood and stream and meadow, Dan and Una make their many journeys back through time, none of which is more impressive than the wonderful eleventh-century Norsemen's voyage to the land of the gorillas in "The Joyous Venture". The best of Kipling's comic tales are also built on journeys charted like children's games – "Brugglesmith" and "The Village that Voted the Earth was Flat". How the mugger-crocodile recalls the delights of his exploration of the Ganges when the Mutiny brought down such a wonderful harvest of drowned bodies is one of the most extraordinary passages in *The Jungle Book*. The child's vision, whether of a world contracted or of a world traversed, lies deep at the heart of Kipling's imagination – and he himself described imagination as a form of imperfect memory. It is hardly surprising that his own adult life often seems torn between the need to put down roots and the need to get out on the trail.

It is exactly such a child's account of himself that he gives us in these first pages of *Something of Myself*: a Bombay of bright colours and strong smells, of the impressions received in walks with his Goan Christian ayah and his Hindu bearer, and, at last, of the compound between his father's house and the Art School where his father taught – seeming so large that "once on the way there alone I passed the edge of a huge ravine a foot deep where a winged monster as big as myself attacked me". But this was childhood, and his father was able to assuage his fears by making up a poem to explain that the monster was only a hen. For Kipling's years in Bombay, unlike the rest of his life, were years of *safe* delight, at any rate in memory.

Kipling knew that not all children, handed over to servants and seen only by their parents on a regular evening visit to the drawing-room, were so happy as he was. This he makes clear in "His Majesty The King", a story of Anglo-Indian childhood. "I don't know," said Mrs Anstell, asked about her little son's happiness. "These things are left to Miss Biddums and, of course, she doesn't ill-treat the child." But, where parents were like Alice and Lockwood Kipling and knew that their own love was needed as well as that of the servants, a little Sahib's life could be very idyllic, however little we may condone the racial and class basis upon which it rested. (I know this from my own experience as a little baas in Durban from the age of seven to eleven years: I have never felt such warm love as I did then from my beloved "Kaffir", George.) Kipling, when writing for his Anglo-Indian readers in *The Pioneer* in December 1885, could take the conventional view of the dangers to English children from native servants in very colourful tones; "in the reeking atmosphere of the servants' huts he soaks in Asiatic vices and meannesses through every pore of his little white skin." [2]

But in his own Bombay childhood he could remember no such perils. It was all bliss. He could go with his Hindu bearer into the temples, for he was "below the age of caste". Below, indeed, the consciousness of caste, class or race – although they had grown instinctive within him as we shall see. But in his conscious mind, it was Paradise. Charles Eliot Norton, the New England scholar, a close friend of Kipling's parents, tells a story of the small child Rudyard at the Bombay hill station, Nassick, walking hand in hand with a native husbandman over a ploughed field, and calling back to his mother in Hindustani, "Goodbye, this is my brother." [3] True or not, the story has the patriarchal, loving tone that would have delighted both Kipling and his father. And this sense of India as the Garden of Eden, before the Fall, never left him, making the Indian peasantry – what most Englishmen thought of as "the Indian people" – his first love, his beloved children for the rest of his life, decades after he had lost all contact with their land, and even in places like Canada where the Indian concern was minimal. His Bombay time, too, made childhood the sacred age from which all growth was a more or less painful lesson of cunning endurance.

An idyll was how he saw it, but that was not how his mother's relations had seen it when she had returned with him to England briefly in 1868 for the birth of her daughter Trix. The little boy of two and a half to whom life with his ayah in Bombay seemed all Heaven, appeared in a different light in his grandparents Macdonald's home in Bewdley. After his two months' stay, his aunt Louie (later Mrs Baldwin) declared herself very fond of him, but nevertheless she wrote, "Rudyard's screaming tempers made Papa so ill, we were thankful to see them on their way. The wretched disturbances one ill-ordered child can make is a lesson for all time to me." [4] The little boy himself was reported to have walked in the streets of the town, crying, "Out of the way, out of the way, there's an angry Ruddy coming." [5] His grandmother Hannah Macdonald wrote, "I cannot think how his poor Mother will bear the voyage to Bombay with . . . that self-willed rebel. I hope his Father will train him better." [6] His gentle uncle Fred wrote, "The little girl is a beauty, but Rudyard, aged three, is already a formidable element in the home." [7]

Even in Paradise itself, at the Sir Jamsetjee Jeejeebhoy School of Art, one of the instructors, a Parsee, Pestonjee Bomonjee (immortalised by name in the story "How the Rhinoceros Got His Skin"), recalled years later that when he had been a student there, the little Rudyard had thrown lumps of clay into the classrooms. [8] And this obverse image is present implicitly in some of Kipling's stories of his little Anglo-Indian boy heroes. Of Tod, the small boy whose familiarity with the realities of Indian peasant life through his intimacy with the servants brings about a vital amendment in a new law about land tenure, Kipling tells us, "it never entered his head that any living human being could disobey his orders." [9] Adam Strickland, in "Father and Sons", admittedly a little Anglo-Indian boy imagined long years after Kipling left India, contemplates suicide because he fears that, having been smacked by his father in front of a woman, his ayah, he has lost caste and suffered fatal dishonour. And it often seems as if, for Kipling, whose adult stoic philosophy centres around acceptance of discipline and meaning found through work, a small child's right to irresponsible happiness remained unquestioned – even Heaven was not good enough for children if they preferred their own homes:

> So through the Void the Children ran homeward
>   merrily hand in hand,
> Looking neither to left nor right where the
>   breathless Heavens stood still.
> And the Guards of the Void resheathed their
>   swords, for they heard the Command:
> "Shall I that have suffered the children to come
>   to me hold them against their will?" [10]

It is the last stage of the elevation of children as sources of imaginative light that had begun when Rousseau and Blake and Wordsworth freed them from the bondage of Original Sin. Yet Kipling's children are, with minor lapses into whimsy, so consistently real, so unselfconsciously revealed to us in their play, that he quite avoids that decadent feeling of self-indulgent empathy with children's ways that so often nauseates in Barrie and A. A. Milne. This is, I think, because he never fell out of love with the small happy boy he had been in India. He never saw a child with an outsider's vision (as he did all the rest of the world), because in the games of that happy child, he instinctively knew, lay the origins of his art, and, therefore, of his own final justification for existence.

Even in old age, he remembered the childish process very exactly, as we can tell from his description of his games: "When my Father sent me a *Robinson Crusoe*," he writes, ". . . I set up in business alone as a trader with savages . . . in a mildewy basement room . . . My apparatus was a coconut shell strung on a red cord, a tin trunk, and a piece of packing case which kept off any other world. . . . If the bit of board fell, I had to begin the magic all over again. I have learned since from children who play much alone that this rule of 'beginning again in a pretended game' is not uncommon. The magic, you see, lies in a ring or fence that you take refuge in." [11] No foster-mother, threatening punishment for naughty boys, could do more than temporarily oust Rudyard from his magic Kingdom, as no policeman could turn Kim away from the gun, Zam-Zammah, where he played at King with his companions, little Chola the Hindu and Abdullah, the Moslem pastry-cook's son. Muhammad Din, the small Indian, played exactly like Ruddy in the narrator's garden in "The Story of Muhammad Din" – "he had half buried the polo ball in dust, and stuck six shrivelled old marigold flowers in a circle round it. Outside the circle was a rude square traced out in bits of red brick alternating with fragments of broken china, the whole bounded by a little bank of dust."

Muhammad Din, however, died like a thousand other Indian children of fever, with the doctor's laconic epitaph, "They have no stamina, these brats." Kim grows up to feel the pull of the Buddhist Wheel, to learn the disciplines of the British Secret Service Game. But we do not feel that he ever learns to answer the question, who is Kim? Nor, I think, did Kipling ever find any satisfactory answer to the question, who is Kipling?, despite all his cleverness and complexity and knowledge of men's crafts, despite all his surface noise and his inner self-disciplined silence. The only thing he knew about himself that gave him identity apart from others was that sometimes, on the large pads of pale blue paper on which he wrote, he could produce, not run-of-the-mill journalism nor even well-made stories and lively verse such as many others could write, but his own special magic, as complete and total in its power over readers as his childhood magic practised within improvised fences of furniture or boxes, or on patches of grass or sand, had been complete in its power over his own childhood self.

6

He called this force, following Plato's account of Socrates, his daemon. It was his one surety of identity. And it is not, therefore, surprising that he so respected and loved children who were his living proof of its existence. Nor is it surprising that a man, who so cultivated and revered this childhood scene, should be exceptional among writers in producing masterpieces for small children like some of *The Just So Stories*, masterpieces for older children like some of the *Jungle Book* stories and of Puck's tales to Dan and Una, and a masterpiece, above all, for adults and older children: *Kim*.

Ancestry

Kipling's immediate ancestry was very distinctive; both his grandfathers were Methodist ministers, and his maternal great-grandfather, James Macdonald, of a Scots family settled in Ulster, had been converted to Methodism by John Wesley himself and had embraced the ministry. Yet the only reference I know of in Kipling's fiction to this Wesleyan heritage is an almost comic one: Aurelian McGoggin, the anti-hero of an early story, "The Conversion of Aurelian McGoggin", is a stiff-necked humanist, a follower of Herbert Spencer, who comes to grief in the Indian Civil Service because, although "he worked brilliantly, . . . he could not accept any order without trying to better it. That was the fault of his creed. It made men too responsible and left too much to their honour." His actual lesson is learnt ironically by one of those morally fitting misfortunes which confirmed Kipling readers tend to call "Stalkyisms", because of the kind of object-lesson practical jokes to which, as we shall see, Kipling and his closest friends M'Turk and Stalky were prone at school. McGoggin aptly succumbs, under the combination of priggish over-work and the terrible heat of the Indian plains, to aphasia which deprives him of any expression of the self he cherishes so much too lovingly. At one point, Kipling tells us of him, "He wanted everyone at the Club to see that they had no souls too, and to help him to eliminate his Creator." And this, it is explained, is due to the fact that "his grandfathers on both sides had been Wesleyan preachers, and the preaching strain came out in his mind". Kipling himself wrote years later to his cousin Florence Macdonald about "Recessional", "Three generations of Wesleyan ministers . . . lie behind me – the pulpit streak will come out." [12]

Kipling's own lifelong agnosticism inclined always towards a reverence for the transcendental. He had a great distaste for the religion of humanity of Comte and the English positivism of Herbert Spencer which so many late Victorians espoused so dogmatically in reaction from their orthodox Christian upbringing. One of his unsigned articles in the *Civil and Military Gazette* of 1884, "On Certain Uncut Pages", professes delight at the unreadable, pompous, self-important quality of the prose of the positivist, Frederic Harison, because it will make the chances of humanity's adopting the shallow religion of humanity very small. Such emphasis upon the individual's value as opposed to the individual's duty will surely, in Kipling's scheme, bring unpleasant retribution from the Gods. Yet if McGoggin is the antithesis of Kipling, there is no doubt that "the preaching strain" came out not only in Kipling's mind but in his writing.

The gospel of work (one of John Wesley's ever-reiterated themes), a hatred of frivolity, earnestness about life's purpose (though never earnestness about oneself, which was a priggish self-importance that life would always punish) – these he inherited from his ancestors. And the language of the Bible in which to clothe them; especially the Psalms, Proverbs, Isaiah, Ecclesiastes – didactic poetry, in fact. This is the superficial inheritance of Kipling from his Wesleyan grandfathers, much of which is likely to stand in the way of the modern reader's easy enjoyment of his prose and verse. But among his deepest complexities is the interweaving of aestheticism and moral purpose. In the last resort, too, Leo the artist in Kipling's parable about life's meaning, "The Children of the Zodiac", and the Girl, his wife, however they hate their artists' mendicant existence, must sing to men, for "whatever does it matter so long as the songs make them [mankind] a little happier . . . whatever came or did not come, the children of men must not be afraid . . . in process of years Leo discovered he could . . . hold [men] listening to him even when the rain fell". The preaching purpose of the art which was the centre of his life Kipling could never quite lay down; this was the final inheritance from his grandfathers.

We know little about the flavour of the Wesleyanism in Kipling's paternal grandfather's home in Skipton where he was to spend a happy holiday when he was sixteen, but when his parents were married at the Anglican church of St Mary Abbots, Kensington, chapel rigidity didn't prevent Lockwood's sisters, the Misses Kipling, from attending. As to the Macdonalds, his mother's family, theirs was a cultivated home, where the music and reading common to so many Victorian households were well above the general standard, where sociability and wit played a large part in life, but in which his great-grandfather's dictates held sway – "never a moment unemployed, or triflingly employed". These were certainly Rudyard's maxims all his life.

Why then did he show so little interest in his ancestry, indeed in the late thirties even firmly but politely dissuade an enthusiast from engaging in genealogical research on his behalf? In part, of course, from his schooldays, and even more from his young manhood in India, he had parted company with the radicalism (however respectable) that clung about much Methodism; more still did he dislike the touch of pacifism in the late Victorian Methodist mind, especially its dismissal of the soldiery as disreputable. As Learoyd, the Yorkshireman of the *Soldiers Three*, says, "There's a vast deal o' fightin' in the Bible, and there's a deal of Methodist i' the army, but to hear chapel folk talk yo'd think that soldierin' were next door an' other side to hangin'." [13] Perhaps there is an echo here of comments by his Yorkshire grandmother and aunts upon the military ethos of Westward Ho, the beloved school from which he came to visit them in Skipton before he left to take up his newspaper work in India.

Yet such talk of their Methodist background as Kipling heard from his parents, who had fallen away from Chapel rigours (like so many late Victorians) not into ostentatious unfaith but into an official but unenthusiastic allegiance to the Church of England, cannot have been without some love and respect. His praise for the American Moravian Brotherhood, those close allies of Wesley himself, is heartfelt in "Brother Squaretoes", "I haven't yet found any better or quieter or more forbearing a people than the Bretheren and Sistern of the Moravian Church in Philadelphia." No, I do not think that the strange fact that Kipling, for whom piety towards the past of mankind, whether historic or pre-historic, and towards his own childhood, was central, should have been so unconcerned with piety towards his own ancestors, is connected with distaste for their religion. There are more powerful reasons deeper in Kipling's philosophy, I think, which would hold him away from digging into family roots. To lay emphasis upon personal heredity would be at once to assert the personal aspect of a man's identity rather than the group heredities of nation, race, caste and place which are man's true strengths and loyalties, and to lessen, by leaning upon genetic determination, a man's reliance upon himself, his absolute accountability for his own actions. It is true that from 1891, when he wrote "The Children of the Zodiac", Kipling does express some anxiety about the inheritance of cancer from his family, an anxiety that was cruelly to torture him when from 1915 he suffered so terribly with undiagnosed abdominal pains; but physical inheritance provides a man with no excuses but to endure. Psychological inheritance leads a man to look into himself and this Kipling wished to evade. As I shall suggest later, it was perhaps his deepest, overriding anxiety.

9

Many of the Macdonald family who have written about his maternal grandmother, Hannah Macdonald – her daughter Edith, her great-granddaughter Angela Thirkell, her great-grandson Lord Baldwin – point to the strain of melancholy, of a sense of unfulfilledness in this talented, loving mother of so many clever sons and daughters. "I wish the lives of my daughters to be fuller, more complete than mine," she wrote.[14] And, indeed, they were. Yet none of her brilliant, lively and beautiful daughters, including Alice, Kipling's mother, seems entirely to have escaped their mother's nervous disposition, although it manifested itself variously in fatigue, psychosomatic illnesses, alternating gaiety and depression, or sudden despairs. And the tension was passed on. Her eldest son, Harry, Rudyard's uncle, whom he met in New York on his first visit to the United States in 1889, had been the most promising member of the family. At King Edward's School, Birmingham, he had been a leading scholar with Burne-Jones who was to remain his friend at Oxford, to which he had gained a scholarship at Corpus Christi College; but he left Oxford without taking a degree. His brother, Fred, who was to reach high office on the Methodist Board, said sadly of him, "the high-strung cord of his endeavour seemed to slacken".[15] He went to make his fortune in New York, but never did so.

To this inherited strain, Angela Thirkell attributes the failure in life of her uncle, Phil, Burne-Jones's son, who she thinks inherited from his mother Georgiana his moods of alternating wit and gloom, malice and repentance. "There was . . ." she says, "coming from her [Lady Burne-Jones's] mother's family, a strain of deep melancholy and self-distrust."[16] Ambrose Poynter, the son of another of the Macdonald sisters, failed to fulfil his promise in a similar way. And Kipling's sister Trix's life went from a youth of exceptional beauty and talent to long years of serious hysteric disorder. To all this Kipling might well have attributed his own black moods, his habitual insomnia, the periodic exhaustions of his vitality, his restlessness. To the fear of it, I suspect, we owe his brilliant pictures of English loafers in India and elsewhere: Jellaludin McIntosh, the drop-out of Lahore, or the terrifying "Thing" that bursts into Epstein's Dive in San Francisco, crying, "I am dying of thirst", whose father is a parson (both notably, like his disappointing uncle, Oxford men).[17]

To the influence of this restless, melancholy strain, we owe surely the perpetual pendulum moving within him from the longing for roots to the longing for escape, for the open road. It is this restlessness that was one of the chief sources of the wonderful, unparalleled *variety* in his writing:

10

For to admire an' for to see,
For to be'old this world so wide –
It never done no good to me,
But I can't drop it if I tried.[18]

With his wife's determined assistance, he did steer clear of the gipsy
road down which he might have travelled, which might have been his
equivalent of the waste of talent that he must have viewed with
sadness in his sister and his cousins; although, despite the brilliance of
many of the stories of his maturity, so much admired by critics in
recent years, there is a price in sheer richness that he surely paid when
he "settled down". It would certainly not have been his way to
speculate upon this unstable inheritance in public. I doubt if he would
have dwelt upon it much in private, partly because he was always wary
of the props that men use as excuses and evasions – and genetic
psychological inheritance is surely one of the chief of these; partly
because he feared what he would find.

Parents

Kipling, then, had no concern for the *idea* of his forefathers. His
acquaintance with any of his grandparents was very limited (indeed,
one grandfather was dead before he was born), too limited to breed
any strong personal love.

For his parents, however, his love, respect and sense of gratitude
was immense. Equally the *idea* of parents in a man's life, in particular
of mothers, as it emerges from his work, is absolutely central. It is
difficult to know how to relate the elevated, almost religious concept
of a mother's place in the life of her son that we find in his stories and
his verse to his own relationship with his mother. Alice Kipling does
not appear to be a woman who would have encouraged such emotion-
alism. She was a devoted and concerned mother – her letters to her
friend and his headmaster, Crom Price, asking firmly why Rudyard's
position in form was so much lower than his position in the school,
show a practical concern in a sphere that would not usually have been
seen as a maternal one in late Victorian times. She has been blamed
for placing her children in the care of strangers at a young age, but, as
we shall see, there are good defences for her action. She has been
universally commended for the close interest she showed in her son's
writings from his schooldays right on to the days of *Kim* (1900).

I think the beneficent effect of his parents' continued influence

11

upon his writing has been overstated; nevertheless, he was lucky to have a mother who cared about writing and cared about his writing, even if her ideas must surely have been inferior to his own genius. But she was an immensely independent woman, with a sharp humour that would not have encouraged any muzzy sentimentalism. She certainly placed her husband's wellbeing and career on a level with her children's, perhaps before them; and, unusually for her time, she was determined to express herself as well. Such a mother is not easily reconciled with the muzzily sentimental idea of motherhood that emerges in such stories as, for example, "A Deal in Cotton", where Agnes Strickland leaves the sickbed of her grown-up son "humming the Magnificat", or of the grown-up hero's mother in "The Brushwood Boy", who "sat down on the bed, and they talked for a long hour, as mother and son should, if there is to be any future for our Empire . . . she kissed him on the mouth, which is not always a mother's property." (He was, as yet, a virgin.) Such over-lush, sentimental passages, along with the equally sentimental poetic references, "Mother O' Mine", and " 'Who'll choose him for a Knight?', 'I', said his mother," are among the uncontrolledly emotional passages in Kipling, things quite different from the carefully controlled appeals to the readers' emotions in, say, the Boer War poems. And in the story "The Knife and the Naked Chalk" (one of the Puck stories) we get a serious allegorical treatment of the basic importance of a man's mother that cannot be smiled away. Here a neolithic pastoral man gains the knife that will protect his tribe's sheep from wolves by giving in return to the Forest People his eye. But the price he pays is, in fact, much greater, for, in his turn, he is treated as a god and must give up the girl he loves. It is his mother who comforts him for his loss. "Whether you live or die, or are made different, I am your Mother." And he comments, "There is only one Mother for the one Son."

There is no direct evidence to connect these pictorial portrayals with Alice Kipling, although Strickland, the Secret Service man who knows all things Indian, does seem to connect with Kipling's idea of his father, Lockwood. Kipling expressed surprise to his cousin, Florence Macdonald, when J. M. Barrie in 1896 published *Margaret Ogilvie*, that a man could make a copy of so sacred a subject as his own mother.[19] Yet despite the fact that Mrs Hauksbee is now known to have been much modelled on a friend, Mrs Burton, the old tradition that Alice Kipling was one of the models seems to me sound, for the character is hers as seen by a son admiring her wit, her kindness and her worldly wisdom, yet not above teasing her a little. How to reconcile this with the other inflated sentimentalities? It is not possible to

12

unravel, but the muddle or mystery does suggest some over-reliant relationship to his mother, if only in his ideal world. To both his parents, I think. I connect it with his dependence upon them at the time of his nervous breakdown in London in 1890–91; and to his father's remark, at that time, that, with all fashionable and literary London at his feet, Rudyard seemed only to want to see his mother.

On his father, Lockwood, the young Kipling made, since fathers are men, more rational, less dehumanising demands. In fiction he has been immortalised in a simple tribute – the kindly, learned curator of the Lahore Museum, who receives the Lama so properly in the first chapter of *Kim*. For the rest, any good, kindly, commonsensical, painstaking and learned figure like the bear, Baloo, in the Mowgli stories may be generally said to represent Lockwood, but may also equally represent Kipling's surrogate father figures – Crom Price, his headmaster, Ned Burne-Jones, his wondrously funny, companionable, beauty-seeing uncle. His love for his father was, with very good reason, intense but not divided between an impossible vision and reality as was his considerable although slightly less love for his mother.

What kind of people were these parents to whom Rudyard Kipling was born in Bombay in December 1865?

Thanks to the research of James Craig in the last few years we have a much clearer picture of Lockwood Kipling. John Kipling (for he did not assume the rather grand use of his mother's surname as his first name until just before he left for India) was born in 1837. Before he was eight he was sent to Woodhouse Grove School near Bradford, a school designed specifically for the sons of Wesleyan ministers – both to suit their meagre stipends and to provide boarding accommodation for boys whose parents were liable to sudden moves on circuit. It was a hard, rough school, with few holidays, teaching was said to be poor, and the tone demoralised. John Kipling was not happy there, though many old boys claimed to have been. The school was intended for boys of eight to fourteen and at fourteen he left. Apart from the difference of distance from his parents, the experience was not so unlike that which Rudyard Kipling was to know when he was boarded out at Southsea at the age of six. Did Lockwood's own experience make it easier or less easy for him to part with his son?

In the year he left school, John Kipling visited the Great Exhibition and, it is said, there resolved to become a craftsman. Certainly, we next find him working at Pinder Bournes, a Wesleyan firm, at Burslem as a designer and modeller, and attending the local art school at Stoke. He then joined a popular architectural sculptor in London – most popular in those days when sculpted ornament of building was at the

13

height of its vogue – as an assistant. It has always been supposed that he worked on the building of the new Museum of Art at South Kensington (our Victoria and Albert Museum), even though his name does not appear on either the Museum's rolls or on those of the Department of Science and Art responsible for its construction, since his figure, bearded and balding already in his early twenties but with his marked gentle and wise look, is one among those included in the terracotta mosaic to be seen at the Museum today.

The picture, as Mr Craig has reconstructed it, is somewhat less exalted but more creditable, in the end, to John Kipling's determination and abilities. It seems almost certain that he was only an assistant responsible for carrying out the actual modelling from the designs of his employer, Godfrey Sykes, who was directly employed in the construction of the Museum. John Kipling's appearance among the others on the mosaic, then, was only a gesture of friendliness to an assistant, not a commemoration by the Museum authorities. In any case the mosaic was executed some years after he had left for Bombay.

What is more important is Mr Craig's suggestion that John (Lockwood) Kipling's connections with the potteries of Staffordshire made him especially useful to the London architect, for he could be employed as a go-between for the manufacturers and the clients. This happily explains the presence, over some time during 1860, in Burslem, of a man who is spoken of as an employee of a London Museum. And it was in Burslem that, in 1860, he met Frederic Macdonald, a twenty-year-old newly appointed Methodist minister and, through him, Alice, Fred Macdonald's elder sister, who was to become his wife and Rudyard's mother.

Alice was then twenty-three, a few weeks older than her future husband. What kind of young woman was she? She was the eldest daughter of a large family of minister's children; all were lively and talented, but she had certainly the greatest reputation for liveliness of them all. She was considered in the family to be "a flirt", had been engaged once or twice, notably to William Allingham, the poet. She was impetuous, witty and sharp-tongued, but George Macdonald had to reprove all his daughters for this fault, though he did so with wit himself. Lord Baldwin tells us that family legend has it that she threw a lock of John Wesley's hair upon the fire (a treasured relic, no doubt, from the days of her grandfather's conversion by the great leader in person), crying, "See, a hair of the dog that bit us!" [20] She played and sang well, as did her sisters; she also composed songs and wrote verses that were well above the average amateur standard. Stories of hers may have been published in magazines even before she married and went to India.

14

It was to be well over four years before they could marry, so that they were both to be close on twenty-eight on their wedding day. It was late, indeed, for a woman in those days. And I think it must have been to this late marriage that Alice referred when she told Miss Plowden she wished that they had met earlier. Certainly her sisters imply in their letters that she was transformed by the sense of being settled at last and to a man whom her parents liked even before they knew of the young people's intentions. The cause of the long engagement, of course, was lack of money. Lockwood as a craftsman mason (however artistic) could hardly have earned much. His father, who died three years before the marriage, was like Alice's father an ill-paid Methodist minister with a large family. It is in the light of the need for a solid job on which to base the risk of marriage that Lockwood's appointment to the Art School in Bombay must be seen.

It has been traditionally implied that the Bombay post which Lockwood secured in 1864 was an important one, and that his influential connections (presumably his future brother-in-law, Burne-Jones) won him the prize. It has also been implied that his supposed position at South Kensington made him a firm candidate for so responsible a position.

All this is probably a part of that genteelising of their past in which most English middle-class people indulge, so ironically diminishing the credit due to them for their determination, abilities and hard work. Lockwood's post at the Jeejeebhoy School of Art in Bombay was not, as it is usually said to be, as principal of a new school. The school was not new, it had been going for over ten years. Lockwood was one of three subordinate teachers appointed to instruct pupils in utilitarian technical crafts – in this case, moulding, the manufacture and design of terracotta pottery and, somewhat lastly, the art of architectural sculpture, for the administrators of the school were very determined that, to be of value to young Indian craftsmen, the teaching must be utilitarian. Far from running the school, Lockwood had perhaps twenty pupils. The pay was poor, but those appointed were told that they could improve their incomes with private work. In fact, Lockwood would, at that date, hardly have been fitted for the wonderful sort of post which legend gave to him. The growth of the legend is sad; it lessens the remarkable achievement of Lockwood and Alice Kipling in building up the distinguished reputation that they held in Lahore when their son Rudyard went out there sixteen years later as a reporter. Their families can hardly have been happy. India was an unknown world to them. They consoled themselves with the vague feeling that the young couple were at least going to Bombay "with its sea breezes" in that otherwise remote, unhealthy sub-continent.[21]

Whatever may have been the doubts with which the family viewed the Indian appointment, the couple themselves appear to have been delighted and eager. Alice's Indian trousseau may have been mocked by her sisters – "a desert hat of the foulest appearance and linen umbrellas . . . The mind of man recoils from the sight, so you see none of her face when it's on and her voice sounds a mile off . . .'[22] – but it is a symbol, I think, of her readiness for new things, her determination, her lively spirits that were to serve her so well in India. They left London in May 1865; in December of that year, Rudyard Kipling was born to them in Bombay.

The financial circumstances in which the small boy lived his first six blissful years cannot have been easy for his parents. Servants, of course, were plentiful, and the grounds of the School in which their small house stood were beautiful enough; there was boating as a recreation. But when, following Rudyard's difficult birth, Alice decided to have her next child in England, there was not enough money for Lockwood to accompany his wife and son. Once again memory lends a rosy hue to this time, for Kipling recalls his mother, returned from a ball, waking him to tell him that the Viceroy had been assassinated. In fact, Lord Mayo was killed when they were in England. And although, no doubt, Alice Kipling did dine out in evening dress, this Proustian picture gives a fairyland touch to his mother's hard-worked life. Lockwood both taught and carried out such private commissions as he could get; he also secured the commission to send in Bombay reports for the important English newspaper, the *Pioneer*, situated far away to the East in Allahabad. Alice had to run the house, try her hand at writing for magazines and local newspapers and, above all, use her exceptional social gifts to assist her husband's advancement. They were laying the foundations of that wide circle of influential people who were to make possible the proper recognition of their talents and industry. It is easy to understand that when Miss Plowden asked some years later why they had left Rudyard and Trix to board in England at so early an age, Alice had given as a primary reason that "she was able to be with John and help him with his work".[23]

Idyllic though his Bombay years with his parents were, and great though his need for his parents no doubt grew to be in the unhappy years when he was away from them, this is less important, I think, certainly to Kipling as a writer, than the years he spent with them in Lahore from 1882 to 1887 when his artistic genius first flowered, the rescue of him for which they were responsible when he collapsed in

1891, and perhaps, also, the support and advice they gave to him as a writer even as late as the first decade of the twentieth century when they were retired at Tisbury in Wiltshire.

This section may finish with a general description of Alice and Lockwood from her brother Frederic's memoirs. He had introduced them to each other in Burslem and knew them again well in their last years. Of his sister Alice he says, "Accuracy of detail was not so much her forte as swift insight, and the kind of vision that is afforded by flashes of lightning," but of Lockwood's ˙intellectual equipment he specially singles out his industry and "detailed knowledge in every branch".[24] Out of this contradiction came a very happy marriage. No doubt Alice's volatile nature with its nervous, hypochondriac under-tow found wonderful support in Lockwood's patient, detailed slower comprehension of life, but he too once said of himself, "I know I look like a holy-holy, but I'm not."[25]

As Mr Lancelyn Green, in his enlightening book *Kipling and the Children*, has emphasised, readers of Kipling's work must remark how this conflict of the qualities of his parents – of quick, impressionistic insight and careful, detailed craftsmanship – makes up the force of his writings.

Southsea

We have now to see Lockwood and Alice Kipling in what a great number of modern readers find a very unsympathetic light. No episode in Kipling's life is probably better known today. To many thousands of the general public because of the brilliant and harrowing television presentation of his story, "Baa, Baa, Black Sheep", which is based on those unhappy years. To academic students because Edmund Wilson's famous essay, "The Kipling that Nobody Read", although now seen as somewhat naively Freudian, was probably the beginning of the critical resuscitation of Kipling's work in academic and intellectual circles; and this essay took these miserable years of childhood as crucial to Kipling's imaginative development.

Before we consider how important the experience was and in exactly what way, the well-known story may be briefly recounted. In December 1871, when Rudyard was nearly six and his sister Trix was a few months over three years, their parents left them in the care of a retired captain of marines, Harry Holloway, and his wife, in a terrace house in Southsea. They had brought the children to England earlier in the year, and they slipped away without explaining to their son (for perhaps their daughter was too young to understand) that they were leaving them for a long time. In fact, it was not until April 1877 that Alice Kipling returned and even then only because she had been warned by her sister Georgiana Burne-Jones that everything was not well with the small boy's eyesight or with his general nervous condition. Nor was it indeed.

Whatever else we may question, there is no doubt at all of the horror of the experience for Rudyard. He made the story "Baa, Baa, Black Sheep" out of it when he was only twenty-three in 1888 and published it in the same year.

It is unique in all his fiction in its closeness to biographical fact or, at any rate, to biographical fact as he still remembered it when he came to write *Something of Myself* at the end of his life – there are very few differences in the fiction and the autobiography. Of course, "Baa, Baa, Black Sheep" was not known to be autobiographical to his readers at the time. Nevertheless, his total reticence about himself and his family in his fiction was broken by the story. The writing of it was extremely painful to him as we know from his friend, Mrs Hill, in whose house in Allahabad he was living when he wrote it.

It was published in *The Week's News*, a supplement of the *Pioneer*, the Indian newspaper he worked for, which was not only read in Europe, but also all over India. The resuscitation of the story, the recapitulation of their son's misery as a topic of the social and club conversation, however the speakers may have regarded it as fiction, must have been very painful to his parents. This is no doubt why, when it was reissued with the other stories of children (all the others laid in India) in the book *Wee Willie Winkie*, Kipling himself, writing in the *Athenaeum*, disparaged it as "not true to life" – yet if it is not the best (I should prefer "The Drums of the Fore and Aft"), it is a very striking story. And belittle it though he may have done, he did reissue it. There was clearly something powerful in the memory of his childhood misery that make him break through the most cherished of his tabus, the privacy of his own life. And so he confirmed when he wrote it again as non-fiction in 1935. So indeed his sister Trix confirmed in her memoirs given to *Chambers's Journal* in 1939 and in a talk on the BBC radio in 1947, even though we may mistrust her memory in old age for exact events of a time when she was so very young. Its compulsive horror made him take his wife to see the house years later, in 1920, after a nostalgic visit to Freshwater in the Isle of Wight, where he had stayed with Caroline and his loved friend, her brother, Wolcott. Perhaps he hoped that she could help him to exorcise the misery. But to no avail. His sister tells us that in 1935 she

18

asked him (surely a little tactlessly) if the terrace house was still standing and that he replied, "I don't know, but if so, I should like to burn it down and plough the place with salt."[26] The hatred comes out in the most oblique ways; for example, in a minor story "Anthony Dawkins", written for the *Pioneer* in 1888, Kipling quite improbably makes the central figure, a vile cockney loafer who drinks and cheats his way through India, born not in London but in Southsea. It is such small references that speak almost more strongly of an abiding horror than conscious denunciation.

What happened in Lorne Lodge, 4 Campbell Road, or Havelock Park as it was called until 1874, Southsea, which Kipling came to call "The House of Desolation", was quite simply that, though Captain Holloway formed quite an affection for the little Kipling, his wife took a violent dislike to what she thought (with some excuse) a very spoiled child and (with a very narrow and conventional understanding) a wilfully backward boy because at six he could not read. She had a son of her own, perhaps six or seven years older than little Rudyard. He appears in both Kipling's and his sister's account as a fiend incarnate – "Dark eyes set near together and black hair plastered with pomatum still make me shudder with dislike," Trix wrote nearly seventy years later.[27] Mrs Holloway probably spoiled her own son; he was certainly a nasty bully. When Aunt Rosa (as the Kipling children were to call her) found Rudyard disobedient to her orders, she punished him severely, with the cane, by shutting him in a locked room, or by sending him to bed – with all the conventional old-fashioned Victorian punishments. And she backed these physical punishments with the threat of a more terrible and lasting punishment for bad boys – Hell, a terrible place of which the little boy had never before heard.

While Captain Holloway was alive, his wife's persecution of the boy was held in check, for he took him for long friendly walks and intervened on his behalf when he thought he was being bullied. But the Captain was not a young man. He had seen service at the Battle of Navarino in the Greek War of Independence in 1827, as a midshipman in the Royal Navy, so that he must have been around seventy. He still suffered from a wound he had received there. In 1874 he died, leaving Rudyard to the tender mercies of his widow and his son.

For the next two and a half years there is no doubt that Kipling suffered greatly. Nor was his unhappiness less because Mrs Holloway, (perhaps longing for a daughter, as Trix shrewdly surmised), treated his sister as though she were her own beloved offspring, although her attempts to divide sister and brother from one another were useless.

Kipling was sent to a local day school, Hope Lodge, which

specialised in passing boys into the Navy, a career which at that time seems to have been intended for him. Here he did not prosper. His general misery and, perhaps, his absorption in reading every miscellaneous piece of fiction or history that he could find in any magazine anywhere now that he had taught himself to read, cannot have helped in his school work. He was never good at figures. He was badly bullied at the school and by young Holloway at home. Faced with taking back bad weekly reports, he suppressed them and lied. When his untruths were discovered, he suffered a punishment like that of David Copperfield at Dr Creakle's School. He was made to wear a placard reading "Liar". (The likeness here to Dickens's invention has made Professor Carrington, who describes the whole Southsea episode splendidly in his biography, add a more recent demur about the probability of this incident, but as I shall explain, I cannot follow him. The whole of Kipling's sufferings as he tells them in fiction and in autobiography seem to me very convincing, but they do need, I think, to be seen in the light of many aspects which were not and perhaps hardly could be clear to Kipling even after he had become a grown man.)

The first question that is always asked today is why did the Kipling parents send away from home children so young and, if they were to do so, why did they board them for payment with a couple known to them only from an advertisement read in the newspaper? The first question arises simply from an ignorance of Anglo-Indian practice. Ostensibly the reason that parents sent their children at an early age back to England was the care of their health, the avoidance of the Indian climate which, particularly given the limitations of nineteenth-century medicine, was perilous, especially in the hot seasons. It was for this reason that Englishwomen had only come out to India in large numbers since the thirties of the century. Even many men, like Kipling's Gadsby, who had sufficient private means, gave up their army commissions or I.C.S. posts to return to England at the request of their wives when children began to arrive. Death, as Kipling's Indian stories were never to cease to remind us, was always round the corner, and children seemed to be the most frequent victims – or was it, one asks, because they were the most tragic? Mrs Kipling, indeed, had just lost her third baby, John, at birth, when the decision to send Rudyard and Trix home was made. Yet we must remember that all her accouchements were difficult, and deaths at birth were, in any case, all too common among the middle classes at home in England in the eighteen-seventies.

In fact it had now become usual for women and their very young children to escape to the hill stations in the heat. When Captain

Holloway explained to the bewildered Kipling children that their parents had left them at Southsea because India was too hot, Trix tells us that they did not believe him, for they remembered being taken up to Nassick, the hill station of Bombay, exactly to escape that terrible ill-famed heat.

The children of English people in the lower echelons of the Anglo-Indian hierarchy stayed there and went to boarding schools like Kim's at Lucknow or up in the hill stations, for example, near Darjeeling. Those children who went there, however, would share their lives with boys of "dubious" social origin and with those Portuguese names that so sprinkle Kipling's stories of half-caste life. To health, then, were added social and racial reasons. Anyone who was anyone would send his children home. Children speaking an Indian tongue more easily than English, or recounting Hindu fables, or mouthing the names of outlandish gods and goddesses, were charming up to, at the most, six years, as, in England, it could be amusing to hear dialect accents or kitchen superstitions from *tiny* children's mouths. But Mrs Strickland begins to worry when little Adam rejects with disgust the Genesis story of creation, for he knows that the world is held up by a turtle ("Son of his Father"). Ayahs, native servants of all kinds were "wonderful with children", but they spoiled them, indulged them too much, especially, given their ideas about women, spoiled the boys too much. Then the standards of all natives were not ours – in matters of truth-telling, of hard work, of hygiene, and (only to be mentioned in intimate club or memsahib gatherings) in sexual life where, as the terrible child marriages showed, they were notoriously precocious. All these prejudices were true, when seen from the English point of view.

The lonely Anglo-Indian child, exiled from his parents to England, goes right back to the eighteen-thirties – see Master Blitherstone, the wretched inmate of Mrs Pipchin's establishment at Brighton in *Dombey and Son*, who is always asking if anyone "could give him any idea of the way back to Bengal". It continued so until our Indian rule came to an end. My second brother was the headmaster of a preparatory school (where I had attended), and I remember in the twenties and early thirties how many of the boys at the school (including some of six or seven years) had to remain at the school all their holidays, when aunts or grandmothers didn't find it "convenient" to have them, or were boarded with the parents of other boys (including my own parents) who were glad of the extra cash, while my brother (the poor headmaster) and my sister-in-law "got away for a week or two at most".

The truth is, I think, that beneath all the ostensible (and sound)

reasons of health and native influences, even of the barely whispered
native sexual precocity, the English remained, throughout their rule in
India, as transient in their final image of themselves, despite all the
home-making of the memsahibs, as they had been in the East India
Company days of "make your lakhs of rupees and come home". It
was to be Kipling's chief difficulty, when later he dreamed of an Anglo-
Saxon Empire, of fitting India, his beloved, into the sisterhood of
Canada, Australia, New Zealand and South Africa. However miserable, however made impotent by retirement to Bognor or Torquay or
Eastbourne, "home" was not just a name for the mother country for
Anglo-Indians, as it continued to be for Australians or New
Zealanders or English South Africans until the Second War; England
was their real home. The earlier, within reason, children were sent
back to England to make sure of their roots, the better. So Rudyard
very reasonably was taken back at six, and Trix (rather less reasonably, surely) at three. At eleven, as we shall see, a school was found
for Rudyard specially designed to train most of its boys to return to
India. It seems an absurd system, but it reflected a time when the
English as a whole were dug into India to stay as long as the mind
could imagine, and yet individual English men and women, although
their families might have served in India for generations, were there
not to settle but to serve their time.

Such was the inexorable reason why children of the Kipling class in
the English hierarchy should be separated from their parents at such
an early age. Nor was this just a snobbish claim to gentility on the part
of a couple like Lockwood and Alice; it was a necessary foundation if
they were to find expression for all their talents and tastes and intellectual powers. Considerable sacrifice must be made, too, to insure this
distinction. The payment to the Holloways must have been a heavy
burden upon Lockwood's meagre salary. This was primarily the
reason why Alice did not return to England to see the children in all
those six years. And we cannot doubt that its emotional cost to the
parents was as great if not as horrible as it was to the children. But
eventually they could claim – and they would be wholly justified – that
the future for their children would be far rosier if Alice could give all
her efforts and great talents to insuring her husband's advancement.
And the prospects for their son through his English education would
be bettered. Yet, ironically, these prospects, which were to make
Rudyard world-famous, came from their Indian connections, not their
English roots.

To the second question – why did the Kipling parents, with so many
near relatives in England, choose strangers (at an expense they could

ill afford) with whom to leave their small children – we have already seen some of the answers. Rudyard's masterful disposition on their visit in 1868 when he was not yet three had not left a good impression on his Macdonald grandparents or on his Aunt Louie or on his Uncle Fred. Alice cannot but have known this feeling on her family's part and surely must have resented it.

When the Kiplings reappeared in 1871 to place the children, Rudyard gave a better impression to the Macdonalds. Even so, the suggestion of Alfred Baldwin, Louie's well-to-do ironmaster husband, was that Trix should live at their house, within range of her grandmother, to be companion to his little son Stanley. And that Rudyard should divide his time between his uncle Fred Macdonald, a very hard-working, rising Methodist minister, and the house of his uncle Burne-Jones. Alfred Baldwin, no doubt, had his wife's poor health in mind in protecting her from the rumbustious Ruddy. However, the Kiplings must surely have felt that it was bad enough to be separated from their two little children, but to separate the two as well would have seemed to break up their little family unit entirely. Indeed, the affection between Kipling and his sister was great, and though time and Trix's nervous illness must have damaged it somewhat, they clearly remained very devoted throughout their lives.

Charles Carrington points out how much Trix's loyalty to her brother, despite her very young age and all the efforts of Auntie Rosa to separate her from the unregenerate black sheep, was to sustain Rudyard amid the persecutions of The House of Desolation. I think much, too, must be said for the strength of Rudyard's love for his small sister. Whether he heard of the plan to separate them and the preference of his wealthy uncle Baldwin and his grandmother for Trix rather than for himself we do not know, but at six not much goes on in a family circle which a bright boy can't conjecture. Certainly the most traumatic psychological aspect of the Southsea misery was the slight put upon his sahib status by a woman's rule, especially after Captain Holloway's death, and this must have been increased by the preference shown for his sister – so good, so bright at her lessons, so much younger and yet able to read. His devotion to her, as hers for him, never seems to have wavered. When, by an unusual chance, it was Trix who had met Auntie Rosa's displeasure, he made up to her for her disgrace by placing two sugar mice, which he had bought with a penny obtained from the servant girl, on her tea plate in the angry Auntie's absence.

His elder-brotherly protective and educative role was no doubt even increased by his need to assert his lost sahibhood. Yet traces of resent-

ment do come through all the genuine love he shows. His pointing out
to her that her acclaimed reading of a psalm is imperfect because she
has read "leather thing" for "Leviathan". His verdict to his mother
after the years of Southsea captivity, when in 1878 Trix's further
education was in question, "Well, it will be difficult. In high falutin'
she beats me, but in solid learning, she can't spell 'shut'."[28] His
remark in his fictional account of those days that his sister was
"deeply religious; at six years of age religion is easy to come by,"[29]
suggests a pious phase in Trix's life that would have delighted Auntie
Rosa; but it also suggests how sorely his sense of the security of their
common front against the enemy must have been tried. But above all
the sentimental story, "His Majesty The King", published like "Baa,
Baa, Black Sheep" in *The Week's News* and in the same year, 1888,
shows surely some welling of suppressed, probably unrealised, feelings
of the Southsea years. In this story a little boy, Toby, called in true
"little sahib" fashion "His Majesty The King", the son of neglectful
and divided Anglo-Indian parents, seeks to gain some of the magic
power of "the wilful four year old, Patsie, who, to the intense
amazement of His Majesty The King, was idolised by her parents"
(the District Commissioner and his wife), by getting hold of her blue
sash in which he decides her power of commanding love resides.
Kipling's unity with his sister was certainly tested in those days, but
misery united them. We may well think that Alice Kipling acted wisely
and humanely in refusing any offers from her family that meant separating her children.

It is also likely that the Kipling parents' strong sense of independence would have found reason to reject each group of relations, apart
from the suggestion of separating the children: the greater wealth of
the Baldwin household; the underlying emotional tensions, which
must have been known to Alice, of her loved sister Georgie Burne-
Jones's household; the aloof temperament of her eminent brother-in-
law, Poynter, her sweet sister Aggie's husband (the suggestion, indeed,
seems not to have been made). As Alice Kipling said in convenient
shorthand to her friend Miss Plowden in 1875, "she had never thought
of leaving her children with her own family; it leads to complication."[30]

If, then, not to their relations, why to the Holloways? We do not
unfortunately, so far as I know, have any information as to whether
the Kipling children were the first of such paying boarders taken by
the Holloways. Certainly no other children were there. It was not until
after Captain Holloway's death that Auntie Rosa asked Alice to help
her to find some more children, presumably because of increasingly

straitened means. We cannot, therefore, tell what references, if any, the Kipling parents took up.

One thing, I think, is certain: the unfortunate aspects of Auntie Rosa, which became evident under the strain of coping with a spoilt, masterful (though intensely interesting and loving) boy, were not likely to be evident to the Kipling parents when they decided to leave the children there. They were not evident, it is clear, to Alice's family. For in autumn 1872, some nine months after the Kipling parents had gone back to India, Grandmother Macdonald and Aunt Aggie Poynter, followed later by Aunt Louie Baldwin and Aunt Georgie Burne-Jones, spent some weeks at Southsea in lodgings, with some pleasant bathing parties shared with the Holloways. Hannah Macdonald, the children's grandmother, a highly intelligent woman, said, "They seem much attached to Mrs Holloway and she seems fond of them."[31] His Aunt Louie thought Auntie Rosa "a very nice woman indeed".[32]

Of one thing neither the Kiplings nor the Macdonald relatives may well have been aware: while they were all making their way into wider, richer, more cultivated worlds, Captain and Mrs Holloway had fallen and were falling in the social and financial scale. Of course they knew that the Captain, as a retired pensioner with vague implications of naval rather than merchant service retirement, needed financially to accept the Kipling children as boarders. But social intercourse rightly covers over the cracks of such sad hopes and fears as seem to have been Mrs Holloway's lot in those years. I do not wish to imply either grossly materialistic or markedly snobbish attitudes on either side, but such things count and counted even more in the eighteen-seventies.

Captain Holloway came from an Oxfordshire family. One of his brothers, who had died young, had been a Fellow of New College, Oxford. Another brother was a lieutenant-colonel. The head of the family was General Sir Thomas Holloway, his eldest brother, who lived, with a spinster sister, in some style at West Lodge, Havant – Kipling remembered it as "everything that was wonderful" compared to The House of Desolation. It may well have been his war wound that caused Captain Holloway to transfer from the Navy to the Merchant Service, yet, whatever the cause, the social decline in the Victorian middle-class world was considerable. We know nothing of his wife's background. But they were clearly "poor relations". From what Kipling says it came to him even as a small boy that Auntie Rosa was involved in some intrigue and hopes that the General would make solid provision for her son. Research at Somerset House has shown that he did indeed do so, but changed his mind, and, when in 1875 he died, nothing was left to his younger nephew. Captain Holloway's death the year before may well, at the very least, have decreased the pension they lived on – as we have seen, far away in India, Mrs Kipling was trying to find more boarders for Mrs Holloway to help her out.

These must have been bad and bitter years for Auntie Rosa, and, by and large, both from the fictional account and from the autobiography, they were Rudyard's worst years with her. Yet these were years of advancement in reputation and fame, to an extent that must surely have reached even Lorne Lodge, of Burne-Jones and of Edward Poynter, Rudyard's uncles; these were the years when the letters from India must have reflected his parents' pleasure at the great advancement both in interest of work and in distinction of Lockwood's new post in Lahore. The yearly holiday at Auntie Georgie Burne-Jones's, the oasis of bliss, as we shall see, in Rudyard's Southsea desert of misery, must have meant for Auntie Rosa and her son the knowledge that this arrogant, deceitful little boy had spent his time in a world quite beyond their dreary horizon.

It had been bad enough when this untruthful child spoke in his lofty, young sahib's scornful way of Hope Lodge, the school that was good enough, had to be good enough, for her son. "He took stock of his associates. Some of them were unclean, some of them talked in dialect, many dropped their h's, and there were two Jews and a Negro, or someone quite as dark, in the assembly. 'That's a hubshi,' said Black Sheep to himself, 'even Meeta used to laugh at a hubshi. I don't think this is a proper place.' "[33] These are, of course, Kipling's fictional words written for a mainly Anglo-Indian audience fifteen or so years after the event. But, if he only succeeded in conveying a part of such feelings to Auntie Rosa about the school to which she (a sister-in-law of generals and lieutenant-colonels, an acquaintance of a Provost of Oriel College, Oxford) had to send her son, she can hardly have loved him the more. And now in these last and most bitter years of Kipling's stay there, while all these aunts and uncles were going up in the world, in what she must have felt to be a dubiously respectable world of arts and crafts and Bohemian living, her own son, a boy brought up to walk righteously, was forced to enter manhood as no more than a bank clerk.

None of this exonerates Mrs Holloway for her heavy-handed treatment of Rudyard, but it does, I think, explain it more than the usual accounts allow.

If Mrs Holloway's social distresses were not apparent to Rudyard's family (and after all, her worst blows came after her husband's death in 1874 and the Macdonald visit was in 1873), so equally I think the other deep division – the religious difference – would not emerge in ordinary social intercourse. Rudyard's parents were not religious people. In so far as public profession went, they were Church people, married in the Church of England. Rudyard was baptised in Bombay Cathedral. But they were no more than conventional churchgoers. Nevertheless, they were the children of Wesleyan ministers. Mrs Macdonald remained a Wesleyan until her death in 1875. Her son Frederic, Rudyard's uncle, was a Wesleyan minister, but of liberal views, happy to associate with Church of England clergymen. The Baldwins were devout Evangelical people who had come from Wesleyan upbringing. Ned Burne-Jones, though unorthodox in most ways, had an attachment to the High Church of England from early Tractarian influences and from the medievalism of his pre-Raphaelite creed.

As a whole, they could be taken as a good sample of the varying strands of middle-class belief in the latter part of Victoria's reign. In some cases there was a return to the Church from the Chapel, that coincided with but must not be thought of as dependent upon a rise in social standing; in other cases there was a shift towards agnosticism that found expression in a lapse of religious practice rather than in any unconventional public expression of disbelief.

One thing that is common to all of them is that, neither in their present professional faith nor in the Wesleyanism of their fathers and grandfathers, is there any evidence of Calvinistic theology. There were, of course, Methodists of Calvinistic belief who had separated off into the Primitive Methodists, but the accent in Wesley's original preaching – and Kipling's great-grandfather Macdonald, after all, had been personally converted by that charismatic man – was much more upon Heaven than upon Hell, and markedly upon Christ as the Saviour of *all* mankind. From Kipling's account the Holloways were churchgoers as his parents had formally become. But this was churchgoing with a great difference. Kipling's account in his old age is rather vague – he was never very interested in the minutiae of English Christian theological beliefs: "It was an establishment run with the full vigour of the Evangelical as revealed to the Woman. I had never heard of Hell, so I was introduced to it in all its terrors . . . The Woman had an only son of twelve or thirteen as religious as she." [34]

It seems very likely that Mrs Holloway was a Calvinist Evangelical of the Church of England, of whom there were a good number. Certainly the shortage of books in the house, the giving to Rudyard of a moral tract, *The Hope of the Katzekopfs*, by a visitor (of which, as one would expect, his imagination made far other things than the author's intentions), the use of collects and psalms to be learned as punishments, imply a puritanism far away from the cultured Wesleyanism in which Alice Kipling had been brought up, let alone the cultured Christian indifferentism in which they had brought up their children. Once again, the small social intercourse would surely have revealed no more than the satisfactory information that the Holloways were good Church people. But it is likely that Mrs Holloway adhered to the Old Calvinist view of unsaved, reprobate children that was Charles Dickens's chief cause for hatred of Dissenters. The incident of the placard "Liar" put upon Kipling after he had concealed his bad school reports seems to agree with this. Charles Carrington has supposed that it grew in Kipling's later memory out of his recall of *David Copperfield* and not out of real experience. But the placard put on David at Dr Creakle's School, "This boy bites", certainly does not come out of Dickens' own experience. His hatred of the Dissenting treatment of children is largely theoretical and not personal. His invention of this punishment satisfactory to Mr Murdstone's "gloomy theology" and Dr Creakle's savagery must have come from general hostile rumours about Dissenting practice. There may have been much more smoke than fire in such rumours. There seems to me nothing to say that Mrs Holloway's reported cruel punishment may not have belonged to just such a puritan fire, however limited in its spread.

There is certainly about all the accounts of these years a sense of Rudyard as the lost reprobate and of Trix as a brand happily snatched from burning. This would account for one of the oddest of all the aspects of these Southsea years – that the bad Rudyard made a yearly visit to his uncle and aunt, enjoying an annual time of delight with his cousins in London, while Trix (as she somewhat reasonably aggrievedly points out) never left Auntie Rosa's side. Could it not be that Trix, whom Auntie Rosa spoke of as her little girl, was not to be corrupted if Mrs Holloway could avoid it? Whereas the wicked little Rudyard needed no saving from the vanities (what those vanities were in reality it is lucky that Mrs Holloway could not know) of the artistic, bohemian household of the Burne-Joneses?

If this was so, it was, indeed, lucky for Kipling that Auntie Rosa could not see her way to saving him, since The Grange, his uncle's and aunt's house in Fulham, was a wonder-house for a child. It is one among the all too many frivolous uncaring shames of our own age that this house, in which one of our greatest novelists, Samuel Richardson, and one of our most curious (though not alas one of our greatest) painters Edward Burne-Jones lived, should have been pulled down in the post-war years. As I remember its external face, it was an elegant, but simple early eighteenth-century structure with Victorian additions (one, no doubt, though I didn't know it, Burne-Jones's studio) and with evident signs of a vanished garden. It was within, however, after the knocker, which Kipling cherished so as a gateway to Paradise that he fixed it later to his own front door in Sussex, had been answered, that the strange wonder-house would be revealed to a child's eyes. Much of it must have been mysterious to him. The great green leaf-patterned walls, with their sudden points of light, the gold and green cabinet, the supposed Giorgione of "Europa and the Bull" glowing in red, would surely have been a wondrous cavern. And from it opened the well-lit simple drawing-room with furniture so plain compared with what a child would see in any other home of the time, with mysterious casts of Michelangelo figures, and Mantegna's "Triumph of Julius Caesar" across one whole wall. And through the long windows the huge old mulberry tree and the shapely evergreens. Upstairs was the studio, always, as Kipling says, with a magical array of unfinished charcoal cartoon figures, only the eyes finished in white staring out of black shapes. The strangeness of his uncle's world could not have been fully realised by a child, even of ten, as Rudyard was by the time of the last of these idyllic Christmas escapes from Southsea. Yet the very shapes – the long-necked, large-mouthed, staring-eyed women, the twisting, lithe Michelangelesque naked men, the sudden brightness of colour, the unexpected detailed flowers and leaves and birds, all these, without any sense of the absurd, muddled, ideal forms that lay behind them, medieval, neoplatonic, pagan, but all romantic – swirling in that long, sweet-eyed, red-bearded head, would seem an enchanter's cave to an imaginative child. And it was in this house that his tiny, cool, grey-eyed Aunt Georgie read to him and to his cousins *The Arabian Nights*. The combination is perfect.

We can get some idea of the pattern of these wonderful times from Georgie Burne-Jones's description of Christmas 1873, at which her children, Phil and Margaret, "had with them their young cousin Rudyard Kipling, now beginning the Anglo-Indian child's experience of separation from his own home."[35] May and Jenny Morris were there, the daughters of William Morris (to Rudyard, Uncle Topsy). Appropriately, the children were entertained to a magic lantern show in the large hall and here they played snapdragon, snatching plums from the flaming brandy. "Charles Faulkner and William de Morgan and Allingham enchanted us all by their pranks, in which Morris and Edward Poynter occasionally joined ... While Mrs Morris, placed safely out of the way, watched everything from her sofa."[36] The very

29

idea of that sphinx-like goddess gazing down upon the scene is extraordinary. Her strange personality must have impressed itself upon
Rudyard in these holidays, for in "To Be Filed for Reference",
McIntosh, the Oxford man turned loafer, refers most irrelevantly in
his drugged wanderings to Charley Symonds' stables – the humble
Oxford place in which William Morris had found his faithless and
lovely bride. What Aunt Georgie doesn't mention, with characteristic
modesty, is the drollery and high-spirited fun which Uncle Ned must
have given to the occasion; nor her own contribution in playing and
singing. She goes on to say, "This is the last time of the kind I remember. By the following Xmas the children's own world had begun, and
it was their turn to amuse us." [37]

This was one of the many values that Kipling got from the Grange –
the importance of making for oneself, making drawings, making up
stories, making up private languages, making up elaborate practical
jokes. No one could be funnier than Burne-Jones – both delightfully
absurd in a way that seems quite modern, and pranksome in the old
Victorian tradition of practical jokes that goes right back to Charles
Lamb. These boisterous outbursts of boyish humour he bequeathed to
his nephew Rudyard far more than to his own children, and, as well,
an uncontrollable enjoyment of his own jokes that doubled him up
with noiseless shoulder-shaking laughter. Kipling was to organise
these practical jokes and his extreme enjoyment of them into his
philosophy and to produce for them a whole series of humorous
stories which always end with the participants crying and spluttering
with mirth.

Burne-Jones, too, was a wonderful comic artist. His comic drawings
were a kind of necessary relief from the high, strained, idealised
eroticism of his "important" painting. They were excellent. And
Rudyard and the other children were treated to a series of comic
adventures of wombats and pigs and pug dogs and also strange absurdities that had more than a touch of Gothic horror in them. But
making for oneself ruled the day, as it was to do later in Rudyard's
parents' home.

It was the best preparation for Kipling's creative powers. Indeed, it
was at The Grange, in one of the holidays from school in 1879, two
years after the captivity in Southsea was over, that he helped May
Morris and his cousins to produce a magazine. In it appears his first
known story (he was perhaps just fourteen), "My First Adventure". It
is a splendid combination of Poe-like delirium and of Burne-Jones-like
humour, in which a schoolboy, walking in delirious sleep, saves an old
countryman from drowning and is taken by the old man for a ghost.

When the schoolboy blows the gaff on this ghost story which the old man tells to his cronies each night, the old man's letter of protest is a direct echo of Mrs Gamp, "When sheeted ghosts turn out to be only lunatic schoolboys, which a nurse or a doctor ought to be discharged for such doings, no characters given and no accounts settled."[38] Already at thirteen, Rudyard showed here his attraction to the weird, his genuine sense of farce, and the mastery of parody which lies below the surface of so much of his work, especially of the verse.

All this making and doing by the children is a great tribute to Burne-Jones himself. But Burne-Jones was to influence Kipling more deeply in the form of his art. Few men can have preserved so completely their ideal dream worlds from any of the realities of life as Burne-Jones. In the last resort, I think, it makes nearly all his painting no more than an empty wonder. Kipling inherited this strong, almost hypnotic sense of a dream kingdom, but, in all but a few over-sentimental stories and poems, his strength comes, even in the most "imagined" of his works, the Mowgli and the Puck stories, or in *Kim*, from the testing of the dream with greater or lesser injections of the real world that seems to threaten it. Where Burne-Jones used his dreams to exclude, Kipling uses them with courage to test his capacity to bear reality. Only, I think, in Kipling's treatment of women does he inherit something of that weakening absolute separation of the ideal from the sensual which makes so much of Burne-Jones's painting null.

Nevertheless, Ned Burne-Jones was one of the two or three men who opened the gates of wonderland for Rudyard. His latest biographer, Mrs Fitzgerald, has suggested that he was the origin of the Lama in *Kim*. I believe that it is much more likely that, in both person and function, he is to be seen as Puck, who opens the way back into History for Dan and Una in *Puck of Pook's Hill* and *Rewards and Fairies*. Indeed, just before his death in 1897, Uncle Ned was sending Rudyard, at his request, lists of English history books to read for his new project. And this new project was to turn into the Puck stories.

All this magical world was made possible by the cool, efficient, reserved management of his aunt. No wonder the Burne-Joneses became for all their lives "The Aunt" and "The Uncle" for Kipling, figures only below "the Father" and "The Mother". And, despite the extreme divergence of their political views from his growing imperialism in the nineties, the close link was never broken.

For Rudyard, The Grange was all a paradise world; yet his sleep there was broken by frightened cries, his cousin Margaret remembered. Auntie Rosa could haunt even there. But he told nothing of the misery of Southsea. "Often and often afterwards, the beloved Aunt would ask me why I had never told anyone how I was being treated. Children tell little more than animals, for what comes to them they accept as eternally established."[39] But the strain of bullying and ostracism *was* telling upon the small boy; the impossibility of saying anything of either world to the other. It left him, I believe, a man forever exceptionally reticent except to children and his very few intimates. More immediately it aggravated an eyesight defect so that his vision was seriously affected. To Auntie Rosa this seemed only another affectation of manhood by a self-important small boy, an evasion of lessons, a very good reason for refusing him the indulgence of his perpetual story-book reading. But, at last, the condition became apparent at Grove House, too. He bumped into trees when playing in the garden. Aunt Georgie took alarm, consulted an eye specialist, wrote to her sister Alice in Lahore that all was not well and that she should come home.

Luckily his father, whose financial means were still small, had recently received a bag of 500 rupees as a special recognition from the Indian Government for his designing of the banners for the ceremony of the Proclamation of Queen Victoria as Empress of India at Delhi on 1 January 1877. With this money, Alice did not need to hesitate for a moment in answering her sister's call. By April she was in England. The story of the little boy putting up his arm to protect himself from an expected cuff when she came to kiss him goodnight in bed is probably the best known, because the most dramatic, of the whole Southsea episode. The whole story appears from outside as the conflict of two eras, a conflict between the idea of childhood liberated, and a precious source of creation that was taking root in the mid-Victorian middle-class world, and an earlier, fast disappearing idea of sinful childhood to be repressed and chastened, as Auntie Rosa believed was her Christian duty.

What was its permanent effect on Kipling? I do not think that we can see it, as Edmund Wilson did, as some lasting maiming of Kipling's genius. But Kipling himself clearly felt it as a continual and frightening memory. He always remembered with horror Auntie Rosa's instruction in the idea of Eternal Damnation. In "With the Night Mail" (*c*.1904), one of his science-fiction views of the future world, the narrator looks back to "the horrible old days when men were taught that they might go to unspeakable torment after death". It even led him on occasion to associate cruelty directly with Christianity. In the story, "They", the blind, childless woman speaks of how she has been laughed at. The narrator comments, "I was silent, reviewing that inexhaustible matter – the more than inherited (since it is carefully taught) brutality of the Christian people, beside which the mere heathendom of the West Coast Nigger is clean and restrained. It led me a long distance into myself."

"These things . . ." he says in his autobiography, "drained me of any capacity for real, personal hatred for the rest of my days. So close must any life-filling passion lie to its opposite." This statement may seem at first sight to be the reverse of true of a man who was throughout his life often to be as vehement as he could be gentle. What other man, even in the height of the hatreds begot of the Great War, could have written the terrifying poem about the Kaiser's suspected cancer of the throat? What other man, when the War had begun and party feuds were to be forgotten, would hark back to the financial scandals that had surrounded the Government when it was the hated Liberal Government, as Kipling did in publishing his fierce attack on Lord Reading's accession to the post of Lord Chancellor in 1915, the poem "Gehazi"? But these and many, many other invectives are not directly personal hatreds, they are calculated blows, however brutal, in public matters. Personal hatred allowed to go unchecked he always sees as a foolish weakness – from "The Watches of the Night", a story of 1887, where we are told, "Now Mrs Larkyn was a frivolous woman, in whom none could have suspected deep hate . . . She never forgot," to the ruin of the talented Manallace through giving his life to personal revenge in "Dayspring Mishandled" (1928).

Certainly he exalts a sustained determination for revenge, for example in the Moslem Malaysian head lascar, Pambé Serang, in the brilliant and terrible "The Limitations of Pambé Serang". Here he rates Asian long memory for revenge above the indeterminacy of feeling, the vague forgetfulness, that underlies much Western forgiveness or Negro generosity. But, on the whole, and in sophisticated men and women, and certainly in himself, Kipling (except in the matter of copyright pirating) eschews personal hatred as a weakness.

As he said in a speech to the boys of Milner Court, the junior King's School, Canterbury in 1929, "You may have noticed that there is not much justice in your present world. There is less outside . . . Too much fussing over abstract justice leads to standing up for your rights . . . Any debt that a man thinks he owes to himself can wait over till the others are paid . . . and . . . standing up for one's rights . . . often ends in leaving a man with a grievance, which is the same as being a leper."

Out of the miserable years at Southsea came "Baa, Baa, Black Sheep". After that Kipling only produced in all his vast output one book rooted in private grievance, the bad novel, *The Light That Failed*, into which he put his bitterness at the final failure of his long, intermittent wooing of Violet Garrard. And this strange episode, as we shall see, all began during his only return to Auntie Rosa's house.

Otherwise, he urged that men should use what might become grievances to assert themselves by all manner of ruses and joky battles with authority. This he did at the school, the United Services College, to which he was sent after his mother had rescued him from Southsea.

One thing more, I believe, is very important about this unhappy period at Southsea. Few writers are more constantly apprehensive of death than Kipling. It is probably why he was so fascinated by the works of Webster and Donne. The fear of death among Western men seemed to him a paramount obsession. "Men say they wish to die but when the time comes they wish to live a little longer."[40] "Every sane human being is agreed that this long-drawn fight for time that we call life is one of the most important things in the world."[41] References of this kind could be found in every period of his work. Two deaths which closely connect to this Southsea time are most important, I believe. Just before he and Trix left the happiness of Bombay to be so mysteriously and cruelly abandoned, as they thought, his baby brother had died at birth. It is hard to think that this unmentioned event and his parents' grief would not have been a mysterious introduction to a terrible time. It was the first death of his life.

And at Southsea itself he was, at least, protected while kind, friendly Captain Holloway lived. To the Captain he owed his entry into the world of Jorrocks, whose sayings are woven into the mesh of his fantasies of school life in *Stalky*, Jorrocks whose comic hunting adventures help to save Frankwell Midmore from the disease of urban bohemianism in "My Son's Life" (1913). The visit to Oxford in 1872 when he saw the Provost of Oriel must have been with the Captain on the way to stay with the Baldwins at Bewdley. This Oxford visit is commemorated in "The Brushwood Boy" twenty years later as a happy time of enchantment. It should be noted too that this happy journey with Captain Holloway led to his only visit from Southsea to Bewdley, after which his grandmother in so changed a tune said, "We were sorry to part with him."[42] After the Captain's death two years later, Auntie Rosa and her bullying son became more bitter and were no longer checked. Rudyard's fate became more cruel. It was the second death that he had ever known and it ushered in what he always spoke of as the most helpless, horrible period of his life.

After Southsea

If Rudyard Kipling, looking back over sixty-five years, had fancifully remembered the assassination of Lord Mayo in 1872 as impinging upon his Bombay childhood, the fancy had a certain oblique foundation. The Viceroy had been killed by a man from the North West Frontier. This event, Mr James Craig suggests, hastened both the establishment of the Mayo School of Industrial Art as a tribute to the late Viceroy's memory, and its siting at Lahore in the Northern Punjab, the disorderly area his assassin had come from. If this is so, Kipling's memory might falsely but also rightly dwell on Mayo, for his parents' move to Lahore in April 1875 was a very important step in the family career. It does not mean that they entered the élite or even the near-élite of Anglo-Indian society, as the British in India were then called (the term "Anglo-Indian" is now applied to people of mixed Indian and European ancestry, who, in Kipling's day, were called "Eurasians"). Anglo-Indian caste order was almost as hard to break as Indian. At dinner parties the Principal of the School of Art (even when he was, like Lockwood, also Curator of the well-known Central Museum) and his wife were among the last to go in.

The Kiplings, it is true, had friends in high places – some of the proprietors of the very important newspaper, the *Pioneer*, to which they contributed, and Rivett Carnac, Assistant to the Commissioner of the Central Provinces, who, among others, claimed to have got Lockwood his job. Their relationship to the highly regarded Edward Poynter of the Academy and to the increasingly famous Edward Burne-Jones, was certainly known. But they were thought of as "arty" – Alice Kipling's appearing without jewellery at dinner parties (surely the wise decision of a handsome woman of slender means not to compete) was regarded as the pose of an artist's wife. Nevertheless, it was the late starting-point (they were nearer forty than thirty-five) of a clever and ambitious married couple.

The Punjab was not rich like Calcutta or Bombay, but it was also not full of established people; it was, too, in its relation to the defence of India and its nearness to Simla, a place where things were happening both militarily and politically. It was a "coming place", as it would then have been called. As Curator of the Museum, Lockwood was not now so confined to purely utilitarian considerations as at Bombay, he was no longer a subordinate but master of his own establishment, and in his museum was to be found an ever-increasing collection of Buddhist sculpture of the Gandhara dynasty which, with its strong ancient Greek influence, was more comprehensible to nineteenth-century artistic taste than any other relics of India. Artists and art historians of all countries would now be consulting him.

When, on top of all this, his banners for the Viceroy, the governors, and the chieftains at the Empress's Proclamation were so widely admired, Lockwood by 1877 was well on the way to being a well-known figure in Anglo-Indian circles. Alice's part in this achievement was, as always, vital. The dialogue reported in connection with her at this time has already a theatrical sound, which by the time of their friendship with Lord Dufferin, ten years later, had become almost pure Wilde comedy. At the Delhi Proclamation in January 1877 the Viceroy, Lord Lytton, also well-known in Victorian literary circles as the poet "Owen Meredith", taking Alice's hands, said, "I hear you yourself worked the angel supporters on our banner. Angels created by an angel ... Who would have thought of meeting Mrs Burne-Jones's sister in India," he went on. Which gave Alice her chance, "Who would have thought of meeting Owen Meredith as Viceroy?" We may smile (I do) but a wife like this was a rare help.

It meant, too, that in the future, when Kipling came to North West India, only five and a half years later, to start his career in life, he came as the son of talked-of people, both envied and condescended to, no doubt, as minor in rank, and all too clever in talk and interests. But the parents' position had also been consolidated at the children's expense, for the seeming lifetime of five and a half years at Southsea of Rudyard's persecution would surely have lasted only half as long if Alice had not needed to stay with Lockwood when he began his new career in 1875. Few Anglo-Indian mothers failed to come to their children every two years – and the Kiplings, who had grown up frugally, would have managed somehow to find the money for her trip, had that been the only barrier.

But now she was home, she made up for it. She was in England on and off from 1877 until the end of 1878 and again for a short spell in spring 1880 to nurse her schoolboy son through a minor illness. Lockwood's position in Lahore now permitted these expenses that, in their Bombay days, would have been impossible. Immediately, too, she took the children from Lorne Lodge to a wonderful long holiday at a farm near Loughton in Essex, within exploring distance of Epping Forest. The manner of their parting from Lorne Lodge is obscure and suggests either that both Kipling and his sister came to magnify the cruelty of Auntie Rosa and her son, or that Alice Kipling failed fully to interpret the meaning of her little boy's arm raised to ward off blows when she came to kiss him goodnight on the first evening of her return. It is true that Trix had been a favourite with Mrs Holloway, adored in what she afterwards described as "a morbid and jealous way".[43] Perhaps she had reciprocated, in the absence of her mother, more than she remembered. Certainly Alice Kipling felt happy to let her daughter spend long periods at The House of Desolation in the next six years. And Rudyard himself paid a visit there to fetch his sister for a holiday to their uncle's in 1880 – with unhappy consequences. Certainly, for the moment, Alice seems to have seen the years at Southsea as something unfortunate rather than disastrous for her son; perhaps she thought he had grown up too much to be under a woman's care, or that he and Mrs Holloway had "got across each other", or that Lorne Lodge was "the wrong atmosphere for him". It seemed an episode that lots of fresh air and farm food and exercise and fun would efface from his memory.

And the children did have fun at Loughton. Their cousin, Stanley Baldwin, an attractive boy with a loving but busy father and a loving but ailing mother, joined them. Nearly fifty years later Kipling and Baldwin laughed over the memory of it all until they cried; but it will be seen that laughter to the point of tears came easily to Kipling. Nor was Kipling's "naughtiness", as Auntie Rosa would have called it, diminished by happiness. Only his youngest, rather formidable, but very loved Aunt Edith Macdonald could control the children one day when they all started to walk out of the dining-room with their fingers holding their noses when the fish was brought in. Management of the children (perhaps worry about what had happened to them in her long absence) proved too much for Alice, who became ill with shingles. As in so many family emergencies, it was her sister Georgie who took charge and nursed her.

Rudyard and Trix went to stay at 227 Brompton Road, in rooms kept by an ex-butler and his wife, where Alice joined them as soon as she was recovered. It was here that one lasting effect of Auntie Rosa's rule manifested itself. Kipling in a typically splendid frightening phrase tells us that "the night got into his head".[44] So began that insomnia and night prowling which, as with Dostoevsky and Dickens, became so important to Kipling's literary imagination and his literary composition. "City of Dreadful Night" is only the most crudely brilliant of the stories that resulted from this misery. For what was our gain was certainly his torture. Loss of sleep lies behind so much of the pure torment in his work, especially in the Indian stories. Once again we may allow his own words to tell us what a torture his insomnia was to him. In an unsigned article in the *Civil and Military Gazette* of September 1886, he describes grimly the Chinese torture of enforced sleeplessness, and adds how well he knows "the elusive thoughts that like Chinese guards will not let you rest".

But otherwise all was fun again. At Brompton Road the two children watched the people passing and Trix tells us that, when she was surprised at how many talked to themselves, Rudyard said that he had always known it. They threw down pieces of coal or walnuts wrapped in paper and were excited to watch even well-dressed people in the street below stop, pick them up and unwrap them. Alice got them student tickets for the South Kensington Museum, to which they went regularly. Rudyard preferred the weapons and ivories; but they both loved the jewels, and they learned the patrol hours so that they could hide overnight in a Buddha and steal them.

Books, at this period, were not much in evidence – no doubt because of Rudyard's eyes – but they read Dickens aloud. Rudyard made up stories for Trix. She tells us that these stories, though they turned into fabulous adventures, always began from something concrete – an old log in the duck pond on the farm perhaps, a gutter on the cat-populated roof at Brompton Road which was put out of bounds by their mother. This building of fantasy from the immediate and concrete was to remain a feature of his inventive approach. His sister was the first child audience whom he at once loved, entertained and taught. And in this she set a very important pattern for some of his most original work.

The whole enchanting period of around nine months with, first, its outdoor carefree wanderings, and then its nose-to-the-window watching, gives to me a great sense of those interludes in childhood between one phase of life and another, which are absolutely recuperative and preparative, because, in them, delicious idling gradually becomes so intermixed with bored dawdling that exit from paradise is made bearable, however alarming the world outside.

For all but the toughest (or the most insensitive), the first months at a boarding public school are hard going. The United Services College was a school of only four years' standing, newly brought into being especially to get the sons, including a high proportion of the less bright or the more refractory sons, of retired officers into the military academies of Sandhurst or Woolwich. It was, therefore, likely to be tougher than most for a boy like Ruddy – imaginative, book-loving, shy, a bit arrogant and, because of his eyesight, unable to take part in ball games. And so, for the first year, it was. He was badly bullied. The first letters he wrote to his mother from school alarmed her and she wrote to the headmaster, "It is the roughness of the lads he seems to feel most – he doesn't grumble – but he is lonely and down."[45] Her sister Georgie hastened to reassure her: her own son, Phil, had been miserable at Marlborough at first, but now he had recovered and was very happy.

Probably both boys suffered more from the customary bullying than their mothers would have cared to guess. Yet Kipling was as lucky with his school as he was with his parents, although, I think, important reservations must be made in both cases. It would not have been so, I am sure, if he had gone to one of the more established public schools. The long-practised machinery of such an institution would either have flattened him into some conventional shape – conformist or rebel – or it would have passed him by leaving him lonely and unadapted to the world. But he was an anomaly in a school that was itself an anomaly and with a headmaster who was an anomaly. During the first year he found two other boys, who, in quite individual and separate ways, shared many of his nonconformities. Together they forged a programme for survival, even for joyous survival most of the time. Major-General Dunsterville, the model for Kipling's hero "Stalky", looking back to his school days half a century later, wrote, "I am sure we were not posing, and we were not setting out merely to defy authority, but almost unconsciously I am afraid that was our attitude. We must have been heartily disliked by both masters and senior boys – and with entire justification." [46]

Kipling's view of his old school was never detached. "The School before its time," he calls it in his autobiography and the title suggests his determination to single it out for distinction. He left the school before he was seventeen. But, when he looked back to it in his thirties, he saw it as an institution which had taught him how to live closely with the world of action and still to be himself. And he rightly thought that his great distinction from most other (certainly English) writers of genius was this close relation to the world of action. With this high sense of what the United Services College had done for him, he came to draw from what he learned there a general recipe for life, especially for the life of men of action themselves. And, at last, to see his old school as the prototype of the best training-ground for the young men who, as he hoped, would, in discipline and devotion, give their lives to the service of civilisation as embodied at that historical moment in the British Empire.

His claim for the school is a large one and clearly enters into the realm of legend. Kipling's account of it is not always consistent. "The School before its time" implies a difference from (and a superiority to) other public schools. United Services College certainly was different, but it is hard to say how different. And Kipling himself (or, at any rate, his fictional "I") goes back on the claim when he says, deprecating the idea that his school and his hero Stalky are unique, "India's full of Stalkies – Cheltenham and Haileybury and Marlborough chaps."

The confusion tells us a lot, I think. United Services College was a very new, very minor public school. The masters who taught there and, indeed, the headmaster had come from posts at other more established public schools of the Victorian, post-Arnold model. The fathers of the U.S.C. boys had most probably been at such public schools themselves. It is unlikely that many of them would have underlined the difference of this school from other public schools; on the contrary, they would have been more likely to underline the likenesses. If Kipling in his real self had spoken the words quoted above in any mess or club in India, words implying that Cheltenham or Haileybury, schools from which a large proportion of army officers had been recruited for over fifty years, were as important in their own way as the United Services College, which had been founded four years before he went there, his "cheek" would have been met with at best an amused smile, more likely, a socially snubbing remark. No doubt he knew this.

It is difficult, then, to make out the truth from the legend about United Services College. Of course, the legend is the more important, for it gives us *Stalky & Co.*, one of his most popular (though not in my opinion one of his best) collections of stories. To understand the art of those stories, it is important to see how fancy is woven into reality. To understand the growth of Kipling's mind and imagination, it is desirable to disentangle (to the limited extent that is possible) his real schooldays from those he looked back to fifteen to twenty years later.

First, then, to try to establish the reality. United Services College was founded in 1874 as a limited company by a group of retired army officers who found the fees of well-established schools, and even more the fees of London army crammers that the more stupid or difficult boys needed in addition to their school years, very difficult to afford out of their modest pay or pensions. The aim chosen was utilitarian – to get boys into Woolwich or Sandhurst without the need of extra tuition.

Kipling, in his fictional work, anxious to underline the difference of his School, makes his heroes very realistic about this point. "We're to get into the army or get out," says Stalky. "And all the rest [he means the usual public school talk of house spirit, or team spirit, or esprit de corps] is 'flumdiddle'." And Dunsterville (Stalky himself) in old age, a little deprecating of the school, certainly, I think, a little embarrassed at the way Kipling has blown it up, underlines the same practical aim and suggests that the unique value of Crom Price, the Headmaster, was the passing-out record of the boys. This was the truth, of course, but I doubt greatly if most of the boys and masters would openly have accepted so utilitarian a version of the school's aims.

But certainly, it must be said, the buildings made little pretensions. "Twelve bleak houses by the shore, seven summers by the shore."[47] (Assonance, or false memory? He was there five summers.) Bleak, certainly. It is rare to see houses (especially terrace houses) which look more inviting from the back than the front, but so it is with these ex-seaside lodging-houses. Westward Ho, in which the school was situated, was a seaside town which had never caught on, built speculatively about twenty years earlier, with a hotel, swimming baths and a very good golf course. Situated on a cliff top, it overlooked Barnstaple Bay, with the old-fashioned Devon market town of Bideford within walking distance. The nine lodging-houses were going cheap. Run a communicating corridor through them and, presto! you had all you needed: a gym, school rooms, dormitories, a few studies, bed-sitting-rooms for the masters (all but one were bachelors) and a house for the Headmaster (also a bachelor). Plenty of room for play-ing-fields – cricket and rugger – ideal for hare and hounds, a swim-ming bath at hand for the winter terms, a long, open beach for sum-mer bathing in the buff (so they would have called naked bathing). Plenty of fresh air. But not plenty of food: all the originals of the famous trio in Stalky & Co., Kipling (Beetle), G. Beresford (M'Turk) and Major-General Dunsterville (Stalky) emphasised this as they loo-ked back in old age. In fact, Beresford, the most sardonic and the least successful in later life, makes good fun of the Headmaster's Sunday breakfasts to encourage friendly relations with the boys which, he asserts, entirely failed because the boys were far too intent on consum-ing any food in sight to say a word.

As in other public schools there were prefects who were allowed to beat, and the school was divided into houses. But in two respects it differed from the recognised public-school conventions: there was no organised or recognised fagging, and the prefects were allowed to smoke. This last was clearly much remarked upon, for Kipling has a whole story of a temporary master who sees in this departure from normal disciplines a likely source of worse sins like drinking or a mysterious hidden evil which Beetle (Kipling) innocently fails to understand. Kipling makes this permissive attitude to prefectoral smoking a positive advantage, for he suggests that such a privilege ensured that young men learned to smoke moderately. But the real reason for this permissive feature was again a practical one. Many young men of seventeen or eighteen, who had failed to pass the Army exams at other schools, came to U.S.C. instead of to an expensive London crammer's. They must have been annoyed enough to miss the liberties of a life in lodgings in London, without the added indignity of not being allowed to smoke. Yet the most striking difference between U.C.S. and other Victorian public schools was in the plain, grim buildings. Other public schools worshipped in mid-Victorian buildings by famous architects – Butterfield's vast Gothic chapel at Rugby, or Carpenter's at Lancing, or Shaw's exuberant mixture of neo-Wren and Louis Treize at Wellington, the most famous of all public schools preparing for the Army, the one to which Kipling later sent his son, John. At Westward Ho there was no separate school chapel and the gym served for a school hall. It is this, I believe, that would have made most mid-Victorian visitors think it a very gimcrack, rumpty-foo – to use their phrase – sort of school.

Obviously, to get results in such a place it was necessary to have an unusual headmaster. Crom Price's history was very different from that of most headmasters at public schools. Like Kipling's elders of his own family, he was not a public schoolboy. He had known Ned Burne-Jones and Kipling's uncle Harry Macdonald at King Edward's School, Birmingham, a grammar school. He had been a scholarship undergraduate at Oxford with them and there, like them, had become involved with Morris, and with Rossetti in London. After taking a degree, he went to study medicine at a London hospital, but gave up before he qualified. For a few years he was a tutor to an aristocrat's son in Russia. Then he returned to become head of the Modern side at Haileybury in 1863; his great success there in language teaching led to his appointment as headmaster by the founders of U.C.S., many of whom were old Haileyburians, in 1874. He had always kept up his relationship with his pre-Raphaelite friends and shared their artistic and even more their literary enthusiasms. He was more widely read than them in French and German literature and, unusually, he, of course, read Russian. His house at Westward Ho was decorated with Rossetti drawings. More curiously, for a headmaster of a public school specifically orientated towards the Army, he shared Burne-Jones's and Morris's radical political views. William Morris's *News from Nowhere*, with its Utopian but inspiring picture of a Socialist England returned to the simplicities of medieval crafts and guilds, has thrown such emphasis upon the domestic side of his political views that his fierce opposition, and in his wake that of his friend Burne-Jones, to any aggressive or militaristic British foreign policy has been forgotten. Yet the Morrisite pre-Raphaelites were staunchly anti-Imperialist and, to a large extent, pacifist. It is possible that most of the parents did not know of his political extremism. A lot of the masters, it seems, were Gladstone followers. (But then, a lot of masters, when I was at Westminster School, professed Socialism.) When he came to honour his old headmaster on his retirement in 1894, Kipling fixed the new Imperialist image firmly on him, "All that the College – all that Mr Price – has ever arrived at was to make men able to make and keep empires." [48] It wasn't, of course, Crom Price's aim, certainly not so in 1874 when the School began: then, it was to make officers for the Army. But, by 1894, and not only in Kipling's mind, the two things were the same. I think that the two men must have exchanged very wry smiles (for they were very fond of each other) when Kipling paid this tribute.

In the month of January 1878 when he brought his new pupil, the son of his old friends, the Kiplings, down to Westward Ho, Crom Price had been busy demonstrating in Islington, with Topsy Morris and Ned Burne-Jones and other pacifists, against Disraeli's support of the Turks against the Russians with its overtones of military aggression. It is not surprising when four years later, in a School debate at Westward Ho, we find the Headmaster opposed to the resolution, "That in the opinion of this Society, the advance of the Russians in central Asia is hostile to the British Power." The proposer of the motion (influenced no doubt by his parents' letters from North West India, where Lockwood was very frontier-conscious) was Rudyard Kipling, aged 16½, and about to leave to take up a newspaper post in Lahore, where no other view of the Russian menace would be possible. But as interesting is the fact that Kipling carried his motion by 21 votes to 9 against the views of the beloved Head – no doubt, many other senior boys had parents in India. If Crom Price could take the minority line in such a public matter, it was not hard for him to make life easier for an unconventional boy like Kipling at the School. And so he did.

When Kipling and his two friends became entitled to a study, they furnished it themselves. They stencilled the walls in olive green and blue with Greek friezes. They bought Japanese fans and searched for bargains of old glass and of Rockingham or Worcester China in Bideford's shops. It was a study for aesthetes. And Kipling's eye, trained by the Uncle and the Aunt and by the Father and the Mother, directed its design. By 1894, when the self-made shipowner in Kipling's poem, "The Mary Gloster", lay dying, he rounded on his pampered son with,

And the things I knew was rotten you said
    was the way to live,
For you muddled with books and pictures, an'
    china, an' etchins and fans,
And your rooms at college was beastly – more like
    a whore's than a man's.

A good many of the parents of boys at Westward Ho in 1880 might have taken the same view of Kipling's study. What is special about Westward Ho (and Crom Price's influence) is that three boys could parade their aestheticism in this way. Even as late as 1935 I remember rooms at Oxford with similar defiant pretensions being broken up by rowing toughs on Bump Supper Nights.

Here, in this study, the boys brewed tea and cocoa, and supplemented the meagre food with what their small pocket money could buy. On occasion, they drank cheap port smuggled in from out-of-bounds Bideford (though when the School Debating Society discussed total abstinence, Kipling – shades of his grandfather – supported it). Most important of all, they read – under Kipling's influence again – all the major poets down to and especially Swinburne. They consumed Ruskin, Carlyle, Emerson, and later (subject of a fierce argument between Kipling and his English master) Whitman. Here Kipling formed his taste for the American humorists, Breitmann (a long-lasting and, I think, harmful love of Kipling's), Twain, and the new craze – Harris's *Uncle Remus*. In Arnold's *Light of Asia* Kipling found his first introduction to Buddhism, later so productive in *Kim*. They made fun of the *Boys' Own Paper* (one of Kipling's best pieces in the school magazine, of which he was editor, is just such a burlesque) and of the popular boys' serials of the day, and, above all, of the mawkish parts of Dean Farrar's *Eric, or Little by Little*. Kipling's repetition of this mockery in *Stalky & Co.* in 1899 led to a letter of protest from the ancient dean, to which Kipling's reply is a model of courteous unwithdrawal: "I can assert honestly that it was no part of any intention to try to injure you with gratuitous insult. Your years and your position in the English Church alike forbid the thought of that."[49] Much of their reading was aloud to one another. And this reading aloud was a special feature of their summer diversion, when, at any possible chance, they crept off, out of bounds, into nearby woods or farms, where in huts made in thick furze thickets or in a shed hired from a cottager, they would smoke illegally (for they were not prefects) but moderately and feel the joys of privacy in defiance of authority.

One aspect of this out-of-bounds life that has not been noticed, I think, in relation to Kipling's work, is how it brought him into contact in boyhood with farm labourers. Many of the locals were still smugglers in those parts; wrecks on the rocks below the cliffs were a local event and the spoils of wrecks, no doubt, were another source for the labourers to add to their pitiful wages; poaching must also have been usual. The boys, out of bounds, and often trespassing, were on the same side of the law as the more dubious locals. A quarter of a century later, when Kipling became first a householder at Rottingdean (still a smuggling town) and then the landlord of the Sussex home of his last thirty years, Bateman's, he retained his sympathies for the errant ways of the farm labourer. Hobden, founded on one of his own employees, became the firm base of the English rural social scene. In "The Land" (written about 1916) he says,

> I have rights of chase and warren as my
>   dignity requires,
> I can fish – but Hobden tickles. I can shoot –
>   but Hobden wires . . .
> Shall . . . I summons him to judgement? I would
>   sooner summons Pan.

This Westward Ho identification with the poor in lawbreaking is very important. In Kipling's code, minor lawbreaking was to be an important bolt-hole for the overpressured man in society; by breaking petty laws, he would be the stronger and more able to keep the mysterious Law that governs all human being. From his schoolday experience surely arises the fact that this lawbreaking is not confined to a class. It includes the Indian coolie and the Pathan and private soldiers and Hobden the poacher (though of course each within his own caste) along with the public schoolboy in that wily "Stalky" outwitting of petty authority that makes living in society tolerable.

From the major recreation of the boys at U.S.C. – organised cricket and football – Kipling was cut off, probably not by eyesight alone as is often supposed. There are a number of witnesses to his lack of co-ordination of limbs in other pursuits. Beresford speaks of his clumsy swimming; his sister of always leading him in dancing; Kay Robinson, one of his Lahore editors, says that Kipling "rode an Arab with which he never established a full and confidential relationship" [50]; it is said that in driving a carriage, his wife usually handled the reins. Whatever the reason, he was excused games, but not watching them. He cannot have been a very enthusiastic compulsory spectator, for, when he was editor of the school magazine, he left descriptions of matches to others. But in his later article for America, "An English School", there is a lyrical account of Rugby football. His school life grew rosy in retrospect – especially as a lesson in English excellence for American readers.

He acted: the Aladdin he played in was not, as often supposed, a schoolboy play, but one simply got up in the study, and in the study too he used to perform a drunk (said by one authority to be Coupeau from Zola's *L'Assommoir* – could it be? More likely, I think, Charles Read's *Drink*) and he played Antony Absolute in a school perform-ance of *The Rivals* – his performance was praised but his huskiness made him hard to understand.

All in all, this mature-looking, eccentric, moustached and bespec-tacled schoolboy was very fully occupied. It is not surprising that his academic results were only mediocre. His French was good, his Latin only adequate, his mathematics poor. All chances of a scholarship to Oxford were out of the question, and the Kipling family finances would not get him there without one. How much did he mind this later? It is hard to say. When his cousin Stanley Baldwin went up to Cambridge, he expressed envy. Oxford men often came out badly in his stories – Jellaludin McIntosh, the loafer living with the half-caste woman and dying of drink and drugs, is a proud Oxford man in the early Indian story "To Be Filed for Reference"; in "The Honours of War", 1911, Kipling tells us of Wontner the Prig, "me he snubbed after the Oxford manner," and so on. Yet long before that he had no need to worry. In 1897, Sir William Hunter took him to dine at High Table at Balliol College, Oxford, when "he received an ovation from the youth below".[51] And in 1907 he was given an honorary Oxford degree along with Mark Twain – surely one of the happiest conjunc-tions of his life.

How much did it matter to his later work that he didn't go to university? In a sense, of course, his philistinism (especially in his early work) is part of his unique quality. Much of his mockery of a modish intelligentsia is telling. Nevertheless, for so clever a man, he was abnormally suspicious of "clever" people. There is an element of grudge and of fear in his attitude. It shows in a foolish treatment of scholarship as a sort of frivolous hedonism: "A scholar may get . . . more pleasure out of life than an army officer but only little children believe that a man's life is given to him to decorate with pretty little things, as though it were a girl's room or a picture screen."[52] He must have known that hard abstract thinking or indeed scholarly learning is not a lazy dilettantism – and, if he did not, two of his great heroes of action, Lord Milner and Cecil Rhodes could have told him so. There is a grudging note here, as of something missed. And that is a defect.

In 1881, however, the decision that he should not compete for the University certainly only brought him bliss. He was released from formal studies. Mr Crofts, his English master with whom he always argued but to whom he still sent all his early articles from India, gave him full run of his personal books. And a little later the Headmaster also allowed him to browse in his own well-stocked library. Here he first read the Jacobean dramatists and the metaphysical poets. Here he first became acquainted with contemporary French fiction. Here he browsed in Isaac D'Israeli's *Curiosities of Literature*. And here he read in French translation Pushkin and Lermontov. The influence of the violence of Webster's theatre, the language and concern for death of Donne and Crashaw never left him. We find him recommending them to the present Lord Baldwin as a schoolboy forty years later. The naturalism of the French, the magpie information of D'Israeli are all influences obvious to Kipling readers. What has been unnoticed is how apt the two Russian authors were for his future Indian career, especially Lermontov with his emphasis on the military life and on the dangers and pleasures of an Empire's frontiers.

At one point, Price was supposed to give him Russian lessons but they did not progress far. I imagine the idea of his working on an Indian newspaper must already have been in the air, for a knowledge of Russian would have been exceptional and invaluable there. Who knows, he might have joined the Great Game with Creighton and Kim.

But to understand how he came to be a journalist so young, we must look at his schoolboy writing and his life in the holidays while at Westward Ho. Before that I must say something of the legend which he made in later years out of his school time. But the account of its reality must end by emphasising once more what a remarkable preparation it was for his artistic genius.

Kipling appears to have begun to think of his schooldays again in about 1893, when he was settled as a married man in Vermont. It was then that he wrote for the American magazine *Youth's Companion* his non-fictional account of the school, "An English School", which he still liked enough to include in *Land and Sea Tales* in 1923. In 1894, while staying with his wife near his parents at Tisbury, Wiltshire, on a visit from America, he went over to the College and made the farewell speech for his old Head. This seems to have set his mind further on the school, for in "The Brushwood Boy", which he wrote on a visit next year by himself to his parents, there is a fairly detailed fictional account of Westward Ho (deleted from the final book version). But the first impulses to make out of his schooldays lively, entertaining, joky stories for boys that would instil his unconventional lessons about life, began to stir when the Kiplings, on finally leaving America, started their new life in a house at Torquay in Devon, the very county in which the school was situated. There, and later at Rottingdean, from the start of 1897 until 1899, Kipling composed ten "Stalky" stories, nine of which were published in the latter year as *Stalky & Co.* Visiting Crom Price in his retirement no doubt helped to kindle the flames of memory. But the didactic impulse surely came from the double effect of his disillusionment with the United States and his growing anxieties about his own country. To the mindless insubordination of the Americans, as he saw it, and the complacent attachment to petty codes and regulations of contemporary England, he proposed his own way of life. It is a code that seeks to give the fullest rein to individual skills, energies and cunning for the evasion of minor rules and the outwitting of lesser authorities, while always upholding a strong sense of the overall need for a higher law or social cohesion to which the individual must submit himself in total self-discipline and responsibility. In *Stalky & Co.* he conveniently brought home the lesson, by constantly overriding the prevailing English public-school ethics, which derived ultimately from the great influence of Thomas Arnold's reforms at Rugby School in the early years of Victoria's reign. A mature boy (and the Stalky trio were in fact, as they are in fiction, strangely mature, or, more truly, like boyish men rather than boys) will not accept the ruling of his life by repeated rotes, whether "pijaws" from the padre, or talks about house honour from the housemaster, or pep talks on the team spirit from the prefects. Within the framework of what the school demands, which we learn from the last story in the book is what service for the Empire (and, indeed, what the preservation of civilised society) demands, though the boys always deflate it in their everyday life to some practical demand like getting through exams, a man or a boy has every right to use any weapon in order to learn what life is really like and to find out how he is best fitted to live it.

On this lower level all is a battle of wits, of cunning, on occasion, of fists. It is a preparation for the jungle life of the world, with many valuable weapons explained which are not conventionally taught to boys, such as how to lie at the right moment and in the right way. Within this day-to-day framework, (1) a boy gets away with what he can. But he also (2) makes no complaint when he is punished, often, as the headmaster frequently explains when beating the boys, "unjustly", for a primary conventional public-school maxim to be overthrown is that life should be fair or just. (3) Life isn't fair. There isn't such a thing as "cricket", except in the minds of immature, self-flattering boys or priggish masters wanting to give a false moral colouring to the battle of life for which they were supposed to be preparing their charges. (4) Masters who foolishly make up easy moral platitudes which treat each boy as though he were the same as another must not be surprised if less conforming boys take advantage of them. For instance when a housemaster tries to make a scapegoat of a boy, by declaring him "a moral leper", not to be spoken to by other boys, he may learn with surprise that his supposed victim is taking every advantage of the seclusion of his moral leperhood to live his own life without regard for the school's conventions. This turning of moral clichés inside out in order to avoid them is for me Kipling at his most sympathetic.

There are other aspects of Stalky's world of which I am less sure. For example, (5) everyone must expect to pay the full penalty of being caught, especially if he is not to blame. A pathetically innocent prefect who is seen being kissed by a girl in the village shop is unmercifully ragged as one in authority who has flagrantly given an immoral example. This appears to me equivalent to press campaigns against purely unfortunate public figures, but then, much though Kipling hated newspaper reporters in his mature years, their ethics had been bred deeply into him from his Indian journalist days. And, again, in another story, some older boys, really young men, throw-outs from a crammer's, having bullied smaller boys, are themselves submitted to bullying by the trio. There is something very distasteful in the systematic torture of the bullies, which is not made any better by the emphasis upon the fact that it is performed coolly without loss of temper.

Here, I think, we come upon a feature of Kipling's work which is always disturbing – the deliberate cruelty of the goodies to the baddies in order to teach them a lesson, or simply as a necessary expression of mastery. It occurs throughout his writing career from an Indian story like "The Mark of the Beast" to a story like "Beauty Spots" of 1932. The former is a very good horror story and the latter is a much better comic tale than is usually admitted. But there are, in each, little give-away phrases which suggest a pleasure in the proceedings which is in subjective excess to the art of the story – "several other things happened also, but they cannot be put down here" [53]; "the first dry sob of one from whom all hope of . . . authority was stripped forever". [54]

Kipling was a fierce man, and a very gentle one, yet there is somewhere in him (as in very many of us) a pleasure in the pain of others.

At the school his dismissal of bullying as immature and stupid did much to lessen its incidence in his last years there; but as a new boy he had been horribly bullied. This may be a clue: those who are bullied, I think, by no means always cherish a relish for their sufferings, but often make a mental swop. Something, of course, may be allowed in "The Mark of the Beast" for the need to make the reader's flesh creep. But the hinting at unspeakable things is surely suspect. Unfortunately, perhaps because he was unconscious of it, its expression is out of key with the power of his art, crude. When it happens he is sadly the ancestor of Sapper and Ian Fleming and the police and criminal television serials at their worst point of sadism disguised as moral realism. This element, which impairs much of *Stalky & Co.*, is less marked in the three or four later Stalky stories which he wrote at various times down to the late twenties.

To complete the picture of the ethical teaching of *Stalky & Co.*, only one other story need be noted. It is the much discussed "The Flag of Their Country", in which the boys are outraged by a jingoistic M.P.'s address, when he expresses from a platform patriotic sentiments that all the right-minded boys know lie too deep for words. The most striking moment of the story is at the end, when Stalky loses his temper, for this is entirely against the cool Stalky creed. He does so when, after the abominable address, Foxy, the school sergeant-major, suggests that the newly formed rifle corps may use the Union Jack that the obnoxious M.P. has left behind. Stalky immediately dismisses the corps and, when Foxy says he may have to report him for this to the Head, "white to the lips, Stalky cried, 'Report, then, and be damned to you.' "[55] Most readers have either praised Kipling's shrewd observation that non-commissioned officers are more receptive of patriotic guff than the future officer class or have objected to the snobbery of that observation. I think that Stalky's unexampled anger tells us something more: Stalky's and Kipling's distaste for the fact, perhaps suggested by the original Sergeant-Major Schofield, the school's drill-sergeant, that Stalkyism, dismissal of empty moral talk and high-flown sentiment, of "flumdiddle", which should be classless, which was the mark of the private soldier heroes of *Soldiers Three*, might not always be so easy for the semi-educated. It is a rare example of the exposure of an over-democratic sentimentality in Kipling's ethic.

The whole ethical scheme is most clearly stated in the story "Stalky", not published in the original *Stalky & Co.*, where we are told, "Stalkyism in their school vocabulary meant clever, well-considered and wily as applied to plans of action."[56] Practical examples are very plainly given in a letter Kipling wrote from Cape

1 Kipling's parents. (*Bateman's*)

2 An example of Lockwood Kipling's work on the Market Hall, Bombay. (*Photo Tony Garrett*)

3 Victoria Memorial, Bombay. (*India Office Library and Records*)

Performance of Drink by Gigger

The Jackdaw Nuisance

Ave Imperatrix Congratulations

A poet ill-conditioned

Chefs de Cuisine Interrupted

Gigger in the Toffee Factory

4 Drawings of Kipling by his Study 5 friend, G. C. Beresford (M'Turk), from *Schooldays with Kipling* (published by Victor Gollancz, 1936): the nickname "Gigger" is from "Giglamp", because Kipling wore glasses.

5 Letter from Kipling to Mrs Tavenor Perry (Mater), a surrogate mother, written in his last year at school, 25 January 1882; he illustrated his letters throughout his life, see letter from

6 Kipling (centre) at United Services College, Westward Ho!, where he was at school. (*Bateman's*)

7 The dining room at Uncle Ned Burne-Jones's house, The Grange, Fulham Road – "a wondrous cavern", page 29. (*Bateman's*)

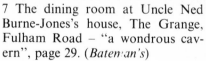

8 Comic drawing of "A Prominent lady on her honeymoon at Rottingdean, August 1893" by Uncle Ned Burne-Jones: he relieved the high-minded idealism of his art by such "vulgarities", and his nephew Rudyard inherited this mingling of the serious and the slapstick. (*Sotheby's*)

9 Rudyard Kipling and his father. (*Bateman's*)

10 Rudyard Kipling in Simla.
(*Library of Congress*)

11 Trix Kipling. (*Library of Congress*)

Town, at Easter 1898, in reply to a "cheeky" request from the editor of the Horsmonden School Magazine, the *Budget*, for a contribution. He proposes "Some Hints on Schoolboy Etiquette". In these practical examples, since he is talking to younger boys then those at Westward Ho, we see the tactics in their simplest guise. For example: "If you have any doubts about a Latin quantity, cough. In three cases out of five this will save you being asked to 'say it again' "; "Never shirk a master out of bounds. Pass him with an abstracted eye, and at the same time pull out a letter and study it earnestly. He may think it is a commission for someone else"; "When pursued by the native farmer always take to the nearest ploughed land. Men stick in furrows that boys can run over." [57]

Major-General Dunsterville (Stalky) applied such maxims to frontier warfare. Kipling applied them to those who tried to penetrate the defences of his privacy. Both met with considerable success.

But, apart from the social teaching, what is the artistic success of *Stalky & Co*? I am surprised to find how many people, including women, look back with delight on their youthful reading of the stories. I find it hard to believe that the book is not now as dead as *Eric, or Little by Little* or *Tom Brown's Schooldays*, which it was intended to supersede. Charles Carrington speaks of its fantasy expressing the daydreams of many schoolboys, of "the witticisms, the ingenuities, the audacities they would have produced if only the world of fact resembled the world of fancy". [58] Fair enough, but, antiquated language apart, I doubt if the daydreams of equivalent schoolboys today could participate much in the life of Stalky. He goes on to compare it as a fantasy to *Tom Sawyer*. If we change this to the greater *Huckleberry Finn*, I think we may see why *Stalky & Co*. does not rank among Kipling's best work. In its language and in its failure to suggest any further dimension to the exploits on the page, it is never poetic, lacks all verbal overtones. And it is the poetry of Kipling's great work, for example, *Kim*, which endures.

That poetry depends in great degree upon his extraordinary sense of place. With all his magical powers he could do little to give life to the studies and hidey-holes of the Stalky trio. It is, as a result, at once the book most dependent upon invented situation and almost the most cerebral. Instead of poetry of language and feeling, or any extra dimension to the described scene, we get an intense literariness and an over-indulgence in reminiscence of books that sustained Kipling as a boy – Jorrocks, Uncle Remus, Pickwick. Perhaps the later "Regulus" (1911) is better than the original stories, because here another boy takes the centre of the stage, a boy less close to Kipling himself, and

51

we are led into a more complex world, that of the courage of the unsure and the over-serious, and equally we are led away from the overcertainties, the cocksureness, the monotony of the exploits of the famous three, with their cardboard foils of master and prefect and irate farmers.

I suffered all too much from a games-worshipping family, yet I think that there is in *Stalky & Co.*, with all its intended liberating ethic, a smug priggishness of the "smart", the resourceful towards the ordinary, the simple pleasures and pains of, for example, the cricket- and football-obsessed schoolboys, which becomes monotonous. It is a kind of high jinks "wake up England" recruiting speech which, like the flagwaving M.P.'s embarrassing oration, is pitched in too loud a key. Perhaps what his niece tells us of the thirty-three-year-old Kipling's delight when writing these exploits, his "What shall we make them do next?" gives us a clue to what seems wrong. It is too self-gratifying. My criticism itself would sound inflated or priggish, however, if it were not for the constant high didactic intention which the author has attached to these stories. Morally he demands much from us, and we have a right, I think, therefore, to demand greater artistic satisfaction.

But certainly he repaid his school for all it had done for him. And especially Crom Price. True, Price had to see himself, a pacific man, turned into a maker of Empire-builders and a regular wielder of the cane when he seldom, in fact, beat any boy. But he is turned, in compensation, from a very nice man doing a difficult job with some strain into a beneficent, all-knowing god, the stalkiest of them all. No wonder, as Sir Sidney Cockerell tells us, when he asked Price how many of the Stalky exploits he remembered, he replied, "Kipling remembers things that I have forgotten, and I remember some things that he would like me to forget." [59] No wonder, too, that when Cockerell told this to Kipling many years later, he commented, "Yes, the dear fellow never gave me away." [60] Few writers have had a headmaster who understood their need so well; but, then, few headmasters have been on to such a good thing in encouraging a precocious pupil.

What, in fact, had Kipling written at school? Price had made him editor of the school magazine. His contributions are interesting. For example, sketches of the life of pre-study boys, "Life in the Corridor", written as though he were describing the natural history of deer, is interesting as pointing (though in reverse) towards the anthropomorphism of the Jungle Books. "Life in the studies" breathes a premature weariness – the boredom of inviting bores to a brew in one's study; the shut-in-ness. This dislike for study life of the fifteen-and-a-half-year-old

Ruddy contrasts with the jaunty enthusiasm for Study 5 life of Kipling at thirty-three.

There is much good stuff for a boy of his age. But one can say no more. Only the unfinished story, "Ibbetson Dunn", written in his last term, has strange overtones which point to the future. It is the tale of a young man called "The King" who lives in a rented hut on the sand dunes, the story of his lonely Christmas festivity. In the bay a ship is in danger of sinking. There is a note of strangeness, of life's intensity and its menace, that suggests the best of the Indian stories. But, of course, the end might well have been some banal rescue heroics. No doubt the shed in the dunes derives from the exciting happy hidey-holes of *Stalky & Co.* but it has a feeling of one of his very best and earliest Indian stories, "The Strange Ride of Morrowbie Jukes", laid in a village of the dead who haven't died but live in caves in the sandbanks of an Indian river. And, in fact, this magnificent, grim parable of the English precariousness in India was written only three years after he wrote "Ibbetson Dunn".

For the most part, however, Kipling's more serious work as a schoolboy was in verse. It was, like some of the prose items, frequently conscious pastiche, and, where it was not, it leaned heavily on great models. Catherine Wright Morris has shown [61] that for all the adult Kipling's Stalky denials to the editors, he almost certainly at thirteen and a half submitted a poem to the popular New York *St Nicholas Magazine for Children*. It is, perhaps, the earliest recording of *Stalky & Co.*:

> We were a dusky crew,
> And each boy's hand was against us raised
> 'Gainst me and the other two. [62]

The poem was refused. But the incident suggests that he may well have sought publication in many quarters during those school years. Apart from local papers, one poem alone saw light, "Two Lives" in *The World*, the editor of which, Edmund Yates, Beresford says, Kipling knew. (If so, it is a fascinating direct link between the schoolboy who so often quotes Charles Dickens and Dickens himself, who had been Yates's staunch patron fifteen or so years earlier.) But the earlier rejected poem of 1879 and a number of others were collected by his mother and published in an edition of fifty booklets in Lahore in 1881 – something which Kipling himself only found out to his embarrassment years later. It is clear that his parents, themselves both contributors to newspapers and magazines, had an image of his future that was a fortunate one for him. To fill out the picture of the schoolboy editor and writer of verses turning into a professional reporter and author we must look shortly at his holiday contacts while he was at Westward Ho.

The arrangements for his first holidays from Westward Ho in 1878 must have been a shock for the boy. He stayed at the school. His father was on his way home from India and his mother went to join him in Florence. Such Italian overland journeys were a familiar feature of Anglo-Indian home leaves and must have been especially attractive to the artistic Kiplings. On the present trip finances if nothing else would forbid them taking the children; about that time even Uncle Ned Burne-Jones, for whom Italy was the love of his life, could not afford a visit. We may believe that Burne-Jones and the Macdonalds were deliberately not chosen as Rudyard's hosts so that Crom Price could get to know his friend's son and new pupil better and help him to settle down. It proved a great success. Kipling tells us that from the first day of the holidays, the whole atmosphere ceased to be that of the school he so hated in his first term.

In recompense, Rudyard accompanied his father to the Paris Exhibition, where Lockwood had some concern (not official, as is usually stated) with the Indian exhibits. Rudyard had a pass into the Exhibition, was given some small pocket-money and left to himself. It seems to have improved his French. Many decades later, when he had long been strongly francophile, he recalled this visit to Paris as the foundation of his love of France. He also, in old age, declared that the sight of Dagnan Bouveret's painting "Death of Manon Lescaut" at the Salon led him to the reading of that book which in turn gave him the central theme of *The Light That Failed*. Both statements have a suggestion of Stalkyish cover-up about them. There was to be much hostility to France between 1878 and his eventual worship of that country. There were other more personal and hidden themes behind the novel. But he obviously enjoyed the holiday enormously – the freedom, the adulthood, the new scene, above all, his father's company. Lockwood wrote to Price shortly after, "I should think that he will always be inclined to shirk the collar and to interest himself in out of the way things."[63] Perhaps it was already this holiday that set the pattern of the thinking of his parents and his headmaster alike about the sort of career that would suit such a boy. One only trusts that they were not typing him too soon.

It was also seen as desirable that he should have a regular home in the holidays when his parents went to India. In these years, Kipling boarded with three cultured sisters – two middle-aged maiden ladies

and a widow – in London, at Warwick Gardens near Addison Road.
They were friends of Alice Kipling's, although Carrington tells us that
she was unsure of the wisdom of the choice. However, once again it
avoided reliance on the family's kindness. In his autobiography
Kipling speaks of the house with great respect. And in its civilised
atmosphere, its associations with literature, the opportunity of meeting celebrities, it had much to offer. Reading his own verses aloud to
the ladies. Discovering Thompson's "City of Dreadful Night", whose
pessimistic romanticism of urban despair influenced much of his own
early Indian work. Here he conversed with the famous African missionary, Mary Kingsley, and clearly found her intrepidity and her
humour much to his taste, for they walked together from Addison
Road to Knightsbridge and back. Here he talked with William de
Morgan the novelist and potter. (About novel writing or about por-
celain? Probably both.) "Somewhere in the background were people
called Jean Inglelow and Christina Rossetti, but I was never lucky
enough to see those good spirits." [64] There is a touch of Kipling's very
discreet irony about this sentence. After all, he was a bookish youth
but he had other more boisterous sides and he was a mature person.

We know from a very unexpected source that the Misses Craik and
Mrs Winnard were a little hard put to it to keep him amused. The
eminent Greek scholar Gilbert Murray, of all people (born in the same
year as Kipling), writes in his *Unfinished Autobiography* for the year
1882, "Once a Mrs Hooper [in fact née Miss Winnard] told us that
her nephew Ruddy was rather lonely in the holidays and would like to
meet another boy. Ruddy came round once or twice and we walked in
Kensington Gardens and talked about books ... I thought him extraordinarily clever and exciting though there was something in him
that repelled me ... He threw stones at a cat." [65] This was a usual
pursuit of Victorian boys, but perhaps unknown to Australia where
Murray had come from. Kipling, it seems, told him about an epic
poem he was writing about Heaven and Hell; but when Murray mentioned it to him twenty years later, he could not recall it. The note is
authentic, for Kipling, so reticent about himself, appears often to have
discussed the works he was composing with others; perhaps this was
but another aspect of his exposing his imaginations within his works
to batteries of facts and technicalities.

It was during some of these holidays from Westward Ho that he
managed to be taken into the Middlesex Hospital (presumably by
some medical student friend). He had told his sister that he wanted to
be a doctor but that a post-mortem had put him off. "Oh! in fact,
Mark Twain has a word for it. I believe I threw up my immortal

soul."[66] His concern with medicine and his friendship with medical men lasted all his life. Indeed in later years, when his own ill-health defied diagnosis, he made many eccentric excursions into the metaphysical and psychological edges of conventional physical medicine that produced some of his most tantalisingly unsatisfactory later stories.

He was, of course, able to spend much time both with the Burne-Joneses, where his cousin Margaret was a favourite as well as her parents; and with the Poynter household, where, like everyone else, he adored his Aunt Aggie. All the same the lacuna in our knowledge of the wanderings of this strange, mature, boyish, clever youth in London is one of the most vexing in all his life. We may be sure from the dialogue of *Stalky & Co.* and from the fondness of Uncle Ned for the music hall that this is when he added the rhythm of popular songs to the rhythm of hymns to produce (in a most unmusical man) a unique sung verse two decades later. But when we think of the excellence of his one later London slum story, "Badalia Herodsfoot", we can only regret that his genius had not matured before he left London; but then he almost certainly wouldn't have gone to India and his unique contribution to our literature would have been lost.

We have another witness to his restlessness at cultured Warwick Gardens in his letters to a Mrs Tavenor Perry. In a letter from school of 25 January 1882, he says, "You don't know the place Westward Ho. I'm afraid I couldn't convey to your mind any idea of its flatness and dullness generally. Nevertheless, I am hardened enough to prefer it to Warwick Gardens."[67] And in May he is writing to her in the excited hope that he may come to stay with her in his summer holidays, for he has heard from Miss Winnard that she and her sister propose to go to Switzerland.

So far as I know, this correspondence with Mrs Tavenor Perry (some letters in the Huntington Library and one in the Carpenter Collection, Houghton Library, Harvard) has not been mentioned in any publication on Kipling. I think that it is likely, from the final address in the Boltons to which he writes to her, that she was the wife of John Tavenor Perry, a well-known architect and antiquary – a likely friend of Lockwood or Uncle Ned. He is probably the "Tav" to whom Rudyard sends messages about pottery and antiques in the letters.

The letters are intimate and he addresses her always as "Dearest Mater" and from Lahore signs himself "Your own graceless boy." They continue until two months after his arrival in India and complain of his loneliness there. They suggest the need for a surrogate mother more than the usual account of his relations with his own mother allows.

He talks to her mainly about school or, in Lahore, reporting assignments. But he also speaks to her in two letters of May 1882 about Flo Garrard. In the first, on 22 May, he says, "It may amuse you to know that everything that has ever existed between myself and the fair F.G. *is entirely at an end*. Draw what conclusion you will from this statement. Aren't I a queerly constructed youth? Reckless is a mild way to put my present state of mind." [68] In his next letter of 28 May, he seeks to dispel her alarm at his news: "A youth has just swallowed his first bitter pill and you must excuse him if he finds it a little harsh in his mouth . . . besides this is merely a temporary 'flick' which, in all probability, is the forerunner of half a dozen more. Very sorry if I've disturbed you in any way by anything I might have said in a moment of weakness – I'm all right now." [69] According to his sister, Trix, Flo Garrard did not break off their understood engagement until after he had been some months in India. Perhaps the coolness described to Mrs Perry was only temporary.

He had met Flo Garrard, who was a little older than him, when he went to fetch Trix away from Southsea in the holidays of 1880 when he was still fourteen. She was a paying guest like Trix at Aunt Rosa's. The attachment, on his side, at any rate, appears to have been immediate and strong. He was physically very mature for his age and emotionally probably very susceptible. His poems written for her in these schoolboy years, "Sundry Phansies" (now in the Berg Library) are, as Professor Cornell says in his excellent *Kipling in India*, more romantic, even more "decadent" than the "Schoolboy Lyrics", but I don't find this very surprising. He was in love with Flo. In any case, much of his earlier Indian work, particularly the *In Black and White* stories, have a *fin-de-siècle* flavour as do all the fragments like "To Be Filed for Reference" that relate to his never realised Indian novel, *Mother Maturin*.

His feelings for Flo Garrard were certainly intense, the miseries of the downs of the relationship great, as more than one of his female relatives, in whom he confided, affirmed.

His parents must have known of his emotional strain, for if he did not tell them (and I suppose he did), his sister Trix would surely have done so. Here was an additional reason to carry out the schemes they had laid for his future. From Alice Kipling's letter to her friend, Miss Plowden, money once more played its part here: "Our income which would be a good one if we were all under one roof does not bear a division and subdivision by exchange – we are really feeling the pinch at present." [70] But Ruddy was in their minds also, Ruddy thirsting for a man's life with a man's work: "if our plan be carried out he will get both when he is eighteen."[71] And so the string-pulling began. Stephen Wheeler, the editor of the *Civil and Military Gazette*, on leave in London, met Rudyard in his school holidays in spring 1882. He must have thought that the sooner this eccentric and literary boy, whom his bosses insisted on employing, came to work under him and learn journalism the hard way, the better. And so Crom Price told him that he was to go to Lahore and work on the *Gazette*. Beresford says that Kipling wanted to stay in London where the literary scene was. But to Mrs Perry, "Mater", Kipling wrote of his anxiety to get out of England. Probably he was divided. In any case, out he sailed for India in September 1882. Far from eighteen years old as his parents had talked of, he was short of seventeen by three months. His last holiday was taken with Trix, partly with his Kipling grandmother at Skipton, and partly with the Aunt and Uncle at their refuge (nearly always packed with visiting relations) on the green at Rottingdean, a seaside Sussex village on the south coast of England.

2 RETURN ON DUTY
TO PARADISE

Kipling's India

At ten o'clock in the heavy, wet heat of an August night, a man, despairing of sleep, which, in any case, does not come easily to his exhausted body and nerves, determines to walk. Indifferent to direction, he will go at random where his stick, thrown in the air, points – a stick that, falling, rouses a hare which runs across a disused burial-ground where "the heated air and the heavy earth had driven the very dead upward for coolness' sake . . . Straight as a bar of polished steel ran the road to the City of Dreadful Night; and, on either side of the road, lay corpses . . . some shrouded all in white with bound-up mouths; some naked . . . and one . . . silvery white and ashen grey. A leper asleep." Two hours' walk to the Delhi Gate and from there but a few steps to the great Mosque of Wazir Khan, where a "deeply sleeping janitor lies across the threshold . . . A rat dashes out of his turban at the sound of approaching footsteps." Ascending a winding staircase of one of the Minars, "half way up there is something alive, warm and feathery" – in fact a sleeping kite. "Doré might have drawn it! Zola could describe it . . . The sleep that will not come to the city . . . Seated with elbows on the parapet of the tower one can watch and wonder over that heat-tortured hive till the dawn." Allah ho Akbar! La ilha Illalah! "Several weeks of darkness pass after this." Then, as the city asleep on the housetops comes to wake at dawn, the man escapes. As he walks away, a voice asks him, "Will the Sahib, out of his kindness, make room? . . . Something borne on a man's shoulders comes by in that half light. A woman's corpse going down to the burning ghat . . . So the City of Death as well as of Night after all." [1] In the native city of Lahore it is the young Kipling's job to look and to report. And, when respectfully requested, to get out of the way of the life and the death he observes.

Near to the Delhi Gate among a hundred ramshackle mould-blotched buildings is an obscure house, called appropriately (and didactically) The Gate of a Hundred Sorrows, where a Chinaman runs an opium den. Kipling, or "I", as he disguises himself in these early stories, is most frightfully knowing about the different effects of opium on men and women according to race – this for the yellow, that for the black, this for the brown, that for the white. But his reportage is swept aside by the compulsive assertion of a half-white, Mesquita. Mesquita lives on a pittance of sixty rupees a month, legacy from an aunt far south in Agra, which he draws "fresh and fresh every month".[2] And pays them to the Chinaman for rent and pipe. Of all the ten original smokers only he and four others survive – all the rest are dead, including one English loafer, McSomebody. The Chinaman's nephew, Tsin-Ling, has inherited the lucrative dream-ship and with it, Mesquita. "Nothing matters much to me now – only I wish Tsin-Ling wouldn't put bran into the Black Smoke."[3] The compulsive need of those being sucked down into Lahore's old city submerges Kipling's knowing "I", gives him the voices he needed, the realisation of the dramatic monologues he has already learned from Browning's poems.

This Delhi Gate is still today a tattered, blotchy, rubbish-filled nook and cranny end of Lahore City. The great Wazir Khan Mosque in Moslem Pakistan seems crumbling and damp-heat-stained beside the memory of the great showplace tourist-filled Moghul mosques we have left behind in India. The road runs here by day, noisy, crowded with bazaar stalls, between which tongas clatter even now. You may observe still – for instance – a boy of sixteen lying on the narrow pavement, his thigh exposed to show an open suppurating wound, from which he brushes flies. And today at any moment a figure may detach itself from the mass, detain you by a skinny hand or glittering eye, and assert its dwindling life in Browning monologue – "Sir, may I ask what do you think of the growing power of women? Everything it seems must be given to the women. I am not a university-educated man, Sir, but to me it seems . . ." At night, no doubt, as in all cities of the sub-continent, the sleepers lie like shrouded dead upon the roofs and the pavements. In London sometimes something still echoes Dickens or Doré, in Paris Balzac or Zola, in Leningrad Dostoevsky, but it is only an echo here and there of a vanished world. In Lahore City, it seems, there could be nothing more to write, for it has all been said by Kipling. Nothing more for an observer, that is, although one's colouring would be different, less echoing Poe and De Quincey, less on the edge of blank verse, but doubtless catching, as Kipling does, that sense of menace, of falling apart, that threatens all, even an Eurasian loafer, even a brash young reporter, when work and duty are put aside. Here on the walls at the entrance to the narrow streets that we have left behind us are still fading notices, "Out of Bounds", echoes of the old Evangelical voice that sought to protect our soldiers' sexual morals – a voice that so riled Kipling back in the eighties when it forced Parliament to abolish licensed brothels for the Army in India; the voice that made him for once only disrespectful to Lord Roberts – how could "Bobs" so impose a chapel-made absurdity on the empty, cruel lives of the soldiers who so adored him?

Here stood the house of Suddhoo, near the now-vanished Taxila Gate. Suddhoo was a very old man with one much-beloved son, now many miles away north in Peshawar and ill with pleurisy. A seal cutter, one of Suddhoo's lodgers, is bleeding the old man white of all his savings for the jaddoo, the sorceries that he performs to save the son's life. As Kipling, "I", friend to the old man, sees at once. Jaddoos, for instance, "in the basin ... bobbing in the water, the dried shrivelled black head of a native baby ... we had no time to say anything before it began to speak ... On the wall were a couple of flaming portraits of the Queen and the Prince of Wales. They looked down on the performance." An impotent British rule. Janoo, a prostitute who lodges there, who "had hoped to get from Suddhoo many rupees while he lived, and many more after his death", also sees scornfully these tricks. But she is in debt to the seal cutter's wealthy moneylender friend. There will never be time to say anything. "She will never tell because she dare not, but ... I am afraid that the seal cutter will die of cholera ... the white arsenic kind – about the middle of May. And thus I shall be privy to murder in the House of Suddhoo." [4] In *The City of Dreadful Night* to look is to be privy to the crime.

As with the escape from the Lahore City fortress, Fort Amara, of Khem Singh, the old rebel of the Mutiny days (days now never mentioned between black and white). In "On the City Wall", the salon of the courtesan, Lalun, looks directly onto the fortress, where young Kipling, "I", visits to observe and listen. Here one day when the Moslem mourning of Mohurrum has turned the city into a battleground of Mohammedans and Hindus, he is persuaded by Lalun's charms to escort an elderly native gentleman through the riots to his friends at the other end of town. The man he has passed by his warranty through the barriers of his friends at the Club and the messroom – the Deputy Commissioner, the Assistant Deputy Superintendent, turned out to quell the riots – is, of course, the bloodstained myth of that far-off terrible year of mutiny, Khem Singh, escaped from the fortress under cover of the riot. He who breaks caste, if only in order to observe, finds himself taken up in action. For action is ever present, if you don't choose it, it will choose you. And the action that chooses you is action against your own kin. But life is sometimes ironically kind to the consciences of would-be observers. Action not only involves, it moves on and discards. Khem Singh "went to the young men but the glamour of his name had passed away ... he could give neither pensions ... nor influence, nothing but a glorious death with their back to the mouth of a gun ... Moreover Khem Singh was old ... and he had left his cooking pots in Fort Amara." [5] So he returns to the fortress and surrenders. Life is always unkind to those whom history has passed by.

Like, for example, Jellaludin McIntosh – McSomebody of the reminiscences of the Eurasian of The Gate of a Hundred Sorrows. "In most big cities natives will tell you of two or three Sahibs, generally low-caste, who have turned Hindu or Mussulman, and who live more or less as such. But it is not often that you get to know them." [6] But Kipling did. "I was admitted to the McIntosh household – I and my good tobacco. But nothing else. Unluckily, one cannot visit a loafer in the Serai by day. Friends buying horses would not understand it. Consequently I was obliged to visit him by night." [7] And there, in his cups, raving in Greek or German, spouting Swinburne's "Atalanta in Calydon", admitting to selling Kipling's Pickering edition of Horace, reviling himself, "I who was once a Fellow of a College whose buttery hatch you have not seen" [8] (the biblical echo, so essentially Kipling's, seems also right for the Oxford drop-out), dying of pneumonia, Jellaludin McIntosh the loafer makes a present to his observer of a huge manuscript – "my work ... being an account of the life and sins and death of Mother Maturin ... If the thing is ever published, someone may perhaps remember this story, now printed as a safeguard to prove that McIntosh Jellaludin and not I myself wrote the Book of Mother Maturin." [9]

It never was published, of course, for Kipling wrote only a part of what was intended to be his great novel of the half-life and low-life of Lahore. From the names dropped in the course of the ravings of Jellaludin McIntosh in "To Be Filed for Reference", we can tell that, connected with it, is the poem "The Ballad of Fisher's Boarding House":

> Since Life is strife, and strife means knife,
> From Howrah to the Bay,
> And he may die before the dawn

Who liquored out the day,
In Fultah Fisher's Boarding House
We woo while yet we may.[10]

All the characters are brought together in the script of the never-made film of the twenties, to be called "The Gate of a Hundred Sorrows".[11] Mrs Carpenter, widow of the American collector of Kiplingiana, tells us that a friend informed her that in the final story of Mother Maturin, the old Irishwoman of the half-world would send her daughter to be educated in England, and that the daughter, married to a civil servant, would return to Lahore.[12] Thus a connection would be established between The City of Dreadful Night and the Lahore of the Sahibs, of the Civil Lines and the Cantonment. Out of this would come a tale of espionage and the selling of the secrets of the British Government. She adds, what Carrington also tells us, that Kipling's decision not to finish the book was much influenced by his father's disapproval. Mrs Carpenter's informant was probably Mrs Edmonia Hill, "Ted", Kipling's landlady and good friend during his time of work on the *Pioneer* in Allahabad. If so, it is quite reliable information. We may certainly believe that he would have told her the plot (as seems to have been his custom even with acquaintances); but that does not mean, of course, that he did not change it in his mind many times in the following years before he finally abandoned it. Lockwood's disapproval might have been because he thought it a bit garish and sensational, or he may have disapproved of its sexual freedom, or he may have doubted the wisdom of discussing the leaking of Government secrets. All these objections would be in the character of a man of good but conventional taste, not without holy-holy qualities, and always sensible of the seriousness of the Establishment in whose favour he stood. But I do not think that we need regret too much the loss of poor drunken Jellaludin McIntosh's masterpiece, for, from its wreck, Kipling made his own masterpiece, *Kim*, which is far more than any simple connecting of opium dens with Government House, the Club and the Mall.

But there was another half-world, another meeting-place of the races in Kipling's Lahore, where the happiness and the sorrow were too deep to be the subject of observation, where only feeling and imagination could suffice. A world that Kipling, unlike the lesser Maugham, knew instinctively, must be too deeply felt for the distancing of an observer, however ironically involved. So Bisesa's "room looked out through the grated window into the narrow dark gully where the sun never came and where the buffaloes wallowed in the blue slime. She was a widow about fifteen years old." A young Sahib, Trejago, wanders aimlessly and hears her singing. There follow duennas and communications by object-letters – bits of broken glass, a pinch of cattle food, even cardamoms, and other odds and ends. "Bisesa was an endless delight to Trejago. She was as ignorant as a bird; and her distorted versions of the rumours from the outside world that had reached her in her room amused Trejago almost as much as her lisping attempts to pronounce his name – 'Christopher'. The first syllable was always more than she could manage." Delicious time passes, then one night after a long interval when Trejago has been too busy to find out why the messages have ceased, he comes to the gully steaming with buffalo dung, the gully of such hidden beauty. "From the black dark Bisesa held out her arms into the moonlight. Both hands had been cut off at the wrists, and the stumps were nearly healed." Trejago, as she tries to warn him, is wounded in the thigh. Now "The grating that opens into Amir Nath's Gully has been walled up." Trejago is "reckoned a very decent sort of man," there is nothing peculiar about him save a slight limp. The story, without Kipling's intercession as "I", has a certain crudeness that follows too easily its didactic opening warning of the dangers of ignoring the colour divides. Yet the effect is powerful enough in its violence, and that effect, I believe, is made more than just sensational by the overtones of a much more sensitive blame that attaches rather to Trejago's condescending passion than to any violation of the barriers of race. Indeed, there is so much to deny the simple racial caution that is declared at the beginning. For example, Bisesa's, "You are an Englishman. I am only a black girl," with Kipling's comment, "she was finer than bargold in the Mint".[13]

It is a good introduction to the much finer paradise lost of "Without Benefit of Clergy", to that most enchanting of houses in the native city where lived John Holden's "woman of sixteen and she was all but the world in his eyes ... Anyone could enter his bachelor's bungalow by day or night, and the life he led there was an unlovely one. In the house in the city ... he was king in his own territory, with Ameera for his Queen." And then comes the baby son, Tota (named for the parakeets who flash like green streams from the evening trees) and "Holden found one helpless little hand that closed feebly on his finger. And the clutch ran through his body till it settled about his heart." He knows, as he tells Ameera, that the white mem-log are not as happy as she. For they give their children over to nurses. "I have never seen that," said Ameera, "nor do I wish to see." Tota becomes "a small gold-coloured little god ... Those were months of absolute happiness to Holden and Ameera – happiness withdrawn from the world . . . By the day Holden did his work with an immense pity for such as were not so fortunate as himself . . . At nightfall he returned to Ameera." And Tota grew. "One evening, while he sat on the roof between his father and his mother watching the never-ending warfare of the kites that the city boys flew, he demanded a kite of his own . . . when Holden called him 'a spark', he rose to his feet and murmured, 'Hum admi hi. I am no spark but a man.' The protest made Holden choke and devote himself very seriously to a consideration of Tota's future. He need hardly have taken the trouble. The delight of that life was too perfect to endure. Therefore it was taken away as many things are taken away in India – suddenly and without warning . . . One mercy was granted . . . to Holden. He . . . found waiting an uncommonly heavy mail that demanded . . . hard work. He was not however alive to this kindness of the gods." " 'Ahi! Ahi!' cries Ameera . . . 'let us all be together as it was before' . . . 'We be two who were three. The greater need therefore that we should be one,' " is Holden's answer. And so it works out. Their love even continues to grow closer until a casual rumour in the Club leads Holden to ask, " 'Is it the old programme then . . . famine, fever and cholera?' . . . Two months later . . . nature began to audit her accounts with a red pencil." But unlike the Memsahibs, Ameera will not flee to the hills before the plague. And so, as "there are not many happinesses as complete as those that are snatched under the shadow of the sword, they sat together and laughed, calling each other openly by every pet name that could move the wrath of the gods". That wrath is proved and Ameera dies. "The quick breathing seemed to show that she was either afraid or in pain, but neither eyes nor mouth gave any answer to Holden's kisses." And so, at last, the landlord, in kindness to Holden's desperation, orders that "the house should be pulled down . . . so that no man may say where it stood".[14] The priests and clerks of the Middle Ages could plead benefit of clergy and receive special trial. Holden and Ameera in their private paradise have no such special rights.

Into that city of dreadful night, Lahore's native city, the sahibs come at their own peril, whether it be for the deathly crowding of Suddhoo's house or the delicious treachery of Lalun's salon or the sweet, heavenly innocence of Ameera's play with Tota. Only one white man makes his way there where he wills: Strickland, Kipling's unconvincing Sherlock Holmes of all disguises. We only hear at second hand of Strickland's exploits among the natives: "He dabbled in unsavoury places no respectable man would think of exploring – all among the native riff-raff . . . When a man knows who dances the Holi-Hukk, and how, and when, and where, he knows something to be proud of."[15]

Jellaludin McIntosh, who has wholly dropped out into the native world, speaks of Strickland with contempt; this reader is inclined to agree with him. The only detection that Strickland performs for us seems to satisfy his own pleasure in his authority rather than to reveal any of the famed nearly superhuman powers of seeing into the native mind that he is credited with. With the warning barks of the dog Tietjens and with the snakes protruding from the ceiling cloth, it was not too hard to find Imray's body hidden above in the roof ("The Return of Imray"). More difficult, perhaps, would be to condemn to hanging the servant who had killed him because he feared that Imray's blessing upon his little son had brought about the child's death. ("He said he was a handsome child, and patted him on the head: wherefore my child died. Wherefore I killed Imray Sahib in the twilight."[16]) But Strickland has no such difficulties. ("Do I hang, then?" said Bahadur Khan ... "If the sun shines or the water runs – yes!"[17]) In "The Mark of the Beast", too, where the planter, Fleet's, drunken profanation of a temple is avenged by some hypnotic spell that turns him into a human leopard, Strickland's contribution as Police Chief is more inventive of action than of detection. When the leper priest who is working the spell is captured, it is Strickland who knows what to do – and "I"? "I resolved to put away all my doubts and to help Strickland from the heated gun barrels to the loop of twine – from the loins to head and back again – with all tortures that might be needful ... Strickland shaded his eyes with his hands for a moment and we got to work. This part is not to be printed."

It is not surprising that such a man of action should be so unconvincing on the only occasion that we do see him in native disguise, for it is in the inactive role of sais or carriage driver which he contrives in order successfully to woo the colonel's daughter ("Miss Youghal's Sais"). And we cannot be very sad, remembering all the similarly brutal heroes of action who have polluted fiction's pages since Strickland's day, when we see how marriage has gelded him, twenty or so years later, in "A Deal in Cotton". "Strickland has finished his Indian service, and lives now at a place called Weston-super-Mare, where his wife plays the organ in one of the churches. Semioccasionally he comes up to London, and occasionally his wife makes him visit his friends. Otherwise he plays golf and follows the harriers for his figure's sake." It is a more terrible fate than the kindly Holmes's bee-keeping retirement. Kipling has a curious power of doing justice, as it seems, unconsciously.

Luckily there is another figure who can move from native city to

civil lines at will. Running over the roofs on some errand of intrigue at
the bidding of the big bully Afghan horse dealer with the scarlet dyed
beard, or camped in the Kashmiri serai where the camel and horse
caravans put up on their return from Central Asia, or striding the gun
Zam-Zammah outside the Museum at the top of the Mall's great
sweep, when carriages roll past, carrying the cream of Lahore's white
society to play tennis in Lawrence Gardens or dance at the
Montgomery Hall – the Little Friend of all the World, Kim, the Ariel
of Kipling's Indian magic kingdom, who goes alike unchecked and
unscathed. I suppose that now, if we could create a figure both so ideal
and so real, we should make him a Tota whose father John Holden
had deserted and whose mother, Ameera, had died. For all his sympathy with the Eurasian world (a sympathy as generally absent from
the Raj of the eighties as it is from India today) which combined
the two races he loved most, Kipling could not so confound order,
though he does make Kim speak with the derided chichi accent of
the half-castes. And, perhaps, the victory of human curiosity and
human attachment in that book over the moral lessons that the author
would impose on them, of the paradox of the benevolent power of mischief and disorder working within the Law, is more fully realised by a
Kim, born of two white parents, naturally at ease with all colours and
creeds, than by any unreal sentimentalisation of the position of the Eurasians living under two quite different racial contempts. Nevertheless,
Kipling had some unusually sympathetic things to say about the mixed
world, as well as some less happy conventional white snobberies. We
may glance at them before following Kim back to the Civil Lines of Lahore,
to the world of the whites in this tour of Kipling's fictional India.

He sees the Eurasians, of course, as they were in a British-
dominated India. And inevitably it is their sense of whiteness that
gives them their moments of victory over their depressed existence. As
with the love of Michele d'Cruze and Miss Vezzis in "His Chance in
Life", where some atavistic drop of Yorkshire blood in the girl im-
poses a demand, as a preliminary to marriage, of a basic salary far
beyond the hopes of her telegraph signaller lover. Beyond the hopes,
but not beyond the courage and the sudden sense of authority that
Michele finds, when without any white man available to take charge,
he quells a religious riot far south in Orissa. And so earns promotion
and his love. This well-told, pleasing tale is especially remarkable for
Kipling's incidental remark about what are now called Anglo-Indians
– "One of these days, this people . . . will turn out a writer or a poet,
then we shall know how they live or what they feel. In the meantime, any
stories about them cannot be absolutely correct in fact or inference."

67

The hope is less likely today than in 1887 when he wrote it. But he repeated it a year later, when, working for the *Pioneer* in Allahabad, he wrote his articles on Calcutta. "All this mass of humanity in Durumtollah [the Eurasian district of Calcutta] is unexplored and almost unknown. Wanted, therefore, a writer from among the Eurasians who shall write so that men shall be pleased to read a story of Eurasian life." [18]

In a story, "His Private Honour", written when he had returned to London as the literary man of the hour in 1891, Kipling "I" allows himself to muse for a page on his dream of an independent British India grown great, "a colonised manufacturing India with a permanent surplus and her own flag". Kashmir he envisages as a military training ground: "there we would plant our much married regiments ... and there they should breed white soldiers, and perhaps a second fighting line of Eurasians." This, at first sight, may seem very condescending; but if we grasp the full implications of that last sentence, we can surely not be surprised at that "perhaps", given the prejudices of his age.

Alas, the young Kipling's dreams were not to survive his departure from India. As time went by, his memory of the country was no less loving, but his picture of it was more conventional. By 1911 in "The Honours of War", Stalky, we are told, had used his well-known joky methods in his Indian days to prevent a chap in the regiment marrying into the half-race – he and some other chaps gave young Elliot-Hocker a bath on his own verandah; "his lady-love saw it and broke off the engagement, which was what the mess intended, she being an Eurasian." And in "Kidnapped", a story of 1887, Mrs Hauksbee, whose exploits usually undermine the more cruelly narrow convention of white Indian society by humane fun, acts with uncharacteristic myopic hardness when she arranges the kidnapping of Peythroppe, a promising young government servant, to prevent his marriage to the Eurasian, Miss Castries. Kipling, indeed, seems disturbed at this humiliation of a half-caste girl deserted at the altar steps, for he gives as his reason, "marriage in India does not concern the individual but the Government he serves", and he makes the jilted Eurasian girl behave impeccably after her sorry treatment. "Miss Castries," he says, "was a *very* good girl."

But enough of the half-city. It has taken us midway from the native city of Lahore to the Civil Lines, to the end of the splendid Mall (even today in Pakistan preserved in its Raj glory, denied to vulgar rickshaws and tongas, a Mall indeed fit for VIP motorcades). Here stands the Museum where for nearly twenty years Lockwood Kipling was curator; within walking distance are the offices once occupied by Rudyard as assistant editor of the *Civil and Military Gazette*; within somewhat further walking distance the probable site of their joint family home. The number of outstanding stories of the tensions, relaxations, strategies, victories, and bloody defeats that ordered the white community life in the Civil Lines of Lahore where Kipling lived and worked from 1882 to 1887 is very small; there are none, so far as I know, of the Civil Lines of Allahabad where he worked and lived for the last two years of his life in India. His tales of the strains of white civilian life are largely drawn from Simla where he spent his leaves and where the Viceroy governed during the hot season. The *Departmental Ditties*, his verses about white civilian life, also concern almost entirely the world of Simla.

The Lahore Club, one of the many noble colonial-classical buildings the English left all over India, appears somewhat anonymously as the scene of introductory, often premonitory gossip, in a number of stories. It is the exchange mart at New Year for the gossip of the lonely horrors of the out-stations, as in the opening of the grisly story, "The Mark of the Beast": "Everybody was there and there was a general closing up of ranks and taking stock of your losses in dead or disabled that had fallen during the year."

It is, however, only the total scene of one tale, "A Friend's Friend", which must, I think, be based upon an experience of Lockwood Kipling before Rudyard arrived in Lahore. Sir Walter Roper-Lawrence tells in *The India We Served* of how the elder Kipling befriended him in his youth as a young government servant of the Punjab in Lahore. He recalls that, as Secretary of the Club, he had to cope with a very drunken English tutor to some Indian prince who arrived at the Pagley Nautch (a fancy dress ball) in the costume of Charles II and behaved very badly. At Lockwood's suggestion, "with the help of some of the servants we lifted him into the bathing-machine conveyance we called tikki-gara. But he jumped out of the opposite door and ran back shouting for Simpkin sharah." [19] The ludicrous (and apparently ineffective) incident, with its pidgin Indian words, especially that for Champagne, is already almost a Kipling story.

But Kipling's "I" 's treatment of a stranger – "a globe-trotter" from England who offended in the same way against the laws of hospitality at a club ball – is more stringent and more effective than his gentler father's. "We corked the whole of his face. We filled his hair with meringue cream till it looked like a white wig ... This was punishment, not play, remember ... We put a ham frill round his neck and tied it in a bow in front . . . We waxed up the ends of his moustache with isinglass . . . We took up the red cloth from the ball room to the supper room, and wound him up in it. There were sixty feet of red cloth, six feet broad . . . We were so angry that we hardly laughed at all." [20] This is the seldom shown anger that we have seen in Stalky's white lips at school after the jingoist M.P. had shouted out publicly sentiments not to be spoken at all. It is an anger we meet again throughout Kipling's work. It is a strange note of sudden intense hatred of someone as the representative of disorder or sometimes of evil mixed with an elaborate schoolboy ritual humour which when it succeeds, as in "The Village that Voted the Earth was Flat", makes completely original farce, but when it fails, as I think it does in "A Friend's Friend", embarrasses the reader as would a sudden loss of temper on a social occasion. But it is a sign that something serious has happened. That a visitor from England (one, too, who up to then had not shown the rather know-all, patronising manner that so many did) should treat the white society of Lahore with light contempt, should show insufficient respect for the white ladies, and, though Kipling doesn't say it, all this before the native servants, is a very high offence in a community that must treat its own rituals very seriously or fall apart. The story fails but the almost hysteric sense of fragility and menace still comes across.

And menace, playfully or grimly treated, is present in the few other stories of the Lahore white world, especially where that world is brought into contact with the natives. As in "Naboth": "he opened our acquaintance by begging. He was very thin and showed nearly as many ribs as his basket . . . a rupee had hidden in my waistcoat lining. I never knew it was there and gave the trove to Naboth as a direct gift from Heaven . . . Next morning . . . he wished to prefer a request. He wished to establish a sweetmeat stall near the house of his benefactor . . . I was graciously pleased to give permission . . . Seven weeks later . . . Naboth brought a blue and white striped blanket, a brass lamp stand, and a small boy to cope with the rush of trade . . . One week and five days later he had built a mud pie place in the clearing . . . he said that God created few Englishmen of my kind . . . Eleven weeks later Naboth had eaten his way nearly through that shrubbery and there was a reed hut with a bedstead outside it . . . Two dogs and a baby slept on the bedstead . . . Two months later a coolie bricklayer was killed in a scuffle that took place opposite Naboth's vineyard." And so on. "Naboth has gone now, and his hut is ploughed into its native mud with sweetmeats instead of salt for a sign that it is accursed."

Sudden benevolent emotion cannot bridge the chasm. But deeper, less casual relationships are also at stake. The white master/Indian servant relationship is, at its best, the solid foundation of human love in two of Kipling's stories written years after he had returned to England in 1889: "A Sahib's War" (1901) and "A Deal in Cotton" (1907). But both are laid in Africa. Distance from his Indian days had sentimentalised Kipling's memory of the servant relationship as it had conventionalised his view of Eurasians. In the stories of his Indian youth the servant relationship is far more precarious. Imray, as we have seen, was murdered by his servant. "Bahadur Khan had been with him for four years. I shuddered. My own servant had been with me for exactly that length of time." [21] And then again Bahadur Khan had killed Imray because he had said that "my child was a handsome child, and patted him on the head: wherefore my child died". And Kipling "I", seeing the little Muhammad Din, son of his servant, playing inventive solitary child's games that are the foundation of artistic creation, gives him full run of the garden. Here the child "meditated for the better part of an hour and his crooning rose into a jubilant song. Then he began tracing in the dust. It would certainly be a wondrous palace, this one, for it was two yards long and a yard broad in ground plan . . . A week later, though I would have given much to avoid it, I met on the road . . . Iman Din . . . carrying in his arms, wrapped in a white cloth, all that was left of little Muhammad Din." [22]

The crown of this terrible hidden gulf between conquerors and conquered is to be found in "The Strange Ride of Morrowbie Jukes", a story written early in Kipling's Lahore days, when he was still nineteen, when perhaps he saw more deeply into the heart of things than he fully realised. It is laid near Pakpathan in the desert areas that border the Sutlej River, some one hundred miles from Lahore. A desolate region for a man to be stationed in the eighties of the last century. By the strangest of coincidences the area might now see many bus-loads of tourists, for it was here in the nineteen-twenties that was excavated the buried city of Harappa that flourished on the River Ravi in 2000 B.C. Strange because in this region on the banks of the twin tributary of the Indus and the Sutlej, Kipling lays his *grand guignol* of the deep sand crater where are shut up those who, apparently dead, came to life in the fires of the ghat. Here they are forcibly kept, as dead to the world as their yet undiscovered neighbours of four thousand years before. Into this crater Morrowbie Jukes, an English engineer, falls with his horse. And here amid the half-starved derelicts, feeding off crows, sleeping in sand burrows, "huddled over tiny fires of refuse and dried rushes", Jukes fights out a survival battle with a

Brahmin, Gunga Dass, whom he had formerly known as a telegraph master. How Gunga Dass, who himself has been driven to eat crows, the most uncleanly thing a Brahmin could touch, goads and teases Jukes, plays upon his hopes and laughs at his despairs ("We are now Republic, Mr Jukes"), in a descrescendo of the respectful manner that he had formerly shown to a sahib, is a masterpiece of inventive telling. Only the inartistic and improbable escape of Jukes at the end of the story prevents it from being among the first dozen of all Kipling's stories. As it is, it remains one of the most powerful nightmares of the precariousness of a ruling group, in this case of a group haunted by memories of the Mutiny not yet twenty years old. And, so incredibly, written by an author not yet twenty years old himself.

Beside these racial nightmares, the nightmares within the small white ruling group seem almost domestic. Yet they are terrible enough. Especially when the Civil Lines of Lahore are left behind for the isolated lives of those – government servants, planters, civil engineers, advisers in princely states – who are dotted about the desert lands or in small hill stations. At a station a day's journey from Lahore, "Saumarez gave a moonlight riding-picnic at an old tomb . . . near the bed of the river. It was a Noah's Ark picnic . . . six couples came altogether, including chaperones . . . Someone had brought out a banjo . . . our amusements in out-of-the-way stations are very few indeed . . . Before we knew where we were the desert storm was on us, and everything was roaring, whirling darkness . . . the thunder chattering overhead, and the lightning spurting like water from a sluice all ways at once." In this setting is played out the humiliation of Maud Copleigh, whom the world and herself think is loved by Saumarez; but he loves instead and proposes to her younger sister, Edith. Hatred and abasement and jealous passion that have to be lived with in a small community, for who knows how long after the duststorm clears. "The air was cleared; and, little by little, as the sun rose, I felt we were all dropping back again into ordinary men and women, and that the 'Great Pop Picnic' was a thing altogether apart . . . and never to happen again."[23] Melodrama though it is, this picnic story has an intense and frightening domestic quality that allows it a place beside that most famous of all English suburban picnics when Emma insults Miss Bates.

More terrible is the fate of the small white hill community in the station of Kashima. "There is but one view in Kashima – a stretch of perfectly flat pasture and plough land, running up to the grey blue scrub of the Dosehvi hills. There are no amusements." Here, into the small white community of an adulterous triangle, are posted Major and Mrs Vansuythen. And both the men fall for Mrs Vansuythen. And the deserted wife and mistress in her jealous agony breaks down and blurts it all out, so that, fatal thing, what could just be lived with privately has now to be lived with publicly. Which is the beginning of all trouble. And, in any case, they are living now with hate not passion. Only Major Vansuythen does not know. And he jollies them along, playing his banjo and singing "in excruciating wise".

It needs, I think, none of Sartre's metaphysical overtones to make of this a frightening *Huis Clos*. The story opens, "and because there is no help for the poor souls who are lying there in torment, I write this story, praying that the Government of India may be moved to scatter the population to the four winds." [24] It ends, "But of course, as the Major says, 'in a little station we must all be friendly.'"

Is there no connection, then, between race and race, or between individuals of the same race in this northern corner of India, the Punjab? A chance contact may go deep, for the moment, as in "In Floodtime", where the hurrying Sahib is held up all night at a ford by rushing floodwater that even the elephants refuse to face. Here he listens to the old Moslem ford guard's tale. It is a grim enough story of his impious wooing of a Hindu girl and his coming to save her in another terrible flood of time past, riding his rival's floating body – "I twisted my fingers in the hair of the man, for I was far spent, and together we went down the stream – he the dead and I the living." But the old man is a solitary and so he can talk. "I see few sahibs. Forgive me if I have forgotten the respect due to them." Even so, "is it likely that the Sahib would speak true talk to me who am only a black man?" Nevertheless there *is* confidence given in that night, even if it is not the Sahib's confidence. Perhaps the old man feels free to speak because "the Sahib takes it [the old man's liquid tobacco] like a Mussulman". All the same, when the flood subsides and morning comes, the old man has to affirm his status. "Money? Nay, Sahib, I am not of that kind."

Sometimes even individual benevolence sticks, as in "Little Tobrah", the eight-year-old boy who is brought before the courts for pushing his small sister down a well, but acquitted for insufficient evidence. In the court compound, "Little Tobrah, being hungry, set himself to scrape out what wet grain the horse had overlooked." Then the Englishman speaks, "Wet grain, by Jove! Feed the little beggar, some of you, and we'll make a riding boy of him yet! See? Wet grain, Good Lord." And so Tobrah tells. "The big beam tore down upon the roof upon a day which is not in my memory, and with the roof fell much of the hinder wall, and both together upon our bullock, whose

73

back was broken. Thus we had neither home nor bullock – my brother, myself, and my sister who was blind . . . There was famine in the land . . . so, on a night when we were sleeping my brother took the five annas that remained to us and ran away . . . But I and my sister begged food in the villages, and there was none to give . . . And upon a hot night, she weeping and calling for food, we came to a well and I bade her sit upon the kerb and thrust her in, for, in truth, she could not see; and it is better to die than to starve . . . I who was empty, am now full," said Little Tobrah . . . "and I would sleep." Here the connection has been made, not by self-gratifying praise like Imray Sahib's of his servant's child, nor by the sentimental sense of affinity with childhood as when the narrator encourages the creative games of little Muhammad Din, nor by the shared bliss of Holden as he and Ameera watch their gold-coloured little god Tota pulling the parrot's tail. All these children die. The Englishman may have fed Tobrah out of pity but he has recruited him for work in the stable. And it is finally work that alone provides reason and connection both between races and within races.

This is the central significance of one of Kipling's best stories, "The Head of the District", which, for a number of understandable but ultimately irrelevant reasons, has been a source of so much hostility to him. In particular, the story has always been a cause of offence to liberal and Indian readers of Kipling.

It tells of the taking over of the government of a Moslem district on the far North West Frontier by a Bengali Hindu Indian, Grish Chunder Dé, M.A., after the death of the able and much-loved English District Commissioner, Yardley-Orde. It does not appear that at any time in the late nineteenth century, Government in India (even at its moment of greatest concern for preparing Indians for home rule) ever did appoint Bengali Hindus to rule over Moslem districts in areas near the frontier where rebellion might at any time break out. It is wholly unlikely that such an idea would have been contemplated (though it must have been rumoured daily and even expected by the chaps in the Lahore Club under, say, the rule of Gladstonian Liberal Viceroy Ripon, in Kipling's first years there). Kipling could just as well have made his point – the ruin of good, long-built-up local government by a hasty or theoretical, misconceived appointment on the part of the central bureaucracy – by making Orde's successor a white civil servant without local knowledge, a chap straight out of England, mistakenly appointed perhaps for his academic or his sporting record. Indeed, Tallantire, the Assistant Commissioner, is chiefly struck on Chunder Dé's arrival with his talking "after the manner of those who are more English than the English – of Oxford and home, with much curious knowledge of bump-suppers, cricket-matches, hunting runs and other unholy sports of the alien".

The quotation is a give-away. As with so many strongly held, intrusive hostilities, Kipling's distaste for the nationalist educated Bengalis was founded in some part upon a real sense of their irrelevance to the India he knew, but it was due also to their modelling themselves upon an England which he had not been permitted to know. To this hysterical onslaught upon the Western-educated Indian must be added the offensive means by which each side is brought back to law and order; Chunder Dé's brother's head, "the crop-haired head of a bespectacled Bengali gentleman", whipped off its body by a loyal tribesman and rolled at the feet of the Assistant Commissioner, and the disloyal blind Mullah teased to death with a knife (the little children, clapping their hands, cried "Run, Mullah, run!").

Inevitably there is too much offence to national and religious susceptibilities, let alone disgust of squeamish readers, for the real purpose of the tensely told, vivid tale not to be submerged. Yet the core of it is the story of the dedicated District Commissioner and of how the tradition of organisation he had bequeathed both to his Assistant Commissioner and to the tribesmen he had ruled, was strong enough to withstand the frivolous appointment of his Bengali successor and the disruptive forces among the tribesmen. The connection between him and both his native and his white allies against disorder is, of course, work. And the purpose of the work is to ensure peace and with it food so that famine may not come and Little Tobrah's sister need not die.

This is the true burden of the lives of the civilian whites, although we seldom see it in the stories. Indeed, we shall only meet it again at the end of this survey of Kipling's fictional India, when we reach the southernmost point of Kim's journey – Benares and the great Mother Ganges – and even on to that old Southern India which Kipling himself only glimpsed from the train window. For, here in Lahore, in the Punjab, another duty than daily civil administration is dominant in the ordinary white chap's mind, certainly in the young Kipling's.

Over on the other side of the canal from the Lahore Civil Lines, where the Kiplings worked and lived, stands the great military barracks of Mian Mir, and about 180 miles further south along the Grand Trunk Road is another vast military cantonment at Umballa (as Kim found to the cost of his freedom). When you make the journey down the empty highway today, passing an occasional government carrier van, it seems that it can hardly have changed since the last decades of

British rule, even back to the days of Kipling and Kim, save that its noisy, human busyness has been replaced by emptiness. The human concerns, where they are evident from a sign or a building, are the same: road-construction, bridge-building, water supply, grain distribution. The animal life is the same, vultures bobbing and praying before a carcass that some infrequent lorry has offered, drongos with their elegant tails and scissor beaks waiting on the wires above for some lesser creature to fall prey to them. Only an occasional 30-foot stone mile post standing in a field or scrub a few hundred yards from the present road tells us that the highway is older even than British rule. The two great cantonments, as far as we may judge from their externals, look much the same as in the days of *Fore and Aft* and *Soldiers Three*. But, of course, you don't care to peer too closely through the wire fences, for these two cantonments are now centres of two separate lands whose hatred for each other bursts forth now and again into short-lived open warfare. But in Kipling's days they were one, and from the life in them came many of the finest of his Indian poems and stories.

> We're marchin' on relief over Inja's sunny plains,
> A little front o' Christmastime and just be'ind the rains;
> Ho, get away you bullockman, you've 'eard the bugle
> blowed,
> There's a regiment a'comin' down the Great Trunk Road.[25]

"The learning is hard in a land where the army is not a red thing that walks down the street to be looked at, but a living tramping reality that may be needed at the shortest notice."[26]

We have seen Kipling and his headmaster on opposite sides over the danger to our Indian Empire from the Russian foe. Here across the top of the Punjab lay the North West Frontier, a mountainous territory with its famous guerrilla-infested passes, the Kohat and the Khyber; and, on the other side, Afghanistan, where only three years before Kipling's coming to Lahore, our British Legation had been murdered at Kabul and only Roberts's (the soldiers' beloved "Bobs") march to Kandahar had pacified the treacherous Emir's land. Expectation of trouble with Afghanistan throughout Kipling's Indian time was real, though it never materialised.

Expectation of war with Russia was less real, though not entirely fanciful, nevertheless it was constant. A phrase in one of Lockwood's letters home to England in 1885 may stand for the general mood of the whites, "We are all agog about the prospect of war with Russia," and he was certainly no jingo. How much the Russian menace to India continued to seem real may be judged by Le Gallienne's comment in his hostile book of 1900 about Kipling's work, " 'When India belongs to Russia, no one will understand Kipling,' said a distinguished poet to the present writer,"[27] which is as though a left-wing critic today were teasingly to ask what relevance the Western European middle-class world has in view of the likely takeover of Europe by the Soviet Union in the near future.

Anyhow, the Indian Army's role in defence of civilised values was much in the minds of the English in Lahore, but throughout Kipling's time (save for those regiments engaged far away in the conquest of Burma) the role of the Army was a waiting one. Kipling's fiction adventured once or twice into imaginary skirmishes on the Frontier, and at least twice into the Burmese battles, but his principal achievement is the fictional creation of the daily life of an army on the alert – mainly the life of the private soldiers. We may suggest why this is so later, but now to look closer at this fictional world.

First, the officers. What of those "Stalkies – Cheltenham and Haileybury and Marlborough chaps", the old boys whose famed Indian military exploits were the object of worship in the studies of Westward Ho? Of the comparatively few mentions, the best, I think, is in "A Conference of Powers", a story of Kipling's bachelor time in London West End digs after his return from India. Here are gathered a number of young subalterns in their early twenties home on leave. One of them, nicknamed "The Infant", recalls a brutal episode of the Burmese War. But more telling than the details of the story is the manner in which the Infant recounts it. Some of this manner, its throw-away modesty, its understatement, its taken-for-granted code has been so exploited by film and parody that it is hard to assess it. "Have you ever seen a crucifixion?" asks a civilian, referring to the famous Burmese atrocities. "Of course not. Shouldn't have allowed it if I had; but I've seen the corpses." But there are touches here and there in Kipling's account of the Infant's demeanour, as he all unconsciously reveals his extraordinary physical bravery and mental Stalkyness, that give to this story a validity that no other of his officer stories possess. For example, the subaltern hero's innate snobbery: "Who was your C.O.?" said Boileau. "Bounderby – Major. Pukka Bounderby. More bounder than pukka . . .' said The Infant. And again, the sudden setting aside of his deference to the old and famous novelist in his audience – his "pull me up, Sir, if I say anything you don't follow", or his " 'fraid I've been gassing awfully, Sir" – when he thinks that the novelist is accusing him of lying. "Cheever [the novelist] brought his hand down on the table with a thump that made the empty glasses dance. 'That's Art', he said, 'flat, flagrant mechanism! Don't tell me that happened on the spot!' The pupils of the Infant's eyes contracted to two pinpoints. 'I beg your pardon,' he said, slowly and stiffly, 'but I am telling this thing as it happened.' " In both these examples there is an authentic smudge on the otherwise saintly image of the modest, unconsciously brave subaltern hero that convinces, as, alas, Kipling's most famous tribute to the subaltern type fails, I think, to do.

"Only a Subaltern" has about it a mawkish, Sunday-school-prize tone that spoils this story of the ordinary, decent Bobby Wick who dies of cholera tending his men. That Private Dormer, whom he has befriended, should burst out, on hearing of his death, "Orf'cer? Bloomin' orf'cer? I'll learn you to misname the likes of 'im. Hangel! Bloomin' hangel! That's wot 'e is!" gives some indication of how the shortsighted, brainy civilian Kipling was not in control of his hero worship for the "Cheltenham and Haileybury and Marlborough chaps" when he wrote this eulogy of them.

As to the officers' mess, the story "The Man Who Was", with its charming Russian spy ostensibly on holiday in India and its officer returned like a ghost to the mess banquet of the White Hussars to show the signs of Russian prison-camp torture, has all the marks of melodrama that made it so successful on the London stage with Beerbohm Tree in the lead. Yet there is nothing more probable than Russian spies in Peshawar in the eighties or than torture in Russian prison camps, then as now. What seems to falsify it is the note of awe with which young Kipling recounts the splendours and traditions of this famous regiment's ceremonial. The East African administrator Lord Lugard's reaction, when he first read the story in 1894, is interesting, because he had known service in the Afghan War in 1880 and the Burmese War of 1886–7: "His knowledge of the barrack room is greater than that of the officers' mess." [28]

In fact, the few stories of officers that are really telling deal not with decent, ordinary, brave chaps like the Infant and Bobby Wick, but with the misfits: with "The Boy", the subaltern who takes reprimands and set-backs seriously and commits suicide, "The Worm", the over-mothered pretty boy, who is the butt of the mess. "The Senior Subaltern meant no harm; but his chaff was coarse and he didn't quite understand where to stop. He had been waiting too long for his Company; and that always sours a man." But the Worm turns to effect, when, in full drag, he descends upon the mess when the Colonel is present and denounces the Senior Subaltern as his faithless, deserting husband. The disguise is detected, but the mud sticks and the Worm is revenged.

The most successful story about an officer is, however, I think, "The Arrest of Lieutenant Golightly", in which a somewhat self-satisfied, extremely dandyish officer falls from his horse in a rainstorm coming down from leave in the hills. Filthy and unrecognisable he is arrested, despite all his protests, as a deserter from the ranks and treated accordingly. Perhaps it is natural that, as in "The Strange Ride of Morrowbie Jukes", Kipling seems most in his stride when the sahib's role is grimly and comically reversed. His sense of life's insecurity is fully satisfied.

And then there are the chaplains – those instruments of torture of Kim: the narrow-minded Church of England padre may truly be said to be the villain of that book (which shows how free from real evil it is). The Roman Catholic padre understands just enough of the depth of feelings of the Lama for Kim to stop the Anglican Bennett from giving him a rupee in exchange for the boy. " 'I cannot see any need why he should wait,' said Bennett, feeling in his trouser pocket, 'We can investigate the details later – and I will give him a ru. . . .' 'Give him Kim. Maybe's he's fond of the lad,' said Father Victor." Neither man, as we clearly see, is, in Kipling's opinion, suited to understand the mysterious in life – whether it be the Lama's quest or the depth of an unusual human relationship. But that is not after all their work. And, perhaps, only in *Kim* does Kipling consistently demand more of men than their work calls for. In the Indian stories we only occasionally see so deeply. And in the army ballads, for the most part, men are judged by how they respond to their tasks. Here the chaplains are acquitted:

> Our chaplain's got a banjo an' a skinny mule 'e rides,
> An' the stuff 'e says and sings us, Lord, it makes us split our
>   sides!
> With 'is black coat-tails a'bobbin' to Ta-ra-ra-Boom-der-ay!
> 'E's the proper kind o' padre for ten deaths a day.
> An' Father Victor 'elps 'im with our Roman Catholicks –
> He knows an 'eap of Irish songs an' rummy conjurin' tricks;
> An' the two they works together when it comes to play or pray.
> So we keep the ball a'rollin' on ten deaths a day.[29]

Truth to tell, the officers (chaplains and all) are to be judged by their function in ordering their men, and "the subaltern is happy who can win the approval of the musical critic in his regiment, and is honoured among the more intricate step-dancers. By him, as by him who plays cricket cleverly, Thomas Atkins will stand in time of need, when he will let a better officer go on alone." [30] An earnest subaltern's life, indeed, is hard; for leadership is all, the rest is flumdiddle.

"We shot all the forenoon, and killed two pariah dogs, four green parrots, sitting, one kite by the burning-ghat, one snake flying, one mud turtle and eight crows . . . Then we sat down . . . by the side of the river and took pot shots at the crocodiles . . . then we drank up all the beer, and threw the bottles into the water and fired at them . . ." "Mulvaney had taken off his boots and was dabbling his toes in the water; Learoyd was lying on his back on the pontoon; and Ortheris was pretending to row with a big bamboo . . ." "There was a twitchin' of the muscles of the right cheek as he sighted; Private Stanley Ortheris was engaged on his business. A speck of white crawled up the water course. 'See that beggar? . . . Got 'im!' Seven hundred yards away, and a full two hundred down the hillside, the deserter of Aurangabadis pitched forward, rolled down a red rock, and lay very still, with his face in a clump of blue gentians, while a big raven flapped out of the pine wood to make investigation."

The first quotation comes from the story, "The Madness of Private Ortheris", in which the little cockney soldier of the Soldiers Three is overcome by one of his periodic hysterical longings to be back in London and is talked out of desertion (and certain shooting at dawn) by his friends over the long, long hours of a roasting afternoon in the rank high grass land by the desolate buffalo-churned banks of the River Ravi that flows by Lahore's cantonment. The second quotation comes from "Black Jack", where, once again by the desolate river's edge, two of the Soldiers Three talk the third out of suicidal action. But this time it is Mulvaney, the talkative, intelligent, drunken Irishman who is being calmed out of one of his black moods in which he is determined to shoot a bullying sergeant – an indulgent easing of deadly constraint that will lead to hanging as sure as any desertion. The third comes at the end of the story "On Greenhow Hill", in which the silent, heavy Yorkshireman, Learoyd, unburdens himself to his friends of a long-ago tale of the death of a girl he had loved. "The recruiting sergeant were waitin' for me at th' corner public house. 'Yo've seen your sweetheart,' says he, 'Yes, I've seen her,' says I. 'Well, we'll have a quart now, and you'll do your best to forget her,' says he, bein' one o' them smart, bustlin' chaps. 'Ay, Sergeant,' says I, 'Forget her.' And I've been forgetting her ever since." Such is the life of Kipling's soldiers. "All their work was over at eight in the morning, as for the rest of the day they could lie on their backs and smoke canteen plug and swear at the punkah coolies . . . It was too early in the year for the excitement of fever or cholera. The men could only wait and wait and wait, and watch the shadow of the barrack creeping across the blinding white dust." Unless like Private Losson, a man could think up the joke of training a green parrot to shout, "'Simmons, ye so-oor,' at the slow-moving butt of the barrack room until all Private Simmons' ample leisure was occupied in thinking of the great roll of fat under Losson's right ear . . . A man could get his hand upon it and tear away one side of the neck; or he could place the muzzle of a rifle on it and blow away all the head in a flash." So Simmons shoots Losson. "And they hanged Private Simmons." [31]

'What's that so black agin' the sun?' said Files on Parade.
'It's Danny fightin' 'ard for life,' the Colour Sergeant said. . . .
After hangin' Danny Deever in the morning. [32]

"Mary, Mother of Mercy, fwhat the divil possist us to take an' kape this melancholious counthry? Answer me that, sorr," Mulvaney asks. And then Learoyd, the slow, heavy man sunk in "what might have been" far back on the Yorkshire moors comes to breaking point at one o'clock of a stifling June night in Fort Amara. "Ah'm tired – tired. There's nobbut water a' ma bones. Leave me die!" [33] And to get him through that night, Mulvaney tells one of his grim battle yarns in which, as always, black reflection is always warring with glorious bloody action. It is a story of the Black Tyrones and, of course, the Pathans. And the Black Tyrones were "the choicest collection of unmitigated blackguards, dog stealers, robbers of hen roosts, assaulters of innocent citizens, and recklessly daring heroes in the Army List". And when the tale "With the Main Guard" is told and dawn is breaking, Mulvaney cries, "I've blandashdhered thim through the night somehow, but can them that helps others help thimsilves? Answer me that, sorr." [34]

But, of course, there is no answer. Mulvaney's intelligence and sensitivity will go on being buried under the endless bouts of drunkenness and next-morning self-reviling. Only his luck in having found Dinah Shadd for a wife has saved him from an endless series of furtive affairs in the married quarters with the notorious sly bad wives. Until a jealous husband shoots and, in his turn, is hanged. As in most of Mulvaney's stories. For his married life to a faithful women seems so exceptional in the world of Soldiers Three. Marriage is more like "The Sergeant's Weddin'"·

> Bowin' like a lady,
> Blushin' like a lad,
> 'Oo would say to see 'em?
> Both is rotten bad.

And Mulvaney will get his stripes and loose them again, and get his stripes and lose them again, and hate the guts of the sergeant when he's reduced once more to the ranks.

> With a secondhand overcoat under my head,
> And a beautiful view of the yard,
> Yes it's pack drill for me and a fortnight's C.B.
> For "drunk and resisting the Guard".[35]

And Learoyd will live coarsely and sullenly and heavily in the memory of something fragile and delicate and refined – the minister's daughter who, dying of consumption, could show that, miraculously, she still cared for him, an illiterate miner, for all that he followed the Devil and had gone for a soldier. And Ortheris, the little, lean Stan Laurel of the group, motherless London slum boy brought up by an uncle, never knowing the love of women, hardest, most bitter, most fly of them all, taking his pleasure in dog stealing and killing: "'See that beggar? Got 'im!'" as he shoots the deserter. "'Happen there was a lass tied up wi' 'im, too,'" says Learoyd, for whom even deserters bring thoughts of the girl who died. "But Ortheris did not reply. He was staring across the valley, with the smile of the artist who looks on the completed work."[36] The killer who has his pride. "My rights! 'Strewth A'mighty! I'm a man!"[37] But there isn't much killing – usually a sitting parrot or a mud turtle.

Kipling's achievement in creating the three soldiers, whose exploits, I think, are best read alongside *The Barrack Room Ballads*, is an extraordinary and fourfold one.

There is a lively picaresque, conventional exterior picture, akin to his account of the Black Tyrones, which takes dog-stealing as the tails of the coins and reckless heroism in battle or skirmish as the heads (or vice versa, if that's how you prefer it).

There is a purely comic series of situation farces in Laurel and Hardy style. In this Kipling, at his best, seems to me a much more interesting forerunner of cinematic vision than in his later complex experiments in visual merging and distancing like "Mrs Bathurst". Sometimes these knockabout pieces fall flat; sometimes they are merely what they were written as – good magazine stories; but

12 The Kiplings' house in Lahore drawn by Lockwood. Mocking friends called it Bikaner Lodge because it resembled the desert princely state, Bikaner. The Kiplings would have no trees or shrubs since they maintained that these brought disease: a typical "cranky" view that marked them off from their ordinary Anglo-Indian neighbours. (*Bateman's*)

13 "As Simla first came into view, I thought of pictures I had seen of Tibetan villages", page 85. (*Photo Tony Garrett*)

14 "We sat down . . . by the side of the river and took pot shots at crocodiles", page 80. (*Photo Tony Garrett*)

15 The railway bridge over the River Ganges at Benares: this bridge is the subject of one of Kipling's finest Indian fantasies, "The Bridge Builders". (*Foreign and Commonwealth Office Library*)

16, 17 The two Viceregal Lodges at Simla in which the Kipling family reached their social heights. Peterhof (now Raj Bhavan) was replaced by a vast neo-Renaissance pile (below) in Kipling's own day. (*Photos Tony Garrett*)

18 Boys by the gun, Zam-Zammah, outside the Museum at Lahore: the scene has hardly changed since the

19 Northbank, the Simla house where Kipling stayed when monkeys raided his room: first identification (it is thought) by Angus Wilson. (*Photo Tony Garrett*)

20 Professor and Mrs Hill at Belvedere House, Allahabad. (*Library of Congress*)

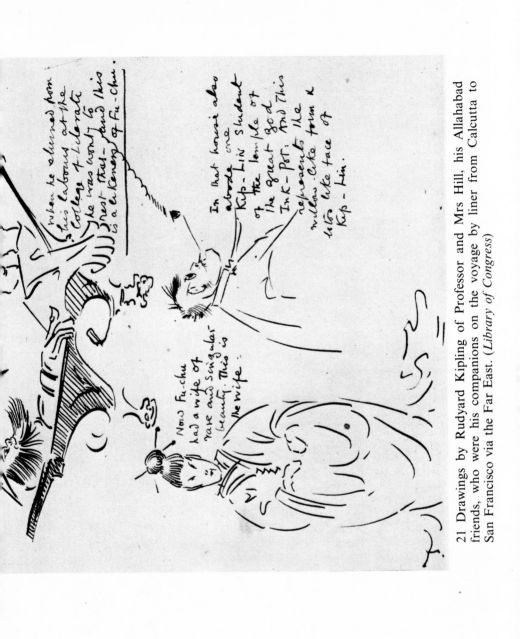

21 Drawings by Rudyard Kipling of Professor and Mrs Hill, his Allahabad friends, who were his companions on the voyage by liner from Calcutta to San Francisco via the Far East. (*Library of Congress*)

22 Blue room at Belvedere House, Allahabad, 1888–9. (*Library of Congress*)

23 Mrs Hill sitting on the trunk of a pipul tree. (*Library of Congress*)

sometimes, notably in the story of Mulvaney and the elephant, "My Lord the Elephant", he creates a continuous motion picture in words that is unlike any other written absurdity that I know.

Then at a third level, we are plunged, often in a recounted story of others, but on occasion in Mulvaney's own reminiscence, into the world of barrack adulteries and treacheries and bullyings and slow persecutions – all the knife-edges from which, from time to time, men fall into murder and court martial and death at humid, sweat-bathed dawn. This is the world "damned from here to eternity" where the Jellaludin McIntoshes of the Army, the gentlemen-rankers, like "Love O' Women", use their shop-worn charms on sergeants' daughters and the governesses of the Colonel's youngsters ("How could I have believed her sworn oath – me that have bruk mine again and again for the sport a'seein' them cry?") before "locomoters attacks us".[38] The Brechtian world of Kipling with its constant half-heard woman's wail:

> I want the name – no more –
> The name, an' lines to show,
> An' not to be an'ore . . .
> Ah, Gawd! I love you so![39]

But behind these external worlds – at their best superbly theatrical or cinematic, at their worst, with a brassily magazine quality – there is a fourth world, a brooding, sad, lost interior world of the three musketeers: the world of the desolate river bank and idleness and regret and pot shots; the world of the prison cell of the long-term serviceman. Here stands "Mulvaney . . . leaning on his rifle at picket, lonely as Prometheus on his rock, with I know not what vultures tearing at his liver."[40] In this world it is not absurd to compare Kipling with Shakespeare, for, along with the exploits of Nym and Bardolph and Pistol, we are also made familiar with the death of Falstaff. And, at its heart, is a mystery that few but Kipling have suggested. Mulvaney may be saved from the knife-edge by his wife's steadfastness, Learoyd by the numbness of a lost past, and Ortheris by the fierceness of lifelong empty loneliness; but what gets them through the days, apart from the mechanical work that is almost done by 8 a.m., is their companionship. It has none of the vocal chirpiness of the schoolboy trio of Stalky. They know each other's hopeless emptiness far too well for that. No easy Victorian emotional, let alone, modern physical explanation fully describes the reality. It's something that grows wherever men need protection from the seemingly eternal and intolerable future in boarding schools and on foreign service and in immigrant bidonvilles. Only Kipling, I think, really caught it in the soldier's lament at the death of his friend:

> 'E was all that I 'ad in the way of a friend
> And I've 'ad to find one new;
> ... Oh, passin' the love o' woman,
> Follow me – follow me 'ome! [41]

And what when battle or skirmish comes to make sense of the soul-killing tedium? With the Soldiers Three it is always in reminiscence – short, brutal, absurd, or effectively half-comic as in the Burmese exploit, "The Taking of Lungtungpen". The meaning of the soldiers' tedious life it may be, but Kipling never sweetens that into glorious heroics. Indeed the most graphic moment in all the battle scenes is when the regiment returns from active service in "Love O' Women". Not the melodramatics of the blackguard soldier Larry's last syphilitic moments in the arms of his seduced girl turned whore, with its strained Shakespearian "I'm dyin', Aigypt – dyin'," but the homeward march of the regiment into Peshawar. "I heard a shout, and thin I saw a horse and a tattoo [a ponytrap] latherin' down the road, hell to shplit, under women. I knew – I knew! Wan was the Tyrone Colonel's wife – ould Beeker's lady – her grey hair flyin' and her fat round carkiss' rowlin' in the saddle, and the other was Dinah, that shud ha' been at Pindi." The best part of every battle is when it's over; and wives are the sign that it is at an end.

Yet characteristically the finest battle scene in Kipling's stories is not a victory but a near-disaster. The story not of the three musketeers but of the two drummer boys, Lew and Jake, in "The Drums of the Fore and Aft". This story is more than usually cluttered with a long, though not uninteresting didactic introduction on the nature of good fighting men. They are, he suggests, "blackguards commanded by gentlemen to do butchers' work with despatch and efficiency . . ." This blackguard view of the army does not tie up entirely with the Soldiers Three, let alone with Kipling's hero, Lord Roberts; he would seem to be reverting to the days of the Duke of Wellington. Yet it may well have been a realistic view of the needs of the mountain pass frontier skirmishes with the Afghans which this story describes, drawn from the near-defeat of Ahmed Khel of 1880, eight years before.

The Fore and Aft, the regiment, is at what Kipling believes is a dangerous stage of literacy: "the percentage of school-certificates in their ranks was high, and most of the men could do more than read or write." As a result, in their first military encounter with Afghans in the Kohat Pass, they waver and break. And the day would have been lost through cowardice if it had not been for the two fourteen-year-old drummer boys, Jake and Lew, who rally them with the tune of "The

British Grenadiers". They do so because they're too drunk with rum
to run away and too drunk with rum to know what they are doing.
"Beautiful ladies who watched the Regiment in Church were wont to
speak of [Lew in the choir] as a darling." And so apparently does the
illustrator who portrays "their last stand" in the famous picture. But
they are little liars, thieves, drunkards and bullies who've never known
anything better than the Army (unlike Rousseau's noble savage, Kim,
who has grown up in the bazaars and on the rooftops). And they die for
it, caught between the two sides' cross fire, and dead drunk. It is a
macabre story of defeat turned to victory, of the powers of drunkenness over cowardice.

> I 'eard the knives be'ind me, but I dursn't face my man,
> Nor I don't know where I went to, 'cause I didn't 'alt to see,
> Till I 'eard a beggar squealin' out for quarter as 'e ran,
> An' I thought I knew the voice, an' it was me![42]

When it comes to fighting which is the purpose of the Army on the
frontier, to back up which is the purpose of the administration of the
Punjab, which is the life that Kipling knew in India, it's the breaking-
point that holds him, the moment when everything seems just about to
crack, the moment when we *almost* ran.

And the same breaking-point magnetised him with civilian Lahore
and, to a large measure, with the third and greatest white world of
Kipling's India, the high society that flutters and flashes round the
Viceregal Lodge and Simla during the hot season. Again and again
one is told today that Simla still reigns – an English town in the foothills of the Himalayas. But it isn't like that. Perhaps it is the number
of Tibetan refugees to be seen working on the roadside as you make the
steep winding ascent from Kalka. Certainly, as Simla first came into
view, I thought of pictures I had seen of Tibetan villages: balconies,
fretted wood, tiled roofs, corrugated iron roofs, fresh paint, dilapida-
tion, all close-packed, all tumbling down the hillside like a large
damaged layer-cake. But incredibly, above this arrested landslide, an
English parish church is confidently in charge of the hill and of the
town.

The centre of Simla, the Mall, the street that rides the ridge of the
hill with the church, is different again. Yes, it does look remotely
English, but a parodied English mock-Tudor Surrey, built by a
German-Swiss who had not been home for years. From the Mall, with
one's back to the town, there are the snow-capped peaks of the
Himalayas. To the left, the ridge winds past the first Viceregal Lodge,

"Peterhof", with its charming Regency-style balconies, and on through trees for about a mile and up to the great Viceregal palace they built towards the end of Kipling's time: an enormous, solid, neo-Elizabethan, English country house, but with an air, perhaps because of its un-English setting, of one of the great English late-Victorian seaside hotels.

Yet despite its several grandeurs, Simla has the feeling of a toy town. There is an unreal atmosphere as you watch the Indian citizens in the Mall, which is a pedestrian precinct, passing to and fro, many of the men with entwined hands, in a Mediterranean passeggiata, past the William Morris Tudor Moot Hall and the Theatre. It is a town put there for people to play in and with. So it certainly was in Kipling's day. Not that life was not hard there then: cheeseparing to keep up appearances, sunlit with hopes of promotion, mouldy-damp with hopes gone stale.

Then, as now, play was only one part of life: today Simla is the governing centre of Himachal Pradesh, province and headquarters of the North West Indian Command. In Kipling's day, the Viceroy brought all his despatch boxes and his vast staff up there in the hot season, to the pretty Peterhof. Lord Roberts, the Commander-in-Chief, kept open house at the other end of the town at castellated "Snowdon".

So when one walks along the Mall, where the façade of Pellitti's coffee-house, the central gossip mart, is still discernible behind flaked paint and rust, and where a photographer's shop still shows some English beauties of 1907 if not of 1887, it is entirely possible, as with no other Victorian author I know, to feel oneself absolutely in Kipling's fictional Simla.

Surely the Sikh army staff officer one passes by the churchyard is today's Ahasuerus Jenkins:

He took two months to Simla when the year was at the spring,
And underneath the deodars eternally did sing.
He warbled like a bulbul, but particularly at
Cornelia Agrippina, who was musical and fat,
She controlled a humble husband, who, in turn, controlled a
    Dept . . .
So when the winds of April turned the budding roses brown,
Cornelia told her husband: 'Tom, you mustn't send him down.' . . .
They found for him an office stool, and on that stool they set him,
To play with maps and catalogues three idle hours a day,
And draw his plump retaining fee – which means his double pay.[43]

Life today in Simla is unlikely to be as worldly-simple as in these sprightly but rather juvenile verses from Kipling's second published volume of poetry, *Departmental Ditties*, suggest. But nor were they then. As we should have found if we had looked in on Mrs Hauksbee in the house she had taken for the season, sometimes alone it seems, sometimes with her bosom friend, Mrs Mallowe.

The stories of Mrs Hauksbee (and they are the main part of Kipling's prose evocation of Simla) have been, I think, as unduly decried in our time as they unduly shocked in eighteen-nineties London. Somerset Maugham's dismissal of her as middle-class and Kensington has tended to set the tone of her critics since the Great War. But this criticism is not only snobbish, but foolish. Apart from the occasional Viceroy like Lord Dufferin and occasional secretaries to the Viceroy like Lord Herbrand Russell (later Duke of Bedford), with both of whom, as it happens, Kipling was on friendly terms, the ruling class of India, and, therefore, of Simla in the hot season, *was* middle-class. Like the middle classes in England, they took on such aristocratic smartness as they could. But unlike the English upper-middle classes at home, they could afford to wear them in their own way, for they (apart from the Viceregal entourage) set the fashion, were the mode. Of course, retirement would come and England and reversal to second rank. Kipling was very observant of this. One of his best contributions from England to the *Civil and Military Gazette* in Lahore when he returned to London was a picture of a retired Indian Civil Service Knight travelling ignominiously on a London omnibus. And the best poem in *Departmental Ditties*, a long monologue put into the mouth of Lord Dufferin – "One Viceroy Resigns" – shows just how a genuine English aristocrat looked down on Simla society, his middle-class top subjects:

> They look for nothing from the West but Death
> Or Bath or Bournemouth. Here's their ground.
> They fight until the middle classes take them back,
> One of ten millions plus a C.S.I.

Meanwhile, Mrs Hauksbee, however "Kensington" or "Brompton", sets the tone.

There is no one of the Hauksbee stories that is among the best of his work, and many of them are bright journalistic pieces for the morning newspaper – where indeed most of them first appeared in the *Civil and Military Gazette*. But then so did some of his finest early stories. But if we are to look at his Indian work as a whole, as a theatre of India as he saw it, which I have been doing in this chapter, Mrs Hauksbee has a very important role to play. As important as Mulvaney and not so very different, for, in general, she uses her wit and intelligence and flair to humanise the hard and lonely white world of Kipling's India.

Mrs Hauksbee's bosom friend (a bosom friend among women in late Victorian society was as important as a man's man in softening the cruel conventional division of the sexes), Polly Mallowe has a husband, Jack, who is in Government service. But who is Lucy Hauksbee? She is, in fact, quite alone. Mysterious in origins, she precedes, both in wit and good intentions, Wilde's Mrs Erlynne of *Lady Windermere's Fan* or Mrs Cheveley of *An Ideal Husband*. They first appeared on the West End stage in 1893 and 1895; Lucy Hauksbee was almost complete by the end of 1888. Of course, she does not trail the dubious pasts of Wilde's mysterious ladies, she remains always respectable, even though separated from her husband – usually a glamorous mother-figure who kindly but firmly puts her protégés in their place when they show any sign of amorousness. But, as a result, her civilising, compassionate mission, to repair broken marriages and secure posts for gifted men instead of favoured nephews of big pots who might have got them, to prise young innocents out of the hands of deathly, predatory women and to ward off snobbish or mercenary relatives from interfering with the true love of their young, can continue from year to year untroubled by scandal. She is far from infallible or unteachable. When we first meet her in 1886 (a story laid in the 1870s) she accepts that Bremmil's wife may be more attractive to him than her witty, worldly self, and is glad of it. At her most serious, she is forced to face the fact that her courage and resources (though considerable) are less than those of a dowdy frump. Her worldliness has marked limitations. She is as surprised as any simple Simla lady might be by the power and range of Government when important documents fall into her hands by chance; but she makes good use of her unexpected new knowledge to help an able man to promotion.

By "Mrs Hauksbee Sits It Out" (1890) she appears to be on easy terms with the Viceroy. In a pleasant little comedy which she (and Kipling) devises, she enlists the Viceroy to distract a snobbish, disapproving aunt from her niece's happy courtship by asking her to be on a Dress Reform Committee.

Her aspirations are wider than the rather mediocre gossiping society she inhabits. She confesses to longing to start a salon. Polly Mallowe, whose knowledge and bitterness about the worth of Simla society, indeed of the nature of English rule in India, go deep, dissuades her:

"You can't focus anything in India, and a salon to be any good at all, must be permanent. In two seasons your roomful would be scattered all over Asia. We are only little bits of dirt on the Hillsides, here one day and blown down the Khud the next . . . we have no cohesion . . ."[44] But Lucy Hauksbee knows it all really, and knows too that it must not be dwelt upon if they are to "manage". So she says, in mockery, "George Eliot in the flesh," to her friend. George Eliot, it is clear, has already become a slightly absurd, over-serious figure even in Simla by 1888. Nevertheless, for all her creaking sprightliness and her only moderately witty wit, Lucy Hauksbee is the most humanistic, George Eliot-like of all Kipling's Indian characters – pathetic rather than tragic as are the Soldiers Three. Yet she has a *deep* pathos, for she clearly knows well the limit of the sweetness and light she can bring to the British Philistines in Simla, since that limit lies in her own limitations and every story brings them home to her. It is not surprising that in "A Supplementary Chapter", published in *The Week's News* in 1888 (shortly before Kipling left India) she appears as a very Firbankian figure at a fancy dress ball as "The Black Death" with a shrieking cicada in her hair.

Outside Mrs Hauksbee's kingdom and the equally underrated comic tragedy of Gadsby's death by marriage, Simla appears only through flashes of lurid lightning as Gothic storms break upon the little hill-perched town. Revellers from evening parties at the Viceregal Lodge can never be sure what figure may meet them on the winding, precipitous road. It may be "The Man's Wife", "a temporarily insane woman, on a temporarily mad horse, swinging round the corners, with her eyes and her mouth open, and her head like the head of a Medusa".[45] She is wailing for her lover who has fallen nine hundred feet down a ravine, "spoiling a patch of Indian corn", and is to be buried three days later in one of the open, rain-filled pits in the cemetery where they had hidden to make their adulterous love. It may be Mrs Schreiderling, forced into a brutal marriage, finding her lover, "The Other Man", dead in his carriage as it arrives from the plains at the Tonga Office – "Mrs Schreiderling kneeling in the wet road by the back seat of the newly arrived tonga, screaming hideously."[46] Or it may be Mrs Wessington's ghost in her "Phantom Rickshaw" haunting her faithless lover Jack Pansay: "Morning after morning, and evening after evening the ghostly rickshaw and I used to wander through Simla together . . . at the Theatre I found them amid the crowd of yelling jhampanis; outside the Club veranda, after a long evening of whist; at the Birthday Ball, waiting patiently for my reappearance; and in broad daylight when I went calling." Simla, indeed, needed all the light and sweetness that Mrs Hauksbee's shrewd maternal wit could bring, for one step too far and the furies closed in on Club and Peterhof and Snowdon and Pellitti's café and the performance of *Fallen Angel* at the Theatre, and their beaks were as merciless as the scavenging vultures down in the plains.

But if you leave the Mall and pass down the sloping road at the other side of the Gothic church (Gothic to exorcise the gothic, perhaps) you come to the bazaar town, to a world away from the Mall. No doubt, on occasion, Mrs Hauksbee and some other ladies would penetrate there to buy native curios, finding it picturesque or, perhaps, like Lady Dufferin, the Viceroy's wife, "amusing". (Lady Dufferin found so much amusing – "the work people are very amusing to look at ... The spectators all crowded into the stand and watched with amusement the ... natives who had no shelter ... Another very amusing race was that ridden by the 'heavy' gentlemen on our staff, persons who had never ridden ... before." [47]) Hither comes Kim in his training for the Game to learn all manner of magic and tricks – of memory, of impersonation, of detection – amid the jewelled marvels of Lurgan's curio shop.

Lurgan was drawn from the mysterious Armenian Jew, A. M. Jacob, who arrived in Simla in 1871. He dealt in precious stones, and had friends in high places, and was only ruined in 1891 after a long-drawn-out legal case with the Nizam of Hyderabad concerning the sale of a fabulous diamond. In the fictional Lurgan's shop, the little Hindu boy, who attends on him, tries to poison him after the arrival of the new apprentice, Kim. " 'Why did he want to poison you?' " asks Kim. " 'Because he is fond of me. Suppose you were fond of someone, and you saw someone come, and the man you were fond of was more pleased with him than he was with you, what would you do?' ... 'I should not poison that man,' said Kim reflectively, 'but I should beat that boy – *if* that boy was fond of my man.' "

Lucy Hauksbee would, no doubt, have heard of the extraordinary A. M. Jacob, perhaps have gone to see his curios and jewels; but she would have been as surprised at such emotions as to learn that Kim or any other boy employed there was learning to be a Government spy.

She would not, however, have noticed a beggar "leaning on the rail of the Mall ... till a policeman told him he was obstructing the traffic." She would have been amazed to learn that he was Sir Purun Dass, K.C.I.E., of whom "all London cried, 'this is the most fascinating man we have ever met at dinner since cloths were first laid' " [48]; she would have been even more amazed if she had been told that his metamorphosis into a Sunyassi, or holy man, was the beginning of his new spiritual existence. (Lady Dufferin, probably, would have found it "amusing".)

90

Purun Bhagat stops that night at Chota Simla in an empty hut and then goes up into the mysterious hills, where Kim was to follow him – hills as mysterious to British Simla in their far reaches where they grow into great Himalayan mountains as the land of Kafiristan, where Dan met his terrible death and Peachey his half-death through crucifixion, was to the British in Lahore. But there is a difference in Kipling's world between the half-savage land on the other side of the Khyber, where only two over-clever loafers would have believed that they could make a kingdom, and the far-away snow-clad Himalayas where two other adventurers (the Frenchman and the Russian) absurdly believed that they could buy with money the Lama's holy book. The one is a treacherous hell, the other a heaven too high for humans, where even the Lama is tempted in his exaltation into anger. I think that, as in so much of Kipling's Indian writing, he is here voicing what most British in India intuitively felt: across the North West Frontier lay threat and trickery and a hell that had to be confined; high up in the Himalayas lay peace and cool and stillness, the unattainable.

But it is notable that, in his work and in his life, the peoples of the foothills of the Himalayas seem to share something of the great mountains' grace. In 1885, he made a recuperative journey there as far as 9,000 feet and was enchanted by the hill people and the beauty of their women. Here, one feels, are people who need nothing save protection from the white world. And, indeed, it is here that two stories are laid showing how absurd and empty, even harmful are the dreams of Christians who would seek to impose their beliefs upon the natives. In Kipling's eyes, this was never other than foolish throughout India, but here in these idyllic hill villages it is seen as actively cruel. "Lisbeth", the heroine of the story that stands first in *Plain Tales from the Hills*, becomes half servant, half companion to the chaplain's wife in Kotgargh. She meets and saves a young English traveller who has fallen by the wayside with fever. And she believes his loving professions of thanks. He will come back to her, and the chaplain and his wife, for the sake of peace, repeat the promise. "'How can what he and you said be untrue?' 'We said it as an excuse to keep you quiet, child,' said the chaplain's wife. 'Then you have lied to me? You and he?'" She goes, of course, back to her people. We are told that when she was an old, "bleached wrinkled creature, exactly like a wisp of charred rag, if she was sufficiently drunk, sometimes she could be induced to tell the story of her first love-affair".

Fourteen years later, in *Kim*, Kipling returned to Lisbeth, disturbed perhaps by the crude violence with which in his youth he had expressed his disgust at her treatment. In *Kim* we see her not as old and drunken but as the handsome ruler of her village people. But even

91

then she can hope for no love from the white world. Kim cannot return her embrace, for he is still serving his discipleship to the Lama and his apprenticeship to the Game. Just as disastrous is the result of the mission of Justus Krenk, Pastor of the Tübingen Mission to the people of the Berbula Hills in "The Judgement of Dungara". This was written in 1888 before the Germans had acquired the satanic quality that they increasingly had for Kipling from 1890. They were seen as well-intentioned, plodding people. But their Mission in Berbula is a disaster as great as Dan and Peachey's kingdom. "The chapel and school have long since fallen back into the jungle," the story ends. But there is a difference, for "The Man Who Would Be King" ends in horror, while the Krenks are driven out by a rather schoolboyish joke (a tribal Stalkyism). It marks the difference of the hills of the Himalayas from the hills of the frontier – and of their inhabitants. It marks the two views of primitivism which alternate in Kipling's mind – half-devils who crucify and half-children who defeat by gigantic practical jokes. In various degrees, this mixture lies in most of the native Indian world which was the most powerful fictional love affair of his life.

There was not much else in India that fed his fiction. Allahabad, where he spent his last two years as a journalist, gave in retrospect (ten years or so later) a memory, as so often happens, of minute particularity – the garden of "Rikki Tikki Tavi" – rather than any general sense either of the life of the important Hindu town or of the grandiose Civil Lines. The Grand Trunk Road, of course, brings Kim south. It is still possible to speak of Lucknow as Kim saw it "from the top of the Imambara looking down on the gilt umbrellas of the Chutter Munzil . . . beautiful in her garish style". But such a view is physically impossible, as I found on my visit there. And, although no doubt the description of the boys and the teaching at the La Martinière College in Lucknow, the original of St Xavier's in Partibus which Kim attends, is likely enough, I doubt if Kipling can ever have seen the school. Its late eighteenth-century Indo-rococo building is one of the most extraordinary legacies of European taste (its owner was a Frenchman) in India and, to my mind, the most beautiful. I cannot believe that Kim, with his sense of the strange and the fanciful, would not have been awe-struck by the curious lions that crown the school's roof. And I do not believe that had he seen them, Kipling could have failed to recreate it through Kim's eyes.

In contemporary stories, Lucknow Railway Station is used as the scene of a bitter parting. Benares has greater reality. Kipling visited there for the *Pioneer* soon after he took up his post at Allahabad. It struck Kim "as a peculiarly filthy city". This rather English tourist's reaction may be considered to be the single example in that book of the palpable effect upon Kim of his years at St Xavier's exemplary public school. He would hardly have survived his nomadic city life if he had usually cared so much about dirt. The atmosphere of the Jain temple at Sarnath outside Benares where the Lama dwells is general rather than particular.

But the Benares visit was not without its imaginative effect. One aspect had an ephemeral life as a story for the *Pioneer* in 1888, later to be the only good story included in the suppressed volume, *The Smith Administration* of 1891. It is a pity that it was suppressed, for it is one of Kipling's most telling blows at a group of people he detested for their insufficient concern for India – the globe-trotters or tourists as we should say now. There was something fundamentally disagreeable to Kipling in the idea of people "touring" India. India must be your whole life or nothing. Later, the possible application of it to himself worried him in 1889 when he himself toured other Asian lands. In the forgotten and suppressed story, "The Bride's Progress", he expresses this feeling most powerfully. No doubt he saw many globe-trotters in his trip to Benares, for a visit to the Ganges funeral ghats has always been a tourist must. In this tale, a young honeymoon couple from England arrive there and we are given the wife's reactions. She watches the details of the burning, floating bodies with growing horror – in particular, a special disgust for conventional English visitors was the sight of pariah dogs eating half-burned human limbs. So far, Kipling is with her, I think. But then she composes herself and puts the scene from her – India, she reminds herself, is only an incident to her on her world tour. It is then that Kipling snaps with irritation: she has taken the part for the whole; she has seen nothing of the grandeur of which this horror is only one face and that one she has not comprehended. India may be only an incident on this idyllic honeymoon; but she is the smallest, smallest incident to India.

More important, however, is Kipling's registering of a particular space of mud on the banks of the Ganges at Benares. During his Indian time the imposing Dufferin (called since 1946 the Pandit Malaviju) Bridge was constructed to take the Grand Trunk Road across the Ganges within sight of the temples of the burning ghats. He reported on its building for the *Civil and Military Gazette* in 1887, the year that it was opened. But the ceremony had been delayed because the bridge had been damaged by flood. In my own experience, the spectacle of the ghat cremations in its juxtaposition of noisy bazaar and silent river, in its vivid colours besides the draining sunshine and heat, and its constant human movement beside the stillness of the dead, heightens the intensity of all one's sense-impressions. A spectator is inevitably moved – either with a sense of dignity (as I was), or with a sense of horror as the honeymoon bride (and, perhaps, Kipling) were. This, I believe, accounts for a simple mudbank in this place being the scene of two of Kipling's most powerfully imagined fictions – the engineer Findlayson's opium dream of the conclave of the Hindu gods on the night when his bridge is threatened by flood in "The Bridge Builders", and the meeting of the grisly "Undertakers" (the mugger-crocodile, the adjutant stork, and the jackal), in *The Second Jungle Book*. The two are closely connected, when the mugger says, "I was faint with hunger. Since the railway bridge was built my people at my village have ceased to love me; and that is breaking my heart." The crocodile's protest, like Mother Ganga's to the Gods, is the protest of Indian natural life against the British order and civilisation, but whereas the Gods are shown to be of longer duration than any British rule (though even they are only part of Brahma's dream), the mugger is wholly evil. And he is destroyed at the end by a bullet from the bridge engineer's gun – "he took about fifteen of my coolies while the bridge was building, and it's time he was put a stop to."[49] But the bridge engineer as a baby had been nearly eaten by the mugger, when escaping with his mother from the horrors of the Mutiny. The floating bodies of that time on which the mugger recounts that he feasted seems to me to prove that the story (and "The Bridge Builders", for surely the engineers are the same men) concerns the Ganges, since the association of bodies with a river is something that is indelibly left by seeing the burning ghats. In any case, together, the two stories are the most powerful evocations of the glory (the company of the Gods) and the horror (the Undertakers) of the Indian natural scene that awoke such fabulous balance in Kipling's imagination.

From Allahabad he made other expeditions for his paper. Only one was productive in memory of art, though all provided first-rate journalism. In November 1887, he visited the Princely States of Rajasthan (or Rajputana, as they were usually then called) and from the journey made the articles in "The Letters of Marque". From all that he heard then must come the excellent melodrama of the princely state (said by Brigadier Mason to be Jodhpur[50]) in that much underestimated book, *The Naulahka*, on which he collaborated with his friend Wolcott Balestier in 1891. In its tension, its sense of sloth and treachery, spoiled riches and corruption, its lurking murder, the state of Rhatore is a worthy predecessor of the Indian Courts portrayed in Ackerley's *Hindoo Holiday* and Ruth Jhabvala's *Heat and Dust*; and it has in addition, as one would expect from Kipling, a superb child portrait, that of the young Maharaj Kunwar.

But the strongest impact of all that Kipling saw in Rajasthan was undoubtedly the ruined palace that was to form the basis of Cold Lairs in Mowgli's jungle. This is one of the most deeply felt of all Kipling's imagined scenes. The ruined city of Amber above Jaipur and the ruined city of Chitor, seventy or so miles from Udaipur, have both been claimed as the originals. Chitor, although under the Indian Archaeological Department and served by a guide, is still more ruinous than the tourist-haunted Amber with its elephant bus. But I do not think that that is the only reason why a visit to Chitor so powerfully conjures up Cold Lairs. (Who, by the way, but Kipling would have found so threatening a name?) At Chitor still come pythons and cobras in season; and the ruin of the Queen's palace, in particular, abounds in crevices and pits beneath the floors that are made for evil lurking, and the stupid monkeys still gather there at nightfall. Even so, to get the full idea of what dreams Chitor in its then ruinous state roused in Kipling, I think a visitor must go to a more deeply buried city like Tughlaquabad, outside Delhi, where as yet no one has conserved or guided and where no visitors save tribes of monkeys come.

"A withered beldame now, brooding on ancient fame." So Kipling celebrated Madras. "Clive kissed me on the mouth." All the south of India was dead to Kipling. A sleeping, outworn world that took no part in the defence from Russia of the civilisation that the English had brought to India. He never saw Madras, and only glimpsed South India from the train on his last visit in 1891, as for four days he travelled up from Ceylon to Lahore.

One long story, written much later when he was living in America, for American readers, embodies his impressions from those four days. But its real importance in his great fictional India is to show how fully he realised that the real basis of Indian life was not bridges and roads and railways, not even military defence, not certainly the private agonies of lonely whites, less still the gothic distresses of opium dens, but the growing of food for the vast peasant population. That he should have laid "William the Conqueror", his only story of Indian famine, in the south is, in part, accidental, because the terrible Madras famine of the late seventies was still much talked of when he was in India. But it is also because he wants to show the young pioneer Punjab not only guarding the old, lazy rotting South India from invasion but coming to succour it when famine strikes. It is an absolute refutation, however, of the idea that Kipling saw only the frills in Indian life. And it is typical that the only other two stories to announce this basic knowledge concerned children. Out of the mouths of babes and sucklings. In "Tod's Amendment" a little boy who

95

knows the real India from being with Indian servants brings home to the great British lawmakers the importance of land to every Indian; in "Little Tobrah", a small Indian boy shows the Darwinian reality of famine when he pushes his little blind weakling sister into the well because she cannot survive. Mowgli's punishment for the villagers who attacked the woman who befriended him is no light one. For, after he has let the jungle into their village with the elephants' aid, the villagers must leave. "They lived year in and year out as near to starvation as the jungle was near to them." [51]

But it is in a bitter poem in *Departmental Ditties* that the young Kipling most clearly announces this basic fact of Indian life. A poem in which Government is not spared at all. "The Masque of Plenty" has been curiously neglected, for it is a highly variegated set of verses in form, as well as explosive in content. "Argument," he writes, "The Indian Government being minded to discover the economic condition of their lands, sent a Committee to enquire into it; and saw that it was good." First, the Government of India in the raiment of the Angel of Plenty sings to the pianoforte accompaniment:

> How sweet is the shepherd's sweet life
> From dawn to even he strays . . .

Then the investigators set out:

> What is the State of the Nation? What is its
> occupation? . . .

But now comes:

> Interlude, from Nowhere in Particular, to stringed and
>   oriental instruments:
> Our cattle reel beneath the yoke they bear –
> The earth is iron and the skies are brass . . .
> The well is dry beneath the village tree –
> The young wheat withers ere it reach a span,
> And belts of blinding sand show cruelly
> Where once the river ran. . . .

The investigator returns with so good a report that the Government of India, "with white satin wings and electroplated harp", sings:

> How beautiful upon the mountains – in peace reclining
> Thus to be assured that our people are unanimously dining . . .

Then hired brass provides:

> God bless the squire
> And all his rich relations . . .

And, at last, comes a chorus of the Crystallised Facts which ends with these lines about the Indian peasant:

> His speech is of mortgaged bedding,
> On his vine he borrows yet,
> At his heart is his daughter's wedding,
> In his eye foreknowledge of debt,
> He eats and hath indigestion,
> He toils and he may not stop;
> His life is a long-drawn question
> Between a crop and a crop.

Young Rudyard Kipling's news "from Nowhere in Particular" is less idyllic than Uncle Topsy Morris's *News from Nowhere*, but it is hardly less disturbing.

Kipling in India, 1882–1889

So much for Kipling's fictional India. What of the life he lived in India itself from the end of his sixteenth year to the middle of his twenty-third?

Kipling landed at his birthplace, Bombay, towards the end of October 1882 and proceeded by train to Lahore, where he was met at the station by his father and his future boss on the *Civil and Military Gazette*, Stephen Wheeler, who had already interviewed him in London. It is so hard to think of the Victorian Punjab apart from Kipling's work that, I believe, we need to remind ourselves that the whole of "Kipling's India" was unknown to him, save what he could have gathered from his parents' letters. He was to make, as I have tried to show, a whole imaginative world out of what he saw in the next seven years, especially perhaps of what he saw in the next four. But he was very young; his parents were very close to him, and both had very forceful characters. There must have been a substantial foundation to his own attitude that came to him from them. The Walter Crane pictures on the walls of the Kiplings' Lahore house, the Indian designs used for the dadoes, the wood fires on cold evenings (to be expected up at Simla but hardly down on the plains), the refusal to plant shrubs in the garden lest they harbour insects and diseases – all these perhaps were a little eccentric. Mrs Kipling sang, as did most Victorian ladies, but she often sang her own compositions for the verses of a poet she had known personally. Mr Kipling read aloud to his wife, as did a large number of the heads of houses – even surely in Lahore; he read Shakespeare, well, of course . . . but he read Browning and Swinburne and Rossetti! Both husband and wife read stories from the magazine *Temple Bar* aloud – a very good choice: but occasionally the stories were written by themselves. They were, it must be repeated, "clever" people. Of course, it was only to be expected from the director of an art school and the head of a museum. A museum that brings scholars from all over the world is obviously an asset to a community, even if one has no inclination to visit it personally. About the encouragement of native styles of design and, perhaps still more, the training of native craftsmen, there must, of course, be two schools of thought. Then Mrs Kipling was related to the painter, Burne-Jones, about whose work, too, there was bound to be more than one opinion. Mr Kipling was a favourite with everyone, tactful and so wise, though there must have been many who chuckled as the ironic edge of some of his remarks went unnoticed by the more simple. Mrs Kipling's wit and charm would be more popular with the men; it is hard to think that someone so impulsive can have wholly disguised her opinion of the women of the British community from them.

But that community was very small. It would be hard to live in it and prosper if you did not fit in. It is true that the Kiplings did not "fit in" in the sense that their ambitions had burst and were still bursting the seams of the position that they occupied in the outwardly rigid hierarchy of British Indian society. The very arrival of Rudyard on the scene, to take up employment at so early an age, was a measure of the economic pressure that Lockwood's mediocre salary imposed upon their way of living. The bringing out of Trix to India early in 1885, at the surely very tender age of sixteen and a half, points up the economic dilemma even more closely. But Rudyard being taken on to the staff of the *Gazette* was also a measure of their well-placed contacts.

After Rudyard Kipling had become famous, so many of those who lived in North West India laid claim to having founded his fortunes that it is hard to sort out the true patrons from the dubious. Nevertheless, the friendship of the Kipling parents with the two wealthy owners of the *Gazette* was well established. William Rattigan, a successful lawyer with a social wife, had reason to sympathise with anyone making their way up the ladder, if, as I suggest below, his career was one of the pointers to *Kim*. James Walker, a banker and transport business man, was a closer friend and probably paid Rudyard's salary in the first year. William Allen, who ran the larger circulating sister paper, the *Pioneer*, down at Allahabad, had for some years been publishing reports and articles from both Lockwood and Alice. Rivett-Carnac, who later claimed to have given Lockwood his introduction to Lahore from Bombay and to have introduced the Kiplings to Allen, was rapidly rising in the Indian Civil Service, and by 1891 was to be an A.D.C. to the Queen. Walter Roper-Lawrence, whom Lockwood had befriended at the Lahore Club when he first arrived from England, was soon to be a Secretary to the Viceroy. Edward Buck was Secretary to the Government of India. David Masson, another partner in the newspaper syndicate, told Goulding, the author of *Old Lahore*, that he had given Rudyard his first chance.

Kipling, in a letter to James Walker in 1911, declining to write verses on the Durbar, adds, perhaps to mollify, that he owes his start in life to him.[52] It would be pleasing, however, if William Rattigan played some part. Certainly, I believe, Kipling owed another more important debt to Rattigan, for his grandson, Sir Terence Rattigan, tells me that his grandfather, who rose to be a member of the Governor General's Legislative Council, was the son of an illiterate Irish private in the Indian Army who had to make his mark on his enlistment papers. By some means his son got to the High School at Agra in the eighteen-fifties and subsequently to King's College, London, and to Göttingen University. Surely here may be a factual foundation, such as Kipling liked to make his imaginative flights from, for what would otherwise seem to be the improbable story of the Irish boy Kimball O'Hara's career.

And these were only some of the influential friends they had made. The brief glorious summer with the Viceroy Lytton at the Proclamation of the Empress in 1877 must have left its mark in local gossip. But with the then Viceroy, Lord Ripon, protégé of Prime Minister Gladstone, they do not appear to have had any contact. Perhaps this was just as well if they were to stand in with the British community in Lahore. Their rise to the heights of Viceregal friendship and royal patronage had to await the coming of the aristocratic, worldly, cultured Lord Dufferin as Viceroy and the presence in India of Queen Victoria's youngest son, the Duke of Connaught.

I am not wishing to suggest that Kipling's parents were in the slightest degree mercenary. Lockwood's ambitions were entirely on behalf of his job, to improve Indian craft and design and make easier the path of good Indian craftsmen. When he was awarded his Order,

99

C.I.E., in 1887, it was by hard work for this cause. But, for all his gentle scholarliness, he was clearly not without understanding of worldly props for his disinterested aims. Alice Kipling, apart from her concern for her husband's career, simply needed a wider, more cultivated, more amusing circle to breathe in. Both were surely very ambitious for their talented children.

Writers on Kipling have, I think, overstressed the unusual quality of his parents, both because he did inherit much of his talent from them, and because they cherished and influenced his writings all their lives (but especially, of course, in these Lahore years when he was so young and living with them). Yet, broadly speaking, in social and even more in political matters, the Kipling parents shared the outlook of the British community in Lahore, though not of the narrowest section of it. They could hardly have had a position from which to burst out if they had not. We hear of them "all agog" at the prospects of war with Russia. Lockwood, for all his zeal for his native students, had a very realistic sense of Indian limitations – Indian contentment with slipshod work, idleness. In his *Beast and Man in India*, he is anxious to point out how unreal is the romantic dream of India that scholars of the old Sanskrit or Buddhist texts (he intends, I imagine, people like Max Müller who never visited India) have created. Since Moslem and Mahratta days, he says, at any rate, cruelty is a marked characteristic of the country. "The Singalese are Buddhists and yet cruelty to animals is one of the marks of modern Ceylon . . . We are apt to judge the results of a creed from the aims of its commandments . . . Yet we ought to know better, for the main stream of our Christian commandments is to lay up no treasure on earth, to consider the lilies of the field, to sell all and follow Christ, etc. In the Christian capitals of the Western world one may see how much of this injunction is obeyed."[53]

The criticism of both India and the Christian West were inherited by his son but the dry tones, the controlled note, the "etc." are far from Rudyard's poetic, romantic vision.

The poet Wilfred Scawen Blunt was a radical in politics, a supporter of the early Congress Movement and so on. It is typical of Lockwood's tolerance and likability that he should have kept on good terms with Blunt. Nevertheless, it is worth noting that when, in 1908, at one of the periodic times of political stress, Blunt wanted to take the pulse of a typical Anglo-Indian, he turned to Lockwood. "Today old Kipling, Rudyard's father, came to dinner and I had a long talk to him about India. I wanted to find out from him, a typical Anglo-Indian, what remedy he would apply to the present condition of things. Like all the rest, however, he has no remedy to propose beyond 'severe repression' for the time being." [54]

In one sense Lockwood, for all his temperate, undogmatic attitude to life, was perhaps more narrow than many less wise Anglo-Indians, for whereas most saw service in many parts of the country, he seldom moved from his posts, first in Bombay, then in Lahore, save for the setting up of exhibitions in Calcutta. He was, like his son, a very bookish man; his *Beast and Man in India* came from books and travellers' reports, not from any first-hand knowledge of Indian cities, villages or jungle.

Kipling, in short, received from his father a conventional if detachedly seen political and social picture of India, as he received from his mother a conventional if sharply seen picture of Anglo-Indian society. What his poetic, turbulent, paradoxical, even, it may be said, revolutionary imagination made of their intelligent conservative view of life must have been, clearly was, a surprise, sometimes an alarm, though always a pride to them.

Carrington has rightly underlined the importance of the Four Square, as Alice called the family of parents, son and daughter, as a centre of Kipling's stasis, the bedrock from which he could venture forth to bruise himself against the real world and return to recuperate. Kipling's most recent critics have followed this further, to make the family the chief of all the group loyalties in Kipling's philosophy, by which a man gathers strength to accept the duties and hardships and indeed the intense precariousness of civilised society. This is all true, though, as I shall later suggest, there are strong gipsy pulls in the other direction whose siren note Kipling knew well and there are crises – notably the change that men make from their father's family to their own – that impose great pressures from the Square. But I think it is also necessary to point out that, though the young Kipling enjoyed exceptional benefit at the time of the genesis of his art in having loving, cultured, interested parents and sister, and, perhaps no less valuable, a well-run, comfortable, well-fed home in a land of back-breaking work, deadly climate and precarious health, the Kipling family at Bikaner House had many of the stresses and strains that all families suffer, possibly more than many because it was made up of four very talented, sensitive people. Kipling himself does not dwell on this aspect of family life, for society cannot afford to underline the tensions of its most cohesive institution. The few family relationships in his stories are somewhat idyllic. Yet he always makes clear that regiments, ships, Masonic Lodges and other essential groups that give man stability, discipline and a sense of security are educative as much through their strains and stresses as through their harmonies. And so,

I am sure, he must have found the family in these years in Lahore.

Certainly he felt ill-at-ease all through the first winter. He needed to keep in touch with his female relations and with "The Mater" as confidants. He was troubled about Flo Garrard's real feelings for him. His father thought the new life, though hard, was a saving alternative to what London night life – "music halls", he calls it – might have done to him had he stayed in England. He may have been right. But young Rudyard, in all the backbreaking routine of his work at the newspaper office, cannot always have agreed. His mother thought the job offered him fine prospects. She was possibly right. But he cannot have been happy to find himself labelled in advance "a young poet", because she had chosen to publish his schoolboy lyrics without consulting him. It was not the best label for a cub reporter.

His parents were worried enough about his moods and his dislike of Lahore in those first months for Alice Kipling to stay in the plains during the hot months of his first year, despite her frail health and although she was overdue in England to see her daughter. And this at Lockwood's determined suggestion. Nor was the situation without its tensions after Trix arrived. If Carrington is right in his shrewd surmise that the lines in *Departmental Ditties*:

> They walk beside Her rickshaw wheels –
> None ever walk by mine;
> And that's because I'm seventeen
> And she is forty-nine,[55]

make open reference to a complaint of Alice Kipling's popularity with the young men by her daughter (the ages fit exactly), we can see how remarkably the family were able to deal humorously with what in a less open family might have been a very serious cause of conflict. But strains there were and some part of the burden of Trix's sad later nervous collapse must be laid upon her girlhood, although she turned most particularly to her mother in later crises of her life.

Whatever the turbulent undertow, in 1884 appeared *Echoes*, a book of parodies by Rudyard and Trix (product of a month in the hill station of Dalhousie), and in 1885 (product of a Simla season) came *Quartette*, a magazine by all four, and containing, for whoever could appreciate it, a work of genius in "The Strange Ride of Morrowbie Jukes". No British family anywhere, I suppose, let alone in India, could have given such proof of the artistic fruitfulness of the strains, disciplines, and the pleasures of domestic life.

Rudyard's life at the newspaper office can hardly have seemed to him so satisfying. Stephen Wheeler, at heart a good friend to him, worked him very hard indeed, throughout the day and often into very late hours when a special item demanded it. Soon after Ruddy had started at the *C.M.G.*, Wheeler was away ill from the effects of a carriage accident and the boy (for he was not yet seventeen) had to run the paper and its good-sized staff by himself. He seems to have grasped the technical processes involved in printing very quickly, as, throughout his life, he was to understand quickly the principles on which things worked in a hundred different spheres. His poor memory and his inaccuracy in detail were equally marked throughout his life. In his art it has led naive Kipling admirers to heights of admiration when he get technical details right and puzzled disappointment when he gets them wrong. None of this matters at all, of course, for like all artists he uses the real world only as bricks to build his own imaginative constructions. Yet he was one of those novelists who needed a mass of "real" bricks before he could erect his castles in the air. Like Zola or Flaubert, the exact weights and shapes of the bricks, the careful figures he had amassed before building commenced, were soon forgotten once he began work. Exact knowledge of technical processes, of course, is more essential to those who must work them. But Kipling did not have to do so. Even in these early days among the printing presses of the *C.M.G.*, he had to know what other men were doing, not to do it himself.

For his journalistic reports, the defects were more serious. This may be one of the reasons, over and above his belief in keeping an airy-fairy bookish young chap's nose to the grindstone, why Wheeler employed the young Kipling on dogsbody work. But the chief reason surely was that there were only two white staff, that Wheeler had accepted this very young man as an assistant, and he quite reasonably was going to use him for the more boring tasks. One, for which Rudyard's good knowledge of French particularly suited him, was the making of abstracts and reports of all that French-language Russian newspapers had to say about Afghanistan and the Frontier – the foreign news that most concerned his readers in the Punjab.

Apart from reporting local events, he was occasionally sent on assignments outside Lahore. In February 1883 we find him, under the penname "Nick", reporting on a fête in Jeypore for the *Pioneer*, and it is interesting to see how much at that early stage he inevitably fell back on his father's Indian concerns. The description of the fête is absurdly taken up with architectural detail. "I'm afraid all this is terribly technical," he writes. And then, beating his father's drum, "Some day it will be accepted as a principle that Indian architecture should be used for Indian buildings." [56] Later travelling assignments were to produce more individual, less influenced journalism, until by the end of his time in India (on the *Pioneer* in Allahabad in 1887 and 1888) his reports from the Princely States, from Calcutta, and from the industrial mining areas on the Bengal border are enormously readable travel journalism even today.

But more important to us is the way in which he used such occasions (or I should prefer, in part sharing Kipling's superstitious belief in artistic daemons, to say, such occasions used him) to produce small moments of intense vision that were to swell into strongly felt, closely imagined fictions. From this point of view, the most important of his five assignments during his employment at Lahore with the *C.M.G.* from autumn 1882 to autumn 1887 was his covering of the meeting of the new Viceroy, Lord Dufferin, with the only recently hostile Amir of Afghanistan. They met in Peshawar, where the delightful Dean's Hotel still gives the feeling of Kipling's time, on the very edge of the mountain passes – the Kohat and the Khyber – into the no-man's-land on the road to Kabul. A sudden irruption of a Russian regiment into the Amir's territory only disturbed the meeting enough to transfer its venue to the more accessible Rawalpindi, only 180 miles from Lahore. This occasion shows the many levels at which the young Kipling's mind was working. On the surface his reports of the meeting and its political significance, helped by his reading of the Russian French-language newspapers, were good enough for one report to be re-published unacknowledged in *The Times*. The surface of the festivities at Pindi remained with him sufficiently for him to produce a decade later a rather whimsical account of conversations between regimental animals – the camels and horses and elephants – which appears as "Soldiers of the Queen" in *The Jungle Book*.

But the journey touched his literary imagination at two much deeper levels. While at Peshawar, he made a journey to Fort Jumrood at the mouth of the Khyber. Most creditably to the Pakistan Government, the formidable ornamental gateway near the customs post is engraved with verses from Kipling. Here, he believed, he was shot at by Pathans and it seems more than likely, for even today the tribes of the neighbouring Kohat pass have found their only appropriate peaceful occupation in turning out replica guns of all times and places for tourists. But the harsh rolling mountain scene was to stir in Kipling's imagination many times.

It produced "The Ballad of East and West" (1889) – "belike they will raise thee to Ressaldar when I am hanged in Peshawar" – that magnificent boyish bravura which announces the superiority of friendship and action over convention and race. It entered more subtly and more powerfully into some of the greatest moments in his stories, as I have suggested. From this border ride, Kipling's imagination must have carried remote and terrible sounds – the prolonged swish of air of Dan's fall for half an hour, thrown from the mountain pass to crash at last on the water below, and the screams of the crucified Peachey. These are the horrors that came to him, I think, from the *visual* scene of the passes.

But something else stirred the depths of the cruelty and terror of his imagination. Here, at last, he was in the regions talked of in Lahore bazaars, the lawless, treacherous land whence came Mahbub Ali, the horse-dealer, a real live disreputable acquaintance (as well as the ambiguous fictional protector of Kim). Here in an atmosphere of intrigue and vengeance, or power preserved by the brutal, irrevocable jesting justice like that of our Tudor age, he found a terrible version of Stalkyism. Where the rough and ready practical joke may put things right in the simple, harsh world of boarding schools, torture and prolonged death agonies are authority's jest in Afghanistan where the slightest threat to the throne may shatter all rule and let loose tribal anarchy. From the bazaars of Peshawar and from talk with those in the Amir's entourage upon this 1885 assignment comes, I think, the cruel teasing death of the blind mullah in "The Head of the District", and the deathly joke of "The Amir's Homily", and at least two powerful neglected poems – "The Ballad of the King's Mercy" (1889) and "The Ballad of the King's Jest" (1890). From these we see that those who suffer terrible punishment are not the open enemies of authority, but those who seek to please the King too much, or talk too much, or carry out too easily his cruel commands, or over-flatter him. Everything and everybody in a world poised on the edge of chaos is suspect, most of all those who are too pliable, who try too hard, the weak links:

> His sire was leaky of tongue and pen,
> His dam was a clucking Khattack hen;
> And the colt bred close to the vice of each,
> For he carried the curse of an unstaunched speech
> Therewith madness – so that he sought
> The favour of kings at Kabul Court.

This young man seeks to please the Amir by collecting tales of Russian invasion and of sedition to warn him. And for his pains, he is tied to a peach tree surrounded by bayonets on the ground below that he may give warning of the Russian invasion he preached too often:

> By the power of God, Who alone is great,
> Till the seventh day he fought with his fate.
> Then madness took him, and men declare
> He mowed in the branches as ape and bear.
> And last as a sloth, ere his body failed,
> And he hung like a bat in the forks, and wailed,
> And sleep the cord of his hands untied,
> And he fell, and was caught on the points and died.[57]

This vision of a brutal justice, at once savoured and casual, that he found among the primitive Moslem world continued to haunt Kipling for most of his life, giving a powerful, yet dreadful, sadistic flavour to the punitive jests with which, in his stories, society protects itself against treachery or weakness in times of danger – the stories of the Boer War or the Great War – giving an extraordinary realism to his imagination when he reaches back into more brutal ages (Roman Imperial, medieval, Tudor) in stories like that of the Roman galley slaves in "The Finest Story in the World" or in many of the best tales in *Puck of Pook's Hill* and *Rewards and Fairies*.

These assignments away from Lahore, however, were only an occasional variation in his hard-packed monotonous office life. After unwontedly staying in the plains with her son to see him through his first season, Alice left for England in the monsoon time of 1883 to fetch Trix back to India. Lockwood was busy with the arrangement of an exhibition in Calcutta for two months. So that, save for a short holiday with his employer, James Walker, in Simla, when he no doubt had his first encounters with the Anglo-Indian hierarchy, the seventeen-year-old Rudyard was on his own.

He had little time for games-playing, even if he had been physically suited for it. H. R. Goulding tells us in "Old Lahore" that Kipling joined B. Company of the 1st Punjab Volunteers, but no one ever saw him at a parade.[58] Goulding, as his commander, had to ask him to make his capitation grant (or enrolment fee) which Kipling did immediately, regretting his lack of opportunity to carry out his duties. In some part, his leisure hours must have been spent brooding about Flo Garrard with whom for a while his semi-engagement dragged on.

After the long, heavy, airless days, print-swimming days that the weak-sighted youth had to spend over his desk, he was faced not with Alice's comfort but with a cheerless young bachelor's life. He was probably both awed and fascinated by the male community of the

Club with its shop-talk, its late Victorian men's near-the-knuckle stories, its political grumbling, its gossip. He was certainly early appalled by the constant threat of death from the many mortal plagues that threatened the white community. A youth, with "clever" parents and a book of poems published by his mother to his credit, would come in, at the least, for a good deal of heavy-handed chaffing.

The story is well known of how he was hissed at the Club one evening because the *C.M.G.*'s editorial had praised the Ilbert Bill by which the liberal Viceroy, Ripon, sought to give Indian magistrates the right to try white offenders. The *C.M.G.*, in general, backed Government measures. Kipling suggests, in his autobiography, that this was because the proprietors were concerned for eventual honours – and indeed all of them became Knights eventually. But it seems as likely that businessmen on a large scale had no wish to offend the Government. They were closer to the broader commercial climate of Calcutta or Bombay. The planters, small traders, minor officials and subalterns who gathered in the Lahore Club, however, saw only affront and threat in the new measure. But for the youth who understood nothing of it all to be on the receiving side of hisses from his seniors can have been no easy moment. Despite all the Club conversation framework of many of Kipling's stories, despite his obvious debt to the shop-talk which he drank in there, Kay Robinson, his later editor, tells us that, three years after this incident, at any rate, Kipling did not go often to the Club. One may think this desertion began early, for, although he was a wonderful listener and a sociable man, he was all his life, I think, sensitive and a man who would do all he could to avoid arguments and rows. In any case, the paper must often have closed too late for Club dinners.

Too tired to read, too tired to sleep, too tired to write, apprenticed to a profession peculiarly exhausting to a man with weak eyesight, it must have been in these lonely seasons of the monsoon months of 1883 and of the hot months of 1884, that the keyed-up, exhausted young Kipling made his long night walks and saw the shadier side of the native quarter.

Increasingly reviewers and critics seem to ask whether in this youthful, solitary life in Lahore, Kipling was not personally involved in the sexual half-world he so wonderfully brings alive. Perhaps no story raises this question more in the ordinary reader's mind than the account of the illicit, blissful ménage of Holden and Ameera, in "Without Benefit of Clergy". There can be no definite answer to this question, of course. One can only say that the complaints of frustration that occur in his surviving diary for 1885 are such as any late-Victorian young man might have voiced in the husband-seeking, glittering female company of the Simla season.

When staying with James Walker in Simla in August of that year, he writes, "Wish they wouldn't put married couples next door to me with one $\frac{1}{2}$ inch plank between. Saps one's morality." And the next day. "Same complaint. This is really ghastly. Only drawback to a delightful visit. His Excellency an angel of the first water." [59]

But the real point is that such a question is a silly one. A writer, especially a romantic writer – and Kipling's extraordinary claim to notice is that he was a romantic working within a stoic framework – creates a world from what he sees and imagines and by no means necessarily from what he experiences in the world outside him.

Given the inevitable frustrations of a young man's life in India at that time, Kipling appears to have been curiously naive, for when, in 1886, after an exhausting newspaper assignment to report the coronation of the new Maharajah of Kashmir, he went on a recuperative walking tour in the foothills of the Himalayas, he chose as his companions a honeymoon couple. But even from this surely frustrating experience he got his bitter marriage comedy of the Gadsbys. It was returning from this trip without his companions that he came close, for the only time so far as we know, with wild animals, in fact with mountain bears. But his inexperience did not prevent him from writing an unique collection of animal stories, in which the wild life is strangely mixed with anthropomorphic fable as in no other author that ever lived.

What it did, however, give him positively was a physical sense of bears to use twelve years later in his fierce political poem, "The Truce of the Bear", a warning against the Tsar's pacific overtures. This poem surely may now be read in other wider contexts – either as warning against sentimentality and patronisingly trusting the wild, or even more against surrendering to a self-flattering sense of pity. But, however we read it, the presence of the bear is inescapable:

> Horrible, hairy, human, with paws like hands in prayer,
> Making his supplication rose Adam-zad the Bear!
> I looked at the swaying shoulders, at the paunch's swag
>   and swing,
> And my heart was touched with pity for the monstrous pleading
>   thing.
> Touched with pity and wonder, I did not fire then . . .
> I have looked no more on women – I have walked no more
>   with men.

Nearer he tottered and nearer, with paws like hands
    that pray,
From brow to jaw that steel-shod paw, it ripped my
    face away!

Yet the same writer could two years earlier have given to the world
Baloo, "old Baloo, who can come and go where he pleases because he
eats only mustard roots and honey," the bear who is in all his movements a real wild creature, but who in fable is the embodiment of the
kind, wise housemaster. Throughout Kipling's work one may see him
try to impose a strict shape and a single law upon exactly such an
apprehended world of monstrous duality as these two embodiments of
the bear.

    1886 was an important year for the Kipling family in general and a
turning-point for Rudyard. The first impact of the Kiplings upon the
cultured new Viceroy and Vicereine, the Dufferins, seems to have been
negative. On returning from the meeting with the Amir in Rawalpindi,
they inspected the Museum and School of Art in Lahore and Lady
Dufferin wrote to her mother, "but there is no use telling you about
things which are everywhere much alike, and in the latter place the
only uncommon sight was a row of juvenile carpenters, about eight
years of age, learning their trade. They begin with carving ... using
their toes almost as much as their hands." [60] However, that hot season
up in Simla, the Dufferins were to discover that the Kiplings were
more "amusing" than the general run of the upper middle class with
whom ruling India inevitably associated them. It is from this season
that Alice Kipling's Wilde-like witticisms begin to be reported, most
notably:

Jealous woman friend: "That was a very long conversation you had
    with his Excellency."
Alice Kipling: "Yes, my dear, and it was as broad as it was long."

                                   and

Malicious woman friend: "What a lot you must have taught your son
    about women."
Alice Kipling: "On the contrary, what a lot my son has taught me."

Alice's young daughter, Trix, too, had exceptional beauty. She
danced well, was sensitive, and her witticisms were also reported:

Trix Kipling: (on being asked by the Viceroy why she was not danc-
    ing) "You see I am quite young, only eighteen. Perhaps when I
    am forty, I shall get some partners." [61]

Her noted powers of quoting Shakespeare and other poets seems to have fascinated rather than have scared the young men. The Viceroy's son, Lord Clandeboys, was among her great admirers. In a letter written to General Sir Ian Hamilton, in his old age in 1942, recalling their shared youth in Simla, Trix says that, for two years running, the young Lord begged her to marry him. His father, and even more his mother, Trix writes, were disapproving and the young man went home to Ireland.[62] One cannot help feeling that Trix Kipling was the real victim of those splendid seasons. She *was* only eighteen. In a year's time she was engaged to John Fleming, seconded from the Queen's Own Borderers to the Survey Department, though Lockwood, at least, was in doubt. After some breaking and renewing of vows, she married him in 1889, after her brother had left India for good. Her childhood had been bound up with Rudyard's. In these few years in India they were the closest friends. Now he went on to the world of fame. She remained to be praised by those two rival giants in India of the 1900s, Lord Curzon and Lord Kitchener. The first said that she was the one lady in India with whom he cared to converse; the second, no famed lover of women's beauty, said that her shoulders and arms were the whitest in India and she did not need to powder them. Yet her life faded away into a cruel nervous breakdown and compensating psychic experiences until as an old lady she recovered to give many lively and sensitive talks on her brother to faithful Kiplingians.

Another of Trix's partners in her best Simla season was the old Queen's youngest son, the Duke of Connaught, just coming to the end of his very successful army service in India. It was probably from this acquaintance that Lockwood got his two most important commissions in England, for the ballroom at the Duke's house at Bagshot and for the Durbar Room at the Queen's beloved Osborne House – not a very happy sugar-cake Moghul decoration which was, however, mainly carried out by his Indian assistant.

For Rudyard himself, these glorious Simla seasons were a heightening of what he knew already. In 1885, the *C.M.G.* proprietors had sent him for a whole six-month stay to cover the social season, so that he was there not as sharing the family's strained resources, but as one invited automatically to every social event. This is when he must have laid the foundation of the Simla stories. "The Phantom Rickshaw", in fact, appeared in *Quartette* that year. He was a frequent guest at James Walker's opulent house and at the house of Edward Buck who was Secretary to the Indian Government. The *Pioneer* and the *C.M.G.* representative at Simla, Sinnett, was said to be in the deepest Government confidence. When, therefore, Rudyard arrived for a month's leave in 1886 to find his family on Viceregal visiting terms (indeed Lord Dufferin himself even "dropped in" on them), he was already well acquainted with the Simla world.

The Dufferins did not find the reserved, still somewhat awkward young man so easy to place in the ranks of this new "amusing" family they had unearthed. But Lord Dufferin, at any rate, came to respect the young journalist's ability fairly quickly. During this month the young Kipling moved much in the inner circle. After the required ice at Pellitti's café in the Mall, he would look in on Walter Lawrence, the Viceroy's A.D.C., at his makeshift office on the Mall, for everyone had to make shift on this annual ascent of Government from Calcutta to the hills in the hot season. At Sunday luncheon Rudyard was, Ian Hamilton recalled, a regular visitor to another of the Viceroy's secretaries, Herbrand Russell, later Duke of Bedford.

One can see faintly stirring in the Indian stories that fascination with political manoeuvre which was to become an obsessive side of Kipling's life from his first visit to Cape Town in 1897 until, at least, the outbreak of the Great War. But, at this youthful age, it appears fictionally only as a rather delightful farce set in the Viceregal Lodge – "The Germ-Destroyer".

In this 1886 season, he first met the witty, intelligent colonel's wife, Mrs Burton, who was to share with Alice Kipling in the character of Mrs Hauksbee, and as the dedicatee of *Plain Tales from the Hills* – to "the wittiest woman in India" – when it appeared the next year. It was now that he walked and talked with the popular Commander-in-Chief, Lord Roberts, who held court at the villa called Snowdon (now only a hospital façade) beneath the opposite hill of Simla, Jakko Hill, to the Viceregal Lodge hill, above the village of Boileaugange.

The culmination of all this glory really came, appropriately, in amateur theatricals in the following year, 1887. Here at Lady Roberts's house was staged *Homes in the Hills*, preceded by a burlesque *Lucia de Lamermoor* with a prologue written by Rudyard and spoken by Trix dressed as a nurse:

> The others who portray poor Lucia's griefs
> Are all in their respective lines the chiefs.
> The army list eluci(a)dates this fact.

But greater was to follow, for the New Gaiety Theatre in the Mall (still busy with rehearsals for a local show when I saw it in March 1975) was opened, at Lady Dufferin's request, with *A Scrap of Paper*. This, very typically of the festivities of the Empire and even still of

111

some of the ex-Empire of today, was a translation of a farce by Sardou, which had been the rage of Paris twenty-six years before. Mrs Burton played the leading role and Rudyard ably supported her as Brisemouche. Once again Rudyard contributed a typical prologue:

> Why "chaste" amusements? Do our Morals fail
> Amid the deodars of Annandale?
> Into what vicious vortex do they plunge
> Who dine at Jakko or at Boileaugange?

No doubt it was the general social success of the Kiplings at this time and the usual alarm that fiction creates in any social circle it describes that, combined with the ambiguous relationship that all journalists have with the public, produced that small but persistent stream of jealous social condescension towards Kipling among some Anglo-Indians which I can remember hearing from grand Indian Civil Service memsahibs in the twenties when I was a small schoolboy. Dennis Kincaid in his *British Social Life in India* tells us that his memsahib grandmother always spoke of Kipling as "a subversive pamphleteer given to criticising his betters".[63] And Sir Francis Younghusband, looking back to his Simla days on the staff of the Quartermaster-General, speaks of Kipling as being, "looked upon with great disfavour by staff officers as being bumptious and above his station".[64]

Kipling was no doubt aware of some of this hostility when he wrote in his preface to *Under the Deodars* – "It may be as well to assure the ill-informed that India is not entirely inhabited by men and women playing tennis and breaking the Seventh Commandment." Indeed, we should remember that Simla was the social centre of well-educated men and women in the Government service. Sir Walter Lawrence, a very gifted man with wide experience, wrote, "I look back on Simla society as the brightest, wittiest, most refined community I ever knew."[65] It must have been imitative, limited and, at best, middle-class, but it was also probably the talented English middle class playing out its social fantasies to their height.

In late 1886, life had also changed for Rudyard in Lahore. Stephen Wheeler, his health worn out, retired to England. There he wrote, in retirement, a warning against the growing power of Indian Congress and the chimera of Indian Independence. His place as editor of the *C.M.G.* was taken by Kay Robinson, a man much nearer to Kipling's age, who had recently come out from England to work on the *Pioneer*. Robinson had already visited the Kiplings at Lahore and had been enchanted by them, though it took him a little time to work through Rudyard's reserve. His physical description of Kipling at that time, written later for *McClure's Magazine* in 1896, is vivid. Among other things he notes how Rudyard at the office, dressed in a white cotton vest and trousers, seemed like a Dalmatian dog because of the mass of inkspots with which he covered himself. He gives us an altogether eccentric young "character" with his "mushroom-shaped" hat and his white fox terrier, Vic, "like a nice clean sucking pig".[66] Robinson, unlike Wheeler, thought Kipling's literary gifts monstrously wasted in routine journalism. To liven up the paper and to give Kipling more scope, he began a new feature – "turnovers" on the front and second pages of the *C.M.G.* They were soon very popular with readers. Among them thirty-nine of the stories in Kipling's first book, *Plain Tales from the Hills*, appeared between November 1886 and June 1887. It is Robinson who reminds us of what critics, who disparage Kipling's early Indian stories, often seem to deny, that a high proportion of Kipling's Anglo-Indian readers had passed competitive examinations far beyond the average readers of magazines in London at that time.

But in autumn 1887, a more complete change came to Kipling's life. He was posted to the senior paper, the *Pioneer* in Allahabad. Here, in the weekly edition – *The Week's News* – he was to be associated with a newspaper that had a good circulation outside India. It has to be said, however, that the fiction Kipling contributed to *The Week's News* between January and September 1888 is disappointing. Of thirty-three items only one is among his best work – "A Wayside Comedy". Six or so have rightly never been reprinted, including his most gratuitously brutal story, "The Likes of Us", a tale of self-righteous army bullying. The last contribution called, indeed, "The Last of the Stories", tells of all the fictional characters who await their authors in a kind of limbo. It is notable chiefly for the strange mixture of novelists who at that time interested him – Balzac, Gautier, Zola, Rabelais, Browning, Stevenson and Twain rub shoulders with Haggard, Besant, Mrs Humphry Ward, Mrs Hodgson Burnett, W. S. Gilbert and Blackmore. He remained all his life an unselective reader; but that is less important than the fact that what he read truly fed and enlarged his imaginative powers.

Had it not been for the impact of the amazing *Plain Tales from the Hills*, he would hardly have gained credit from these publications although he was writing much splendid fiction, for example, "Baa, Baa, Black Sheep", in the Allahabad years.

Yet these two years are finally more productive of good journalism than of good fiction. His work on the *Pioneer* was broadening his knowledge of India, forcing him to defend, sometimes rather desperately, and occasionally to relinquish, the Punjab view, bringing him constantly into conflict with a new Indian nationalist world, particularly in his visit to Calcutta, bringing him into contact, both fascinated and repelled, with an older Hindu India when he visited the Princely States of Rajputana, and with a new industrial India when he visited the great railway depots, opium factories and coal mines of the Patna area. All this clash of the new and the old India was to be heightened and, indeed, petrified into rigidity when he came to London a year later and heard what he felt to be dangerous and ill-informed liberal talk about the nationalist future of the country that was his emotional centre. It was then that he wrote his most talked-of polemical pieces – "India for the Indians", published in the *St James's Gazette* for December 1889 (shortly after he arrived in London), and the more famous, "The Enlightenment of Pagett, M.P.", in the *Contemporary Review* of summer 1890. In this second piece he received much assistance from his father, returned on leave and equally disgusted with what he felt to be such vague liberal London talk about the country he knew.

In the former article, inspired by his growing sense of the white British Empire (Canada, Australia, etc.) which was to become the centre of his thought in the next decades, he predicts a takeover of India for its own good by Anglo-Indian administrators and soldiers based upon Kashmir, men determined to save all they had done for India from being ruined by a handover to incompetent Western-educated Indians by ill-informed, self-indulgent Englishmen. It was a dream that was to reappear at odd moments over the next years. Its unreality, I think, was in the end to lead him to leave India out of all his Imperial political schemes of the next decades, so that she might remain enshrined in his heart untouched from what he had known in his wonderful youth. A notable feature of this article is the first appearance of a gushing, sentimental tone which he puts into the mouth of all his liberal or radical opponents – "Where's the dear delightful Nationalist Congress with all its boundless possibilities?"[67] It is feeble journalese at this stage, but it was to be an effective mockery of the silliest liberals in his political allegories of the early nineteen-hundreds and an even more telling travesty of the speech of London bohemia in such stories as, "My Son's Wife".

The second story, in which a well-intentioned M.P., Pagett (very different from the globe-trotting radical M.P. of the same name so vitriolically attacked in his poem) comes to stay with an old school

114

24 Lurgan's house in Simla: the disreputable antique shop where Kim learns the disguises and memory tests that prepare him for "The Great Game". (*Photo Tony Garrett*)

25 The New Gaiety Theatre in the Mall, Simla, was opened with *A Scrap of Paper*: Kipling played the leading role. (*Photo Tony Garrett*)

26 La Martinière School, Lucknow, originally the rococo home of a rich Frenchman: it was the model for Kim's school at St Xavier's – yet surely Kipling cannot have seen it for he must have known that the monstrous lions would have drawn Kim's attention. (*Photo Tony Garrett*)

27 An Irish boy's carving of his name (Kim's?) on the step of La Martinière School. (*Photo Tony Garrett*)

28, 29 The Mall, Simla, as it is today. (*Photos Tony Garrett*)

30 Chitor, the ruined city of Rajasthan, the principal model for Cold Lairs, the most powerfully evoked scene in the Jungle Book tales. (*Photo Tony Garrett*)

31 Milestones from Moghul times still mark the Grand Trunk Road. (*Photo Tony Garrett*)

33 Covers of Kipling first editions. (*Grenville Taylor Collection*)

34 A Royal Academy version of Mowgli: "Mowgli and Bagheera" by E. J. Detmold, 1902. (*Bateman's*)

35 "A Sylvan God" by Arthur Wardle.

36 A Royal Academy interpretation of Kipling's dreamworld of children: "The Land of Nod" by Charles Sims.

friend, District Commissioner Orde (who had already appeared in "The Head of the District"). Pagett's naive opening remark at breakfast, "The National Congress . . . must have caused great excitement among the masses," gives his host, Orde (and Kipling) the rather too easy opportunity to produce witnesses from among many types in India's agriculture, finance and industry utterly to refute the wretched Pagett's remark.[68]

The piece is not without its merits. Kipling makes some telling points – the complete failure of the English liberal to recognise the deep acceptance of disaster and death as the natural lot among Indian people as a whole, the power of the Indian family, and, something that contemporary Indian government would applaud, the need of a strong government to protect India from the selfish interests of foreign (including English) investors, above all the essential importance of the Indian land cultivator. But all this is vitiated by his too persistent belief, firstly that educated minorities have no real force or influence in society; and secondly, that political power ultimately lies with the man who supervises the man who does the job. This anti-intellectual bias, however ethically or emotionally sympathetic in its respect for those who bear the weight of administrative or executive responsibility, was unfortunately a grave misreading (or perhaps a determined misreading) of the nature of power in a rapidly expanding democracy based upon a rapidly expanding education – India potentially, England actually. Its full effect on his social thinking is better seen later in its general application to his political concerns in the next two decades.

In general, his deep imaginative sense of India seems to get increasingly blunted and narrowed in scope in so many of the articles he wrote in Allahabad. He had, I think, great difficulty in focusing the new wider Indian perspective he met there and in Calcutta in this last year and a half of his Indian journalistic career. What he wrote about Congress itself, and indeed about the Indian and especially the Bengali clerical class, seldom rises above schoolboy sarcasm. He refuses really to believe that they are more than the absurd (though also dangerous) instruments of their foolish "intellectual" English supporters like Allan Hume, their first Indian National Congress President. Of all his many articles against Congress and his invented babu Bengali lawyer, Mr Chuckerbuti, very few give clues to his superb imaginative powers, let alone add respect for his political realism. One, however, "A Little Morality" (published in the *Pioneer* in January 1888), an attack on the usual English literary education of Indian boys – *The Faerie Queene*, Charles Kingsley's *Westward Ho!*, "Hypatia", pages of Chaucer, "Empedocles at Etna", *The Rape of the Lock*, *King Lear* and

Macaulay's *Lays of Ancient Rome* – not only makes a good if obvious point, but suggests how deeply his own integration with what he reads is shocked and disgusted by an unfelt literature imposed from without. It goes a long way to explain his contemptuous suspicion of "culture" as a *deus ex machina* to transform society; although, no doubt, sour grapes at not having received a university education played some small part here too.

He is, let it be said, quite as contemptuous of those English who suppose that they can acquire Indian culture equally superficially, as we see in a very funny *Pioneer* story of May 1888 – "The Mark of Solomon", in which he takes a Mrs Ringdove to an Indian village play so that she may get ideas for her "oriental" amateur production to be performed soon at a hill station. Her bewilderment at the heroine with a slight moustache and the Sudanese slave with his boy wife, whose jokes the gallery so adore, is beautifully told and makes this one of his unreprinted Indian pieces that deserves to be placed in the canon of his work.

But the main impression is of his bewilderment by the complexity of the India he had now to take in. The contradictions between old and new that he absorbed then and never resolved are very important, for they inextricably entwined the contradictions upon which his political and social philosophy ultimately foundered. Thus, in his visits to Patan in Hyderabad State, he observed with approval that the Indian caste system was in decline and the Brahmins a dying class. Yet in his journey to the Princely States in 1887 he becomes remarkably affected by the old Hindu way of life, and the effect again is strangely dual – his sensuality and his puritanism are locked in battle. At Chitor, the ruined city, he writes, "the first impression of repulsion and awe is given by a fragment of tumbled sculpture close to a red daubed lingam . . . What is visible is finely and frankly obscene." By the spring of the tank, he finds "the loathsome Emblem of creation . . . It came upon me that I must go quickly out of this place of years and blood." [69] But he came back to see it by moonlight.

The travel articles on Calcutta and industrial Patna are less powerful works of imagination; the satires on Congress sittings are heavy-handed; the diatribes against the crime and prostitution of Calcutta's red-light district have all the conventional Gothic and sermonising that we find in Dickens's similar journalistic escapades with the London police to Limehouse; the paeans of praise to the machinery and the technicians of India's mines and railways are marred by that showing-off of technical terminology that was nearly always to mark his treatment of machines.

But the whole picture is torn in two directions – praise for the British for being rid of child marriage and suttee and famine coupled with a hatred of anything that threatened the deep and deathly peace of India's ancient mystery, praise for modern technology and crafts-manship coupled with loathing of the brash spirit that could turn Indians into hybrid monstrosities by imposing upon them alien Western ideas and learning. It was a pull between the past and the present which went on throughout his life long after India had become only a persistent memory; and, inclining now this way, now that, gave us some of the best of his poems and stories. It was equally a pull that in the nineteen-hundreds led him to associate passionately with the radical right in English politics in an ideal programme whose con-tradictions could doubtfully have been resolved in practice.

Perhaps, if, by some chance, Lockwood and Alice had moved with him to Allahabad, his father, at least, would have guided him into some apparent incorporation of the rest of India into his old Punjab outlook. Politically, perhaps, it would have been more sober in its expression (something of the undoubted solidity of argument in "The Enlightenment of Pagett, M.P." is probably due to Lockwood); but this would have been surely an arrest of his artistic development. Lockwood's views were no doubt "broader" than his son's. They approximated more to the respectable liberal conservative attitude (as we would now call it) which many ardent Kiplingians adhere to, and, indeed, try to impose upon their author. But Rudyard's convictions were too deep, too passionate and, finally, too chiliastic for measured conventions. His vision was the poetry of tension, not of "give".

At twenty-three, it was time that he plunged out on his own. As it was, after a short period of residence at the Allahabad Club and the lucky chance of a first-rate Moslem servant to put domestic order into his natural untidiness, he met, through the introduction of Sir Edward Buck (head of the Department of Agriculture in the Government) a Professor and Mrs Hill and, after a short acquaintance, was invited by them to live in a suite of rooms at their charming house, the Belvedere. His meeting with the Hills was also to change his life. It was a lively comfortable house, made that much more piquant because the hostess was something he had never known before: an American. He con-tributed a sketch of his life there to the *Pioneer*, "A Celebrity at Home", and, even in little details like the fact that Mrs Hill never ate porridge, we can see his pleased sense of emancipation from the received English customs of the Anglo-Indian world.

Aleck Hill had been appointed to the newly-formed Muir College by Lord Salisbury's government, to run the observatory and to

117

investigate his meteorological theories about the density of rainfalls at the various levels of the Himalayan foothills. It is clear that Hill, who was a keen amateur photographer, gave to Kipling a new visual dimension, but also, more importantly, he argued with him and teased him about the dogma of his opinions not as a parent figure but as an elder brother. And Mrs Hill, Edmonia, always called "Ted", was an attractive sister-figure of a type very new to him – the boyish, adaptable, companionable American girl of the kind he was much to admire a year later when he visited the States.

Much has been written about Mrs Hill's big-sister influence on Kipling. Much less has been said about Alec Hill, who was so close to Kipling at Allahabad and in the months of travel that they made together on Kipling's way back to England via the Far East and the United States. The "Prof", as Kipling calls him in his travel articles was, however, a man of character and it seems worthwhile quoting some opinions about him expressed by former Indian pupils in *A History of the Muir Central College, 1872–1922* (edited by Professor Amaranatha Jha, and published in 1938). Some idea of his humorous approach which Kipling comments on can be seen from this reported dialogue – "I well remember this Professor's beginning his first lecture to a First or Third year class by quoting a dialogue thus: 'What is the matter, Mama?' asks a boy. 'Never mind' answers his grandmother. 'What is mind?' asks the boy. 'No matter' replies the grandmother." Another Indian ex-student tells how Hill once paid the College and Examination fees of a poor student. Hill, apparently, often helped to get jobs for his students. He adds the following story: "I was once preparing lemonade in the Science Laboratory and to my surprise Mr Hill happened to come in. I was in a fix. Mr Hill asked me what I was doing. I said, 'To tell you frankly, I am preparing lemonade and want to see what will be its effect on the stomach.' He smiled and said, 'This is a very interesting experiment and I would like to perform this experiment myself.' He took a bottle of lemonade I had prepared and after tasting it 'It does show a good chemical manipulation. I have got a hand soda-water machine at my bungalow, if you use it in this experiment you will succeed better.' Next day he brought the machine and gave it to me. From that day we used to perform this experiment at leisure and Mr Hill used to take part in it." It is not surprising that when Hill died so suddenly of typhoid, his students, despite some opposition from authority, insisted on "carrying his coffin from the carriage to the grave". A man who made such a relationship with Indian students must have been as much a liberalising influence on Kipling as was his unconventional American wife.

Ted Hill published an account of Kipling's stay with them in *Atlantic Monthly* in the year of his death, 1936, much based on her contemporary letters to her mother and sister in the States. She admired him from the start, though with an amused observation that saw him essentially as an eccentric Englishman. Her kindness, her attractive personality and her admiration for his work won his confidence, for he gave her his own version of his career – he spoke with evident thrill of having a sonnet published in the *World* when still at school, he stated that his coming to India had been due to the Aunt and Uncle's fear of his running wild in London's West End, he told her the Southsea background of "Baa, Baa, Black Sheep". She noted with amusement and some slight disapproval his capacity to draw people out and to use their talk for fiction and his somewhat snobbish attitude to the small hill station, Mussoorie, where he visited the Hills.

It was the Hills' photographs and accounts of the Seonee jungle, which they visited, that gave Kipling much of the scenic background for *The Jungle Book*. Most important, the Hills surely set his mind more firmly on a world outside India.

Reports were coming now of critical appreciation of his work in London. Not only Kay Robinson in Lahore but Alice Kipling were urging him to test his powers in London, the literary heart. And, it is less often noticed, forces were working to make his position in India less easy. His articles on Congress had led to an assault upon him in Allahabad and a lawsuit. His prose piece on Lord Dufferin handing over to Lord Lansdowne had caused some offence in high government circles. Even beloved General Roberts must have been unpleased at the picture of his naive sentimental view of his tommies which ironically opens the horrific story of bullying in the ranks, "The Likes of Us". It was, perhaps, to remove a brilliant but increasingly embarrassing reporter that Sir George Allen suggested that the *Pioneer* pay his passage for a trip abroad in return for articles. And now Ted Hill, recovered from meningitis, also needed a spell away from India. All worked together to take Kipling back with the Hills to England via East Asia and the United States. It freed him for a new life and a wider, more demanding artistic scene. It also saved him from wasting himself trying to resolve the insoluble contradictions of India, yet it also ended the unique and most enduring total imaginative experience of his life.

After a farewell visit to his parents in Lahore, he set off with the Hills from Calcutta by liner bound for Burma, Singapore, Japan and San Francisco in March 1889. He was never to return to India save for a short visit to his parents in Lahore in 1891.

But he was never to forget it. More immediately, of course, it was the presence of Tamil servants that he noticed in Burma and the likeness to Anglo-Indian life of the British scene in Singapore botanical gardens. In the United States, a Negro waiter incurred his hatred by speaking of Indians with contempt, and he met with delight some babu gentlemen in an Atlantic coast hotel. Back in England, he mostly expressed his disgust at London life through stories told by fictitious Indian characters.

And the influence unfortunately did not die with the years. He filled his South African stories with quite inappropriate Indian characters as moral catalysts. Yet he refused to accompany the Prince of Wales to India in 1905 or to stay with the Viceroy, Lord Curzon, for the Durbar in 1907. Viceregal Lodge was not his place in India, he said; and surely he did not want to see a changed and changing India.

Only when the Great War came could he write happily of the Indians again, as the Gurkha and Sikh soldiers showed their bravery in the Western trenches. Perhaps his letter to his old friend Mrs Hill, speaking of his visit to Egypt in 1913, the nearest to India that he ever travelled again, tells us best of the major part of him that remained confined in the wonderful imaginary world that he made out of his six years in the land of Mulvaney, Mrs Hauksbee, Kim and Mowgli: "I felt as though I was moving in a terrible, homesick nightmare and as though at any moment the years would roll away and I should find myself back in India. But it is 25 years and 26 days since I left it." [70]

In any final consideration of Kipling's stature as a writer, he must, I believe, stand or fall by his fictional India. In that I include not only all the short stories of Indian life, but *The Barrack Room Ballads*, *Naulahka*, the two *Jungle Books*, and, his masterpiece, *Kim*. He wrote many fine individual stories in his late years, some of greater depth and many of more remarkable technical skill than his Indian work shows. It has been customary since his death for his admirers and, indeed, most of his critics, to set their main attention upon these later stories, and, since they had been neglected by serious critics in the twenties and thirties, at the time of their publication, this later attention has revealed many, many buried treasures. But some part of this subsequent appreciation of his later neglected work is the result of contemporary taste of the thirties and forties as much as the undiscriminating praise of his Indian work in the nineties was a product of that time.

What recent critics (since his death, that is) have so admired in his later stories have been their psychological depth, their dexterous, complicated, often elliptical narration, their "maturity", by which they usually mean a new strongly-felt compassion and an expressed concern with the metaphysical. It was natural that critics and admirers of Kipling should wish to emphasise these aspects of his work at a time when he was cruelly and foolishly neglected. These were the elements that appealed to the dominant literary critical schools of that time, probably to themselves. But we have gone away from the belief that the "greatness" of fictions depends upon the depth of their psychological insight; that technique is a matter only of the dexterous arrangement of narrating voices; that "maturity" can be so easily defined that it may be chosen as the touchstone of fictional greatness. We owe great debts to Henry James, to Percy Lubbock, to F. R. Leavis, but we have moved away to use, if we wish, fable and word-play and farce and alienation, innumerable dexterities of presentation, a wider range of depths and shallows than they allowed for; and, I should hope, a consciousness that our new ploys and ways of seeing are no more dogmas than were those of the earlier systems.

It is no longer necessary, then, to seek in Kipling's work these special qualities found more markedly at the end of his life. And we are likely to see more imperfections in those late stories, masterpieces though some are, to find some pretension and muddle and unnecessary obscurity where many Kipling scholars have discovered weight and depth and rewarding difficulty. I have not often in this book examined or contested the views of individual Kipling critics. Academic Kipling criticism, I believe, has led to a great deal of most interesting and stimulating discussion of Kipling's themes, but it has done much less to illumine and reflect the strange and powerful quality of Kipling's imaginative picture of life. The special quality of that vision is its uniqueness; the things he looked at and the ways in which he looked at them are very different from those of other writers. And his particular vision is more strongly concentrated, more complete in the Indian work than elsewhere.

Perhaps the shift of emphasis in contemporary appreciation may be most happily illustrated by Jorge Luis Borges's introduction to his *Dr Brodie's Report* (1970). "Kipling's last stories," he writes, "were no less tormented and mazelike than the stories of Kafka or Henry James, which they doubtless surpass; but in 1885, in Lahore, the young Kipling began a series of brief tales, written in a straightforward manner ... Several of them ... are laconic masterpieces. It occurred to me that what was conceived and carried out by a young man of genius might modestly be attempted by a man on the borders of old age who knows his craft." [71]

Kim *and the Stories*

It is this Indian vision that Kipling will surely above all be remembered by, for the British Indian scene (native and Anglo-Indian) is a composition of relationships that no one else has ever put on paper, and no one else has ever made into a consistent social metaphor for human existence. A very strange man expressed himself here through a very strange, now historical, phenomenon. Against this, the obvious imperfections of the young Kipling's mind and the crudities of his craftsmanship in the early stories seem of little importance. The brashness, the assumed man-of-the-world voice, the club-gossip, the know-all "I" narrator, the occasional puritan's leer, the arch Biblical pastiche language and the even more arch forays into pseudo-Arabian Nights narration – all these are minor flaws in a great East Window that shines and glints and darkens and dazzles as nothing else in any literature. There are some truly inferior stories among the scores of his Indian tales and more mediocre ones, and enough masterpieces – but the vision should be taken as a whole from the first tale, "Lispeth" in *Plain Tales from the Hills* to her reappearance in *Kim* – should be taken good and bad alike, with *Departmental Ditties* and *Barrack Room Ballads* thrown in. One must be grateful to Andrew Rutherford, for example, for making a selection of Kipling's later stories for the two Penguin volumes (though I do not always agree with his choice), but the Indian work must stand as it is, in all its imperfections and its glories.

I have suggested its quality when I wrote about Kipling's India. I do not think it would enhance that overall impression to examine in detail the felicities and faults of individual Indian stories. This must be done with his later work in order to trace the various directions in which his creative spirit moved in search of the freedom it could never find. But Kipling's India speaks for itself. The *Jungle Books*, I think, need a short explanation, for they are very odd. And, of course, *Kim*, his most magical work, one of the oddest masterpieces ever written, demands our full scrutiny.

Three of the seven stories in *The First Jungle Book* and five out of the eight in *The Second Jungle Book* concern Mowgli and his jungle empire. For many people Mowgli, Baloo, Bagheera, Kaa and Co. *are* the *Jungle Books* – a kind of Greyfriars. But the merits of the individual Mowgli stories vary very much. Only a few, and perhaps only parts of these, show Kipling at his very top form.

The interest in the Mowgli group as a whole cannot really be a literary one. It is connected with his pervasive idea of the Law which is expressed in them more continuously than in the rest of his work, although hardly less obscurely. But first I should mention the two or three non-Mowgli stories whose excellence has been overshadowed by that attractive jungle predecessor of Kim.

"Rikki Tikki Tavi" has rightly commanded some attention because the fight between the mongoose and the snakes takes place in that clearly seen backyard bungalow compound which is Kipling's visual forte; but it is marred surely for modern readers by the whimsical intrusion of the human family.

"The Miracle of the Purun Bhagat" is a very fine story. It tells of the Indian Minister who rises to be the toast of London's smart dinner tables and to win the K.C.I.E. and who then changes overnight to become a wandering Sunyassi or holy man. It has been hailed as Kipling's tribute both to educated India and to the Hindu way of life. And so it is both; but it has also been pointed out that the dénouement of the story, when the holy man, up in the foothills of the Himalayas, leaves his anchorite's rock cell to warn villagers of an impending avalanche, is a tribute to the Western code of action rather than to the Hindu way of passivity. This is surely right, but it is also no chance mistake of Kipling's. He is attempting to pay tribute to both systems and yet to suggest that the Western creed of human concern will assert itself in a crisis.

Whether he is right or not, the story convinces. It is surely a curtain-raiser to *Kim*, in which the Lama's Wheel and the Great Game (East and West) meet in one man, Purun Bhagat.

Apart from its excellence as a story, the most curious feature of "The Miracle of Purun Bhagat", to me, is how Kipling's verbal picture of the Hindu holy man talking with the beasts in his cell, brings to mind some stained glass picture of St Francis and the birds, as it might have been painted by his Uncle Ned Burne-Jones. It is perhaps just a little too delicately beautiful to stand beside Kipling's other tributes to the Indian natural scene where the fierce roughness of life always shows through. Is this perhaps why he incorporated a story of such adult concern in a book on the surface intended for "juveniles"?

"The Undertakers", the story of the river-bank predators – the mugger-crocodile, the jackal, the adjutant stork – is unique in his work, for, in the hypocritical dialogue between these three ruthless cowards he creates a wonderful interchange, humorous and stylised, that might come out of Ben Jonson's *Volpone* or *The Alchemist*.

Yet the accent, for all their unevenness, must fall upon the Mowgli group. In the first place, these stories make the most central statement about The Law, that ill-defined, yet absolute and categorical barrier that stands between man and anarchy, and, more importantly, between man and the probably meaningless death and destruction that await him and all his works.

This concept of the Pervasive Law that must rule all human action, with its accompanying doctrine of stoic social duty to back it up; its alleviation of that stoicism by means of Stalkyish cunning and tricks that mock a too solemn or too slavish interpretation of The Law's Dictates and by means also of group loyalties, more or less mystic (Freemasonry, Mithraism, clubs, regiments, professions, crafts – above all, families), has necessarily attracted the attention of sociologists. For it goes plain against the historical optimistic progressive strain that usually informed all English social thought in Kipling's day, derived from Locke and Bentham. Lord Annan has interestingly shown how close Kipling's approach is to Continental social philosophy of the time. But I agree with Mr Sandison in thinking that Lord Annan, in his intentness upon this different aspect of Kipling's thought, has placed too much emphasis on Kipling's political (in the widest sense) view of man, on society as being more important than the individual in Kipling's work. If my impressionistic sketch of Kipling's India has at all succeeded, it will have shown how the proper centre of that strange world *is* the individual, the lost, scattered individuals – unsure of their identities – "Who is Kim?" – finding temporary security before the inescapable and probably final fact of death in duty and suffering with dignity and in keeping out anarchy. As Mr Sandison says, contrary to Lord Annan's view, Kipling doesn't subordinate the individual to society, he invents a rigid social rule (The Law) to shield the individual (and himself) from a constant nagging anxiety about his ultimate fate. Indeed the whole of this book is intended to suggest that Kipling's art is suffused with a personal and mysterious despair and apprehension of exactly this kind.

Where I do not agree with Mr Sandison is in his condemnation of Kipling's violent hostility to those – frivolous like the Bandar-log the monkeys, brutally unlawful like Shere Khan the tiger; or cunningly parasitical like the jackal – who seek to evade The Law, to demand more for the individual than Kipling's grim role. For Mr Sandison, this is a central defect in Kipling, a dog-in-the-manger hostility to those who have tried to seek more personal fulfilment, perhaps more pure pleasure. Part of this, it is true, is due to Kipling's innate puritanism that makes him hostile to hedonism. It is often disagreeable. The superior beauty of *Kim* or of some of the Mowgli tales or of Purun Bhagat's tale (the three are linked in many ways) comes from the absence of this constant apprehensive condemnation of those who do not accept the restraints that Kipling's own anxiety places upon the human race. But then, in varying degrees, these three works try to fuse the real world with the Garden of Eden, Kipling's dream world of childhood. Yet, in the main body of his work where the individualists and pleasure-seekers are fiercely condemned as frivolous, dangerous, overweening or a source of corruption, it is not, I think, as Mr Sandison would suggest, from any grudge of Kipling's against those who try to get more out of life (and sometimes succeed in so doing) than he does. It is an essential part of his anxious, doom-threatened world that man should take on his duty, even if it be, as in "The Children of the Zodiac", Leo's duty of singing his poems to the people to alleviate their lot for the little time left them before Death closes in, should follow The Law for other men's sake and his own so that they can forget the probable oblivion ahead in the orderly exercise of a patterned life. The condemnation, then, of the Bandar-log, and the Black Rat at the Mill Dam, and Aurelian McGoggin, and the Wax Moth, and the Mugger, and Shere Khan, and Jellaludin McIntosh is not just for their selfishness and frivolity but because they will bring horror to themselves and other men if their anarchic behaviour spreads. But finally, I am not sure, interesting though these speculations about The Law are, whether they throw so much light on the excellencies of Kipling's work, upon the way he creates his magical effects. With Shamsul Islam, I would say that Kipling was neither a thinker nor a sociologist but primarily an artist.[72]

The chief glory of his art in the Mowgli stories lies in his extraordinary combination of the natural and animal world with the world of the humans. Baloo is a bear and a housemaster; Bagheera is chiefly a leopard but a wise, sensual man more worldly than the bear; Kaa is primarily a python, delighting in his coils and glistening skin, lusting to chase and kill, but he is also an exceptional and clever man, knowing himself yet accepting The Law, perhaps a true intellectual as opposed to the Bandar-log who are monkeys and "intellectuals"; the jackal is Mussolini's forerunner, and Shere Khan Hitler's, as wartime telegrams between the Kipling Society and General Wavell rightly suggested.

It is a strange achievement, a brilliant artistic bluff, where words and thoughts veer towards the human and movements, vision and feeling are as near to animal as a writer can hope to guess. And, of course, the whole is made credible by the extraordinary evocation of the jungle itself (which perhaps Kipling had only seen in the photographs that the Hills brought back from Seonee) and the powerful effect that Chitor's ruins had upon him. The law in this world is exact but far from Darwinian; we need note only that no animal will attack another at the pool in time of drought.

Into this world comes the lovable, strong, highly intelligent wolf-cub boy, Mowgli, who learns the simple Law which in more complicated form he will have later to follow in human society. And, by his superior human intelligence and compassion, eventually also wins mastery in the animal world. The Law of the jungle is absolute and can be followed by the animals with comparative ease, for they do not know tears or laughter, the things that make man's life both more glorious and more complex and far more painfully burdensome among human beings than has ever been known in the Eden of Kaa and Baloo, however bloody and terrible many of the deeds that happen in the jungle.

All this about The Law is interesting, but as far as Kipling's art goes, it often gets in the way, with too much didactic moralising. In *The First Jungle Book*, only one story is reasonably free from it and that doesn't really get going until halfway through. "Kaa's Hunting" contains one of the most horrible scenes in all Kipling's work – and that work contains many such. It is the picture of the Bandar Log monkeys swaying helplessly towards their doom in the great ruins of the King's palace in a hypnotic trance induced by the coiling and looping of Kaa, the python's body and his "never stopping, low humming song". It is made more terrible by the jungle fact that, were it not for Mowgli's human unsusceptibility to the snake's enchantment, Baloo and Bagheera, Kaa's erstwhile co-hunters, would inevitably sway towards their death with the monkeys. For, in the jungle, all alliances – and bear, python and leopard have hunted together to rescue Mowgli – break up when the kill is on. It is made, indeed, even a little too horrible by a certain relish with which Kipling recites the awful fate of the frivolous, mischievous monkey folk.

The best Mowgli stories come in *The Second Jungle Book*. The manoeuvres by which Mowgli lures the ravening hordes of dholes, the red dogs from the South, to their death and the battle between the dholes and the wolves is one of the best action narratives in fiction.

The crown of the two books is "The King's Ankus", Kipling's best use of myth in all his work. The story opens deceptively and purposely as the most sensually idyllic of all the scenes in this Eden, with Mowgli "sitting in the circle of Kaa's great coils, fingering the flaked and broken old skin that lay looped and twisted among the rocks just as Kaa had left it . . . It is very beautiful to see – like the mottling in the mouth of a lily." This lolling in the python's folds during the heat of the day gives way to the evening visit to the jungle pool. "Then the regular evening game began – of course Kaa could have crushed a dozen Mowglis if he had let himself go . . . They would rock to and fro . . . till the beautiful, statue-like group melted in a whirl of black and yellow coils and struggling legs and arms." But the jungle paradise of learning life's laws and strengthening the body is always circumscribed by what even the wisest of the animal-preceptors, even Kaa, the python, doesn't understand; such unknown dangers nearly always relate to men and their ways.

So it is in "The King's Ankus". Mowgli, sleepy and relaxed after his wrestling, expresses his content: " 'What more can I wish? I have the Jungle and the favour of the Jungle. Is there anything more between sunrise and sunset?' " It is then that Kaa, who loves the boy, as all his animal protectors do, pours into Mowgli's ear (serpent-like) the knowledge of something new. A very old white cobra, that lives deep beneath the ruins of Cold Lairs, guards a mass of objects (Kaa could make neither head nor tail of them) that have been in his care for centuries – they are, the old cobra says, things "for the least of which very many men would die". Mowgli is sure that these new things "*must* be a new game", but Kaa declares, "it is *not* game. It is – it is – I cannot say what it is." It is, of course, the treasure of the kings who once ruled in the ruined city, gold and jewels in abundance, described by Kipling in a restrained *Yellow Book* manner that is as pleasing as it is fitting.

The white cobra is one of Kipling's most fascinating creatures. In it he suggests that sense of something repulsive and frightening that, if we are honest, we must admit to find in some very old people. His situation is immediately pathetic to us – an old lost creature, faithful to his duty, not understanding that the world above is not still a wonder city of kings and palaces and royal elephants, not knowing that the jungle has taken over. But the cruelty, the venom that lies beneath the pathos soon shows itself, as he seeks to entrance Mowgli with the treasure, as all humans are entranced by gold, and then to make sport, in killing the trapped boy. "Is this not worth dying to behold? Have I not done thee a great favour?" he asks, and then calls to the angry Kaa, "See the boy run. There is room for great sport here. Life is good. Run to and fro awhile and make sport, boy." But the cobra is impotent as well as old, his venom has dried up. Mowgli scorns to kill him, as he also scorns the royal jewels and coins he does not understand. His curiosity only bids him take the jewelled and golden ankus or royal elephant yoke. And in a day, he sees four men lose their lives in lust for it. At last, he takes it back into the cobra's deep den. He is not yet ready to leave his jungle Eden, perhaps the sight of what gold does to men has even deferred his instinctive urge to grow towards manhood by a story or two.

But at last it comes in "The Spring Running", where Bagheera the leopard, seeing the boy in tears, says that he will soon leave the jungle for human life, for animals don't know tears. This final story is a moving, if a little disjointed piece. Mowgli goes off to assume later his proper human duty under The Law as a member of the Forestry Service of the Indian Government of Her Majesty (told in "In the Rukh", a story published earlier than the *Jungle Books*). But, in fact, Mowgli, the wolf boy in the jungle, is surely only the shadowy if delightful precursor of Kim, the street arab, who knows all guiles yet remains in Eden innocence, a far more delightful hero, for, unlike Mowgli, his zest for life is not the product of bodily health and physical content only, but of an endless desire to see and know new things. Kipling takes his myth of Eden away from the world of animals, where Mowgli is the master of the Jungle, to the scene of the Grand Trunk Road so rich in human variety, where Kim is something much better than a master – The Little Friend of all the World.

It is rare to find readers, Kipling fans or others, who are not captivated by *Kim*; it is equally rare to find many who can offer any detailed account of their enjoyment of the book. "Oh! *Kim*, of course, is a magical book," is the usual general account that follows a detailed discussion of his other works. And so it is. I shall try here to account for its magic.

Kipling's mention of it in *Something of Myself* is at once proud and slightly dismissive, as though he were not quite sure how to account for the extraordinary thing he had made. Indeed, I wonder if he did realise quite how strange a masterpiece he had produced during those eight years or so. *Kim* had first inspired his imagination in the early days of his married life in Vermont, that halcyon time when Josephine was the summit of his delight – a young baby that was his own. The novel had continued to fire his fancy through all the bitter sweets of the failure of his American dream, and on beyond the nightmare of Josephine's untimely death in New York. At last he had finished it at his parents' retirement home in Tisbury, happily recalling the Lahore family times, his father advising on Buddhism, his mother teasing him on his failure to invent a plot.

It was the longest time that he took to write any book. It was said to subsume the unwritten novel, *Mother Maturin*, that Lockwood disapproved of; and this alone can excuse Lockwood's interference. It has a deeper connection with great fictions of the past than any other of his work. He himself was aware of the picaresque connection with

Cervantes – surely because the Lama and his chela, Kim, are so happy
a recall of Quixote and Sancho Panza, a deeper, more original recall
than Pickwick and Sam Weller. He succeeds overall in something that
Dickens dared not attempt, that no writer, I think, has tried. For in
Kim himself, he unites the knowingness, the cunning, the humour and
the appeal of The Dodger, with the gentleness and goodness of Oliver
Twist, a seemingly impossible task. And I think that the scenes where
Lurgan, the antique dealer of Simla, instructs Kim and the Hindu
boy in various memory games and competitions in disguises to
prepare them for espionage work must have been written with at least
some half-memory of Fagin's instruction of Oliver and the boys in
thieving. As to the rich and various Indian life of the Great Trunk
Road which is so vital a part of Kim's pleasure in novelty and variety,
it owes something, I think, on its didactic side to Kipling's loved
Pilgrim's Progress; but the didactic side of *Kim* is always played down
– one of the reasons for the book's greatness – and the Great Trunk
Road owes more to another of Kipling's favourite works – Chaucer's
Canterbury Tales. But I name these impinging masterpieces of the past
not to suggest any derivative quality in *Kim*, for it is its absolute
originality that is its making, but rather to suggest the sort of literary
heights in which we are travelling in this strange work.

The most striking feature of *Kim* is sounded early on, when we are
told that Kim "did nothing with an immense success". "He lived in a
life as wild as that of the Arabian Nights, but missionaries and
secretaries of charitable societies could not see the beauty of it. His
nickname through the wards was 'Little Friend of all the World' . . .
he had known all evil since he could speak – but what he loved was the
game for its own sake." His two small companions playing on the gun
outside the Lahore Museum are a Moslem boy and a Hindu, "Chota
Lal . . . His father was worth perhaps half a million sterling, but India
is the only democratic land in the world." Kim's superiority to them
both is at once declared when the strange figure of the Tibetan Lama
appears on the scene, for Chota Lal is afraid of him and the Moslem
boy despises him as an idolator, but Kim is immediately drawn to him
– he is new.

And his love of the new, this thirst for fresh experience and changing scenes persists in Kim's young life: on the Grand Trunk Road,
"there were people and new sights at every stride – castes he knew and
castes that were altogether out of his experience"; and with the important Sahiba's entourage (the Wife of Bath's world) "this was the life as
he would have it – bustling and shouting, the beating of bullocks and
the creaking of wheels, lighting of fires and cooking of food, and new

sights at every turn of the approving eye . . . India was awake and Kim was in the middle of it." Colonel Creighton, who sees Kim as good material for the Spy Service, knows at once how to attract him: "In three days thou wilt go with me to Lucknow, seeing and hearing new things all the while." When Kim sleeps among Mahbub Ali's horses and unwashed men we are told, "change of scene, service and surroundings were the breath of his little nostrils".

I know of no other English novel that so celebrates the human urban scene (for English novelists are all touched by the Romantic country worship) except for that utterly dissimilar book, *Mrs Dalloway*; and when one reads of Kim's thoughts, "this adventure, though he did not know the English word, was a stupendous lark", one is reminded of the opening passage of Virginia Woolf's novel (Clarissa's thoughts as she steps out into the streets of London): "What a lark! What a plunge!"[73] It is a note of delight in life, of openness to people and things that is maintained throughout the novel and is the essence of its magic.

Kipling's passionate interest in people and their vocabularies and their crafts is, of course, the essence of the magic of all his work. But in all the other books it tends to be marred by aspects of his social ethic – by caution, reserve, distrust, mastered emotion, stiff upper lips, direct puritanism or the occasional puritan's leer, retributive consequences, cruelty masquerading as justifiable restraint or bullying as the assertion of superiority. None of these is present in *Kim*.

Kipling's social ethic, it is true, is there in Kim's apprenticeship to "The Game", the British Secret Service in India. This is the way that, as a sahib's son, he will serve the British cause. This has stuck in the gullet of many liberal critics, notably Edmund Wilson. But I think that fine critic and lovable man was misled by his strong dislike for British Imperialism.

True, Kim will be serving British rule, but this must be read within the context of Kipling's belief that the two higher values in the book – the richness and variety of Indian life and the divine and spiritual idiocy of the Lama – can only be preserved from destruction by anarchic chaos or from despotic tyranny by that rule. This is directly underlined in the scene when Kim bears the letter to Creighton from Mahbub Ali that tells of the plotted rising in the North. The Lama, thinking of how far he has come from his monastery, laments, "Alas! it is a great and terrible world!" And Kipling immediately writes, "Kim stole out and away, as unremarkable a figure as ever carried his own and a few score thousand other folks' fates around his neck." In short, the Lama in his spiritual revulsion from the world, innocently does not know the real and terrible dangers that threaten the ordered society in which he can safely seek his sacred river; but Kim, by his involvement in The Game, can help to preserve that holy man whose spirituality he can glimpse and love but never hope to achieve. And let us note, it is a game, however terrible a one, in which Kim, by his strange street-arab status of friend of all the world and night climber across rooftops, is peculiarly associated – a game in which he must be able to carry maps in his head and remember a hundred objects seen and be able to pass disguised as twenty or so other people. These powers make him perfect material for a spy; the same powers made Kipling a great writer of fiction.

But, if the moralising side of Kipling is only lightly present in *Kim*, implicit in The Game, the corruption of Kim's world is always implicit rather than stated. The world Kim moves in is no ideal one. Only the Lama in his innocence mistakes the generous prostitute for a nun. It is a world of lies – Kim knows the Lama for a rarity because he tells the truth to strangers. Physical danger is constant and real. Human life is not held in high regard – Mahbub Ali is prepared to sacrifice Kim's life to get his message to Creighton, yet he loves Kim strongly and jealously. Few of the fifty or so vividly realised characters are without his or her faults, but most are made generous and loving by contact with Kim and the Lama. Yet Kim is never above the ordinary dishonesties and tricks of daily life. As the Lama says, "I have known many men in my long life, and disciples not a few. But to none among men, if so be thou art woman-born, has my heart gone out as it has to thee – thoughtful, wise and courteous; but something of a small imp."

And it is not Kim's virtues alone that win him the friendship of all the world. He is remarkably physically beautiful and, in a way that is successfully kept by Kipling from being fully sexual, flirtatious with all and sundry. It is part of his worldly guile. The prostitute in the train is won over by him as is the other prostitute who dresses him up when he escapes from St Xavier's School; the Sahiba's motherliness has an earthy tinge; the woman of Shamlegh yearns for him. In Lurgan's shop, as I have said, the jealousy of the Hindu boy has obvious sexual overtones; as I think does the jealousy of the horse-dealer, Mahbub Ali, for Kim's overriding devotion to the Lama. Yet all this sensuality is without an explicit sexual tinge. I do not believe that this is Victorian self-censorship upon the part of Kipling. It is certainly not an avoidance of the subject in a book ostensibly intended for the young, for the scene where a prostitute tries to steal from Mahbub Ali is quite explicit. It is, I think, one more aspect of the purposeful attempt by Kipling in this novel to create a world that is real and ideal at one and the same time. Nor is the absence of overt sex offensively evasive as a modern critic might think; it is just a natural part of the innocent-corrupt world in which Kim lives.

As to evil, it is strikingly absent, as may be measured by the unimportance of the "villains", the Russian and French spies. They are bad men, we know, for they offer violence to a very good man, the Lama. But their retribution is not the savoured brutal one of so many of Kipling's stories. They merely pass out of the novel, mocked by all the Himalayan villagers as they make off with their tails between their legs. Their humiliation is like that of Trinculo and Stephano on Prospero's magic island in *The Tempest* and we bless the babu Hurree Singh, who mocks them, as we bless Ariel. In default of true evil, we must judge the English chaplain, Bennett, as the villain, for he lacks all concern for freedom and variety, virtues so surprisingly celebrated by Kipling in this book. It could be said that this absence of real evil prevents *Kim* from vying with the great novels of the past as a "mature" book; but, in compensation, it must surely be said that this creation of an innocent world of guile makes it an unequalled novel.

Nirad Chaudhuri has said that *Kim* is the very best picture of India by an English author; and I am sure he is right. But rich and convincing though the varied Indian characters are, and splendid though the evocations of the Indian scenes are from the Jain Temple outside Benares to the Himalayan foothills, it is yet Kipling's own India as Kim is Kipling's own street-arab and the Lama Kipling's own Buddhist. Many Indian critics, notably K. Jamiluddin in *The Tropic Sun*, have pointed out that Buddhism is a very strange choice of religion to represent India, from which it has been absent for centuries. No doubt, Kipling was a bit influenced in his choice by his desire to draw on his father's special knowledge; but I think he was even more concerned to pose his own version of self-abnegation against his own version of commitment to the world as represented by Kim. The Lama and Kim make a most delectable Prospero and Ariel. And it is no sparring partnership for either, since the Lama's greatest erring from The Way is in his attachment to his Chela, and Kim comes close to exhausting his adolescent physical strength in bringing his master down from the mountains. The story of Kim and the Lama is, in the last resort, beneath all its superbly realised human and topical detail, an allegory of that seldom portrayed ideal, the world in the service of spiritual goodness, and, even less usual, spiritual goodness recognising its debt to the world's protection. It is the culmination and essence of all the transcendence that Kipling gained from his Indian experience. In it alone of all his works he does ask, "Who is Kim?", although he cannot answer the question. In a sense, his answer is the book itself, for it is the best thing he ever wrote.

3 VANITY FAIR

Coming to the Fair

On 9 March 1889 Rudyard Kipling left Calcutta on board the S.S. *Madura*, in the company of Aleck and Ted Hill, bound eventually for San Francisco. The journey took about a week short of three months, of which four weeks were spent in Japan. This liner holiday was the first of what was to become a most necessary form of escape and recuperation in his nerve-beleaguered life. His constant anxiety, his sense of the fragility of the human condition and his apprehension of the threat to the order he respected were all assuaged in the ordinary way by the simple doctrine of duty, of application to hard work. But, of course, the strain that overwork imposed did as much physical and nervous harm as it gave moral reassurance. The cruise on the liner was to prove as valuable a recuperation from work and *Angst* for Kipling as it was for so many other overworked English and American descendants of puritans from the eighties until the Second World War.

But Kipling's incessantly active and powerful imagination could not rest like the overworked brains of business tycoons. I believe that liners (and, indeed, all ships) were a powerful solace for him, because, while they took him away, not from work, for an imaginative writer can hardly cease to work to order, but from routine pressure and anxiety, they could sufficiently replace the ordinary life of duty because they were, in themselves, societies in little, and, moreover, societies always needing to be vigilant, always "in peril" on the sea. But with a difference, for whereas, on land, it was everyone's duty both to be vigilant and active, and to obey, on the ships the passengers could leave the vigilance and activity to the crew, all they needed to do was to relax and, in an emergency, to obey.

And we have another confirmation. A passage from Arnold Bennett's diary has often been quoted in which a woman is reported as

134

saying that Kipling was disliked by the officers on the Union Castle liners by which he travelled to and from Cape Town in the first decade of this century because, while being friendly, and, indeed, markedly interested in the workings of the ship, he would report any officer he thought neglectful of his duties. This sounds like one, or at most, two cases worked up into a generalisation; but it is not incompatible with the view he would take of society, and, therefore, of its miniature version, a liner. Indeed, the sensitive complication of relationship between a liner's crew and its passengers, with its need for combined association and demarcation, is exactly the sort of moral situation that engages him in every aspect of society. In the midst of life we are in death is his constant assertion about man's daily being; and though the dangerous days of the sailing ship were long past, still there remained a sense of "for those in peril on the sea".

His comments at the time of the sinking of the *Titanic* bear this out, for he clearly saw the whole of that terrible disaster as an allegory of man's pride and frivolity. "Lest we forget" is a phrase peculiarly alive to the apprehensive on liners in those days, in jet planes now. Kipling did not live to hear of the jet-set, but he would have approved greatly the pejorative implication in the term. Yet, feeling the liner to embody the very anxiety state from which he was seeking assuagement, he could perhaps surrender himself completely to the physical and nervous rest that he was again and again to need so badly. Relaxation was strengthened for such a man by the thought of the order and vigilance and routine that made it possible.

But, apprehensions apart, on this first trip, certainly, he enjoyed himself. He was young. It was his first escape from a loved and loving family. He was with a man he liked who teased him out of his more extreme moods, and with a woman he admired, yet who surely knew how to prevent his admiration getting out of hand. He was going towards an unknown fame in London – and fame is always nice to approach; but if its quality is uncertain, it is pleasant to delay meeting it. The liner trip was, as such things should be, a long interval. True he was a globe-trotter – something rather irresponsible that he had always reprehended in India. But he consciously guarded himself against this charge, for he was to report all the time to the *Pioneer* on what he saw – and, as he wrote in his first article, "my destiny is to avenge India from nothing less than three-quarters of the world".[1] After all, he remembered always those intolerable travellers who had told him that he was too near to India to judge. And then these reports (now making the last half of the excellent travel book, *Sea to Sea*) were not just amateur jottings, but the work of a professional

135

journalist who genuinely needed the money to finance his voyage. He was writing for the audience back home in India and he kept this in mind.

For this reason, it is not always possible to gauge how far his constant comparison of what he sees in the Indian scene is dictated by his sense of his readers. But my impression is that he writes in this way because this is how he sees it – the joy of hearing a Punjabi voice in Rangoon, the Tamils there who delight him by recalling India but annoy him by speaking English (though he wouldn't have understood if they'd spoken Tamil); in the heights of Hong Kong, he *does* actually find Mussoorie and the intention *is* the Simla one of putting Hong Kong in its place by the comparison; in the midst of the extreme humidity of Singapore's orchid gardens he *does* come slap up against an Indian station "not quite as big as Allahabad, and infinitely prettier than Lucknow", with the memsahibs and Thomas Atkins unchanged, and so on.[2] No doubt, some Anglo-Indian readers long out from home would share his disgust at the passengers' peremptory treatment of a white woman when they simply bawl "Stewardess!", but those whose memory of Victorian England was more adult would hardly be surprised. One is constantly reminded that he is coming to London and the wider world as an Anglo-Indian who had left England when he was a schoolboy, whose whole short adult life is Indian.

It is this, perhaps, too, that accounts for the shocked boyishness of his tour of Hong Kong's red-light district. His readers in Allahabad and Lahore will perhaps agree that "to one who has lived in India there is something shocking to meet . . . Englishwomen in the same sisterhood,"[3] but there must have been some smiles in the Club, if not a gleam of laughter in Mrs Hauksbee's eye, when they read, "Very many men have heard a white woman swear, but some few, and among these I have been, are denied the experience. It is quite a revelation."[4] The strange quality of this article on the Hong Kong prostitutes is that it should have been written at all for late-Victorian newspaper-readers, but also that it should be written by a young man who so completely confesses his own naïveté. It all serves to remind one that, at twenty-four, Kipling had already created an imaginative world that can stand comparison with that of all but a few great novelists, and yet, for all that, he was about to meet success and fame in sophisticated London with much of the equipment of a schoolboy.

Inevitably he does all he can to fight off such new experiences as he cannot assimilate to his Anglo-Indian vision. He is struck, very struck, by the beauty of the Burmese girls, and finds himself admiring the physique of the Burmese men. But then he remembers the dacoit bandits of the Burmese War and their brutalities and he calls in his father's and his uncle's old love, Swinburne, for explanation: "Is there not in the *faces* of the beautiful Burmese girls something of those cruel Roman empresses, the 'lolloping, walloping women' that Swinburne sings about?" The Japanese aesthetic appreciation of the beauties of nature gives him pause to wonder: "it is an astounding thing to see an Oriental so engaged; it is as though he had stolen something from a Sahib." [5] But he comforts himself: "Japan is a great people ... her artists [play] with life and death and all the eyes can take it in. Mercifully she has been denied the last touch of firmness in her character that would enable her to play with the whole round world. We possess that – we, the nation of the glass flower shade, the pink worsted mat, the red and green china puppy dog, and the poisonous Brussels carpet. It is our compensation." [6] And that, one cannot help remarking, of all those who despised Study 5 for its Japanese fans.

But the reassurance is more and more called for as the voyage proceeds. This is the most peculiar feature of Kipling's first world journey. It is – and one truly feels this in his writing – a great new enlargement of the world for him. And yet, from the very start, he travels as though he were at bay. When he leaves Calcutta, he wonders whether a Russian man-of-war may intercept his steamer. "Let Armageddon be postponed, I prayed, for my sake, that my personal enjoyment may not be interfered with." [7] The sentiment is a satirical reflection upon the nature of globe-trotting; but its fears are none the less real. And then from Penang onwards, the Russian menace is replaced by the yellow peril – the Chinese in Penang "were the first army corps on the March of the Mongols. The scouts are at Calcutta, and flying column at Rangoon." [8] He tries to tease himself about his fears. The Chinese boil their babies, he is sure; others say that what he has seen are sucking pigs, but he knows better: "Dead sucking pigs don't grin with their eyes open." [9] By the time he visits Canton, he declares, again with an unconvincing air of self-teasing, "These people ought to be killed off because they are unlike any people I ever met before. Look at their faces as they despise us. You can see it, and they aren't a bit afraid of us, either." [10] Professor Hill tries to tease him out of his fears, saying this is "an intemperate libel on a hard-working nation!" Then Kipling makes a most revealing comment: "He did not see Canton as I saw it – through the medium of a fevered imagination." [11]

At Singapore he had begun to formulate the English Imperial dream that was to grow until it became the centre of his life in middle age – the "army of a dream". He starts sadly by deploring the unsuitability of tropical countries (poor India!) for extensive English permanent settling. This keeps the tropical colonies dependent on the home government instead of self-government. "Is this sedition?" he asks. Otherwise they would all break free and then, "all the freed states who have learned their lesson by over-spending," would come together. "Within that limit Free Trade, without, rancorous Protection . . . It would be too vast a hornet's nest for any combination of Powers to disturb." It is not for yet. Canada, Borneo, Australia all say, "We are not strong enough yet, but some day we shall be." [12] It is a vision, of course, of a young man to whom echoes at least of Seeley's dream of *The Expansion of England* (1883) had percolated; but it looks forward also to Kipling's future heroes, Cecil Rhodes and, above all, Joseph Chamberlain. What is important to notice, however, is how in Kipling's case it grows out of the sense, that he had learned in the Punjab, of being endangered by the enemy. And this was to underlie his Imperialism even at its most exultant and on-going.

It is not surprising, then, when he arrived in San Francisco, that among the host of conflicting thoughts which the excitement of the American scene brought to him was the reassurance that San Francisco harbour could offer no effective resistance to the British fleet.

But Kipling's American experience, although it brought very little fruit to his art, plays such a large role in the formation of his general social and political ideas, that I think it best to depart here from strict chronology. I shall discuss this first four months' travel in the United States in the section which describes his ill-fated attempt to live in that country three years later. For the moment, we will accompany him straight to London, where he arrived in October 1889.

At the Fair

One thing he did bring from America with him to London. He was engaged, or semi-engaged, to Caroline Taylor, Ted Hill's sister. He had stayed with their family in Pennsylvania. The Taylor family had been very congenial after his wanderings and the young Caroline the most congenial part of it. Now, however, in London, he had to part from Caroline, for she was accompanying her sister and brother-in-law back to Allahabad. It meant that the young Rudyard, alone in London, had two families to pine for in his beloved far-away India – Caroline and the Hills and his own Kipling family in Lahore.

London, with its strangely mixed memories of seven years before, did not wear a happy guise:

> The sky a greasy soup tureen
> Shuts down atop my brow.[13]

He had not sold any of his work in America. His finances, apart from the articles he sent back to the *Pioneer*, were scanty. But he had not suffered severance from the solace of his parents' protecting love to fall into the arms of surrogates, however deep his affection for Uncle Ned and Aunt Georgie Burne-Jones, or, indeed, for Aunt Aggie Poynter (whom at her death in 1906 he called "the dearest, sweetest of my mother's sisters"[14]). He must have sensed tension at that time between the beloved Aunt and Uncle Burne-Jones, despite all their love for each other; and to take help from Aunt Aggie would be to make himself indirectly beholden to his monumental and tetchy Poynter uncle, whom he delighted to mock in private. In any case, he knew how far his political ideas were from the Burne-Joneses and his social aims from the Poynters.

He chose to live, as he tells us in his autobiography, very close to the bone, although the famous story of his Aunt Georgie's maid, Annie, visiting him at his rooms on what he regarded as the pretext of mending his socks and sewing buttons on his shirts, may surely have been the tactful ministering of his Aunt to a lone and very undomesticated bachelor rather than any amorous desires of Annie. Yet it is significant that the members of the family he saw most were his two cousins around his own age, Phil Burne-Jones and Ambo Poynter, both young men of talent, vainly seeking to make their way apart from their famous fathers. They envied his independent bohemian bachelor existence and he helped and advised them. He wanted, quite naturally, the elder brother's role, not the nephew's. He had come to London to find success, not home from home.

He established himself in rooms in Villiers Street, Charing Cross, far from the Brompton–Fulham–Earls Court world that had been his boyhood London (and in which his parents immediately settled when they came home on leave eighteen months later); far, too, from the smarter Mayfair–Kensington world of the Poynters; far, also, from the districts in which lived most of his would-be patrons in the English literary scene – Walter Besant, Sidney Low, Edmund Gosse, Andrew Lang and the many other late-Victorian men of letters who were ready to help and advise him as a newcomer.

Here he challenged the literary world to come and get him – with a notice on his door, "To Publishers, A Classic while you wait." [15] Here, in a loose dark suit, buttoned to the neck like a workman's blouse, and a fez without a tassel, surrounded by Japonaiserie and fishing tackle and a rifle and tobacco jars and military prints, he challenged everyone to place him: the artist? the sportsman? the subaltern? the bohemian? the young man about town? His evenings were spent at Gatti's music-hall across the way; his food was most cheaply bought in the pub next door, and his articles show that his knowledge of "town" was much derived from the music-hall frequenters in the bar and, as he tells us himself, from the lively cockney barmaid.

All in all, his life-style presented a brave and teasing puzzle to publishers, editors and critics determined to place him. And the challenge preserved his independence, which was what he mainly wished. But, like all young men challenging great cities from impoverished lodgings, from Rastignac through Pendennis and Copperfield to Raskolnikov, the stance is a costly one in loneliness and strain, and the city cruelly indifferent. Both physically and nervously, this year did much to increase the tension of an already tense personality. On top of these pressures were posed the miseries of unrequited love. It was not surprising that breakdown came near. Yet, in its immediate purpose, his lonely challenge to London succeeded. It won him fame without surrender.

The story of Kipling's relations with the literary and publishing worlds relates more to the general English literary history of the nineties and to the complicated bibliographical history of his works than to the inter-relation of the real world and the imagined in his art which is my central subject. Nor does London's literary scene play much part in the themes of his books. It appears only twice in his prose work. In *The Light That Failed*, the distasteful scene of the baiting of the cardiac art publisher must have relieved Kipling's feelings a good deal about the few publishers who actually pirated him and the many more who, he feared, might do so. The second appearance is a tribute, but a markedly reserved tribute, to his senior literary colleagues, probably to Thomas Hardy. This is the character of Eustace Cheever in the story, "A Conference of the Powers". But the eminent novelist, Cheever, whose stories have so delighted a subaltern on leave from the Burmese War and who is himself so amazed by the reality of the war as told by that subaltern, appears as deficient in a sense of the reality of the world outside England as he is devoted to his craft. In one of his *Letters of Travel* of 1892, Kipling said, "There is no provincialism like the provincialism of London." [16] And one feels that he thought the eminent men of letters who welcomed him in 1890 and 1891 were, like

Cheever, nice old boys but, as far as the world went, provincial.

Even those who befriended him, like Sir Walter Besant, he was prepared to attack when he thought they were damaging his interests. There was in his attitude to these literary seniors a certain amount of wrongheadedness, and it was certainly not tactful. But a young man of independent genius and belligerent views could not have surrendered to such men. Their politics were safe, and his were not; their world was cosy, his was raging within him; they were domestic, he was untamed; they were correctly and organisedly bookish and he was a random devourer of books that excited him. He mistrusted them as much as Lawrence mistrusted literary London when he came there from Nottingham more than twenty years later. But where Lawrence vituperated, Kipling mainly held at a polite arm's length. This, I think, was because Lawrence wanted to master the literary world, whereas Kipling simply wanted to be left alone in order to reach a much wider public. Indeed one of the chief reasons why he was wary of his conquest of the literary world in those two extraordinary years, dating perhaps from the *Times* leader upon his work in March 1890, is that they accepted him only on their limited literary terms and he was looking for something much more.

It was not only that the appreciation of his work by men like Andrew Lang was so partial and so safe; it was also that they sought to anaesthetise him. For example, some of them placed him with Pierre Loti as an aesthetic painter of the Orient, giving England her picturesque India as Loti had given France her picturesque Indo-China. And so he was, of course, but he was much more. They welcomed his soldiers – especially Mulvaney – but with exactly the sort of patronage that Kipling would resent, if only because his own picture of the ranks, superb though it is, cannot be wholly acquitted of a whiff of patronage, but a patronage born of understanding is different from the globe-trotter's patronage. They mostly reprehended Mrs Hauksbee and the scandals of Simla with a moral shockedness and talk about Zola that seems absurd to us now.

Kipling was drawn to Zola's work from early days, I am sure. The references to *L'Assommoir* alone tells us this. But he was alarmed by Zola, not, I believe, for the realism or the frankness, but for the element of sensuality in his work. It is notable that in a passage from *From Sea to Sea*, he recognises quite rightly that this element in Zola is at its strongest in *La Curée*. He was frightened of his own sensuality, I think, although in part it is what makes "Without Benefit of Clergy" one of his finest stories. Yet he must have disliked the nineties critics' constant tendency to set him a little above Zola in morals which perhaps suggests a little below him in art.

The London critics' praise of him was sincere and full. By 1891, indeed, the excitement in literary circles about his work was a laudatory chorus. This alone, of course, was daunting for a young man. Universal praise is always alarming, for clearly it will not last and yet it seems to demand constant new offerings to keep it going. But, over and above that, such praise is nearly always founded on a misunderstanding and Kipling's was particularly so.

The critic Justin McCarthy's account in his memoirs of how he came to appreciate Kipling is very friendly but very revealing in this respect. He tells of picking up some stories of Kipling's – it could either be *Life's Handicap* or *Soldiers Three* from the account, probably the latter – with little interest, "then the conviction grew upon me that here at last was the man I had long been expecting, and that the life of the Englishman in India was revealed by the touch of the new enchanter's wand. I need hardly say that the enchanter was Rudyard Kipling." [17] He goes on to say that he soon found that his admiration was shared by everyone he talked to. And he pays high tribute to Kipling's modesty at this time of new celebrity when he first met him: "there was no affectation about him, not even the affectation which tries to ignore one's own success and to make believe there is nothing really in it." [18]

But then comes the rub. Some time later, McCarthy tells us, "I met at an English country house a man who had made for himself a most distinguished name in one of the departments of Indian administration. We talked about Kipling and, of course, we both admired his writings, but my new acquaintance expressed some wonder at the fact that I had not found myself out of harmony with most of Kipling's ideas on Indian subjects . . . Up to that moment I had not concerned myself in the slightest degree as to what Rudyard Kipling's theories might be about this or that department of Indian rule, or indeed as to whether he had any theories on the subject at all. To me he was the delightful painter of life and manners in India; the painter whose touch was never heavy and whose colours were never dull; the spirit-stirring ballad singer; the humorist and the realist who could sometimes dream dreams and see visions." [19]

Now, surely this is all very well. There is nothing that compelled McCarthy to share Kipling's views on India, or even to be interested in them beside the aesthetic pleasure he got from the shape and language of his stories and poems. But not to notice them is an absurdity.

Kipling inevitably must have felt some unease at the Savile Club, where they all made him so welcome and yet saw only aesthetic beauty and humour and stirring metres in his work. Of course, he was a devout craftsman and an aesthete – the nephew of his uncle, the son of his father. Of course he had visions and dreams. But those visions and dreams concerned the world he lived in.

Later, towards the end of the decade, when Kipling became a "popular" writer, his Imperial vision in its crudest form was, too often, taken for the whole of him. But that Imperial vision was far more than the political surface or even the Empire itself that embodied it. You may disagree with it. I usually do. But, if one is to appreciate Kipling, one cannot ignore it as his admirers of the early nineties mainly did. And, of course, such selective admiration was bound to crumble, as it did at the end of the century when Kipling reached a much wider audience.

There was one man, W. E. Henley, the right-wing Tory editor of the *Scots Observer*, who was more sympathetic to Kipling's general ideas. Kipling's letters to Henley are nearer to intimate than most of his letters to writers. But they are also reserved almost entirely to literary or political affairs. He knew Henley's splendid early hospital poems from his Indian days and admired them. But, I think he must have seen how Henley's poor crippled body ached to be powerful in the literary world and that, with all his bonhomie and Victorian–Rabelaisian hearty comradeliness, he was a poor thirsty man who needed able young writers to be his disciples. He had to remonstrate with Henley so that he should not be used as a "personality" and one peculiarly the property of the *Scots Observer*. "Henley is a great man," he told Trix, ". . . but he is not going to come the bullying cripple over me after I have been in harness all these years."[20] He found the dinners given by Henley, when he came to London from Edinburgh, more congenial than the starchier entertainment of most literati. Henley's world was nearer to that masculine vigorous Bohemia which he must have had in his mind when he chose the Villiers Street life. Something of their quality may be reflected in the Torpenhow episode in *The Light That Failed*. Yet finally, Henley and his world meant the world of journalism and Kipling had every intention of putting journalism behind him. It was also a world that smelled of failure and Kipling intended to have success.

He was glad of the showcase that Henley provided for him. But Henley should have been glad indeed for what Kipling gave to him to put on show, for into the *Scots Observer* went some of the best of the *Barrack Room Ballads*, starting resoundingly with "Danny Deever".

As to mixed social life, it is worth noting, I think, that the two literary hostesses whom he cared for most were Mrs W. K. Clifford and Mrs Molesworth, both writers of children's books.

It is time, then, to consider what picture of London Kipling gave in his journalism in these two materially rather grim, yet sensationally successful years.

London, as he saw it, is to be found, as far as journalism is concerned, in the *Letters on Leave* he contributed to *The Week's News* of the *Pioneer* in Allahabad, in one or two pieces in the *St James's Gazette*, and in the story, if it can be so called, "One View of the Question", published in the *Contemporary Review*. "In Partibus", the poem from which I quoted at the beginning of this section, is the best known and the most succinct account of his hatred of the city he had come to so hopefully.

> But I am sick of London
> From Shepherd's Bush to Bow.[21]

It is a London in its hateful aspect largely of streets and of literary or smart salons – the claustrophobia of the outsides of buildings and their insides. One senses him like an animal unsure of its own strength and of its new territory, venturing forth with all guards up, retiring to its den to hide and lick its wounds, driving all intruders angrily out of that den. This jungle aspect, indeed, is the one overall impression of life as portrayed in *The Light That Failed* which reveals that that unhappy novel is the mistaken work of a young man of genius. It must have been something of the same London that he had left when he was sixteen, of the celebrity-studded studio of the Uncle and the more demure but celebrity-frequented home of the Misses Craik, of mooching and discovering in the streets; but now he was the celebrity himself and determined not to be pinned down. His anonymous exterior self (always so important to Kipling) was adapted to the Anglo-Indian Club or the newspaper office, not to tea crushes or book talk at the Savile Club. His inner being was torn between family security or married security and the frightening insecurity of his need to stand alone and find the measure of his own power.

All his life, Rudyard Kipling was to seek some junction between the boy that remained whole inside him and the man he had grown into. It is the pattern of most romantics and some of his best work was done in trying to solve the puzzle. But he was too young for such a return to boyhood now, at twenty-five and twenty-six. Yet he was also aware that he had to find himself before his fame had put a mould on him. The nagging of some longer work, the fear of becoming an ephemeral magazine man if he remained with stories and verse, the pressure of poverty, fear of a new "clever" world, fear of loneliness, overwork, all pressed together upon him in this year and a half to produce a hatred of London (and he condemned all England with the city).

This hatred emerges quite differently in two fine poems: "Winds of the World", with its savage attack on "the poor little street-bred people", and in the smoother "Tomlinson", with its hatred of urban civilised nullity.

He was only able to forget all this strain and despair at the music hall, as he probably had when he was sixteen. From here came the rhythm of his greatest works of this time, The *Barrack Room Ballads* (though their peopling came largely from India). But the strength of the *Ballads*, like that of the London musical hall songs they echo, is the determined hilarity in which the strain and despair find release.

In considering the hostile picture of England that Kipling offered in his journalism at this time, it is necessary to remember that for the most part it is offered to an Anglo-Indian audience. It is, perhaps, to reach the subalterns and the planters that, for example, he plays down his familiarity with contemporary French literature, with which, after all, he had been fascinated since his browsing in Crom Price's library at Westward Ho. When, in an article, "Three Young Men", in *Letters on Leave*, he attacks an "arty young man" he has met, he tells how this youth chattered of Guy de Maupassant, Paul Bourget and Pierre Loti and adds disingenuously that he then obtained novels by these authors and that "unwholesome was a mild term for these books".[22] The reply that he claims to have made to the young man's boasting of his knowledge of French modern novels, that he himself "only knew *La Vie Parisienne* and Zola in translation with pictures" is more of an imaginary subaltern's snub to the book talk of "long-haired things in velvet collar rolls" than his own reply was likely to have been.[23]

Yet, even so, the outlines of his distaste, even disgust, are the same when he speaks to his Anglo-Indian readers in *The Week's News* of the *Pioneer* as those he addresses to sophisticated English readers of Frank Harris's *Fortnightly* through the mouth of his fictional Indian Mohammedan visitor to London in "One View of the Question". The particulars, perhaps, vary a little – Anglo-Indian audiences are given more account of the follies of smart, cultured society – particularly in an amusing article, "On Exhibition", where he describes his own experiences as a lion at a party with two women talking about him over his head on a sofa. Here he develops that special sort of silly feminine voice that he was to use to good effect in all satirical accounts of progressive or bohemian circles almost up to his death – "Was

Mulvaney *quite* real? Oh, how lovely! how sweet! how precious!" [24]

This ecstatic, silly "cultured" hostess voice he ridicules in "On Exhibition" is virtually that of the Black Rat and the Cat in "Beyond the Mill Dam" (1902), his principal satire upon the inability of the Tory old guard to adapt themselves to a changing world. It is important, I think, in understanding the political changes that were going on in him in these years to realise that these attacks on cultured society were probably as much aimed at the world of the Souls, of Balfour, of the intellectuals in the Tory world as at anyone. Hence perhaps the famous verse in which "the long-haired things . . . moo and coo with women folk about their blessed *souls*".[25] That world of cultivated, witty but romantic aristocrats, the Souls, the Percy Wyndhams, the Horners, the Gaskells, even Balfour himself, were very close friends of Uncle Ned Burne-Jones despite his radical liberal politics. It was to live within range of the Percy Wyndhams in their famous house, "Clouds" designed by the pre-Raphaelite architect, Philip Webb, that Lockwood and Alice, on their retirement from India towards the end of the decade, settled at Tisbury in Wiltshire. Here would have been an easy family entrance into Conservative society that Kipling might have been expected to welcome, yet, I suspect that from the very first he felt ill at ease with the rather precious, in-turned, English county flavour of the Souls' world, and this estranged him from the main, traditional stream of English conservatism. His reaction as he reports it to his Anglo-Indian readers, however, like his reply to the arty young man about French novels, seems a little manufactured for his "plain man" subaltern audience. A young lady was present at this soirée, it seems, who was going to India and, to her, Kipling was about to give the only useful advice he could offer (to take light underclothing to tropical countries) when a sudden silence in the company cut him short for "the English only wear their outsides in company".

But the frivolous and the artificial and those with smart second-hand opinions are not the only culprits in the upper class. He attacks "the university smile" with its "sorrow that you can't march with progress" and its special representative in the young man who does social work in Toynbee Hall, the London East End social mission, and "knows everything that should be done for the poor".[26] (It is ironical that only a few years earlier Milner, one of Kipling's future Imperial heroes, on coming down from Oxford, gave all his spare energies to Toynbee Hall work; yet not surprising, for the new Imperial movement, the radicalism of the right, was to draw converts from every source.) Kipling had little doubt what should not be done for the poor. In his *Letters on Leave* he analyses as fiercely the faults of the

English working class (he seems to have drawn his information in great degree from chat at his Villiers Street tobacconist) as he does those of their superiors. Working men, above all, he thought, lacked pride and independence: "thousands of men meeting publicly on Sundays to cry aloud that everybody may hear that they are poor down-trodden helots, the 'pore working man'. Its the utter want of self-respect that revolts." He goes on to speak of a young housepainter cousin of his tobacconist's who approves every form of lawlessness: "Of himself as a citizen he never thinks, but of himself as an Ishmael he thinks a good deal . . . He has no duties to the State, no personal responsibility of any kind, and he'd sooner see his children dead than soldiers of the Queen."[27]

If we leave aside the sin of despising army life that the cockney working man shares with so many other Englishmen – Wesleyan tradesmen or publicans who show Tommy the door – we may, at first sight, see some contradiction here between Kipling's hostility to cockney individualism, cynicism and rebelliousness and his love of the cockney music hall, of Nellie Farren and Fred Leslie, his solaces at this lonely and perplexed time. One *Letter on Leave* called "The Great and Only" is a paean of praise to the music hall and its superiority to the "new theatre" (Gosse made him go to Ibsen's *Hedda Gabler*).

Certainly in the very interesting letters to J. B. Booth about the old music-hall that he wrote in the late twenties and early thirties, he appears to recognise these rebellious, irreverent qualities in the songs that he and Booth looked back to nostalgically. "Personally, I date from 'Kafoozelum', which, by the way, is a work of art. Do you remember that it was cheerfully attributed (on the cover) to the Bishop of London? Fancy what would happen now if anyone tried a game of that sort?" And again, he writes, "Yes, the old lot *were* gloomy. I've heard 'Don't go down the mine, Daddy' intoned from end to end at a revel of agriculturists – *with relish*. And in the S.A. campaign Tommy moaned all through the sing-songs."[28] But this, in fact, is not a recognition of the cynical individualism that underlay much Victorian cockney humour so much as a recognition of the sort of collective griping and irreverence that sustained the Soldiers Three in their hard life. And it is, of course, exactly to the hardships and bitternesses of military life that Kipling adapted the music hall so blithely and jauntily in the *Barrack Room Ballads*. Of the communal life of mines or factories he never knew anything, but in the slums of London he saw only a wild and dangerous individualism threatening the fabric of society, and he found the individualism of the suburban commuter, the world of the clerks, only better in that it threatened no violence.

This vision of London is important, I think, for the permanent effect it had upon his social and political outlook and for the immediate effect it had upon his attitude to his own life. And it was heightened and given a kind of resolution by his final analysis that what was wrong with English society was that it feared death too much and accepted death's reality too little.

But, before tracing these strands through his life and his writing in these momentous two years in England, I must point out an odd and important reservation in his hostile attitude to the cockney masses – his very real feeling for the women of London slums. It is an odd reservation, because as we shall see, events in his personal life at this time produced in him a savage misogyny which was not wholly to die away for many years to come, and completely ruined the unbalanced novel, *The Light That Failed*. It is an important one because it produced one excellent and totally unexpected story, "The Record of Badalia Herodsfoot" (November 1890); one of his most famous ballads, "Mary, pity women" (collected in *Seven Seas*, 1896) and "An Imperial Rescript" (1890), the first of his series of brilliantly sustained attacks upon Kaiser Wilhelm which reached a crescendo of beautifully organised hatred in the Great War. Somehow, and through some conversation with working women (was it with the barmaid of whom he speaks in his autobiography?) he acquired the belief that some cockney women had a constancy and a purpose in life through their love of their men which the men themselves in their drifting individualism and idle rebelliousness lacked and which his own bitter experience did not allow him to find in women of his own class.

Badalia Herodsfoot, the East End slum girl, is one such woman. She is superior to her fellows, for her devotion to the brute who kicks her out of his home gives her some sense of values beyond herself. On the other hand, when she helps the missionaries, though she lacks their religious faith ("there ain't no God like as not, an' if there *is* it don't matter to you or me, an' any'ow you take this jelly"[29]), her greater realism makes her the first social worker to dispense benefits to those who need them and not to scroungers. She is practical and she expects and accepts death, even though it comes to her from the violence of her man. In short, like the soldiers and the Indian natives for whom officerly or paternal care is proper, and unlike the disorganised, Ishmael male slum dwellers, she is worthy because she lives her life under some code, however misdirected. The story is a little sentimental but still greatly superior to the mass of realistic stories of London slum life that appeared under the influence of Zola in the nineties from Arthur Morrison or the writers for the *Savoy*. It certainly is a more

than adequate revenge upon the Toynbee Hall young man who told
Kipling what should be done for the poor; and it is the first really
successful expression of that deep compassion for lonely and unloved
women that ran alongside his superficial misogyny and outlived it to
produce some of the finest stories of his last twenty years.

"Mary, pity women" has also a sentimental touch, yet in its mixture
of crude sexual passion and pathetic desire for respectability:

> You'd like to treat me fair?
> You can't, because we're pore?
> We'd starve? What do I care!
> We might, but *this* is shore!
> I want the name, no more –
> The name an' lines to show,
> An' not to be an 'ore . . .
> Ah, Gawd! I love you so!

it seems to me to have greater truth than the long series of proudly
amoral "My Man" popular songs from Brecht to "Can't help loving
that man" and "He's my Bill" to which it has given birth.

"An Imperial Rescript" has an interest of another kind, for it is his
first tilt at the young Kaiser Wilhelm who was to become his personal
devil. But, curiously, the poem antedates his identification of Germany
as the inevitable enemy of Anglo-Saxon world order. Russia (heritage
of the Punjab) was still Public Enemy Number One. In so far as return
to the English scene modified this it would have been to replace Russia
with France, from the early days of Napoleon III still the target of
periodic warnings of England's vulnerability to invasion. Indeed, a
copy of *Invasion and Defence* by F. N. Maude, with France our
hypothetical enemy, is in his library at Bateman's and, as it was published in Calcutta in 1888, he was probably well aware of the French
bogey in his Indian days. Germany, in so far as she emerges in his
work up to that date, is either mild or humorous like the German
naturalist he met on the liner in Asia, called in fiction Hans Breitmann
after his favourite German-American comic writer, or mild and
humourless, like the German missionaries in some of the Indian
stories. The occasion for satire of "An Imperial Rescript" was ironically nothing to do with the battle of world forces, but with a quite
different fear of Kipling's at that time. In 1890, the young
Emperor, taking on the dismissed Bismarck's paternalistic labour
role, made an international appeal to working men to aid their
weaker brethren:

> The strong shall wait for the weary, the hale
>   shall halt for the weak; . . .
> Ye shall march to peace and plenty in the
>   bond of brotherhood – sign!

The working men of the world, as Kipling portrays it, seem likely to respond to this dangerous Utopian appeal, this further weakening of self-reliance.

> When – the laugh of a blue eyed maiden
>   ran clear through the Council hall.
> And each one heard Her laughing as each one
>   saw Her plain –
> Sadie, Mimi, or Olga, Gretchen, or Mary Jane,
> And the Spirit of Man that is in Him to the
>   light of the vision woke;
> And the men drew back from the paper . . .

In short, the common sense and pragmatism of working women the world over saved the day.

The poem is in language and thought a perfect example of that occasional muddled immaturity that makes one suddenly realise how young and bewildered, beneath everything, the precocious author of genius was in areas unfamiliar to him. But it further points his excepting of working-class women from his general black picture of London.

Working women, all the same, were only a small exception in their greater realism and subordination of self among the degenerate mass of English society, as Kipling diagnosed it, in London in 1890. One thing underlay everything – the trivial aristocracy, the second-hand thinking intelligentsia, the deluded do-gooders, the narrow-minded inturned middle classes, the insular army-hating traders, the soured self-indulgent poor, above all, the debilitating class hatreds and suspicions that weakened and disunited the nation. The Indian Mohammedan narrator of "One View of the Question" puts it clearly thus: "If they desire a thing they declare that it is true. If they desire it not, though that were Death itself, they cry aloud, 'It has never been.' " As Kipling himself says in "The Finest Story in the World", "The Western World which clings to the dread of death more closely than to the hope of life."

One of the best of the *Letters on Leave*, "A Death in the Camp", tells of the effect on London society of the death of a man of seventy, prosperous, having lived a happy life, leaving a well-cared-for family.

150

Everyone is shocked. It is the subject of talk at every tea party and dinner party to which Kipling goes. And, at last, he understands why, the cause is fear, because "it was only in the next street that it happened". Remembering India, he tells them – "Run about and see what death really means. You have described such death as a god might envy." [30] And, of course, in a score or more of his stories of Indian life that he gave to the English reading public in the early nineties, he tells them of Death ever present, death of children, death of young men on the edge of attainment or at the peak of their powers. Against this he sets Tomlinson, who, in his Berkeley Square house, has so little positive to his credit, whether of action or thought, that when he dies neither heaven nor hell can find a place for him. It is for such men that the streets are covered with straw so that their passing shall be unharmed by the sound of the horses' hooves.

It is a fair indictment. But, perhaps, not quite realistic about London's slums. For though mortality, especially infant mortality, was lower there than thirty years earlier, in, say, the sixties, and, of course, far less than in India, it was still very high. Perhaps this is partly why, unconsciously, he excepted from his indictment the working women who acted as nurses and layers-out in the slums.

Nevertheless, the refusal to face death as inevitable is something that strikes him most forcibly, in contrast to India. In "The English Flag" (1891), the street-bred people (and let us remember this meant all classes in the island) are reminded that:

> Never the lotos closes, never the wild fowl wake,
> But a soul goes out on the East Wind that died for
>   England's sake –
> Man or woman or suckling, mother or bride or maid –
> Because on the bones of the English, the English
>   flag is stayed.

General Gordon's death in Khartoum and the defeat by the Boers at Majuba were very much in the minds of Gladstone-haters like Kipling in 1890 and the belief that ignoble peace was the cause of the rot of the nation was knowing one of its periodic resurgences, as it had in the time of Tennyson's "Maud". Kipling, indeed, in an unsigned article published in the *St James's Gazette* as early as January 1890, a few months after his arrival in London, saw the sacrifice of war as one of the only hopes of uniting the nation and being rid of the canker of class division. In "What it came to: an unequal tax," he tells us, "and the lists came in day after day . . . the Duchess cried on the housekeeper's neck, for they had both lost husbands; and the Duchess's daughter wept with the lady's maid, for they had both lost lovers," and so on. " 'Well, what about those blooming aristocrats that lived on the sweat of your brow?' said the British Public. 'Ow, there ain't much wrong with them,' said the Masses ... 'And what about those Brutal and licentious Masses?' said the British Public. 'They're all right, when you let 'em alone,' said the aristocrats." [31]

The idea of war as a permanent social solution is, of course, naive, and any apparent glorification of war, after two world wars, is extremely repulsive; but it was not an uncommon attitude of the last half of the nineteenth century in all European countries among sections of the intelligentsia. In fairness to Kipling, he was already preaching the dangers of such nationalistic euphoria by 1897 and, after the Boer War at least, his hope for such a social solvent centred around the creation of a national defensive army and not upon the equal sacrifice of human life. He had expected Armageddon from the mid-nineties at least. When it came in 1914, he was not surprised. But though, like everyone else, the endless toll of lives at the front overwhelmed him, he had anticipated far more of the terrible reality than say, the Souls in England or the Futurists in Italy or Apollinaire in France. Only for a moment, in these bewildered two years of his arrival in London, did he suggest that war could be a panacea. Increasingly from the mid decade and entirely after 1902, he saw it only as a terrible inevitability if there was no renewed sense of national duty. But it must be said that this belligerent strain in Kipling increased the revulsion of some critics at the time, culminating in Robert Buchanan's article in 1899, "The Voice of the Hooligan",[32] and surely added to the revulsion of the many old-fashioned Victorian readers like Lady Emily Lutyens, granddaughter of Bulwer Lytton, who wrote in 1891, "I thought his books so dreadfully vulgar, besides being dull. People seem so fond of horrors now and such unnecessary horrors."[33]

More disturbing than the unsigned article "What it came to" is the glorification of war in *The Light That Failed*, but as this is more an attempted solution of his own personal desperation in these years than any proposal for national regeneration, we must now look shortly at what had happened in his private life – shortly, because its only expression in his writing is this inferior novel.

His half-engagement to Caroline Taylor, with her background of a Pennsylvania small-town Methodist College, of which her father was Principal, had run only a short course. Charles Carrington, who has seen their correspondence, suggests that it was very much a young man's rather gauche wooing. He gives a letter containing Rudyard's account of his religious beliefs sent to Caroline, in which, while paying tribute to the force of the Christian creed, his honesty succeeds only in producing a near-deistic affirmation. Carrington convincingly suggests that "On Greenhow Hill", with its largely unsympathetic account of the Yorkshire Methodists' incapacity to appreciate the hero, Learoyd, must have signalled to the Taylors the impossibility of the marriage.

Certainly "Badalia Herodsfoot", published in the autumn of that year, after the semi-engagement had passed into limbo, expresses an admiration for Roman Catholics over other Christians for their practicality and breadth of view (though hardly an approval of *any* Christian body). It was to remain his attitude to the Christian sects, certainly in *Kim* in 1900, probably until political issues like the "Irish Question" and the papal neutrality in the First War were to weigh with him against the Catholics. It was not a preference that could be easy for any Methodists in those days; and would perhaps be harder for the Taylors to swallow than a measure of Socinianism in his views.

Shortly after the break with Caroline, Aleck Hill died very suddenly. Kipling maintained a correspondence with Ted until her death in the nineteen-twenties in a leafy, well-heeled suburb of Baltimore. But it was friendly rather than intimate. She never met Kipling's wife, so far as I know. Whatever her boyish charm, so new to him in Allahabad in 1888, may have contributed to William, the Anglo-Indian heroine of "William the Conqueror", which he wrote for the American *Ladies' Home Journal* in 1895, the fire of his admiration had been satisfactorily and safely transferred to her unmarried sister Caroline and it died away with the end of his understanding with Caroline.

In any case, all such fires were now to pale, indeed had surely begun to pale before he broke with Caroline Taylor, beside the sudden rekindling of his old passion for Violet Garrard. It had always waxed and waned. Before he left school he had written to Mrs Perry, "Mater", that the engagement was all over. Yet after he was in India he still wrote about it to his cousins and talked of it to his sister as a continuing understanding. The apparent end had come in a letter from Violet (or Flo as she was called) to him at Lahore some time before the summer of 1884. Now it seems that he met her again in the street in London and his old passion was reawakened. His sister, Trix, coming on her first trip home as a married woman in February 1890, found her brother broken by the strength of his feelings for Violet and the unlikelihood of her responding. I think that Trix's view of Violet Garrard has been a little over-easily accepted, as though it were some kind of external evidence to give justification for the violent misogyny which his hopeless passion led Kipling to give way to in *The Light That Failed*. Trix charged the unresponsive Flo with being "naturally cold" and with being obsessed with painting "her very ineffective little pictures".[34] But Trix was a loving sister who perhaps felt a certain guilt that the schoolboy Rudyard's great affection for herself had made him brave the memories of the House of Desolation again when he was fourteen, and that this very courageous sign of his love had been rewarded by a meeting with a girl who continued, after more than a decade, to make his life miserable. She is, therefore, hardly a fair judge of Flo's nature or her artistic ambitions.

Whatever the girl–boy attachment, there is no evidence to suppose that Flo was still alive to it when she met him again by chance in February 1890. Years later, it seems, she spoke of it as *his* infatuation. A visit that Rudyard paid to her in May 1890 in Paris, where she was sharing a studio with a friend, Mabel Price, certainly gave him no encouragement. The fact that she was apparently still with her friend over thirty years later may lead one to wonder whether he had not, by chance, embarked upon a romantic quest that was stillborn from the start. But enough conjecture has pursued the unfortunate Miss Garrard, simply because a young man of literary genius fell deeply in love with her in his early youth.

This is not to minimise the pains (and, one hopes, some months of great happiness) that his love for Flo Garrard brought to Kipling. Nor to be surprised either that he should have suffered its reawakening, when they met by chance six or seven years after she had broken with him, or that he should have kept it to himself in later years. (What business was it of anyone else's? And was it not truly buried by the subsequent years?) Charles Dickens, in his late teens, had known an equally absorbing love for Maria Beadnell and an equal suffering when she jilted him. He had expected a return of the passion when she re-entered his life thirty years later. We may call his case more absurd than Kipling's, if we wish to see the eccentricities of sexual love in an absurd light. But he was more happy than Kipling in the use that he made of his passion in his imaginative writing. He waited to tell of his disappointment with Maria until he was a mature married man and produced, therefore, in the story of David Copperfield and Dora a picture of youthful infatuation which is damning but yet still loving and very alive. As to his foolish hopes of finding his girl-fiancée again in a stout middle-aged matron, he created from these his greatest "divine idiot", Flora Finching.

Kipling was less lucky. Hedged in by loneliness and overwork, disillusioned with the great London world that was ready to lionise him,

154

alarmed beneath his assumption of adult scorn at the unshaped prospect before him, torn between the equally siren voices of coterie fame
and quick journalistic riches, aware that he had much to learn in craft
yet aware too that all the craft in the world wouldn't guide him if he
lost touch with his inner inspiration, his desperation needed a
scapegoat. He found one in Flo who could easily wear for him the
guise of a familiar and shoddy *fin-de-siècle* artistic myth – the *femme
fatale*, the *belle dame sans merci*, the vampire that sucks man's life
away, a spurious fancy who dodges a few years later in and out of the
Yellow Book and the *Savoy* and the drawings of Aubrey Beardsley.
This comforting fantasy alone would have made poor work, imitative
of its period. But it could have been one way in which the young
Kipling could have got rid of his pre-Raphaelite inheritance, for his
youthful passion for Flo Garrard, I think, may well have been sustained by all the fantasies of medieval courtly love and Arthurian
idylls in which Uncle Ned Burne-Jones found artistic expression for
his own easily infatuated nature, much to the detriment of his painting.

Something of this kind might have satisfied a less complex man than
Kipling. Indeed, seven years later, in 1897, he turned out a poem along
these lines to accompany his cousin Phil Burne-Jones's melodramatic
picture, "The Vampire" (painted under an obsession with that
goddess siren symbol of the nineties, the actress, Mrs Patrick
Campbell):

> A fool there was and he made his prayer
> (Even as you and I!)
> To a rag and a bone and a hank of hair
> (We called her the woman who did not care)
> But the fool he called her his lady fair –
> (Even as you and I)

But Rudyard's "lady fair" was not the centre of his real quest,
which was not in truth a pre-Raphaelite one. For all that he was in
fact pouring out fruitful and good work at this time, he was in search
of assurance that he was still in touch with the sources of his inspiration. In his overcharged imagination the two became mixed. And the
result is a farrago of misogyny and false heroics and self-pity. *The
Light That Failed* is a *fin-de-siècle* decadent tale with death as its
outcome but this would hardly matter (or at any rate it would have
made nothing worse than a modish, mediocre work) but that the mode
was not Kipling's. For him, if death there was to be, then that death

must be exalted, not melancholy, and, to point the misogynist moral, a manly, heroic death in battle that would wash the mouth clean of woman's petty concerns and selfish ways with a good draught of healthy soldiers' blood. The whole makes a novel that would be very distasteful if it were not absurd.

I do not propose to examine *The Light That Failed* as closely as most critics of Kipling have done. Much has been written about its debt to Scarron and to the Abbé Prévost's fine novel, *Manon Lescaut*, but I suspect that Kipling spoke of such things in his autobiography because he did not wish exploration of the private motives which have now been fully discussed again and again. One of its defects – a certain brutality, evidenced both in the scene with the cardiac publisher and in the treatment of the women characters – was already apparent in his earlier Indian work; it is only more intolerable here because the whole book falls apart and, therefore, its justification seems less.

The idea of the lasting destructive romantic attachment, which Kipling may owe either to Uncle Ned Burne-Jones, in his life and art, or to the family history of his failed uncle, Harry Macdonald, who had experienced such a passion in youth, must surely have been in his mind all through the pains and pleasures of his love affair with Flo. Yet, in *Plain Tales from the Hills*, it is only once, in the story of young Dickie Hatt's ruin through love for a shallow girl, that he lays blame on the woman. In "The Other Man" and in "The Phantom Rickshaw" he turns the idea to artistic success by treating it as a setting for Gothic horrors. And in "On the Strength of a Likeness" he lays blame fair and square on the man. Indeed, contrary to the critical opinion of the nineties which still lingers, Kipling's early work, I think, is largely marked by his extraordinary understanding of the unfairness of women's lives, with his sympathy and liking for them. The blind, self-flattering misogyny of *The Light That Failed* comes, then, as a peculiar surprise and disappointment. Happily, after an interval of fourteen years, he returned to the theme of abiding passion and, although not immediately successful in giving it imaginative shape, he eventually made from it the best of his stories of English countryside, "The Wish House", and the most powerful of his stories of the Great War, "Mary Postgate".

But it is not only his absolute refusal to see the heroine, Maisie (Flo), as a human being, with rights and needs of her own. The picture of the vengeful model who (Hell hath no fury like a woman scorned) cuts to pieces the hero Dick Heldar's masterpiece, "Melancholia", is equally melodramatic nonsense. The "Melancholia" itself, with its overtones of pre-Raphaelite admiration for Dürer's masterpieces, is an unfortunate choice to illustrate the original genius of a young painter of the nineties. Indeed, the whole picture of the painting world is totally outdated. To have set Dick Heldar's battlepieces against Maisie's determination to study in Paris as a contrast between true artistic instinct and shallow amateurism is, to say the least of it, unfortunate at a time when the French Impressionists were gaining their first recognition in England through Whistler. But then the Father and the Uncle, to say nothing of Uncle Poynter, later President of the Royal Academy, were hardly good guides to the vital strains in contemporary painting.

To balance all this misogyny we have the idealised world of men's men. Such a happy bachelor society is liable to be misunderstood today. But Victorian sexual divisions created worlds unfamiliar in these days when men's clubs in London can only survive by providing for women guests, when "men only" bars are disappearing even in outback Australia. But "a man's world" and "man's talk" (like "bosom friends" for Mrs Hauksbee and Mrs Mallowe) provided a necessary relief from the artificiality and tensions of much pre-1914 mixed company. Kipling was, in great degree, "a man's man" as the phrase went, with a taste for technical talk and broad chaff and broad humour. But, as a young man, perhaps more in theory than in practice. As we know, he had avoided the Lahore Club to escape bores and arguments. He was pleased to be enrolled at the Savile Club in London and to attend Henley's dinners, but he kept his distance from both circles. It was the officers' mess which he didn't know that he wrote of with eagerness. Dick Heldar's all-male circle in *The Light That Failed* comes out of du Maurier's *Trilby* which contains a portrait of his not greatly loved Uncle Poynter as a youthful student twenty years before; the rest it owes to memories of Study 5 at Westward Ho. But one could forgive the unreal quality of all this – the elaborate horseplay, the mannered schoolboy affectation of language – if it were not for the wretched sentimental mothering of each other with which Dick and Torpenhow and the Nilghai assuage each other's wounds received in contact with the deadly other sex. This reaches a nauseating height after the jilted Dick goes blind. Given Kipling's bad eyesight, the blindness is an understandable symbol for fear of loss of creative power but its melodramatic effect is disastrous. And this effect is finally compounded when the blind hero dies in a Sudan battle surrounded by scenes of carnage. ("Oh, God has been most good to me.")

Yet Dick's death in the Sudan does point to a very real dilemma in Kipling's life at that time, even though it provides an embarrassing end to an embarrassing book. Earlier in the novel, the hero pleads with Maisie over two or three pages to come East with him to exotic lands where they may paint together. "You'll see for yourself what colour means, and we'll find out together what love means, and then, maybe, we shall be allowed to do some good work ... You're half gipsy ... and I – even the smell of open water makes me restless. Come across the sea and be happy?" The passages are naive but they alone in the book have some of the poetry that the Indian stories have led us to expect. They are, I believe, a cry from the heart, for escape, for the feelings and sounds that had made his earlier work. It was a dilemma that was to press upon him for all of his life, and, until he found the English countryside and the English past after the turn of the century, something that pressed upon him most cruelly, making no home possible, rejecting all roots. It is, of course, the dilemma of a great many artists. And, to this, Kipling added the same dilemma (with different causes) of the expatriate. It is, indeed, one of the aspects of Kipling's art that has drawn me, as a half South African, to his work. It was not only to tug at his creative self, but at his political self, affecting his attitude as much to America, to India, and to the "white" colonies as to England. And it bit deep into his whole estimation of himself as a man. On the one hand, there were loafers and globe-trotters and remittance men – and he had written of their doom, even though in his condemnation there is deep sympathy. On the other hand, what do they know of England who only England know? Even so late as "Gipsy Vans", he ends:

> Unless you come of the gipsy race
> That counts all time the same,
> Be you careful of Time and Place
> And Judgement and Good Name:
> Lose your life for to live your life
> The way that you ought to do;
> And when you are finished, your God and your wife
> And the Gipsies'll laugh at you.

For a man married thirty years the tone is curiously ironic, although I think by that time he had long learned that the "gipsy race", as far as he was concerned, existed inside himself and not in the outer world.

However, the lifelong problem was at its most acute during the crisis point of 1890, and not the less so, because, as his plea to Maisie (Flo) tells us, he was as desperate not to be alone any longer as he was to renew his imagination from what he believed to be its true fountain. As we shall see, it was not to be his last appeal to someone to accompany him on the long trail. Perhaps, also, though he wanted to return East, he did not want exactly to return to the family square.

For the moment, however, his loneliness was to be greatly assuaged, for, spurred on by a telegram from Rudyard himself, his parents arrived in London on leave in May, and set up house in the time-honoured family district of Kensington. Here, in the Earl's Court Road, Rudyard could taste, when Villiers Street grew too solitary, the intimacy of home again, even of the Square, for they were sometimes joined by Trix (her husband was also on leave). Here Lockwood helped him in giving England a lesson in the true problems of India with "The Enlightenment of Pagett, M.P.", here he probably also supplied some details of Yorkshire Methodism from memories of his youth for "On Greenhow Hill". Here Alice is said to have helped to give force to the key lines of "The English Flag".

Yet, even with the beloved parents' nursing of the pains of over-work and publicity, Rudyard's nervous strain reached a breaking point. The *Athenaeum* of 4 October 1890 announced, "We regret to hear that Mr Rudyard Kipling has broken down from overwork. He has been ordered to take a sea voyage and sailed on the P. & O. steamer *Shannon* for Naples on Thursday. His illness will probably delay the publication of *The Book of the Forty Five Mornings.*" The choice of Naples confirms my sense that he was still homesick for India, for here he was to be the guest of Lord Dufferin who had presided as Viceroy over the Kiplings' happiest times at Simla. Already when Kipling had visited Paris in late 1889 for a short holiday soon after his arrival in London, he called on Dufferin at the Embassy, modestly announcing himself as "the son of Mr Lockwood Kipling". Now he went to stay with this cultured Tory peer at his villa in Sorrento, which, as Ambassador in Rome, he used for relaxation.

The visit was a delight to Kipling, as he remembered forty years later. Yet, four years later, Sir James Rennell reports the famous young Rudyard Kipling (on a visit from America) at Lord and Lady Cranby's with Balfour as a guest. "In such company the conversation did not flag, but our guest of the evening R.K. was rather contemplative." [35] He was sitting next to his hostess, a beauty and a Soul, later Duchess of Rutland, sculptress and mother of Lady Diana Cooper. Cultured Tory aristocrats of stay-at-home English high society were one thing, cultured Tory aristocrats who had governed India quite another.

He returned from Italy refreshed, but, of course, to the same dilemma. His father noted that, amid all the host of notabilities who sought his acquaintance, amid all the requests for work from his hand, he seemed only to care for his mother.

159

This seems the moment to mention a problem much discussed by Kipling scholars, that of the two versions of *The Light That Failed*, because the two solutions offered throw emphasis upon the dilemma which was increasingly underlying all his anxieties. His final choice in this dilemma was ultimately to decide the external shape, at any rate, of the rest of his life.

The Light That Failed was published first in America and England in *Lippincott's Monthly Magazine* in January 1891, a magazine that in the previous year had published another inferior autobiographical fantasy by a major author – Wilde's *Dorian Gray*. Kipling's novel in these versions had a novelettish conventional ending in which Maisie repents of her rejection of Dick and they are married. In March 1891 what the author called the original conception appeared in book form published by Macmillan – in November 1890 it had been used by Lovell in America in the copy they deposited in Washington for copyright. Here, as we have seen, Maisie is peremptorily dismissed from Dick's life and he goes blind to die amid the glorious sands of the Sudan battlefields. A most interesting article by Margaret Newsom in the *Kipling Journal,* drawing upon an earlier article by Charles Carrington, suggests that the first more conventional and surely less objectionable version was urged upon Kipling by his mother.[36] This was what an old friend of the Kipling family had told Professor Carrington. Mrs Newsom goes on to suggest that when Kipling then published the more objectionable version of the novel, he appended as an attempt to appease his mother, the famous poem, "Mother O' Mine":

> If I were damned of body and soul,
> I know whose prayers would make me whole,
> Mother o' mine, O mother o' mine!

This poem has usually been seen as a comment that when other women fail, a man's mother may be relied upon. I have already written of the mother-worship which can certainly be found in Kipling's work and which would lend credit to this usual view, but I like Mrs Newsom's suggestion for it lends support to my suspicion that perhaps Kipling, however much he fell back on his parents for support, however much he was to welcome their comments and assistance to the end of their lives, was becoming restive, perhaps with himself, for this reliance. He was, after all, now twenty five years old. The reference to *The Book of the Forty Five Mornings* in the *Athenaeum*'s notice of his illness suggests that he was still intent upon publishing some version of his novel *Mother Maturin*. What Mrs Hill tells us of the plot as he told it to her suggests that when, under Lockwood's persuasion, he abandoned the book, we lost a conventional spy story, with oriental trimmings and gained a unique work, his finest work, *Kim*. Nevertheless, however much we may think the judgement here of Alice and of Lockwood superior to their son's, however much we may declare, as most of his biographers and critics have done, that he was lucky in having parents who could so foster his talent, there comes a time (and early too) when a writer wishes to fall by his own misjudgement rather than stand upon someone else's good one. It may well be, as Margaret Newsom suggests, that the bitter ending of *The Light That Failed* was that moment.

But there is a rival claim to Alice Kipling's for the sweetening of the novel in its first version. It has usually been accepted that this was due to the commercial instinct of Kipling's new friend, the literary agent in London for Lovell, the American publisher of *The Light That Failed*, Wolcott Balestier. Edmund Gosse lays claim to introducing Kipling's work to Balestier; but Kipling himself had first met this young American early in his return to England at the house of Mrs Humphry Ward, one of the best-selling English authors whose American publications the young Balestier managed. It was this function above all that had made him so popular and new a phenomenon upon the English literary scene, this and his extraordinary personal charm.

On behalf of the American firm, Lovell & Co., he made decent contracts for English authors' American publications at a time when lack of copyright still allowed for the pirating that had incensed great English authors from Dickens to Kipling.

It is hard to get a picture of people long dead whose reputation rests largely upon charm. But it so happens that we have an account of Wolcott by Arthur Waugh (father of Alec and Evelyn) who worked for him in his youth for £1 a week. We also have a testimony to him at the time of his death in 1892 by Henry James. And on one vital point they are in total agreement: Arthur Waugh speaks of Wolcott's "chameleon power with people"[37]; Henry James of "an extraordinary subtlety of putting himself in the place of the men – and quite as easily, when need was, of the women of letters".[38] Now this chameleon power was a marked trait of Kipling himself. It might, instead of drawing the two young men together, have kept them apart. But their empathies were so different – Wolcott got on naturally with writers, Rudyard with almost anyone else, Wolcott was in love with London, Rudyard very much out of love with the city. Kipling's empathy with so many kinds of men was, I think, through silence and listening; Wolcott's, as Waugh describes him – "tall, pale, very thin, quick eyes, sharp voice, marked U.S. accent"[39] – seems likely to have been through volubility.

Yet their discretion and humour must have drawn them together, for James writes, "he was a well of discretion and it was charming and interesting in him that even when he was most humorously communicative his talk was traversed by little wandering airs of the unsaid". He took infinite trouble for his clients and James tells how when a play of his was being presented at a Lancashire theatre (an agony surely for James), Wolcott made "a long and loyal pilgrimage for purposes of support . . . on a wet winter's night".[40] And all this work, James said, was for love of the drama of business, of doing his job well, of money to be made to secure himself freedom in life. And, indeed, Waugh tells us that, in his eagerness to make honourable, useful deals for English authors, Wolcott often found himself ahead of Lovell's remittances and had to find advances from his own pocket. When it is added that, after a deeply felt row over the publisher Harper's piracy of Kipling's work, Wolcott set about securing authorised American editions, it is not surprising that the two young men became very close friends. Nor indeed that they collaborated in a novel together, for if Kipling in his sense of loneliness asked for companionship on travel, how welcome must have been the chance of congenial companionship in that most frightening and exhausting of journeys – imaginative creation.

The usual explanation of the two versions of *The Light That Failed*, namely that Wolcott with a knowledge of the magazine market (and why not a fear for his friend's grotesque self-revelation in the bitter version?) persuaded Kipling into publishing first in a conventional "happy" form, is very likely. I do not believe that this necessarily conflicts with the likelihood of Kipling's mother urging the same course. It only means that Rudyard's sticking to his own guns in the end was doubly heroic and wrong-headed, and yet, instinctively right for an artist. That Kipling's future collaboration with Wolcott was much in his mind when he wrote the happy-ending version of *The Light That Failed* is very probable, for the manuscript at Princeton University (a gift of great solemnity to his publisher, Frank Doubleday, in thanks for all he had done during Kipling's nearly fatal illness in New York in 1899) has on the verso of one of the pages references to "Doc Tarvin" and to "Kate Sheriff", and other rough notes which clearly relate to *Naulahka*, the novel he was to write in collaboration with Wolcott.[41]

This novel has usually been dismissed as an inferior work unhappily written with an inferior writer. I agree with Kingsley Amis in thinking that this conventional judgement is mistaken. *Naulahka* is not a masterpiece, but it is excellent reading. The American first section laid in Colorada, written by Balestier, who spent some time in the South West States after he left Cornell University, is very fresh and workmanlike. The hero, Nick Tarvin's determined wooing of Kate, the heroine, away from her supposed vocation as a mission teacher in India, though a bit contrived in plot, is free of the misogyny and self-pity of Dick Heldar's story. It was easier for Kipling to engage in an informed attack on missionaries (old butts of his Indian stories) than on art students. And the Indian section, laid in a Princely State, gave free rein to Kipling's dark imagination of princely intrigues that had been roused by his visits to the ancient ruined cities of Amber and Chitor. It also gave him a chance to create one of his best child portraits in the Maharaj Kunwar, the ruler's son who is threatened with death by secret poisoning.

After Wolcott had established himself in London, he brought over his mother and his two sisters to keep house for him in Kensington. For a short time they were joined by their rather wild brother, Beatty; but more of him later. The Balestier family were by origin French, from Martinique, whence their grandfather had come to make his fortune in Chicago. He married the daughter of an old Connecticut family, the Wolcotts, and settled in a spa town, Brattleboro, Vermont. Wolcott's mother was the daughter of an eminent judge, legal adviser to the Emperor of Japan, and had settled in Rochester, New York State, where the children were born. But the centre of the Balestier family still lay in Brattleboro where lived their formidable grandmother, now a widow, Madame Balestier, as she was called locally.

Kipling, it is said, first met Wolcott's elder sister Carrie in her brother's one-room office at Dean's Yard behind Westminster Abbey. He visited them in Kensington. And later he stayed with them in their rented house at Freshwater in the Isle of Wight. The judgements of Carrie made by Kipling's parents, who met her before they returned to India, do not appear enthusiastic, though Lockwood at least was to be a frequent visitor later to their married homes. In extracts from letters to his Aunt Baldwin on his marriage day, Kipling speaks of their "having gone through deep waters together".[42] This may be a reference only to Wolcott's death, but Charles Carrington says on "personal information" that the affair did not run smoothly. Apart from his parents, we may suppose that Carrie's mother must have been anxious about how this new friendship of her daughter's would be viewed by her formidable mother-in-law, Madame Balestier, back home in Vermont.

In any case, no official engagement seems to have been announced. Kipling was still overworking all that year of 1891, receiving solace from his parents' customary interest, and relief from shared imaginative work in the making of *Naulahka* with Wolcott. In May he made a short visit to America with his minister uncle, Fred Macdonald. The purpose of this visit was to see his eldest uncle, Harry, in New York, once the bright hope of the family, now an ailing man whom failure had cut off from his family in England. Rudyard had already met this uncle on his way from India to England, and had liked him. But the decision to make a recuperative journey with this purpose is perhaps significant, for Harry had taken the gipsy road and Harry had married and settled in America. Also symptomatic of Kipling's anxious, ambiguous frame of mind is the fact that he travelled incognito, but then acted so openly that reporters were awaiting him on the dock at New York. Fame? Privacy? England? America? Gipsy? Settled man? A question-mark must have hung over everything, and, meanwhile, his fertile imagination went on working at full speed. *Life's Handicap*, containing some of the best stories he ever wrote, appeared that year: although there was old work in it, the main part were stories written in these tormented two years, and four or five contained experience that he had known since India.

Wolcott, always weak-chested, also seems to have been ailing from overwork, for, in addition to everything, he was now involved with Heinemann in an attempt to rival Tauchnitz by publishing English and American works on the continent of Europe. If we may trust the manuscript of Kipling's poem, "The Long Trail" in the Berg collection in New York Library, he urged his friend to join him on the gipsy trail, to leave the tents of Shem (the business world of Europe?) and go south on the long trail with him, for this manuscript version is addressed to "dear lad". But when Rudyard left on 22 August for the Cape, Wolcott did not go with him. Mr J. Primrose has traced this last bachelor journey of Kipling's most exactly[43] and we can now see how little time he could give to the daughter countries of the Empire that he visited – a fortnight, time enough in the Cape to become a familiar with the Simonstown naval station which was to be so important in his later life, just time enough, perhaps, to have seen his future hero Rhodes, but not to have met him; twelve days in New Zealand; a few days only in Australia, mainly in Melbourne; then, with General Booth of the Salvation Army as fellow-passenger, on to Colombo and so four days by rail through the South India he didn't know, back to his parents in Lahore by the second week in December. A voyage that, as he said to reporters, was "only for a loaf and to see pretty things". A strange prelude to a momentous event.

But before we come to the climax, there are two aspects of this bachelor voyage which must be noted.

The first is that the ostensible reason he gave for this voyage south and east was that he intended to visit Robert Louis Stevenson in Samoa. Indeed, there is every reason to think that he intended to do so, but found in New Zealand that the journey would take too long. Stevenson half-expected him. James wrote that he supposed Kipling had already arrived at Stevenson's home. Stevenson, too, had gone on the long trail. But he had done so, much to the disapproval of the bohemian literary circle of W. E. Henley, with an American wife. The connection with R. L. Stevenson goes deeper than this obvious parallel. In 1892, after Kipling had married and, indeed, when he had once more set out on the long trail but this time with a dear lass, another author was being pressed by Stevenson to visit him – J. M. Barrie. Stevenson, in tropical exile, hankered after Edinburgh, as Kipling in London hankered after India. He writes to Barrie in November 1891, "It is a singular thing that I should live here in the South Seas under conditions so new and so striking and yet my imagination so continually inhabits that cold, old huddle of grey hills from which we come."[44] And in July 1892, he wrote again to Barrie, "Mount, sir, into 'a little frigot' of 5,000 tons or so and steam peremptorily for the tropics . . . Mr Barrie, sir, 'tis then there will be larks!"

The bringing together of these three best-selling authors in this context is striking, for it shows up the greater maturity of Kipling. All three had that quality of boyishness, that romantic urge to turn their back on reality and give themselves up to dream adventure. It is a central clue to their popularity in the last decades of the Victorian age, for throughout the eighties and nineties, and even after the Boer War, the middle classes, with the solid-seeming foundation of dividends, rents and consols, were only too happy to be reassured, as they were at *Peter Pan* in 1904, that the artist's vision in which they could share was "always to be a little boy and have fun". Stevenson, in his marvellous boys' world, gave signs of greater maturity as in *Weir of Hermiston*, but illness and physical weakness were too much for him. There are buried even in the pathology of poor Barrie's life and work some glimpses of a fuller life. But Kipling alone maintained the romantic boyish vision, the child's view, and, as no other author I know of, save now and again Charles Dickens, fused it with all the realities, the horrors and the splendours of adult life.

The second thing to note is that the many sea voyages that he made between leaving Calcutta in 1889 and returning to England to marry in 1892 have an importance of their own. They were reflected in some good stories that he wrote in these years, stories that now led away from India and its themes to themes he was to explore in the next century. Four such stories are worth some examination. The first, "The Limitations of Pambé Serang", was published in *Life's Handicap*, the other three – "The Disturber of Traffic", "The Finest Story in the World", and "A Matter of Fact" did not appear in book form until the publication of *Many Inventions* (an equally rich collection) in 1893, but all four were composed in these dark London years. And all were influenced by the sea.

I have already spoken of "Pambé Serang" as an example of Kipling's respect for the perseverance of emotions, even destructive ones, over the transient, meaningless quality of much generosity or compassion or patronage; even though the title, "The Limitations of Pambé Serang", admits the ultimate self-destructive goal of any murderous impulse under the law. Pambé, the serang, a kind of bosun on a liner, is a Malay, but born in India. Nureed, the stoker, is a Zanzibar Negro. Nureed, in a fit of drunkenness, insults Pambé, then the next morning apologises. But Pambé doesn't accept such apologies, such changes of mood. Before the voyage is out, Nureed flees Pambé's wrath and deserts, but Pambé pursues him all over the world. At last, starving and ill, Pambé lies in a Christian mission room in the East End docks. Here he hears Nureed's voice in the street below and begs the English Christian missionary to bring him up. Nureed has made money and greets the sick Pambé with Negro generosity and patronage. He sees at once what the Christian gentleman does not, that Pambé is desperately poor and he goes to give his old shipmate money. "Hya, Pambé. Hya! Hee-ah! Hulla." He bends over the sick Pambé in gay, matey Negro greeting. "How beautiful," says the Christian missionary, "How these orientals love like children." But Pambé knifes Nureed. " 'Now I can die!' said Pambé. But he did not die. He was nursed back to life with all the skill that money could buy, for the Law wanted him; and in the end he grew sufficiently healthy to be hanged . . . Pambé did not care particularly; but it was a sad blow to the kind gentleman." It is a powerful story both in its telling, and in its revelation of Kipling's overwhelming fear of sentimentalism.

But it is also very interesting for its revelation of the way that Kipling combined experience to shape his tales. The shipboard scenes clearly come from his voyages, but the stoker, Nureed, I think, is drawn from a Tamil whom he met at the London docks, as he tells in one of his *Letters on Leave* to the *Pioneer*. This Tamil, who worked for him at Villiers Street for nothing, only wanted work and keep until a ship arrived with a Lascar on board whom he was waiting to kill. India, even South India, has this constancy of purpose. Yet the Christian missionary surely connects closely with the clergymen do-gooders in "Badalia Herodsfoot" and Kipling's dislike of the young man from Toynbee Hall "who knows everything that should be done for the poor".

"The Disturber of Traffic" is said to have been composed by Kipling while staying with the Balestiers on the Isle of Wight. Certainly the framework of the story is laid in a Channel lighthouse, in which "I" spends a night of fog listening to the keeper's story of strange doings in time past in another lighthouse far away in the Java Straits.

Many of Kipling's Indian stories had been told in a framework, for example most of the stories of the Soldiers Three or the story of "The Man Who Would Be King". But the Soldiers Three stories have a framework of friendly patronage between Kipling ("I") and the tommies he supplies with the beer and tobacco. Peachey and Davot have a specific framework to their tale of Kipling the journalist and the newspaper office. Other stories again, in which the "I" is less clearly Kipling, have a club-room yarning opening which recalls Conrad's Marlowe and was to be made a stereotype by Maugham.

But the Channel lighthouse is something different. The "I" (if Kipling he be) is there on sufferance, he has to prove himself by an understanding of the lighthouse-keeper's technical language. There is almost a menace in the air: "I looked at Fenwick, and Fenwick looked at me; each gauging the other's capacities for boring and being bored . . . He fenced cautiously to find out the little that I knew and talked down to my level, 'till it came out that . . . Hereupon he ceased to talk down to me, and became so amazingly technical that I was forced to beg him to explain . . . This set him fully at his ease; and then we spoke as men together, each too interested to think of anything except the subject in hand." This more elaborate frame, of conversation entered into as a kind of campaign, was to become an increasing feature of Kipling's stories, sometimes with remarkable effect, sometimes with an over-elaboration and consciousness of craft that stifles the story.

The story this time is surely the outcome both of his voyages and his naval talk at Simonstown. It tells of the growing madness of the lighthouse-keeper Dowse in the Flores Straits near Timor after a long period of isolation with a strange half-human, half sea-gipsy native, an Orang-Lamt, called Challong, as his sole companion. His insanity takes the form of misleading ships away from the channel that he is supposed to guard. The Prospero–Caliban relationship declares Kipling's fascination with Shakespeare's *The Tempest*, a play which must concern all creative artists deeply. It also introduces the theme of obsession which was to reappear often in his work. But the coming together of Prospero and disordered wits, of magical powers misused speaks, I think, for his deep anxieties about the direction in which he was to guide his own artistic force. There is even, I suggest, a fear that Challong (Caliban), the animal side of nature, may play too large a part in the preoccupations of a Prospero, an artist, isolated as is Dowse, the Java Straits lighthouse-keeper. And yet, as we know, there is a desperate longing to escape not only from urban civilisation but from the civilising forces of the group, of the Square and so on. But *not* alone . . .

It is a horrible and purposely puzzling tale, carefully told without clear definition. And when the fog disperses in the Channel, the puzzle of the dreadful events in the far-off straits disperses too: "the sun rose and made the dead sea alive and splendid . . . he smelled a smell of cows in the lighthouse pastures below. Then we were both at liberty to thank the Lord for another day of clean wholesome life."

"The Finest Story in the World" is said to have been aroused by his cousin Ambo Poynter's ineffectual search to express himself in poetry. No doubt the London clerk who has visions half-recaptured of his previous lives as a Roman galley slave and in a Viking ship comes from Poynter's search to express himself to his famous cousin. The metempsychotic theme itself comes from Indian days and is given a special and very well-realised ironic twist by the fact that rational interpretations of it are offered by an educated Bengali. But the real core of the story lies in the clerk's recalling, both in prose and in verse, of the atmosphere of the Roman galley. It shows Kipling being led by concern for navigational techniques into a period of time that was to be the setting of some of his best later historical work – the Roman Empire. And his power of evocation is already fully formed as it emerges. This is no longer the pastiche of the few historical Indian stories, like "The Dream of Duncan Parsenness", but a detailed awakening of the past which is more powerful, because its hesitant building up in the clerk's mind reconstructs Kipling's own searching for a mode of evoking the past. " 'Can't you imagine the sunlight just squeezing through between the handle and the hole and wobbling about as the ship moves it?' . . . 'I can, but I can't imagine your imagining it' . . . 'How could it be any other way? Now you listen to me. The long oars on the upper deck are managed by four men to each bench, the lower ones by three, and the lowest of all by two. Remember it is quite dark on the lowest deck and all the men there go mad. When a man dies at his oar on that deck, he isn't thrown overboard, but cut up in his chains and stuffed through the oar hole in little pieces' ... 'Why?' I demanded amazed, not so much at the information as at the tone of command with which it was flung out ... 'To save trouble and to frighten the others.' " It is Kipling in communication with his creative self. Although he wrote no literary criticism, few authors have said more of value about the creative process in many of his stories and some of his speeches.

The last of these four stories, "A Matter of Fact", is in framework a not very good joke against American journalists, but it contains one of his first and best pieces of crude poetic writing of the kind that we should now call science fantasy. This is the death of the grotesque and blinded sea monster thrown up from the ocean's depths by an earthquake and wounded by a passing liner, and with it, the moving cry of misery that comes from its mate. The passage expresses Kipling's deep sense of pity with a clear force, that is impossible where he is concerned with human beings and with all the tabus that he holds necessary against indulgence of feeling for the individual.

But, however productive in imagination his journeys were, Kipling was now to learn that we are not masters of our own lives, however we climb on the gipsy van. Far away in Dresden, where he had gone on business, young Wolcott Balestier died suddenly of typhoid that he had brought from England. Sudden death from man's failure to master his environment was, ironically, not confined to far-off tropical places. Wolcott had, no doubt, worked away the strength to resist it. His mother and two sisters were with him at the end. Alec Waugh tells us that Carrie Balestier claimed that she knew her brother was very ill when he wouldn't allow her to ring a second time for the maid. A characteristic Carrie observation, I suspect, compounded of humour, bitter feeling and held-in emotion. Henry James came out there to help the three women and we have luckily his account of Carrie's behaviour on her beloved brother's death. He is obviously puzzled, even alarmed by her reserve and her force of character, but wholly admiring of her courage and determination. It is a judgement we are to hear repeated over the years.

Rudyard probably heard of Wolcott's illness at Colombo. When he joined his parents in Lahore, he was there long enough to look again at the settings of his old stories and to write the visit up for the *Civil and Military Gazette*. We have a drawing of him attending a Bazaar. But news must have come of Wolcott's death and Carrie's request for his presence, for he left before Christmas. Now Alice must have

known that the Square was finally broken. Kipling stopped at
Bombay long enough to see his old ayah (did he think he might never
visit India again?). Then he sailed for England. He arrived on 10
January 1892. And on 18 January he and Carrie Balestier were
married at All Souls' Church, Langham Place in London, with only
one relation present – Ambo Poynter. In February the honeymoon
couple sailed to America on the first lap of an intended long trail
around the world which was to be as frustrated by chance as his
bachelor pilgrimage to Samoa.

Land Without Hedges

Kipling came to his wife's homeland with affections and prejudices,
quite independent of hers: they were formed first by his boyhood and
continuing devotion to American literature, especially American
humour, a reading, I suspect, unknown in the well-read Englishman of
his time (as was his often disguised knowledge of contemporary
French writing). This fictional world had then been checked by reality,
when he crossed the United States from San Francisco to
Pennsylvania on his journey from India at the end of 1889.

He had left behind in the States from that visit a reputation as a
visitor more sour in his comments than Mrs Trollope or the young
Charles Dickens half a century earlier. He had sent back letters for
publication in India describing his trip across the States, to Allahabad
under his contract with the *Pioneer*. Since they were not copyrighted,
most of these letters were copied in some important American newspapers, although they were supposed to be exclusive to McClure's
Chicago *Daily Tribune*. And, now that he was much better known, the
whole series were pirated by an American publisher, Ivers, as
American Notes. The official publication of all his Indian, Asian and
American letters of that time as *From Sea to Sea*, from which some of
the more violent disparagement of America had been left out, could
only have partly removed the general impression of an angry, hostile
young man.

Yet discerning American readers must not only have admitted the
justice of some of the criticism, but have seen (except perhaps in the
sections on Chicago) that the young Englishman found much to like
everywhere, and, more importantly, that under everything he wrote
was a longing to love, a disposition to wonder and to admire, a hope
that he would find here a freer and larger way of thinking about
Anglo-Saxon civilisation, a tougher more pioneering spirit united with
the sort of easy culture that he found in his friend Mrs Hill, a power of

170

hard work, openness to risk, and acceptance of life's hardship which he feared (and he was right) he would not find when he got back to London.

I suspect that he hoped to discover in America some variation of his dream of an Anglo-Indian separate country based on Kashmir. He hoped to discover such virtues in the Republic and, of course, also hoped not to, for the Republic was not part of the British Empire which, now that he had travelled through Burma and Singapore and Hong Kong, increasingly occupied his terrestrial dreams. Indeed, like all foreign countries, America was a potential active enemy, as well as, with its huge immigrant population, an inherent enemy because of its growing cosmopolitan quality. But surely, he still hoped, whatever the historical, the racial and the customary differences that marked off the States from their mother hive, the two great Anglo-Saxon lands could find a common purpose in the better ordering of the world by their superior powers of obedience and self-sacrifice.

The failure of the United States of reality to answer to this dream was only part of a long process of disillusionment that Kipling, with other British visionaries, was to experience in the coming decades. The process was a long one, perhaps only finally brought home when the Great War, that had united the Anglo-Saxons in discipline and self-sacrifice, was followed by a peace in which the components fell apart in competition and demands for separate rights. This long journey of Imperial hope and disillusion which was to occupy so much of Kipling's surface time from now almost until his death can only be sketched in this book, for it only indirectly fed his writing (save in a few excellent satirical poems and prose fables which make him the first heir, if not the full equal, of Dryden and Swift in a country where political satire has, on the whole, been of a lower order).

But it cannot also be neglected completely as it has been by most writers on Kipling. Some critics, underestimating the potential force and the actual intellectual capacities of what used to be called right-wing Imperialism, but is now more satisfactorily named right-wing radicalism, in Edwardian England, perhaps because it never won power and failed in its aims, have preferred to ignore this aspect of Kipling's thinking, dismissing his political ideas as silly and immature. All revolutionary views, whether of the left or right, are silly and immature unless and until they succeed. Kipling's, of course, where they are successful, filtered through the imagination. He was an artist not a thinker. And, too, even when they appear most impersonal, his political and imperial concepts spring from his own agonising sense of personal isolation, of man's lonely, futile-seeming journey from child-

171

hood's wonder to death's eclipse. But that, again, is only to say that he was an artist, not a thinker. And that, in the ideas of the Right Radicals, of the Imperialists, he was to find a programme of activity that accorded with those deep personal inner fears and desperate hopes that were the source of his art.

Nor was the practical programme "silly". These critics forget, that if Joseph Chamberlain had not suffered a stroke at the height of his powers, or if Bonar Law had been a less unsuitable leader, Kipling might have been the Laureate of a powerful British Imperial movement (however short-lived that power would necessarily have been). His extreme views were shared with differences of detail by the intellectuals of the right of his time – by the *Spectator* and the *National Review*, by the St Loe Stracheys, Amery, Milner, the Maxses. To dismiss the views of such people as "silly" or "immature" is to equate maturity with the politics of the centre, of compromise. It's a tenable position, of course, but a very smug one which has left the centre, all too often and in too many countries, not knowing what has hit it. Repugnant some of the many strands of thought in the political views of Kipling and his associates from the mid-nineties may be (they certainly are to me), and muddled and impracticable many other strands must surely be judged to be; but many of the strands in their diagnoses of what was wrong with society appear perceptive and just. The trend of their general social hopes, if we except certain racialist assumptions, especially about Africa, which were common to most people of that time, certainly not excluding the Fabians, is often more sympathetic than their vehement expression suggests. These political hopes must be considered seriously if we are to understand their pressure upon Kipling's imagination for the rest of his life, the small but often strikingly good material he produced to propagate them, the dreams of genius that he pursued to illustrate them less directly, and the gentler mood that often marked his best later work as he came inwardly to accept their defects. On the other hand, great attention has been paid to his political ideas by recent more academic writers about him, but it seems to me that in recognising their originality they have too greatly abstracted them. It is clear that, in contrast with the main streams of English political thinking of his age, Kipling (like his more intellectual associates) conceived of society in terms nearer to the great Continental social theorists, Weber, Pareto and Durkheim, laying emphasis on groups within society rather than the historical or ethical development of society as a whole. But there is a danger in this approach to Kipling through his ideas. It is inevitably, I think, disruptive of the imaginative impact of his work. Seeing his ideas first and *then* tracing them in his stories and poems, Lord Annan, important though his insight has been, inevitably finds the work more didactic, less fully imagined than I believe a less abstract reading of it allows. The ideas are there, but though they are not "silly", they are confused, more confused than those of most intelligent Imperialists, journalists and politicians of his time (though less confused than those of Cecil Rhodes). Indeed, there was often speculation about Kipling's meaning by the young Leo Amery or Maxse, or any of Lord Milner's brilliant young men. The poet of the group, as usual, was often gnomic to those who sought clear indications for a policy of action. And, of course, this was because Kipling, like all artists, above all romantic artists, which for all his reserve he was, spoke out of his own inner conflict, although that conflict and the code he had devised from it absolutely forbade his emergence into the tensions of his stories in his own person (save as a bystander narrator device). It is this that Professor Alan Sandison, Kipling's harshest yet finally most completely appreciative critic, has emphasised in his essay, "The Artist and the Empire". The very balance of the title is correct. And, if we were to seek analogy with European counterparts, it should be with romantics like D'Annunzio rather than with European social theorists.

From the moment that Kipling left India in 1889 one part of him looked at everything he saw and asked: is it to be the corner-stone in the Anglo-Saxon fortress (from 1911 or so he would increasingly have been willing to say Anglo-French fortress), that must be built to shore up the world against the forces of despotism, anarchy, frivolity, meaninglessness? Of course, the political question sprang from his own desperation, from his own version of the prevalent terror in a world from which God had been removed. Yet its political form was a wholly serious one. And each land or idea that he came upon failed to prove that corner-stone. India, from which it all started, soon had to be forgotten, since his love and respect for its old native culture gave it no place in this new white man's world. England, when he reached it, was found to be built upon shifting sands. America, above all, was to remain a delusive hope for most of the rest of his life.

His experience of Americans on the liner going from Calcutta to San Francisco in 1889 was in itself formative. He already knew, of course, Ted Hill and admired her, admitted the teasing of her and her husband, though perhaps a little puzzledly, for English admirers of American humour in books must surely always be puzzled at their first impact of American humour in fact, so near is it and so far from British humour. But, for the rest, it is unlikely, with his distaste for globe-trotters, that he had talked with many Americans in India. Now

173

he was a globe-trotter himself and many of his fellow globe-trotters were Americans. There is one incident he relates about the attitude of the Americans on the liner to the Queen's birthday which seems to leave him puzzled about how close the Anglo-Saxon link really was to the ex-colonists: on the one hand they are so courteous, on the other ... But more important was the presence of a young spoiled American boy on board, the child of rich Americans in the age when Chads and Isobel Archers were first making Europe aware of their riches, where (Ta ra ra boomdeay) sweet Tuxedo girls, we see, pride of high society, were buying their way not only into Ascot's royal enclosure but into the peerage (Ta ra ra boomdeay). This spoiled boy, out of control, noisy, pert, blasé, was almost everything that was blasphemy to Kipling's concept of childhood as a wonder time, with a vision of its own that transcends the grown man's. It is a measure of his love for children that he should have saved that vile child up in his mind not to punish him but to redeem him six years later in *Captains Courageous.* But it was not a happy introduction to the land of the free; it suggested that the manly American liberty which he had hoped might oil the rusting wheels of England's complacency could have turned into meaningless, self-indulgent licence.

And so, in between endearing bouts of a young man's delight in being alive in a new and fresh world, Kipling found it when he landed in San Francisco. His indictment is not unlike Dickens's fifty years before, after he had left the Anglo-decency and gentility of New England. Lawlessness above all. Kipling managed accidentally to see one Chinaman stabbed and practically invited the sight of another by paying a visit to a Chinatown gambling den. The harshness of many American voices (especially women's). Spitting, boasting, impertinence of customs men and hotel clerks, and Negro waiters who outrageously dared to pity the lot of Indians; the garrulity and the indecent prying into private affairs by journalists, "to whom I returned answers mendacious and evasive".[45] This list is in large part that of Dickens, and Kipling specifically commends *American Notes* at this juncture as one of Dickens's best books. And, of course, like Dickens, as time passed, Kipling felt increasing rancour against American disregard of copyright, although his full fury did not burst until his row with the American publishers Harper's in London a year later.

As a lover of the variety of America, I yet think that if one went, unprepared, this could be a superficial judgement by an Englishman even now, save for the spitting. American politics, he learned, were corrupt and disorderly. The only Englishman he met in San Francisco was a lost gentleman loafer, quoting English literature and ruined by a hard-hearted girl in England (shades of Flo Garrard!). He made the episode into a story characteristically called "Her Little Responsibility".

Perhaps in contrast to these faithless girls far away in England, Kipling maintained throughout an encomium on American girls – "I am hopelessly in love with about eight American maidens." [46] This dissipated any too strong feeling that he may have had for Ted Hill who had now gone on to her Pennsylvania home. "They are clever: they can talk ... they are self-possessed without parting with any tenderness that is their sex right. They have good times, their freedom is large and they do not abuse it." [47] Here, at last, we feel a beneficial effect of America in loosening the uptightness of a deeply anxious young man. In the end he regretted leaving San Francisco – the men were so clever, the women so witty. But what hit the American headlines, of course, was his opening broadside when he landed, about the indefensibility of San Francisco harbour against British naval might: "I saw with great joy that the blockhouse which guarded the mouth of 'the finest harbour in the world, sir,' could be silenced by two gun boats from Hong Kong with safety, comfort and despatch." [48] The quotation marks alone suggest to me that the Americans were as unappreciative of Kipling's brand of humour as he was of theirs.

And there is little doubt that he carried away some fixed ideas of international anarchist conspirators against the British Empire hidden away in San Francisco's back streets, for they form the background of the tense story of the Irishman spy in the Indian army ranks, "The Mutiny of the Mavericks" (1891). Here the pathetic Irish American villain whom the regiment strings along to his death is "devoted with that blind rancorous hatred of England that only reaches its full growth across the Atlantic".

He was warned, as he travelled north, against speculation in real estate in the Washington State boom, and invested some money instead, at the request of a young Englishman, in British land in Vancouver (mistakenly as it later turned out). In the national parks of the Far West, the American tourists appalled him by their overpraise of their own country (something surely now largely vanished) and by their lack of pride in their army. A formidable Methodist American matron fell foul of him by alarming a colony of beavers, animals whose instincts of colonisation, industry and construction were peculiarly sympathetic to him. In the Chicago stockyards he suddenly strikes one of those peculiar notes of horror resonant beyond the words he uses, which are so impressive in his work, when he tells us of

175

a woman in red and black with red shoes who came to watch the Chicago pig and bullock slaughterhouse. "She looked curiously with hard, bold eyes, and was not ashamed."[49]

Nevertheless, when a supercilious young English gentleman warned him that he couldn't be too careful whom he talked to, he burst forth in a torrent of anger. "Wait," he cried, "till the Anglo-American-German-Jew – the Man of the Future is properly equipped. He'll have just the least little kink in his hair now and again; he'll carry the English lungs above Teuton feet that can walk forever; and he will wave long, thin, bony, Yankee hands with the big blue veins on the wrist, from one end of the earth to the other. He'll be the finest writer, poet, and dramatist, especially dramatist, that the world as it recollects itself has ever seen. By virtue of his Jew blood . . . he'll be a musician and a painter too . . . He will be a complex and highly composite administrator . . ."[50] It is nice to think that English upper-class snobbery and philistinism could then wring from the young Kipling so unabashed an eulogy of artistic creation. After that generous outburst, one is glad to think that his stay with Ted Hill's family and her sister Caroline's fulfilment of his admiration for American girlhood made such a happy climax to this first visit to the United States. Indeed most of what he saw this time on the Eastern seaboard delighted him, save for a literary colony that he visited with Professor Hill. The climax, perhaps, was a successful interview with his hero, Mark Twain, although, characteristically, when *A Connecticut Yankee at King Arthur's Court* appeared at this time, Kipling was quoted by American newspapers as receiving it unfavourably. Facetious treatment of English history was not what Kipling wanted from the man he revered as the creator of Huck Finn and Tom Sawyer. And, of course, he was right.

When, then, in February 1892, Kipling arrived in New York on the first leg of an indefinite honeymoon long trail, he was face to face with a familiar love–hate, but the accent was strongly on the love. Except for New York. New York was never to be to his liking, how could it be, with its sense of impermanence, its cosmopolitanism? Now his former dislike for its lawlessness is formulated more fully. The city has become "the shiftless outcome of squalid barbarism and reckless extravagance".[51]

But, in any case, the whole renewal of the American experience was only to be momentary – a short stop to see those of Carrie's family who had not met Rudyard and then on – on the trail. The Kiplings seem to have had no firm plans beyond their honeymoon journey. Both England and America had family associations that were as

176

daunting as they were welcoming. The main thing was that life was opening up for both of them, not only with all the family prospects of marriage but with all the green signals now showing for a spectacular literary career before Rudyard. At the same time marriage brought down for both no doubt – but we are concerned primarily with him – safety curtains against a possible roving, lonely open future as terrifying as it had at times seemed tempting to him. The marriage of a young man with prospects often has this double aspect. But few men can have needed a mainstay as Kipling did, for, if he dreamed sweet dreams, he was also possessed by terrible nightmares. In Carrie, there is no doubt, Rudyard found the firmest of anchors, but he also found a partner whose own nerves were often taut from the bleakness of the world she saw around her.

The newlyweds made a short trip (only a three-day stay) not to Rochester, the upstate New York industrial city, where Carrie and Wolcott had been born and bred, but to the Balestier family stronghold in Vermont, to Brattleboro. The town, until somewhat after the Civil War, was a much-frequented spa, many of whose visitors were wealthy families from the Southern States. With the decline of Southern mercantile wealth and of the fashion for hydrotherapy, Brattleboro became popular as an excursion centre for New Yorkers visiting the Vermont hill country. Main Street still has many buildings of Kipling's day, and many more typical of the American small town of the twenties and thirties. The prominent Freemasons' Lodge must have been much the same when he attended as now. The railway station is recognisably the one he used. The street is dominated by Brook's Hotel which in the heyday of the spa accommodated luxury-class visitors. Renovated much since then, it still has that late mid-nineteenth-century French château look which we associate with big seaside hotels in England. At that time it would, somewhat incongruously but charmingly, have had a New-Orleans-style cast-iron verandah and first-floor balcony. The street is not beautiful, but few American small-town main streets are. It would have been more beautiful then, but not, I think, to Kipling.

What certainly captivated him in 1892, as it must any visitor today, is the glorious hill and wood country in which Brattleboro is situated and through which runs the fine Connecticut River. I can bear witness to the enchantment of the setting. For this was my first visit to the upper New England states, to Maine, New Hampshire and Vermont. I have, in any case, a prejudice in favour of the Pacific coast or the Southern states of America; and I had heard such extravagant praises of the reds and yellows of the maples of New England in the fall that I

177

approached the whole journey with scepticism. I do not easily recall such immediate enchantment as that scene provided. And the visit to Brattleboro came after Maine and most of Vermont when I thought my enthusiasm had been exhausted. It was not so. Not, that is, three or four miles outside of town, just across the parish line in Dummerston.

Here Madame Balestier then lived in Beechwood, one of those large elegant colonial-style houses (built in fact in 1868) which make the countryside of the East of the United States the one part of the world where imitative architecture has brought not vulgarity or whimsy but elegance. The large house stands today as it must have done then, as almost all American farms or country houses or suburban homes stand, surrounded by open garden and meadow. For an Englishman the first surprise of living in an American suburb or village is the openness to neighbours of one's daily life. It makes a walk through an American suburb a delight to the passer-by – the garden and house are laid open to public view, by contrast to an England hidden behind hedges and fences. This openness and neighbourliness always delights me after England's daunting privacies – at least over two months or so ... I do not think that it was ever a delight to Kipling.

But the first thing that strikes one at Beechwood is not the house or the meadows or the garden, but the stunning view across wooded hills to Mount Monadnock. Here Rudyard and Carrie were driven by her lively, hospitable, hearty younger brother, Beatty, on their arrival on 12 February in a 30 below zero snow-storm. Beatty was but two years married and lived in a house called Maplewood on his grandmother's estate. Here the Kiplings stayed for their first three-day visit. Kipling, in his new carefreeness, was exhilarated by the weather which was of a kind quite outside his experience, and then, when the snow cleared, overwhelmed by the beauty of the view in the cold sparkling air. He and Carrie agreed that they must have some part in this scene. At first Beatty wished to make them a wedding present of some acres of his own. But Carrie, knowing her brother's insecure financial circumstances, with a wife and a small girl, dependent in great degree on Madame Balestier's indulgence towards her charming youngest grandchild, insisted on a legal purchase giving the Kiplings ten acres to which Beatty reserved the pasture rights. It was a three-day visit of one young couple to another young couple's home, given extra delight to Rudyard by the presence of a child. Too short for Carrie and her new sister-in-law, Mai, to feel anything but the communication each to the other of her own wedded happiness. As to Mount Monadnock,

37 Caroline Balestier

38 Caroline Balestier before her marriage to Kipling in 1892. (*Bateman's*)

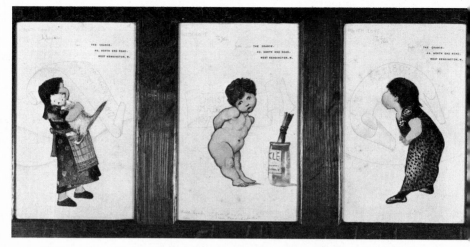

39 Sketches of the three Kipling children by Sir Edward Burne-Jones, made in 1897. (*Bateman's*)

40 The three Kipling children in London, 1898. (*Bateman's*)

41 Kipling by Shepheard. (*By kind permission of the Kipling Society*)

42 Architect's drawing of the eastern elevation of Naulakha, the house in Vermont designed for the Kiplings in 1892. (*Howard C. Rice*)

43 Kipling clearing rubbish away from his new well. This drawing, published in the *Boston Sunday Globe*, was made from an unauthorized photograph taken by one of the well-digging crew. (*Howard C. Rice*)

44 Main Street, Brattleboro, Vermont. (*Howard C. Rice*)

45 Kipling's study at Naulakha. The inscription above the fireplace –
"The Night cometh when no man can work" – was modelled in plaster
by Lockwood Kipling when he visited Rudyard in 1893. The plaster casts
on the mantel shelf were a gift from Joel Chandler Harris. (*Howard C.
Rice*)

46 Kipling in his study at Naulakha. (*Library of Congress*)

47 Sketches by John Lockwood Kipling made during his son's convalescence, Lakewood, New Jersey, 24 April 1899. (*Doubleday Collection, Princeton University Library*)

so loved of Emerson, one of Kipling's idols since schooltime, they would find there a holiday home? a fishing hideaway? At any rate, a place where they could repeat, whenever they wished, this idyllic visit.

Now they went on their way. Up from New York through the near mid-West, that Kipling already knew, in order to cross into Canada. In the articles he then wrote of America, love was certainly predominant in the love–hate mixture. Yet already, before they crossed over into Canada, a little British note creeps into his comments. In St Paul, Minnesota (far south from his post, one would have thought), "A man of the Canadian mounted police swaggers through with his black fur cap ... his well-fitting overalls, his better set-up back. One wants to shake hands with him because he is clean and does not slouch or spit, trims his hair, and walks as a man should." [52] "It's Oh to Meet an Army man who ... hogs his bristles short!" [53] in fact. It is the first time that Canada registers as a centre of value. The impression was to last as they crossed by the Canadian Pacific Railway through the Rockies from Winnipeg to Vancouver. It survived the discovery there that the young man who had sold him land in 1889 had sold him a pup. Indeed, Canada, despite set-backs Kipling attributed usually to French-Canadian interest, was of all the Imperial or Anglo-Saxon hopes of Kipling's life the most lasting. It was not only her response to England's call in the Boer War and in the Great War, other white colonies and his beloved Indians could show that. It was, I think, her constant resistance to the siren voice of the States that, despite all the disappointments over British immigration discouraged or Imperial preferences unfulfilled, kept Canada a constant source of hope to Kipling's political dreams.

But now he and Carrie left Vancouver for Japan to stay with friends in Yokohama. Here, to his great pleasure, Carrie was as distinguished a guest, as the granddaughter of Japan's legal adviser, as Rudyard himself – something all too rare in the long years ahead as Rudyard's fame grew and grew. But here also something happened that not only brought the indefinite long trail to an end, but which was markedly to decide the balance of the Kiplings' future married life.

One day in Yokohama, as he tells us in his autobiography, he went into the local branch of his bank, the Oriental Banking Company, to draw the equivalent of £10. When the manager urged that it might be convenient to take more, "I answered that I did not care to have too much cash at any one time in my careless keeping, but that when I looked over my accounts I might come in again in the afternoon. I did so, but in that little space my bank, the notice on its shut door explained, had suspended payment." The loss was total. Cook's happily refunded their fares. The Canadian Pacific Railway took them back across Canada free of charge. His credit was excellent. His work was in high demand, the future rosy. But the fact was that for the moment they were broke. When they returned to Carrie's family they were not the glamorous pair who had set out upon that magic journey that had no special end, but might possibly take in a visit to the famous Robert Louis Stevenson. On the contrary, they were a penniless couple, the Balestier girl with her English-fangled ways and her unknown husband whose occupation was the mysterious idle one of writing. They had come to live upon the charity of Madame Balestier and her family, who, in any case, were strangers of French origin and high and mighty ways who dressed for dinner and drank wine, and lived in an unneighbourly manner beyond the town boundaries. Save, of course, for Beatty, the good mixer.

Kipling, in his autobiography, makes it clear that this was how he felt the folk of Brattleboro looked upon him and Carrie; and he is surely largely right. It is unlikely, however, that the Kiplings were at all aware of this as they spent the first idyllic year of their marriage in little Bliss cottage, usually a hired man's house, leased from Carrie's mother. To crown that blissful dawn and make it very heaven for Rudyard, a daughter was born to them – Josephine, his best beloved.

He did not work much and it is pleasing to note that this slave to the work ethic was happy in idleness and this haunted man could lie peaceful without dreams demanding to be turned into art. Money, however, was not slow to come in, always in larger sums as his sales leaped ahead. For Carrie Kipling, however, orderliness and economy seemed natural. And now she, who had, after all, suffered a honeymoon of failed land speculation and failure of bank credit, took charge not only of household accounts but of all expenditure. She also took on in these earlier days a good deal of business correspondence – where she showed herself not only a good businesswoman, but, from the few of her business letters I have seen in collections in America, a friendly, tactful, concerned but firm correspondent with publishers and magazine editors.

Although Rudyard, to a great degree, handed over what he calls the "ways and means", the Yokohama incident must have further weighted the balance in himself against the gipsy and in favour of the prudent, hardworking heir of Methodist forbears, though the conflict was never resolved. It seems likely that, as time went by, he associated the insecure gipsy with his old journalistic days, for he spoke to a journalist friend in South Africa of the profession's "training to prevent the formation of habits of thrift, to make men careless of the future".[54] When he spoke to the Savings Committee at Folkestone in 1918, he said, "It takes something of a man to save, and the more he saves the more of a man it makes him."[55] And as Rector of St Andrew's University (an honour he found most congenial), he said in 1923, "May I take it that you, for the most part, come as I did, from households conversant with economic strictness which have taught us to look at both sides of the family shilling."[56] In his 1918 Savings speech he remarks, "The man who says he never worries about money is the man who has to worry about it most in the long run."[57] And, as late as 1932, a man squandered and fallen to Rowton House doss-house level is among the souls in the Purgatory Station of "Uncovenanted Mercies". Between economy and penury there seems little choice. Yet the habit of economy does not appear natural. In Kipling's account, it would lose its character-building value if it were. It is just one more of the disciplines needed in order to come through.

Carrie remained throughout, then, even after the advent of secretaries, as strict a supervisor of the business side of Kipling's literary life as she was a strict, "difficult", and Victorian manager of the household with its many domestic servants – cooks, nursemaids, hired men – that began to enter the Kiplings' life as soon as their fortunes expanded. From now, perhaps, begins to build up the image of a wife-dominated ménage, which Rudyard seems often to have fostered, for example in his remark to their Brattleboro friend, Miss Cabot, when she asked to what hotel they were going in New York – "Why bless you, I don't know. I'm no more than a cork on the water when Carrie is with me."[58]

They began, at once, to build upon the plot they had bought from Beatty. Henry Rutgers Marshall, the architect they employed, was not the happiest of choices. He was the sort of nineties "original" architect who had all the idiosyncratic urge of a Frank Lloyd Wright or a Philip Webb without the genius of the first or the high talent of the second. In addition, Kipling himself imposed upon the house the general features of a great ship towering above the wooded pastures.

The house was named Naulakha to honour Wolcott, but with the spelling corrected from the one passed for the title of their novel by Wolcott, who was unfamiliar with the Indian name (nine lakhs of rupees) Rudyard had chosen. The view towards Mount Monadnock is superb, but beside the gracious openness of the conventional colonial mansion "Beechwood", opposite down the hill, the Kipling house must always have seemed like a fortress on the hill, even before the present un-American hedges grew to the great secretive height they have today. Inside, the casual visitor (or, indeed, the appointed one) had to run Carrie's guardianship of all ways that led to Rudyard's study. Formidable privacy to the stranger without the gates, it must have been idyllic for the writer within, who had a great deal to get onto paper.

The years from 1893 to 1895 are richly productive years for Kipling. They produced one of the most splendid of the Indian administrative stories, "The Bridge Builders", and all the great Mowgli stories. At last, by 1895, the Indian vein seems to be wearing a little thin. "William the Conqueror", a tale of famine in South India, is only a pale reflection of his previous tributes to the administrator engineers Orde and Findlayson. It was written for the American *Ladies' Home Journal* to introduce a new type of heroine to them. Yet curiously it seems more like a tribute not to the memsahibs but to the intrepid, easy-going, boyish American girls he much admired – to the memory of Ted Hill, it is said, but I wonder if it is not a tribute to his own wife's staying power and guts, for if Carrie's figure was far from boyish, she had (as Henry James and her father-in-law had both seen) a man's courage and tenacity that had already served Kipling well in a financial emergency where a more feminine Victorian girl would have been helpless. But the Indian impulse had still to give its fullest power: he began at Naulakha to work on *Kim*.

It seems clear that, in the beautiful features of his Vermont home with a vegetation, a climate and an animal life totally remote from India, he was able at last to abstract himself from all the crowding particularities of his Indian memories and to envisage great symbolic scenes – the ravaged tombs of Cold Lairs, the gathering of the Hindu Gods at the riverside or of the horrible predators on the sandbank, the jungle in the time of drought, the massacre of the dholes or yellow dogs, and from there to return in *Kim* to Indian humanity, but without the claustrophobia of barrack or club room or dak bungalow, to see India's people entire on the Great Trunk Road. The last vestiges of the gossipy or the know-all voice which sometimes prevents the Indian stories from moving into the world of poetry, have gone. A visionary takes over, but with a vision that, unlike some of his more prophetic political poems, has no impeding echo of the Old Testament to come between the reader and the life of what is seen. Nor, as with too many later "dream" stories like "The Brushwood Boy" or "They", a vision flawed with whimsy or self-pity. It is the crown of his great Indian work and, however disastrous the experiment of American living was to prove to be, its remoteness from all that was English as well as all that was Indian made that culmination possible. After the Mowgli stories and *Kim* his vision was only once again to acquire such intensity and, more important, such homogeneity, a sense of a world seen in separate dreams that yet make a whole, and this was to be in the best of the *Puck* stories. After that, he produced great stories, fine verses, but they were always fragmented, unattached, lonely works of art.

The Vermont years, too, produced some fine verses, especially the continuation of the army poems in the second lot of *Barrack Room Ballads*. These still echo India, though in at least two there is a sharp rebuke to what he had seen in England of the neglect of the ex-soldier who had fought for her:

> A man o' four and twenty that 'asn't learned of a trade –
> Beside "Reserve" agin' him – 'e'd better be never made
> I tried my luck for a quarter, and that was enough for me,
> An' I thought of 'Er Majesty's barricks, an' I thought
>   I'd go an' see.
> Back to the Army again, sergeant,
> Back to the Army again.
> 'Tisn't my fault if I dress when I 'alt –
> I'm back to the Army again.[59]

and:

> So if me you be'old
> In the wet and the cold,
> By the Grand Metropold, won't you give me a letter?
> Give 'im a letter –
> Can't do no better
> Late Troop Sergeant-Major an' – runds with a letter!
> Think what 'e's been
> Think what 'e's seen.
> Think of 'is pension an'
> Gawd save the Queen![60]

Kipling's radicalism was still strongest when it came to civilian treatment of the army. And so was his sense of man's desolate lot. There is no doubt of Kipling's personal happiness in those first Naulakha years, in his wife, in his baby girl, in the affairs of the farm, in the unfamiliar wild flowers and birds, in physical exercise – driving and snow-golf and fishing – in his growing but happily distantly heard fame. Yet two of the best of these late Barrack Room Ballads offer sad alternatives to men:

I've taken my fun where I found it,
And now I must pay for my fun,
For the more you 'ave known o' the others
The less you will settle to one;
And the end of it's sittin' and thinkin',
An' dreamin' Hell-fires to see.[61]

or "The Sergeant's Weddin'":

Escort to the Kerridge,
Wish 'im luck, the brute!
Chuck the slippers after –
(Pity 'taint a boot!)
Bowin' like a lady,
Blushin' like a lad,
'Oo would say to see 'em
Both is rotten bad?

Beside the intensity of the great Indian fables and the bitter music-hall jauntiness or lament of the ballads, the material that Kipling got from America itself is thin. Much of his spare outdoor time at Naulakha was given to horses – to carriage-driving with Carrie, to attending to the salting of the horses with his brother-in-law, Beatty. Carriage-driving, of course, was not new, he had had his horse and trap, the Pig and Whistle, at Allahabad, but the atmosphere of the Vermont countryside life was essentially horsey. Out of this came his fable about American labour politics, "A Walking Delegate". This conversation-piece among horses, where the agitator from the Far West is shown up for an empty braggart, has been praised for its comprehension of the various American dialects spoken by the horses. It may be true to American speech of the early nineties, but the spellings seem to me to bear only a marginal relationship to the accents of the South, New England, New York, the West and so on of today. Certainly the political observation appears to be superficial, though vehemently felt.

But the light that "A Walking Delegate" throws upon Kipling's art goes deeper, for it shares its failure with one of the few really unsuccessful *Jungle Book* tales, "Her Majesty's Servants", a conversation between horses, mules, camels and elephants of the Indian Army. Why are these stories so inferior to those which deal with wild animals, even the lesser ones that concern animals remote from Kipling's knowledge like the arctic animals of "The White Seal"? I believe it is because his imagination is too much reined by the failure of "place" to set him free from the world of his daily life, of his conscious adult life. Mowgli's jungle works, because it frees Kipling, and it works at its fullest when, like a child's imagination, like Muhammad Din's as he plays in the bungalow garden, Kipling's fancy can find a small place to make the universe. It is not necessary, however, that Kipling's creation of his men-animals should take place in the wild. "Rikki Tikki Tavi" is good and authentic, for though the mongoose and snakes live around and under the human house, they are wild creatures, and it is exactly those wild creatures that live secretly in his own domain that most fill a child's imagination. I remember how the snakes and the rats beneath a South African house, built on stilts against white ants, filled my dreams as a boy, for they had their own life, were only occasionally glimpsed and yet were there. Hence surely the power of rabbits until quite recently in children's stories; and, despite their diminution in numbers, the extraordinary success of *Watership Down*. The more this child's transformation of place seeps into Kipling's great animal fables for adults, the better it works. Hence the success of later political animal fables like "The Mother Hive", where the mysterious life of the bees that fill the hive in his garden works into the human social lesson he preaches, giving it a looseness, a life which otherwise might be strangled by the confines of the political sermon; or even in "Beyond the Mill Dam", which gives life as a child might to the hidden place where on Kipling's own estate the Black Rat and the Cat live out their secret lives by the rotting mill-wheel. This sense of a secret world known only to the author and the animals, a secret imparted by the creation of a small total world from the territory of animals, is lacking when animals are too domestic, too bound up with the lives and purposes of men – it accounts for the failure of Kipling's attempts in his last years to bring alive the world of dogs in *Thy Servant – A Dog*.

In such stories as "The Walking Delegate", however, the horses are alone, yet their paddock has no secret from man and the illusion doesn't work. That the political fable itself is probably based upon insufficient knowledge of American life is not important, I believe; political fables are simplistic things and need no elaborate detailed knowledge. They cut most deeply where prejudice is strongest, and Kipling's prejudice against American labour leaders was very strong. No, the failure of America finally to act upon Kipling's mind is seen, I think, in his failure to produce a fable from the wild life, although it fascinated him greatly. Perhaps, if he had been able as he wished to find some way of keeping beavers at Naulakha, he would have found the secret world to embody his feelings. The American natural scene had to wait fifteen years before it was truly celebrated in his story, "Brother Square Toes". And, ironically, this was a celebration of the Amish Lancaster county of Pennsylvania, Caroline Taylor's and Ted Hill's state, not of Vermont, where he had hoped to make a life among Carrie's people.

Kipling also produced at this time two stories in which engines and parts of engines are given an independent life, or rather a life dependent upon each other, to serve, in each case, as an allegory for human society. I have seen these two stories praised highly by engineers, sailors and railway men. Indeed, while I have been writing this book, I have received a letter from a train driver stressing the value of this part of Kipling's work. No doubt, for my correspondent, Kipling's story of American locomotives, "007", works well; and for ships' engineers, his dialogue between the machine parts of a steamship, "The Ship That Found Herself", is a delight. But this satisfaction of the specialists cannot hide the fact that in "007" and "The Ship That Found Herself" we have information without the illusion of life.

Kipling's concern with machines is very interesting in itself, for it looks to be a foretaste of a literary movement at first sight very remote from him – the Italian Futurist movement of the first decades of the twentieth century. Yet it is not so remote as it would seem. Marinetti and his followers were romantic defenders of Italy's Imperial conquests in North Africa, and Kipling, at the end of his life, like many another right-wing staunch opponent of Hitler, was an outspoken supporter of the Italian cause in Abyssinia. Marinetti and his followers sang paeans of praise to death in battle, to the music of guns, that are both sillier and more romantic than anything Kipling could have produced even in his most romantic-aggressive mood in London in 1890. Yet to deny all connection between his thinking and that of the Futurists would be mistaken, I think. Although much of the style of the writers who heralded Mussolini's Italy has a scented, flowery romantic flavour beside Kipling's writing, there is much that he would have found attractive in it. In a letter to William Heinemann, he speaks of his admiration for D'Annunzio.[62] And in his library at Bateman's there is a copy of Marinetti's *La Bataille de Tripoli*, published in French in Milan (1912), where we read, "la guerre seule hygiène du monde et seule morale éducatrice".

Yet we have only to look at the work of the Futurists to see how totally different is their glorification of machines from Kipling's interest in them. One side of Kipling wanted to be rid of what he thought a dead part of contemporary civilisation. And machines may have seemed to him the phenomenon that could sweep complacency away. But far more of him was traditional, and machines appealed to him as instruments of greater order, not as the romantic destructive forces the Futurists lyricised. Equally, Marinetti and his followers exalted machinery above human values. This would have been as repugnant to Kipling as it would have seemed ridiculous. In his poem, "The Secret of the Machines", after celebrating all that modern machinery can do:

> We can pull and haul and push and lift and drive,
> We can print and plough and weave and heat and light,
> We can run and race and swim and fly and dive,
> We can see and hear and count and read and write!

he adds explicitly:

> But, remember, please, the Law by which we live,
> We are not built to comprehend a lie,
> ... If you make a slip in handling us, you die!
> ... We are nothing more than children of your brain.

It is only because Marinetti and his followers hold an extreme view of art as an autonomous value that they are able to exalt machines as they do. Yet their aesthetic approach to machinery produces, as well as much bombast, some genuine lyricism. Kipling's position is both more honourable and more sensible, but, on the whole, it makes him less able to use machines as an independent subject for fable as in "007" or "The Ship That Found Herself". The trains, like the horses, may echo man's arguments, and the parts of the ship may act out a play that recalls the interdependence of men in a well-ordered society, but the fable doesn't work in any of the three cases, for Kipling is merely using man-controlled creatures – steam-engines, pistons, dynamos, plough-horses, carriage-horses – to illustrate human truths. The illustration is simply reduplicative and destroys the imagination, whereas wild animals living out their mysterious lives may be moulded into human actions and each is strengthened by the other.

The only successful treatment of ships during this American period of his life is the story "The Devil and the Deep Blue Sea", which uses modern piracy as a gesture of disdain for the world as it is organised (whether in London's salons or New York's offices or Brattleboro's main street). This is a recurrent gesture of Kipling's when he feels oppressed. The story has perhaps the most casual-seeming terrible ending of any in his work. But the finest celebrations of machines are to be found in his two imitation Browning monologue poems, "McAndrew's Hymn" (1893) and "The Mary Gloster" (1894). And here he celebrates not the machines, but the men who work them – a Scots ship's engineer and a hard old, tough-living, rich shipowner on his deathbed. Both are positive hymns to the life force. They work perfectly. And one sees well why a man who could encompass the whole meaning of an individual life in a single poem would find the intricacies and necessary *longueurs* of novel-writing uncongenial.

The celebration of the ruthless life-force of a self-made man in "The Mary Gloster" is really the only work of these Vermont years that fully suggests any strong influence from his newly adopted country, even though the self-made man of the poem is an Englishman.

Admiration for the self-made American industrialist, indeed, is one of the two central themes of his only purely American work of distinction, *Captains Courageous*. This novel, in which the spoiled American boy who had so disgusted him on his journey from Calcutta to San Francisco in 1889 is redeemed in the person of the hero, Harvey Cheyne, is, if marred by a little too much undigested technicality about cod-fishing, Kipling's one book that can truly be called "a book for boys". It is filled with a real love of the vigour and mixedness of America as represented by the cod-fishermen with their various national origins (including a Negro) and by the spoiled boy's self-made millionaire father, as it is by hostility to American lawlessness and self-indulgence as exemplified by Harvey's spoiled upbringing by his mother.

In February 1896 Kipling made some fact-finding trips for this book with his Brattleboro doctor friend, Conland, to Gloucester, Massachusetts and to Boston where the cod fleets lay at anchor. These were his happiest American days, but also some of his last American days, for by the end of August he had left America in distress.

It is clear, looking back, that the attempt of the Kiplings to make their life in Carrie's native country was doomed from the start. We can trace rumblings of the earthquake that broke the ground beneath their feet back to the second year of their stay – but when the break came, it came suddenly and violently. How did it happen?

First, it must be said that if Kipling was in love with the Vermont scene and the peace it gave him, he was never in love with the society around him. A letter to W. E. Henley as early as October 1892 shows this: "Never you mind about my being in America. If you saw this life of ours and didn't happen to know your geography, it could be Africa or Australia – or another planet. I have what I need – sunshine and a mind at ease, peace and my own time for my own work and the real earth within reach of my hand, whenever I tire of messing with ink. Good stuff will come out of this in God's time and if nothing comes then I shall have led a sane clean life at the least and found new experiences. Half my time in town [i.e. London] was spent in hearing and telling how good work was to be done, which is extremely interesting so long as you have not much to do. The farmers here do exactly what I did, but their club is the lee side of a barn door, and their art the how and why of farming. Therefore are their fences gapped and therefore do mortgages come upon them, and their young stock die. There is no very great difference between men after all." [63] And by January 1893 he is writing more directly: "Me and the aborigines are excellent friends but they can't understand why I don't come to chicken suppers and church sociables and turkey sprees. The farmers are delicious but there is a local society by the side of which Pogrom, Scudder and the others [unamiable characters from the American chapters of *Martin Chuzzlewit*] are pale and watery shadows. Dickens never did better work than his *American Notes* and the more I get to know the land, the more do I stand astounded at my own moderation ... The moral dry rot of it all is having no law that need be obeyed; no line to toe; no trace to kick over and no compulsion to do anything. By consequence, a certain defect runs through everything ... all innacurate, all slovenly, all out of plumb and untrue ... barbarism plus telephone, electric light, rail and suffrage; but all the more terrible for that reason. I like it. When I have done with seeing what I want to see, I shall be in possession of a few interesting facts. Then, O Henley, the band will begin to play." [64]

It never did, of course. Despite the later stories of individual loved–hated Americans in England, or in the South African War, or in the Great War that were to be among the most bitter attacks in his work, America itself figured no more than the little I have discussed. What silenced him? Was it his continuing hope for America's adhesion to an Anglo-Saxon civilising world mission? I doubt this, for his anger at American failure to cooperate in the coming years was often very great. Was it a sense that this was his wife's country to be respected as such? A little, perhaps. Was it the extremely strong ties of friendship he had had with a few Americans? Ted Hill from the past; Dr Conland and Miss Cabot in Vermont; Uncle Ned's old friend, the critic, Charles Eliot Norton, the New England literary mandarin whom he placed alongside his uncle and father as his mentors in life (yet his doubts about the old New England cultural élite were as strong as those about the pre-Raphaelites); Theodore Roosevelt and John Hay, the American politicians in whom he saw hopes for his world dream;

Julia Catlin and her daughters, first met on holiday from Vermont in Bermuda, holiday friends who became very close and were later a special tie with their beloved France; Sam McClure, the magazine editor; and, above all, of course, Frank Doubleday, his publisher and warm friend. Certainly, as so often happens with Englishmen who go to the United States, the individual friendships he brought back were some of the strongest in his life, but I doubt if they could have withstood Kipling's daemon.

No, I think the anger as much as the love for America remained to the end and found occasional voice in outstanding stories and poems. But America itself, the feel of the place, the world in which his Naulakha fortress was set, faded away after a year or so's nostalgia once he returned to England. And his letter to Henley suggests why: he had work to get on with – the *Jungle Books*, *Kim*, the *Barrack Room Ballads*. For four and a half years he lived on American soil but his imagination was still in India. He resented the intrusion of his neighbours who wished to welcome him to their country and its ways. In any story of Kipling's a man so situated, so blind to the society he depended on, would have to face Nemesis. And so Kipling, and his wife, who had her own dislike for the Vermont scene, did.

But Naulakha was not only a stronghold for keeping the local society of Elijah Progrom and Scudder out, it was also a fortress to be held against the invasion of the American press which his growing celebrity inevitably invited. Nor were his own sharp journalistic comments, past or present, calculated to make their incursions more friendly. Stories abound of the Kiplings' war against American reporters' invasions – in particular of one woman journalist taken exhausted from the winter's snows and cossetted when she was thought to be an innocent traveller, but turned out again into the blizzard when she proved to be a prying reporter. It is true that the Kiplings' great natural generosity of heart turned to stone when anyone intruded on their privacy; and their American experience petrified this attitude in them for the rest of their lives. Already in the letter just quoted, Kipling writes to Henley of American reporters: "They can by merely writing about it, knock all the beauty, honour, wit, wisdom and reverence out of everything in the world, and leave behind only the smell of an over-heated ante-room or of a hollow booth. Yet, individually heaps of them are fascinating." [65]

He wanted America, especially, I think, its independent and irreverent qualities, as a counterpoise to the dead, stuffy world he found in England. He sought again in the United States the refreshment he had found in Wolcott Balestier in his London misery. Even in his most

190

hostile poem, "An American" (1894), (an atrociously bad piece of work) he sees the nation saved and destroyed by its humour:

> But through the shift of mood and mood,
> Mine ancient humour saves him whole –
> The cynic devil in his blood
> That bids him mock his hurrying soul;
> That bids him flout the Law he makes,
> That bids him make the Law he flouts . . .
> That checks him foolish – hot and fond,
> That chuckles through his deepest ire,
> That gilds the slough of his despond
> But dims the goal of his desire.

Paradoxically, it was the roving, gipsy side of him that hoped to be satisfied in the vast world of the United States, yet he settled there as a married man among small-town folks – and wanted to be left alone. It was certainly not to be. As he once complained, America knew neither liberty nor equality, only fraternity.[66] The "goodfellow" was the bane of the American nation – there were the reporters and the locals and the New York visitors to Brattleboro all wanting to be matey with this new celebrity.

The pressures upon him came from without and from within his little Vermont world, and when they coincided it was too much for him. And his revulsion was ironically reinforced by his experience of England in 1894 and 1895, when he had spent holidays short enough and yet long enough to taste the pleasures only of parental company in retirement and to know London only as a place where he now received honours that with his English traditional inheritance could never be equalled in his eyes by the most immense fame in New York or Washington.

In any case, he was sarcastic about the New York literary world when he went there in 1893: "They have an intensely literary society there – same old names cropping up week after week at the same old parties, same old gags; same old dishwater as it might be in any city we could name – allowing for local colour and the necessity of Creating the Great American Literature."[67] As for Washington and the political scene, when Carrie was convalescing from a serious stove-scalding, they stayed there in spring 1895. Rudyard was entertained at the White House by President Cleveland – "reeking bounders", he found the Presidential company.

And, at last in the summer of 1895, the two storms burst together.

Nationally, the United States became involved in a dispute with Great Britain over the Venezuela/British Guiana frontier. Cleveland adopted an aggressive policy. Kipling's anger was only exceeded by his alarm. He confidently expected war. In his letters of that time, he speaks of preparations to escape into Canada and of making provisions that would keep Carrie and his loved Josephine from starvation. To add to his alarms for his family, by the fall his wife was expecting another child – their daughter Elsie, born in February 1896. All through that autumn and winter, the Anglo-American row went on. And, of course, it spilled over into their local life. We read of him walking out of the house when even his close friend, Miss Cabot, retorted sharply to his harping on the British Navy's capability of taking New York. The friendship of Dr Conland, who delivered Elsie, must have been most precious to him at this time and the visits to the cod fleet to research *Captains Courageous* a heaven-sent relief.

All this Anglo-American tension, no doubt, played its part in heating up the row with his brother-in-law, Beatty, which had been brooding for at least a year. Basically, it was Carrie's row with her brother (or possibly more with her sister-in-law). Beatty was becoming more and more irked at his growing dependence on the Kiplings, partly through their "friends' agreement" over the land, partly through the need he was in to accept paid jobs from them. Carrie, in her turn, a hard worker who was therefore a hard mistress, was more and more unwilling to put up with her brother's slovenly work and easy-going drunken idleness, especially no doubt because they were at her husband's expense. Carrington's notes of Carrie's diaries show her recording each minute payment that she makes to her brother. Both the Kiplings tended to think that Beatty was an absurdly irresponsible child. But in Brattleboro he was seen as a good mixer, a good guy – and so from all accounts he was, outside those who had business dealings with him. But not for Carrie, whose sense of responsibility, as well as decorum and a touch of puritanism, he outraged.

Relations had begun well. When Conan Doyle came with his brother to stay with the Kiplings, they ate Thanksgiving dinner in 1893 at Beatty's house – for Thanksgiving is a time for American hospitality as any visitor knows, but also for fraternity and mixing. It is to be noted that Conan Doyle, who liked the Kiplings, had nevertheless come in part to beg Rudyard to moderate his criticisms of America. But then Conan Doyle enjoyed lecturing to the Americans as they loved to hear him, whereas Kipling told Major Pond, the lecture-tour impresario, that unless he was on his beam ends, he would never lecture and added, "America is a great country but she is not made for lecturing in." [68] By 1895, such visits to Beatty's house were a thing of the past, and the coolness even affected the Kiplings' relations with Carrie's grandmother. Locally people began to talk. In March 1896, Beatty brought shame upon them by petitioning to be made a bankrupt. In May, the famous scene took place between Rudyard and his brother-in-law. Beatty, driving in his carriage in the local lanes, met Rudyard on his bicycle and in the angry argument that followed, he threatened that he would kill him some day. The scene would be farce if it were not so sad. Unbelievably, and against all the teaching of Kipling's art, he turned it into a full farce by charging his brother-in-law before the court in Brattleboro the next morning with threats of murder.

At Beatty's trial which followed, Rudyard could only emerge in an absurd, even dubious, light.

"Were you afraid of being shot?"

"I had an objection to it." ...

"Ordinary business matters your wife takes care of?"

"Yes." [69]

There was much play with Carrie's fortune to come through her mother from Judge Smith, her grandfather. Kipling was driven into appearing to say that he had come to America to assist "the boy" (Beatty was only four years younger than himself). And he had clearly talked of Beatty in this way to a local colonel at Brook's Hotel ... "Oh! Beatty is his own worst enemy. I've been obliged to carry him for the last year, to hold him up by the seat of his breeches." [70]

When Beatty was remanded until the fall, Rudyard, unbelievably but with characteristic generosity, offered to go bail for him. Of course, Beatty found the bail himself. The national press didn't have to be malicious to harm the Kiplings now; and only the Boston *Globe* appears to have been so. As to Brattleboro, the ordinary citizens rejoiced to see folk who dressed for dinner (the old grievance against the Balestiers) and kept an English coachman in livery shown up in so poor a light. Beatty was the beloved prodigal son of everyone. Only some of the grander citizens backed Rudyard, their distinguished guest. The Kiplings did not wait for the fall, they packed up, said a tearful farewell to Dr Conant and their few friends and, on 29 August, they left for England. They returned to the United States only once in 1899 when tragedy overtook them there.

The Vermont episode is very strange and, in some ways, very illuminating about Kipling as an artist as well as a man. It is possible to sympathise a lot with him over his desire for privacy and his distaste for small-town life, yet it must also be said that he lived in a fantasy world when he supposed that he could set up a fortress in which to dream his wonderful Indian world in such a house as Naulakha, a few miles from Brattleboro, however lovely the setting. Perhaps all artists, certainly all romantic artists, have this capacity suddenly to become oblivious of the world around them. Yet it is peculiarly ironic in Rudyard Kipling because of the teaching of his writings. From some of the earliest Indian stories onwards characters who try to make their own law, to live for themselves, are surely punished. Aurelian McGoggin learned the lesson, so did Holden in the death of all beauty, and Wressley of the Foreign Office in years of wasted talent. And the theme was to remain with him.

I think that Kipling was gnawingly aware of the irony, but managed to suppress it by all the cunning in his possession (and he was a man who trained himself all his life to cunning). This, I think, is the explanation of "An Error in the Fourth Dimension" which he wrote while at Tisbury on a visit to his parents in 1894. This story has been much disliked as cruel. And, at first sight, it does seem a needlessly ruthless crushing of a pleasant butterfly. The story tells of a cultivated young New York millionaire's son, Wilton Sargent, who "set out to be a little more English than the English. He succeeded to admiration." He buys a large English country house to hold his collection of *objets d'art*, plays the cultivated squire and is a great addition to the county. Back in New York "they howled . . . that he was an unpatriotic Anglo-maniac". Everything goes well until, wanting suddenly to go to London, he flags the Express train that runs near the edge of his estate. Nemesis overtakes him in the form of British law and order that knows nothing of millionaires' whims. " 'Suppose you flagged the Empire State Express or the Western Cyclone?' . . . 'Suppose I did. I know Otis Harvey – or used to. I'd send him a wire, and he'd understand it was a ground-hog case with me. That's exactly what I told this British fossil company here.' " But England knows no such millionaire mateyness, no fraternities above the law. And Wilton is driven out. He returns to America, to the plushy, gadgety millionaire world of the Hudson River which was the Golden Age America Kipling had an especial love–hate for . . . "the twelve hundred ton ocean-going steam yacht Columbia, lying at her private pier, to take him to his office, at an average speed of seventeen knots – and the barges can look out for themselves – Wilton Sargent, American".

It's a beta-plus story in the measure of Kipling's art. But it surely throws light on Kipling's disquietude at his own position in America. By dwelling on the impossibility of "real" Americans settling in England it not only highlights the lawlessness he so hated in the country he had adopted, but in attacking a common feature of the nineties – the invasion of Europe by rich and cultivated Americans – it seems to banish thought of a rare case of the opposite – a celebrated Englishman making his home in the States. For Kipling was before his time.

Like Wilton Sargent, he was driven out of his ill-chosen Eden, though, unlike Wilton, he never perhaps truly settled down in his native paradise. The whole Vermont incident, working so strenuously against all his teaching, shows how, despite the loud and persistent voice of Kipling the social moralist, Kipling the dreamer and artist was a much stronger force. And for her part in plucking the apple, Carrie came into exile from her native land.

Before the curtain closes on the Kipling drama in the Land without Hedges so repugnant to their sense of privacy, I must just sketch the tragic New York epilogue of 1899 in which Mrs Kipling plays so heroic a role. The whole episode is so ironic, so impossible in our day, and finally so simply sad that it both holds the imagination and distracts the attention from any one of its aspects.

The Kiplings had found the wet, cold winter of England in 1896/7 very trying; Josephine, a very American girl, had not settled down. For Rudyard, with his Indian experience of the annual departure to the hill stations, a change of place once a year was natural. In January 1898, the Kiplings went to Cape Town in South Africa. But in 1899 they set off instead for the United States. Carrie had not seen her family for two and a half years, and now she had a baby son to show to her mother and to her sister Josephine. She was to pay cruelly for her natural desire.

The Atlantic crossing was a bitter, stormy winter one. Not long after their arrival, the children fell ill with whooping cough. Carrie herself was ill for a few days. Then, on 20 February, Rudyard became very ill with congestion of the lungs. All this in a New York hotel. When, early in Rudyard's illness, little Josephine came down with a high temperature, Carrie decided to send her to the Long Island house of their old Kipling family friend, Lockwood de Forest. Now Rudyard's illness reached its crisis and his doctors could give no hope for his life; then the crisis passed and he recovered. But, unknown to him for some time, little Josephine had died.

Carrie's competence and courage in such a crisis seem to be beyond praise; and, if in after years, as critics increasingly suggest, she was to become a limiting factor in her husband's life, it is well to remember how she met for him, in turn, the crisis of Wolcott's death, the bank failure, and the death of their loved daughter, aged nearly seven. Her position alone in the Grenoble Hotel with a desperately sick husband and a few miles away a daughter dying on Long Island and two other young children to care for also, was much alleviated by the devotion of many American friends; in particular Kipling's publisher Frank Doubleday (and, no doubt, by the presence of her sister and mother). She was well served medically, too.

But the horror was aggravated by three things – by the knowledge that Rudyard's last days had been made miserable by one of the wretched piracy struggles with American publishers, in this case Putnam's, which had for so long poisoned his relations with America; by the news that her brother Beatty had greeted their arrival by a statement to the Press that he intended to sue Rudyard (so much for good guys and good mixers); and, at the last, by the siege which she underwent in that nightmare hotel suite from newspaper reporters from all over the world.

It is this and the flood of telegrams that present so extraordinary a phenomenon to us today. It would not have happened if Kipling had fallen desperately ill only three years before. But in 1897 and 1898 he had written in turn "Recessional" and "The White Man's Burden", which I discuss in the next chapter. These poems had turned a popular, very well-known writer into a controversial figure of world fame.

Writers, it is true, had been the pop stars of the nineteenth century. Reporters had hung around the St James's Hotel in Jermyn Street, London in 1832 when Sir Walter Scott lay stricken there on his homeward journey to Abbotsford from his ill-fated European tour. The deaths of Dickens and of Tennyson hit every headline. Zola's involvement in the Dreyfus case and his flight to England, only the year before Kipling's New York illness, combined politics and literature as an international event. But the clamour that surrounded the Kipling agony at the Grenoble Hotel outdid them all. Never again was a writer to be such international news, save perhaps for Tolstoy's flight from his home, for though Bernard Shaw constantly hit the headlines, there was always something organised, some showmanship in his newsworthiness. In turn, boxers and pop stars were to take the headlines that Kipling had held. And, in a degree, not quite they, either, for Kipling's was the concern of the highest (the Kaiser) and the most highbrow (Henry James) as well as the world at large.

Every writer (everybody?) likes celebrity. I do not think that Kipling, before these events of February 1899, for all his occasional barking at reporters, was an exception. Perhaps, if Josephine had not died, the Kiplings would have recovered from being a world spectacle, even though it was an intrusion into their deepest private life. But, with no rejoicing possible, even when Rudyard recovered, the public interest became a horrible association with their darkest hour. Rudyard never got over Josephine's death, and became obsessed with the sanctity of privacy. But if Rudyard with all his resources felt so, what of Carrie, a reserved woman who had borne the main impact of these horrible weeks alone? It does much to explain what the world found difficult in her in later years.

Nor could they leave America until Rudyard had quite recovered. Lockwood came over to be with them; Watt, Kipling's agent, to help in sorting out the copyright quarrels. Rudyard, looked after by a splendid nurse, Margaret Ryerson, went to convalesce at a hotel in Lakewood, New Jersey. One may end the episode comparatively cheerfully by quoting a very characteristic letter, about the hotel waitress, to his publisher Frank Doubleday (his beloved "Effendi") which shows his resilience, at any rate on the surface: "I had a long talk with her. Waiting at table is *her* game and she tells me with pride how she can take eight different sets of orders at once and not mix 'em up in her mind. This is her point of pride and she speaks of it with the air of the craftswoman. Curious how all human nature's alike." [71]

The Kiplings never returned to the United States and Carrie only saw her mother again on their Canadian tour in 1907. The irony of Josephine's death in New York was fully apparent to Rudyard. In a letter of 31 July 1899 to his old friend Mrs Hill, when he had returned to England, he wrote: "I don't think it likely that I shall ever come back to America. My little Maid loved it dearly (she was almost entirely American in her ways of thinking and looking at things) and it was in New York that we lost her." [72]

4 UNDER-REHEARSED
FOR ARMAGEDDON

A first-class dress parade (The Boer War).

When Kipling returned to England in 1895, he was not the seven days' wonder of 1890, not the literary rocket whose imminent fall as a spent stick the critics were prophesying, not the haunted, overworked angry young man who had left on the long trail for Samoa in 1891, although inside him, of course, the conflicts were not resolved and were to find new artistic and political forms in the decades ahead.

Perhaps the most clearly positive result of his four years stay in America had been his changed attitude to England. Two of his best Jungle Book stories – the wonderfully repulsive "The Comforters", and his moving tribute to Hinduism, "The Miracle of Purun Bhagat" – were written when staying with his parents in their retirement. Here, too, he miraculously recaptured his obsessive dream of the land of the dunes in "The Brushwood Boy", although in writing the story when he returned to Vermont he incorporated an embarrassingly sentimental attitude to the mother he had left behind. Here in the humorous story, "My Sunday At Home", ostensibly a leg-pull of an over-solemn American doctor travelling in England, he wrote the first of those superb impressionistic Constable-like accounts of the English countryside caught in a particular moment of English weather.

There seems little doubt that he was immensely happy staying at his parents' house, despite his grumbles at the weather. It was a typical idyllic compromise between the patterns of life that were pulling at him: here he was, married and a father, yet the old safe, encouraging parental nest was still his to return to. Alice and Carrie, no doubt, found the life a strain, when Carrie accompanied her husband to Tisbury. Indeed, when the younger Kiplings returned to England, they never seemed to have contemplated settling near the old Kiplings at Tisbury. Rudyard took Carrie to London for expeditions during their

198

long 1894 visit, and the month's visit of 1895 was divided between Tisbury and London. In London, they stayed at Brown's Hotel, the scene of their wedding night, but also a typical compromise, for here stayed the country gentry on visits to London and also wealthy, cultivated Americans. We must remember how extremely American the Kiplings must have seemed in many ways. As late as March 1896, Rudyard's audience at the Anglo-African Writers' Club were struck by his American accent.

Yet now he also felt happy to dress up for all London occasions, to participate in the Season. Not only is he accepting being a celebrity in England as he could not accept being a literary figure in his bohemian days, but he does so with glee. There is something most touching in his letter to American friends, when he and Lord Roberts (the great Commander-in-Chief he had been privileged to ride with, his host at Simla's imposing Snowdon before whom he had acted for charity) were guests together at a Royal Academy banquet in 1894. Maybe his Uncle Poynter *was* Director of the National Gallery and his Uncle Ned, the great Burne-Jones, but *he* was there in his own right. "It was some fun as I am only twenty-nine." [1] How seldom did he permit himself the natural self-congratulation of triumphant youth! But I think there is more to Kipling's happy acceptance of London and Brown's in those holidays to England from Vermont.

Every man who is not to be a gipsy (and let us remember that, in, India's caste system which so much influenced Kipling in his view of society, gipsies are untouchables) needs his exact place in society; even writers if they are not to be bohemians (gipsies). In England, perhaps even today, but certainly up to 1939, this meant fitting into a class. Lockwood and Alice had in Tisbury (isolated and bleak though their house appears to be today) found a close, comforting, flattering society to live in range of. As Charles Carrington points out, the presence of the Percy Wyndhams (one of the influential families of the cultivated upper-class Souls) at Clouds nearby was like a continuation of, or rather a return to, those idyllic Simla days when the Dufferins reigned. Indeed, anyone who has driven up both the rhododendron-lined avenue leading to the fabulous neo-Jacobean Viceregal Lodge at Simla and the rhododendron-lined approach to Philip Webb's fabulous creation, Clouds, can tell how Alice's visits to the Wyndhams in her retirement must have brought back the golden days of Viceregal receptions and her *tête-à-tête* with Lord Dufferin. The Wyndhams, of course, were old friends through brother-in-law Ned. So far as I know, Kipling was on good terms with them but, when his father died at Clouds in 1911, he speaks of them particularly as friends of his parents. As he increasingly grew impatient with the Tory old guard's Imperial policy and Balfour's cultured *fainéantisme*, so he must have tolerated the Souls less easily.

In any case this was not the world he was looking for. He did not want to be any sort of aristocratic client. Neither of the Wyndhams nor of the Morrisons nearby at Fonthill, though he seems always to have been a good friend of Morrison and a book about William Beckford's Fonthill in his Bateman's library is almost as incongruous with the popular idea of Kipling as is Marinetti's tract.

But when he and Carrie "did" the London Season from Brown's in these years, I see in their conventionally dressed figures the social world in which they were eventually to find their place after 1903 – not the aristocracy, but the country gentry, a mixed body of landed families and retired colonial administrators, distinguished service officers and so on.

I remember seeing this world in top hats and frock coats, in picture hats and slightly dowdy smart dresses, at the Royal Academy Summer Exhibition when I was a London schoolboy in the late twenties – it was, by then, their swan-song. The men bronzed, some of the women evident ex-memsahibs, all, as my brother showed me, touched with "county", making their way across the road to Fortnum's to shop, but not, as they would even by the late thirties, returning that night to their homes by train or motor car. No, stopping, as their class had from early Victorian times, at a family hotel like Brown's, or, if they were men alone, at their clubs; not, as more middle-class professional people from the provinces might stay, at Kensington hotels; never, as the aristocratic neighbours of Alice and Lockwood at Tisbury, opening their London houses. There *is* a slight social backsliding in the Kiplings' London pattern, when in Jubilee Year of 1897, before the birth of their son, John, they stayed at a hotel in High Street, Kensington (the old family stamping-ground of his boyhood). But the normal London pattern of their life – not a place to live in but a place to accept when needed, of the world comfortably and decorously viewed from a suite in Brown's or from a window of the Athenaeum – seems in the main to have been established before they had discovered the country life that traditionally went with it. It is an important moment, for this life-style, when finally established, inevitably influenced Kipling's work as well as his day-to-day existence.

Their first choice of St Mary Church, in the environs of Torquay in Devon, was a disaster. They were homesick, especially Josephine, for America. Presumably Rudyard chose Devon out of love for his old schooldays – he wrote most of *Stalky & Co.* there. But the wet West

Country winter weather of 1896/7, however mild, was all that their New England acclimatized bodies most rebelled against. " 'Bloody British' is the only word for it," he wrote to Charles Eliot Norton, and added, "Torquay is such a place as I do desire acutely to upset by dancing through with nothing on but my spectacles." [2]

It was not the dead respectability of retired professional classes that Rudyard was seeking. Rock House, the place they had rented, mysteriously depressed them, but ultimately to some effect, for it produced nine years later his best psychic story, "The House Surgeon", Kipling tells us in his autobiography. By the summer of Jubilee Year the Kiplings had revolted and left Torquay, but they had not found yet their social identity. It was also at Dartmouth on the Devon coast, that Kipling made his first connection with the Navy, which was to grow into one of the central artistically productive strands of his life until after the First World War – a strand, alas, that produced only badly flawed work.

In 1897, Jubilee Year brought many triumphs. First at Oxford. His host, Sir William Wilson-Hunter, was an eminent retired Indian administrator and historian of India. He was the man who had given Kipling his first friendly notice in English journals – a praising if somewhat patronising review of *Departmental Ditties* way back in 1888 in *The Academy*. Now Kipling stayed with him at his impressive house, Oaken Holt, near Oxford. Kipling's bread-and-butter letter reflects, I think, a real impression, for effusion was not his manner: "And so I am back to earth again, the richer for the rest of my life by those three wonderful days with you." [3] Sir William and Oaken Holt, indeed, may stand for the very type of man and house which were to make up Kipling's social world increasingly for the rest of his life after he settled at Bateman's in 1903. But there was an additional reason for his delight. Sir William took him to dine at High Table at Balliol College and here he was given a standing ovation by the undergraduates in the Dining Hall. The dinner was followed by a special Bach concert in College in his honour. Kipling's total lack of musical appreciation will hardly have made this a pleasure in itself, but the whole incident must have done much to erase the sense of loss which I am sure that he felt when, as a boy, he knew he could not go to Oxford. Ten years later Oxford gave him an honorary doctorate, and in 1908 Cambridge followed suit.

On top of Oxford's applause came one of the greatest professional-class establishment honours of late Victorian England – he was elected to the Athenaeum Club, and not just in the ordinary way, but under Rule II, which allows for special election on grounds of distinction. He was the youngest member. Among the General Committee at that time there were only two literary men, but their names take us back to his days in London in 1890 – Sir Walter Besant, the beloved, Sir Sidney Colvin, the detested. But it was Henry James who seconded him, as he had heard already from his aunt, Georgie Burne-Jones, the year before his election. He wrote to James to thank him: "I'll be a bishop in gaiters yet." [4]

Soon after his election he dined at the Athenaeum with Cecil Rhodes and Alfred Milner, two men, so opposite, who were to be his successive hopes for his Imperial dreams in the coming fifteen, most politically agitated years of his life. His reference to the occasion in a letter to Dr Conland in Brattleboro is boyish: "And talking of smashes and their results reminds me that we are going to London in a few days to meet Cecil Rhodes at dinner. I think it will be rather larks." [5] But this should not blind us to his awareness of the importance to him of the Athenaeum and all it stood for in a new world of relationships. As he writes to Stanley Weyman, "The Athenaeum (Golly what a club – I've been afraid to enter it for fear the hall porter would kick me out) is good enough for me – and London in Jubilee is unspeakable Tophet." [6]

If he must be in London during Jubilee then the Athenaeum's distinguished fellowship is to be his refuge from the fraternity of London's teeming streets, where mateyness reigned almost as much as in Main Street, Brattleboro. But, in fact, he and Carrie took refuge in Uncle Ned's and Aunt Georgie's seaside house, North End House, in the secluded fishing village of Rottingdean, on the high chalk cliffs of England's Channel coast, near Brighton. Here, loud, jubilant shouts of London's rejoicing at her own greatness could not be heard.

I remember that my father, like most late Victorians no great lover of the old Queen whose sixty years' reign was being celebrated, nevertheless recalled Jubilee London with great delight and with the chorus:

> We all got drunk and went upon the spree
> When going with the Missus to the Jubilee.

Kipling, like my father, his exact contemporary to a month, was not particularly fond of the old Queen, but for this frivolous, boozy approach to jubilation for the nation's greatness, he felt the greatest dislike. All the puritanism of his ancestors revolted against it, his artistic dislike for promiscuous, unselective fraternising, his fear of disorder and intemperance, above all, his apprehensions of disaster brought on by overreaching and vainglory, all rejected it. The fear of pride punished touched, I think, the deepest nerve in his personality, an almost superstitious apprehension of disaster brought on by taking for granted, by failing to recognise that all hopes and all securities rest upon the thinnest of ice. It is not surprising that his verbal reaction when it came should echo the Old Testament tones of the old religion, however little he believed in it rationally, for it came spontaneously from a deep level in him when his fears were painfully touched. And, on a conscious level, he no doubt regarded a formal, traditional "religious" (i.e. god-fearing) form as appropriate for any public statement in time of emergency. Hence came "Recessional". "Lord God of Hosts be with us yet, lest we forget, lest we forget."

The curious thing (and it is typical of the endless paradoxes which mark Kipling's life) is that, having written this, his most famous public utterance, he should have thrown it into the waste-paper basket. Perhaps even the act of utterance seemed to him a dangerous presumption that might threaten the nemesis it sought to avoid. It was retrieved for the world by Sally Norton, the liberal daughter of his New England mandarin surrogate father, and by the advocacy of his pacifist, radical, beloved Auntie Georgie Burne-Jones. These two ladies persuaded Carrie and Rudyard that the poem should be posted to *The Times*, where it duly appeared. Indeed, "Recessional" has always been seized upon by those anxious to suggest that his Imperialism, his belief in the law-keeping mission of England in a precarious, threatened scheme of things, was more liberal than is generally supposed.

This is quite to misunderstand the sentiments of the poem. The active role of the lawmaker, the mission to preserve the weak, is no less implied in "The Recessional" than in the poems that have been seen as more grossly imperial. It is simply that here, as the climate of 1897 demanded, he stressed the need for humility, for awe, for simplicity and decorum in those who have been given so high and heavy a task to perform. He was, of course, pleased that his beloved Uncle Ned and Auntie Georgie should be able for once to feel at one with him. But when his radical cousin J. W. McKail wrote, praising the poem, he drew back from McKail's interpretation. There was no question that, however she needed a lesson, Britain would "pull through not without credit". And – a little dig at his cultured radical professor cousin – "it will be common people – the 3rd class carriages – that will save us". Years later, too, in a letter to his friend Rider Haggard, he expresses anxiety about the passive, retiring view of Britain's role that interpreters had too often found in his poem.

What is most striking, however, is the tremendous reception given to the poem when it appeared in *The Times*. It was, of course, an upper- and middle-class public that responded. But not only did he clearly touch a chord in the serious dissenting provinces from whom he usually was politically divided, but it was clear that, jubilation over, all but the most frivolous of even the more vocal patriots felt that here was a proper rebuke to frivolous levity. Two things, I think, may account for this: the underlying mood of the nation was apprehensive and anxious in this hour of apparent high prosperity, as Kipling was by temperament and direct conviction; in this time when churchgoing was first eroding and religious doubt and indifferentism were spreading in all classes, a vaguely religious exhortation was exactly fitted to meet the vague anxieties of ordinary men and women about their slide away from church and chapel.

To his American reputation was added "The White Man's Burden" with its special appeal to the United States. In 1898, the year after the Jubilee, America still held a central place in Kipling's scheme of things, nor did his growing interest in South Africa seem anything but an enlargement of the bond he had in common with Teddy Roosevelt and forward-minded Americans. We may see, as a typical unifying hope, his bringing together Theodore Roosevelt's friend, John Hay, the Ambassador to St James's, with Cecil Rhodes at a dinner at the Savoy Hotel in London in that year.

Early in 1898 had come the United States' war with Spain over Cuba. Here surely was the chance to bring the two nations together to replace the old worn-out colonial mercantile world of Spain and Portugal, the world of the East India Company and before, not to say the narrow in-turned world of the two Boer Republics in South Africa, with an Anglo-Saxon Imperial mission that would be wide-thinking and modern – as he and Roosevelt (or Hay) and Rhodes were wide-thinking and modern. And sensible of duty, of the burden and sacrifice that history had imposed upon the two nations at that moment in giving them such power and opportunity, the sacrifice that he had seen made by the district commissioners and subalterns and engineers in India, he made his clarion call to America:

> Take up the White Man's Burden –
> Send forth the best ye breed –
> Go bind your sons to exile
> To serve your captives' need;
> To wait in heavy harness
> On fluttered folks and wild –
> Your new caught sullen peoples,
> Half devil and half child.[7]

Such an admonition, intended in a spirit of comradeship in arms, was not altogether popular in America – or not with those who saw no special link between their political and commercial, even their patriotic needs, and those of the old, decadent England. It is hard to tell how much Kipling realised this, or how much he still regarded American patriotism as an overflow of Anglo-Saxon sentiment, save for the small but, alas, ever-growing number of Irish or German or Slav immigrants mainly in cosmopolitan New York or Chicago or in the lawless Far West. In any case, his message to America was the positive side of his Imperial creed, as "The Recessional" was the negative side of the coin. And both were, in great degree, surely addressed to himself.

Anyone who has read his work sensitively knows that children and devils, even, I think, "fluttered folk and wild", are the uncontrolled source of what he calls his "daemon", his deepest creative impulse. Upon that impulse, to shape it and preserve it from destruction by evaporation, he spent all his energies in craft and organisation and polishing and control. And he knew that about neither – genius nor powers of craft – must he ever be braggart or boastful, for fear the powers would depart from him as they had from other sloppy, vainglorious artists: it was his deepest superstition. "The Recessional" voices this fear, "The White Man's Burden" speaks of the other great trust of preserving the voice that gave us Mowgli and Kim and the Puck stories and of ordering it into a voice of art, not an empty self-indulgent gipsy song.

Of course, Kipling meant every word of his Imperial beliefs and gave most of his surface active life to them, but I am sure that the excess of the tensions they produced, his political frenzy in the years 1900–1914, can only be fully understood if one grasps that his fear of anarchy or foreign tyranny, his hopes of a sane, ordered Pax Britannica, a Pax Anglo-Saxonica, or, at last, a Pax Franco-Britannica were also a reflection of the deep inner struggle between the anarchic, romantic childlike force of his creative impulse and the ordered, complex, at times almost self-defeating pressure of the craft he imposed upon it.

By a curious chance, from 1897 to 1901 or so, his underlying fears and needs spoke to the underlying needs and fears of a great part of his countrymen as never again. He spoke almost directly to them in terms of the Imperial tensions that they both knew. Of course, to a literate and numerically limited section of them, for "The White Man's Burden" appeared, like "Recessional", in *The Times*.

Both, too, were written at Rottingdean. For here, after the birth of his son John, in August 1897 in Aunt Georgie's house, the Kiplings had settled in an old rambling timbered farmhouse, The Elms, just across the village green from the Burne-Joneses. Here they remained until September 1902, when they moved to Bateman's at Burwash in the depths of the far East Sussex countryside. It was only then that they found their social identity, or, rather, for Kipling as artist, his necessary social camouflage. It was only then that they finally sold Naulakha to Miss Cabot, although their determination never to settle in the States must have been final after the tragedy of 1899.

The five-year stay at The Elms could only really have been provisional. For Rudyard, at first, it brought the happiness of the presence of the Aunt and the Uncle, and of the visits of his parents, of many other relations and of Crom Price and his children. It meant the frequent presence of his cousin Stanley Baldwin to whom he was growing close, for Baldwin was married to Lucy, daughter of the Ridsdales, Rottingdean's squires. It gave him his own family of four in the centre of his loved and inherited family. His unwillingness to relinquish his childhood roots is very marked. How happy Carrie could have been under such Kipling–Burne-Jones scrutiny seems more questionable, but, perhaps it meant an intercourse with those who mattered so much to Rudyard – the Mother, the Aunt – in a general family setting that was easier than formal visits. For so housekeeping-obsessed a woman, the sprawling, upstairs–downstairs nature of The Elms must have been a trial but also a challenge.

Tensions with Aunt Georgie were to grow in the Boer War, though never to diminish Rudyard's love for her. But, for the moment, they were drawn very close by the sudden death from heart attack of Uncle Ned, for Aunt Georgie needed her nephew so badly. He could lend her help with the memorial of her husband to which she devoted her widowhood (perhaps the best of all family biographies I have ever read – loving, touching and yet perfectly organised). The family pressures, then, were for the moment welcomed. As to nearby Brighton's trippers, they had not yet begun to press upon The Elms as they began to do when the century turned.

In any case, any sense of claustrophobia was removed by three new elements in Kipling's life that gave him a sense of an expanded sphere, of a fuller range of sensibility, above all, of a connection with the world's future rather than, as with Rottingdean, of his own family past. These three spheres were, in ascending importance – the hiring of a motor car and the beginning of a lifelong delight in motoring (1899); a summer cruise with the Channel Fleet (1898), the continuation of the interest aroused in the Navy at Simonstown in 1891, and the beginning of a close association that was to culminate in his publicity work for the Navy in the Great War; last, and most important by far, a visit with his family and Lockwood to Newlands, a suburb of Cape Town, to escape the winter of 1897/8 which was to lead to his wintering at the Cape every year until 1908, save for the unfortunate visit to New York of 1899. All these were safety-valves for him, and the Cape was perhaps even more important to Mrs Kipling as a world away from England and her in-laws. But their importance to his well-being were not to be matched in his art, though each produced its share of tales and verse which must be shortly described.

Motoring, that activity which has increasingly given the paradox of privacy combined with participation in the outside world, to millions of people, has been a source of inspiration to many writers. It improbably unites Kipling to Virginia Woolf. I, like them, am an ardent passenger motorist, and I can speak for the unique combination of absorption in the passing world around and of nervous relaxation allowing the creative imaginative process to work subconsciously as the surface mind is diverted, that passenger motoring provides for the novelist. For Kipling, I think, it had a special value as a means of release from the study and the home while retaining the privacy, the separation from the intrusion of strangers which he came obsessively to value. In fictional form, it is connected with his increasing identification with the Sussex countryside (the "place" so vital to his art which seems to have failed to reach his imaginative centre in Vermont). A discussion, then, of his motoring stories and the curious way he turned them into piratical instruments of Stalky-like revenge on an overweening society, is best left to his life at Bateman's as a country gentleman after 1903.

The cruise in the Channel in 1898 started a firm association with the Navy and naval officers vital to his political concerns in the coming years. But his interest, of course, lay back in his friendship with Captain Bayly and his meetings at Simonstown Naval Officers' Club in South Africa in 1891; if not further back to his walks in Southsea with Captain Holloway. And we know from Admiral Evans of the U.S. Navy that Kipling, during his American time, had shown an equal interest in American naval vessels in New York.[8] At the time of the Jubilee in 1897, the British Fleet was still the source of pride that it had been for two centuries. But to many critics, alarmed at Continental threats to our colonies and our trade, it was beginning to seem quite inadequate to our expanded concerns. German rivalry was not as yet seen as the sole danger. Even Kipling had strong fears of France, his loved nation from 1910 or so, as one can see from the story of the French spy disguised as a Portuguese castaway on a British naval vessel in "The Bonds of Discipline". The Frenchman's over-ingenious imagination makes him an easy prey to the crew's powers of Stalky spoofing once they grasp that he is a spy (an over-ingeniousness, it must sadly be said, matched by the over-ingenious method of Kipling's narration which was to grow in the last decades of his life). This story was published as late as 1903. Nevertheless, Germany maintained its position as chief enemy in Kipling's mind, even above the Russian bear, from the mid-nineties onwards. In this he was more constant, more sure that there could be no compromise than even his three Imperial heroes, for Rhodes had sought the Emperor's friendship before the Jameson Raid and included Germans among the Anglo-Saxon recipients of the Rhodes scholarship, Milner had through his parents strong cultural associations with Germany, and Joseph Chamberlain, when in power, sought fruitlessly three times to conclude an Anglo-German agreement.

But, as the new century progressed, very many more than Conservatives in England became so alarmed at the German naval menace that the Liberal Government was compelled to add eight dreadnoughts to our naval strength in 1909. The "We want eight, we won't wait" campaign that forced this unpalatable increase upon a government that wanted the money for social reform (foremost among the opponents of such naval increase was Winston Churchill!) has a music-hall sound that must have delighted Kipling. But his own advocacy of naval increase had long preceded the national mood. And he had been able to plead the Navy's cause with professional skill, for his friendship with naval officers and his participation as a guest in naval exercises had made him an amateur expert on naval engineering and naval economy, the accuracy of whose fictional accounts of ships and their workings still arouses controversy among professional sailors.

And he loved the life on board as an honoured guest. Here in naval craft were communities far closer to his view of society than even the liners that, we have seen already, were so congenial to him. Far smaller communities, at any rate on the naval ships in which he was a guest; crews united not only by caste discipline, but by craft, vocabulary, danger and their own law. True, the danger does not, as in a liner, immediately involve others than themselves, but, in the wider view, the British Navy protects the whole community, the liner's crew only a disparate and motley body of relatively frivolous globe-trotters. Their law – Poseidon's Law, as Kipling calls it – is a very special one. On board they must abide absolutely by the logic of navigation, by the

logic of the machine-gods who serve them. Machines, as Kipling has
told us, "cannot tell a lie". But sailors, too (especially those serving
the cause of civilisation's law in the Navy) must not tell a lie – as
Poseidon says to all sailors in the poem:

> Behold a Law immutable I lay on thee and thine;
> That never shall ye act or tell a falsehood at my
>   shrine . . .
> Ye shall not clear by Greekly speech, nor cozen from
>   your path
> The twinkling shoal, the leeward beach, or Hadria's
>   white-lipped wrath;
> . . . The soul that cannot tell a lie – except upon
>   the land,
> In dromond and in catafract – wet, wakeful, windward-eyed –
> He kept Poseidon's Law intact . . .
> But once discharged the dromond's hold, the bireme
>   beached once more,
> Splendaciously mendacious rolled the Brass-bound Man
>   ashore.[9]

The language is as obscure as it is pretentious, and hardly fitted to
bring home their duties to more than a handful of sailors, but the
situation he describes is a special and glorious case for The Law as put
forward in *Stalky & Co.* Absolute vigilance and duty when at sea,
total *laissez-faire* for larks and lies and anything else when Jack's
ashore. A kind of "in school" and "out of school" ethic for adults.

But, even in school, there is need for some sense of gusto so that
duty can be carried out without priggish tension. Unfortunately, I
think, Kipling's position as an honoured guest on board paradoxically
told against his getting the emotional balance of naval life right, as his
more distanced position as a hearer of tales and a casual observer
served him so well in gauging the mixture of gaiety and despair in the
lives of the Soldiers Three. He was nearer to the scene, but as a well-
known writer and a guest of honour he saw only the side of life on
board that was intended for public view – the duty and the larks that
lightened that duty. I am sure that he took his visits very seriously,
that he listened with close attention – perhaps, he even suspected at
times, over-attention, for he gets in a crack at himself, when Pyecroft,
the petty officer who is the Mulvaney of his naval stories, says in
"Their Lawful Occasions", "I know 'e's littery, by the way 'e tries to
talk navy-talk." As the officers' guest, he was not, perhaps, best placed

to absorb the ratings and petty officers who are the core of his naval stories. The result is that all the many Pyecroft naval tales have a kind of jocosity, a sort of "out on the spree" quality that sets them far, far below the adventures of Mulvaney, Ortheris and Learoyd, who even at their most comic picaresque have that ambiguous, amoral quality of Shakespeare's Pistol and his associates, have also the dark despair that gives their positive performance of duty a depth that goes far beyond Sunday school morality.

This makes Pyecroft an empty narrating device, compounded only of comic knowingness, cockney accent and of naval jargon, in the stories of adventures aboard ship like "Birds of Paradise" and "Their Lawful Occasions", and, more dismally still, an intrusive, unfunny "funny" voice in the tales of motoring larks on shore, "Steam Tactics" and "The Horse Marines", the last of the Pyecroft stories, published in 1910. The truth is that Kipling did not know the life of the man he was describing and so he cast him in careful, arranged farce, often on shore. A sailor's peacetime life, at any rate on the lower deck, must have had much of the sadness, the tension and the reduction of humanity that he captures so wonderfully in the Mulvaney stories which probably reproduce only what he heard.

Kipling was not concerned to plead on behalf of the ratings or the petty officers or indeed the officers, but to interest the general public in the Navy itself, to pass on his own enthusiasm for a neglected Service, not to pass on his compassion for neglected men. Reading these naval stories, published in popular magazines, so full of jargon, one wonders how much he can have fulfilled even this socio-political aim, for who but naval men or engineers could stay with such stuff, however larky? As artistic productions, they are among his worst.

His longing to find a private world to match his own passion for privacy, his longing to find a secret society that would match his own Freemasonry, his longing to find a loneliness that would match his own creative isolation, must have seemed miraculously answered when he was allowed to penetrate that rare world of Her Majesty's ships at sea in peace time. "Life out of which this [the Navy's] spirit is born has always been a life more lonely, more apart than any there is," [10] he told the Naval Club in 1908. And he went on to note how only from the turn of the century, with the arrival of Marconi's wireless, were fleets in touch. I think that naval privacy and isolation defeated the empathy even of Kipling's extraordinary powers of making himself one with other men. He went on board as an honoured guest, he was even chaired by the crew, but he remained apart. Yet he loved the peacetime Navy enough still to write about it when he was on holiday in Jamaica in "A Naval Mutiny", as late as 1931. It is another elaborate farce that fails.

Pyecroft's voice is one of the things that finally deadens the over-complex, over-revised South African story, "Mrs Bathurst", which has aroused so much praise. But the failure of "Mrs Bathurst" is part of the history of Kipling's close association with South Africa from 1898 to 1908 which we must now look at. The letter of Lockwood Kipling to Mrs Trotter, who kept the boarding house at Newlands, Cape Town, reserving rooms for Rudyard, Carrie, two children under five, one nursemaid and one governess, is dated 16 November 1897. It is worth noting as showing how the family travelled even when their destination was a boarding house. It masks, I think, Carrie's strong sense of economy united with her Victorian attitude to domestic help. It was to last all her life. Lockwood rather engagingly adds that he may come out himself, "but a mere single man can be put anywhere".[11]

This first visit to South Africa must have been largely made to avoid the winter. The Simla habit died hard with the Kiplings. The parents had visited Florence in most winters in their retirement. Carrie, as well as Rudyard found the damp, so unlike New England, a great trial, and Josephine, an entirely American child, was miserable in England's stuffiness. But Rudyard had more definite troubles with his health. The doctors, he told Conland, have told him that his liver is not at fault, but "the colon is rather distended with wind. Also you smoke too much."[12] Can it be that the gastric disorders which were to cause him such pain and misery from the Great War until his death were giving their first evidence?

Alfred Milner was now Governor at the Cape, his first Imperial appointment of power. Expected by the Salisbury Conservative Government that had appointed him, even by the great Imperialist Colonial Secretary Joseph Chamberlain, to find some means of making a settlement with Kruger, the Boer President of the independent Transvaal Republic, that would give status to the many British subjects in the mining towns, he was learning that his task was impossible. The mixture of cunning evasion and moral certainty of their cause with which the Boers entered negotiations that to them threatened annihilation of their godly rule, was increasingly intolerable to Milner's essentially academic yet equally exalted nature. Uncle Ned, who knew Milner through his friend Mrs Gaskell, a cultivated Souls hostess, had given Rudyard an introduction to this man, whom he liked personally as much as he disliked his Tory politics. But Milner was too busy to see much of the Kiplings, as he wrote to Mrs

Gaskell: "I saw practically nothing of him, though I should have liked to do so, for he is the most companionable of creatures . . . I fancy he saw a lot, and I am very glad that he saw through that utter imposture, the simple-minded Boer patriot, dear to the imagination of the British radicals." [13]

Back home in London, Kipling, speaking to the Anglo-African Writers' Club, made his views clear: "The Transvaal . . . a state . . . hopelessly inept and crippled, except for the efforts of the energetic but oppressed men who are trying to make it prosperous" (i.e. the British residents). He went on to make clear what his position would be in the future, "Under some misapprehension about Continental help, the Boer in the Transvaal may rise and give trouble. If they do, then will be the time to scoop them out." [14] It is hardly likely that Kipling would not have taken this view, for if he saw little of Milner on that visit, he saw a lot of his other hero, Rhodes. Cecil Rhodes, who was usually ill-at-ease with women, got on well with Carrie. In the last month of their visit (March 1898) Rhodes arranged for Rudyard to make a visit up to the territory of Rhodesia, which he saw as the first step in his dream of an all-red British route from Cape Town to Cairo. Rudyard made the trip to Bulawayo and the Limpopo River on his own – an increasingly rare event in his life since his marriage. It clearly stimulated him greatly. Of all *The Just So Stories*, "How the Elephant Got his Trunk" is the most visually seen and it was on this expedition that Kipling saw "the great, grey-green, greasy Limpopo".

As a result of the expedition, Rhodes's South African dream seized Kipling's imagination. Years later, in 1908, when he finally left South Africa in despair, after the apparent triumph of Afrikanerdom in the creation of the Union, it was, above all, the cutting off of Rhodesia from the south, the visible end of Rhodes's dream, that he mourned.

If we may trust his letter to his old friend Mrs Hill written in July 1899, he still considered spending the following winter in India: "It's impossible to stay through the English winters now, so I suppose I may as well try India as any other place." [15] But this may only be a means of stressing his old tie with her. At any rate, events intervened. In October, President Kruger (perhaps under some misapprehension about Continental help) issued an ultimatum that set the war machine in motion. At first Kipling's prophecy of British victory, made to the Anglo-African Writers, seemed wide of the mark. In the following months the Boers advanced into Natal, inflicting a series of defeats on the British. British forces were besieged in Mafeking, Ladysmith and Kimberley. In the last, Kipling's hope for the future, Cecil Rhodes, was imprisoned.

At home, Kipling immediately responded to the situation by publishing "The Absent Minded Beggar" in the new vast-circulation *Daily Mail* newspaper, before October ended. This poem, which was recited on stage and music hall and in drawing-rooms all over the country, is an extraordinary reflection of Kipling's abiding concern for the decent treatment of Learoyd, Mulvaney and Ortheris, perhaps, with its accent on the cockney Tommy, especially for Ortheris. It is, of course, a recruiting song. And also in its famous lines –

> Cook's son – Duke's son – son of a belted Earl –
> Son of a Lambeth publican – it's all the same today!

it asserts that somewhat nebulous dream of an England undivided by class differences, united in patriotic service which was to be at the centre of Kipling's social thinking in all his high hopes for the next six or seven years.

But its direct purpose was to raise money for soldiers' dependants, and it raised over a quarter of a million pounds. He took nothing for it. It is this persistent concern for those on whom the burden of his Imperialist dream fell that makes one warm to Kipling, I think, even when that dream is less than sympathetic.

Certainly it won the hearts of the soldiers on behalf of whom he had spoken. It is not surprising, then, that Kipling should have wished to be at the scene of their action and of his hero Rhodes's drama. The family left for Cape Town, where they stayed at the Mount Nelson Hotel, still today one of the last shadows of the old gracious-living hotels of the Edwardian era of travel. It is here, with all the crowd of war correspondents, wives of distinguished serving officers, and political observers, that we see Kipling first in that atmosphere of general political gossip and alarum that, I think, was to be the bane of his Cape Town life in the coming years, the atmosphere that most stood between him and South African life itself, the atmosphere that made him write to Mrs Hill in 1906, "my half year at the Cape is always my 'political' time, and I enjoy it"[16] – the atmosphere that, in the end, prevented his imaginative creation from using his South African experience in a way that gave more than a tantalising glimpse of what might have been.

The brilliant young Imperialist Leo Amery, then a correspondent for *The Times*, speaks of being "for some weeks Kipling's table companion at the Mount Nelson". His description of Kipling's talk, "jerky and full of swift changes and vivid illustrations,"[17] seems to be a picture almost of his very political social life at the Cape and, indeed, of his public image in England until 1914 – intense, at times frenetic, ardent, subject to extremes of hope and despair and very muddled. But, in this visit of 1900, he was summoned away from his family and Cape political wrangles to closer experience of the War. Indeed it was the first and, perhaps, the only time in his life that he was to be within sound of battle gunfire.

In March 1900, Lord Roberts, on invading the Orange Free State, which had secretly been helping its sister republic, the Transvaal, commandeered one of the leading newspapers in the capital, Bloemfontein, the *Friend of the Free State*, as a newspaper for his soldiers. He put it under the charge of various leading correspondents, somewhat to their embarrassment in view of their commitments to their own leading London papers. One of them, Perceval Landon, of *The Times*, invited Kipling to join them and he arrived in Bloemfontein on 1 March and stayed working in the office until 1 April. We have a very full account of this short return to journalism from Julian Ralph, an American correspondent, who was one of his co-editors. From the very first, Kipling resumed his old life with delight, insisting on reading all poems from Tommies himself, composing some rather simple war fables about animals for the paper, and generally entering into a relationship with his co-editors reminiscent of his schooldays in Study 5. He greeted Landon's birthday, for example, with an appropriate piece of chaff in verse:

> Tell the smiling Afric morn,
> Let the stony Kopje know,
> Landon of The Times was born
> One and thirty years ago . . .
> Whisper greetings soft and low
> Pour the whisky, deal the bun,
> Only Bell and Buckle know
> All the evil he has done.[18]

He had been put down as a working editor – "Well, I should have been offended if you had not. Where's the office? I want to go to work as soon as I've finished my grape jam."[19] The office, when he saw it, made him cry, "It's quite like old times in India!"[20]

Yet, for all the memories and all the larks his return to the newsroom allowed him, he had no real wish to look back – it was exactly then that he told Ralph that journalism was "training to prevent the formation of habits of thrift; to make men careless of the future".[21]
The visit to Bloemfontein, in short, was seen clearly as a sight-seeing

214

trip along the gipsy trail, but no real indulgence in his gipsy strain.

He tried hard to be a private man, but he was inevitably the great celebrity. Gwynne, another of the editors and Reuter's correspondent, had announced his arrival in an issue of the *Friend*: "Today we expect to welcome here in our camp the great poet and writer who has contributed more than anyone perhaps towards the consolidation of the British Empire." [22] It was inevitably a time of pride for Kipling, not least because, at any rate as far as the soldiers were concerned their gratitude to him was no heady rhetoric. Ralph's account of Kipling's visit to the hospitals distributing copies of the paper – "His name is whispered, 'God bless him! He's the soldiers' friend' " [23] – has, of course, a touch of the Victorian legend of Florence Nightingale, but like her story it is founded on solid devotion that can withstand debunking. His means of disposing of embarrassing adulation, too, have a touch of "celebrity" about them – at the Free State Hotel:

Admirer: Is it possible that I have the honour to meet the author of "The Absent Minded Beggar"?

R.K.: Yes. I have heard that piece played on a barrel organ and I would shoot the man who wrote it, if it would not be suicide. [24]

Yet Kipling's capacity to break through to a personal intimacy when he felt at ease is once more illustrated in the *Friend* office. It was not just a matter of saying, "Now, what shall I do? Write a poem, fill out cables, or correct proofs?" [25] He did all these things and he also made close friendships with his fellow editors in these very few days.

Of course, they were men after his heart. They were his perfect mixture – Julian Ralph, an American, was the very symbol of that possibility of the Anglo-American world partnership which he still hoped for; Gwynne of Reuter's was a tough, assured reporter of many military campaigns, a mountain climber, a man of action; Landon, of *The Times*, was an Oxford man, scholar and amateur poet, trained for the law (he had, when the Army moved on from Bloemfontein, to return to England for reasons of health). No Study 5 composition could have been better.

Ralph died a few years later, but Landon and Gwynne were to remain close friends and political colleagues. Gwynne, after 1911, became the editor of the *Morning Post*, the extreme right-wing newspaper nearest to Kipling's heart, and their correspondence reflects, despite Gwynne's strong anti-semitism, their shared despair at the turn of world events, right into the nineteen-thirties. Landon had a cottage on Kipling's land at Bateman's and was his companion on his visits to the front in the Great War.

The lasting results of so short an initial association remind us of that quick-working and enduring charm with which he grappled close to himself a wide range of friends all his life. These friendships were a precious part of his life, and he would only relinquish them, as he was later to do with Beaverbrook, when he believed that some absolute betrayal of principle had taken place. Because of his hypersensitive feelings about privacy, they have almost no reflection in his fiction. The information he evoked by this strange power of intimacy fed his work; the persons who gave him the information never.

The regular fictional portrayal of each other that happened in, say, the circle of Lawrence, Katherine Mansfield and Huxley, he called "the higher cannibalism". But even the more usual occasional fictional transformation of friends hardly occurs in his work. The absence of characters drawn from the mix of life cannot be called an impoverishment, it is simply one of the things that makes his work, certainly after the Indian period, so wholly different from that of other serious writers. Yet if he used people very little directly in his work, his imagination fed most directly from his power of identification with them. What he paid for this in negative capability, in terms of suppression of himself, he only begins to reveal to his readers (and perhaps to himself) in the stories of his last years, when he enters his own work through the character of St Paul.

His days at the Bloemfontein office, then, were a celebrity's public lark from which he snatched some very vital private friendships. His only sight of battle was an equally public trip, but from it he snatched moments of vision that give life to his few Boer War stories, though they are not enough to outweigh the mass of extraneous detail that his pre-South African attachments and his political purposes imposed upon them.

In his autobiography, over thirty years later, he recalls this visit by Cape cart (a canvas-covered, one-horse, two-wheeled carriage) with Bennet Burleigh, the *Telegraph* correspondent, to the scene of a small skirmish at Karee Siding (part of Lord Roberts' mopping-up operation before the Army advanced from the Free State on to Kruger's base in the Transvaal). Even here, looking back over so many years, we get this vivid phrase: "a small piece of hanging woodland filled and fumed with our shrapnel much as a man's moustache fills with cigarette smoke."

But his singular visual power and his creative, coalescing imagination were separated by an iron curtain of political dogma in these years. It is typical that the most fully *seen* story of the war, "The Way That He Took", should peter out as a boy's story, a simple account of a military ruse to avoid ambush. Yet, in the more adult Boer War stories, the vision is seldom there. Once, however, it is unforgettable, the description in "A Sahib's War" of the shelling of the old Boer pastor's house by Australians, in revenge for the killing of a young British subaltern: "And the face of the house folded down like the nose and chin of an old man mumbling, and the forefront of the house lay down." This surely comes from the Cape-cart jaunt to the skirmish of Karee Siding.

In general, the Boer War stories are very disappointing, save for the light that they throw on the shaping of Kipling's social and Imperial thinking. Kipling's greatest hatred during the Boer War, as, indeed, later in the Great War, was for the undeclared enemies rather than for the declared ones. Neutrals, foreigners fighting for the Boers, the supposedly friendly Boer farmers of the Free State, above all, the cultivated Cape Afrikaners whose sympathies, of course, were often more with Kruger's Transvaal than with the British to whom they had sworn allegiance.

His fiercest attacks, "A Burgher of the Free State" and his article, "The Sin of Witchcraft", contributed to *The Times* on his return to England in April 1900, are direct polemics against Free State traitors and Cape traitors, as he saw them. These are understandably loaded, for they are journalism composed, so to speak, in the heat of the battle. Yet the same distracting themes inform "A Sahib's War" (December 1901) and "The Comprehension of Private Copper" (October 1902). By the time the latter was published, Kitchener's concentration laagers of Boer civilian women and children had succeeded Roberts's military victories and the war had, indeed, been ended for six months. Kipling had contributed his curious backhanded olive branch to the defeated Afrikaners, "Piet":

> Me an' my trusty friend 'ave 'ad,
> As you might say, a war;
> But seein' what both parties done
> Before 'e owned defeat,
> I ain't more proud of 'avin' won
> than I am pleased with Piet . . .
> I've known a lot o' men behave a dam' sight worse
> than Piet . . .
> Ah there, Piet! with your brand new English plough,

217

> Your gratis tents an' cattle, an' your most
> ungrateful frow,
> You've made the British taxpayer rebuild your
> country seat –
> I've known some pet battalions charge a damn
> sight less than Piet.

The tone of disgruntled patronage is not attractive; but Kipling, by attaching his writing so completely to political policy in these years, too often undermines his own art.

That we cannot accept Kipling's simplistic distinction between loyal and disloyal Boers under British rule, in a war where the enemy was of their own race, is not the reason for the failure of these stories. In my own case, if I were to have to share Kipling's political standpoint to appreciate his artistry, this book could hardly have been written.

It is necessary to go behind the particular. Treachery and its punishment are inherently most dramatic themes. The subject of "A Sahib's War", the enticement of a small British detachment by the hospitality of a Boer pastor and his wife, and the prearranged sniping in which the commanding subaltern is killed, is neither improbable nor dramatically unpromising. The violence with which the treachery is answered is shocking, but then Kipling means to shock us and, as always, he knows how. The demoralised collapse of the treacherous or the bullying is for him a necessary demonstration of the victory of the good. Hence we are given the collapse of the pastor's fat old wife when she believes that she and her beloved idiot son are to be killed: "She followed upon her knees and lay along the ground, and pawed at my boots and howled ... the woman hindered me not a little with her screechings and plungings." But this is a war story and the narrator is a brutal man, a Sikh veteran.

Equally in "The Comprehension of Private Copper", when the tables are turned on the cultivated Dutch burgher bully who has been torturing the English tommy, Copper, the description of his breakdown into hysteria is detailed. The comment by one of the tommies, " 'E screams like a woman," is brutal and contemptuous. But it is not this clinical realism, which has shocked some readers, that is wrong. In fact, it is quite right, for it brushes away all the mass of irrelevance, sometimes propagandist, sometimes factual, with which Kipling's wandering thoughts and feelings have embroidered the incidents, and wonderfully concentrates his mind on the reality of the tensions of war which are the centre of his imagining. But the success of the brutality only, alas, highlights the discursiveness of the rest.

218

What has his old theme of the loving relationship between an Indian servant and the little white sahib, which he has brought with him from his Bombay childhood, to do with South Africa's war? Or even the devotion of a Sikh non-commissioned officer to his British officer which takes us back to *Plain Tales*? There *were* Indian troops from the British Indian Army serving in Africa. Kipling may have been right to think that there should have been more. But it is an irrelevance. Of the real and large community of Indians in South Africa he showed no awareness whatsoever. In all his winter stays at the Cape, he never visited Natal where the large Indian trading community now lived – perhaps it was as well, for the advocate of their cause was Gandhi, a Babu lawyer. His concern for Indians in "A Sahib's War" is merely a sentimental nostalgia. What could have been a clearly seen and terrible story of war's brutal necessity is smothered by extra dimensions.

The same floating Indian memories are even more out of place in "The Comprehension of Private Copper". Here the Transvaal burgher who captures Copper and tortures him is given a chi-chi accent, a dark complexion and a plover's-egg eye so that we are forced to conclude that his father who settled in the Transvaal was a Eurasian rather than an Afrikaner. And this, in fact, undoes Kipling's propaganda against the treacherous rich Boer farmers. The only reason for this muddle seems to be the desire to provide Private Copper with memories of his Indian service, for his captor's broken Eurasian chi-chi accent, as he taunts him, recalls an incident at a regimental dance in Umballa, the main military cantonment in the Punjab.

And Kipling adds another confusing irrelevancy to this in the story. At this time he found himself increasingly at odds with the English ruling classes, both in England, as we shall see later, and in South Africa, where he thought (as many did) that the upper-class officers were in great degree responsible for our early disasters. He has to incorporate this point, also, when Copper, an enlisted tommy of Sussex farm-labouring stock, is reminded by his Boer tormentor's drawl of the son of the Squire of Wilmington when he caught Copper poaching and kicked him. The conflict between upper-class tormentor and uneducated tommy victim works very well in a somewhat Stalkyish way. When the renegade burgher says, "My father found out who was the upper dog in South Africa" (meaning the Boers), " 'That's me,' said Copper valiantly, 'If it takes another 'alf century, it's me and the likes of me.' " Kipling is striking a note on behalf of the common soldiers who, he believed, should people South Africa as immigrants when the war was over. But if he really wanted to incorporate this class conflict, he should have made the confrontation one directly between a British officer and a private. His sense of discipline and decorum inevitably avoids such a mutinous enormity. So we are left with the utterly improbable figure of a rich young white South African farmer who speaks and looks like an Indian but also has the drawl and the culture snobbery of a young Etonian squire. Against this, the very real and sympathetically realised figure of Private Copper doesn't stand a chance of coming to life. Kipling has too many points to make and too many hang-ups from the past to be rid of.

And so it is with the other stories. "The Outsider" never gets beyond the point that a rector's son with private means makes a bad officer, while Thrupp, the vulgar trader from the South African mining Rand, makes a good private. The Regular Army in South Africa, in fact, is useless, the volunteers are the relevant men. The attack upon the English upper-middle class here goes farther than anywhere else in Kipling's work, for Seton, the useless subaltern, is shown to have been wrong from the start of his life – he despised his nurse for being a woman, a master at school because he was poor, and a boy at school for boating instead of playing cricket. Good points to attack in conventional Edwardian public-school types, but the story is a feeble one.

For the rest, "The Captive" has been highly praised, but here we are confronted with all the growing faults of Kipling's later work – over-technical language, too elaborate a framework of narration – and there is none of the compensating depth that makes the best of his later stories so fine. He starts with a splendidly visual opening picture of a prisoner-of-war camp by the Cape seaside, but this is all swallowed up in the story of an American enlisted on the Boer side and how he learns that he has been wrong. Too much goes into getting exactly right the American narrator's voice. And it is a complete irrelevance. Once again South Africa and the War are lost in propaganda – for American readers – and nostalgia – for America itself. It does however contain the memorable phrase, voiced by a British General, "It's a first-class dress parade for Armageddon."

The South African stories, then, are spoiled by muddle, because Kipling's social and political ideas were at this time increasingly confused by the contradictions in a complex world that would not arrange itself according to his simplistic vision. They are muddled also because he had not yet truly found a mine of imaginative richness to replace India. Inevitably, nostalgia for India (he had not yet completed *Kim*), or regret for the failed treasure-house of America fills in the gaps in his incomplete imaginative engagement with the South African scene.

Cecil Rhodes had given a beautiful one-storeyed Colonial Dutch house on his estate to the Kiplings on a life tenancy. The Woolsack was a delight to the whole Kipling family. It was almost rebuilt to Carrie's taste. Here she spent much of her happiest time, inwardly relieved, perhaps, to be away from the Kipling family atmosphere of Rottingdean, able in South African conditions to relax from that tense, careful housekeeping which too often marred their English homes. For the children, Elsie and John, it was clearly a Paradise garden. And Rudyard, too, relaxed and wrote first some of *The Just So Stories* and then some of *Puck of Pook's Hill* and *Rewards and Fairies*. The first is a monument to his happiness with his own and all other children – and a first-rate children's book. The Puck stories are too often seen as a tribute to his children, but, in my opinion, as I shall hope to show later, they are, at their best, his next great imaginative revelation after his Indian world had finally dried up with the completion of *Kim*. But only the first, in part, has anything to do with South Africa. Indeed there is no more paradoxical picture in Kipling's life than that of his visiting the Cape Town library to check and sharpen his pictures of medieval or Elizabethan England, for his stories of England's history. His body was at the Cape, his mind wandered over the South Downs of the neolithic age or the Romney marshes of sixteenth-century smuggling. The nearest he got to his geographical reality in those stories was the gorilla land of West Africa in early Norman times. In truth his imagination was busily building up a cyclic past history of man's fight against disaster to compensate for the collapse of his present dream, of which South Africa was only a part, but a rapidly crumbling part.

He produced only one post-war story laid in South Africa. It has been highly praised and, as he clearly spent much effort upon fashioning it, it must be discussed. This is the famous "Mrs Bathurst" which has aroused as much puzzle-solving among his devotees as the unfinished *Edwin Drood* has among Dickensians. But, although important work which breaks new ground is often likely to puzzle the most sensitive and perspicacious readers, puzzle in itself is no merit in literature. My impression is that admirers of Kipling have understandably but mistakenly seized on the difficulty of not knowing what Kipling really means in "Mrs Bathurst" in order to insist that he, too, can be "difficult" like authors so admired by highbrows. But the "difficulty" of Mrs Bathurst is of little interest, for, in the last resort, the story is empty.

A naval warrant-officer named Vickery, of whom we know next to nothing save that his dentures are ill-fitting, deserts from his ship at Cape Town and disappears. We know that in the preceding week he has been obsessed night after night by the chance appearance in the news on the cinema screen of Mrs Bathurst, a New Zealand hotel-keeper, who is beloved by a large number of seamen who visit Auckland. Of her we know a little more – the way she puts her hand up to the curl behind her ear, her generosity to her seafaring customers, her long memory for faces she has seen years before, her blindish way of looking at people. For the rest we are told that she has a mysterious appeal – "It", the first use of Elinor Glyn's later famous term for sex-appeal. To this story, given by Vickery's shipmate, Pyecroft, is added the information from Hooper, a South African railway inspector, that beyond Bulawayo, on the way to the Zambesi, two bodies have been found, two tramps it is thought, turned to charcoal by the lightning of a great thunderstorm. Both disintegrate on touch. One has the false teeth and tattoo marks of Vickery.

What does it mean? Why is he there? What has he done to call down such wrath? Who is the other? Is it Mrs Bathurst herself? The answer to the last question seems, pretty certainly, no. But if Vickery's dead mate is somebody totally unknown to the reader, what is the meaning of that? The questions remain and will remain unanswered.

But an insoluble mystery is only effective if it matters. And what happens to Vickery doesn't matter because we know nothing of him; indeed, what happens to Mrs Bathurst doesn't matter much to us, although her generosity and amiability may make us hope that she did not leave her hotel in Auckland in order to be struck by lightning in a teak forest on the way to the Zambesi River. This story is the only one of Kipling's that rouses in me this sort of easy irony, because, whether he was conscious of it or not, it is very pretentious. Mr Amis has suggested that it fails because Kipling, in his passion for paring down his work, has rendered it unintelligible. He may well be right, but I think it is more likely that it never had much meaning.

Kipling has taken the idea of the fatality of elective affinity, of the devastating persistent attraction of one particular woman for one particular man, or vice versa, that haunted him from his Indian story days through *The Light That Failed* to the superb "Wish House", and tried to reduce it to some mysterious element that defies analysis. If he had any idea of bringing such a theme alive in words, he could only have done so if he had built up the two central characters until we knew enough of them both to recognise that what happened between them was something more than themselves. Instead of that we know next to nothing of them, and they are presented through the interchange of narration of three different men, the chief of whom is unfortunately Pyecroft, the petty officer whose voice ruins so many of Kipling's naval stories. It is true that here his voice and his carefully organised irrelevancies are not as maddening as usual because they are less loaded with jargon than in the naval tales and less sustained by "jaunty" than in the motoring tales; all the same they are an obstacle rather than a help. All the skill that should have gone into creating Vickery and Mrs Bathurst goes into realising the actual quality of talk of Pyecroft and Hooper, which includes a good deal of irrelevant gossip.

No climax, however dramatic and horrible, can repair this rambling narrative. Nor, though it is excellently done, is the sense of reality of the railway siding on the Cape seaside, where the narrating goes on, enough to pull the story together. Clearly this bit of Cape seashore Kipling knew completely, but he wastes it. And I cannot say that I am convinced by those who would place the story high among his works, because it not only introduces the cinema at a very early date, but also imitates the art of cinematography in the way that it cuts and dissolves in a new fashion. Indeed, I am by no means convinced that it does, for it seems to me that the cutting in and out of narration and back to the narrated scene is merely an elaboration of what we find in such earlier Indian stories as "On Greenhow Hill".

I do not wish to mourn too much for what Kipling did *not* get out of South Africa. I have already suggested the degree to which he exhausted himself by his natural empathy with others, his alertness of ear and eye, the washing-out of strength that negative capability induces. His Cape Town winters were a rest from this. Another and more curious imaginative process was taking him far away to Roman Legions in Northumbria, Talleyrand in Philadelphia, or the plague in seventeenth-century Sussex. And to unique, marvellous effect. But even if South Africa had been only a time of relaxation with his children, writers need such times. It is tantalising, however, to read the suggestions for articles and stories he made to G. W. Black of the *Cape Argus* in a letter of 10 April 1908, from The Woolsack, just before he finally left South Africa in disgust at increasing Afrikaner control:

He sketches the following plans for Cape Town tales:

(1) A Malay Laundress's account of her Mecca pilgrimage told on her own stoep.
(2) A night talk among tramps in the old Cape Town cemetery.
(3) The walks in the city of one of the Little Sisters of the Poor.
(4) Salvation Army Captain, fresh from the Transkei, talks with a Salvation Army girl (of the Cape) who has worked in the city and has her own opinion of the natives.

(5) A Kaffir train going out to location and the talk along the train.

(6) A sale in the market square, a study of the Jews there, the broken-down houses and the riff-raff generally.

(7) A child born and growing up on top of Table Mountain. At last seeing the trains, cars etc. that he has watched so long – a sort of "Young Savage Crusoe" close to civilisation.

(8) A dock study. Crowds (?) and boarding houses and the great silence and emptiness of the docks as well.

(9) The small school teacher – her loneliness and helplessness.

(10) A morning at the tram power-station – talk of drivers and conductors and the great cars sliding in and out.

(11) Adventures of small boys along the foreshore of the Woodstock drainage pipe. The cheerful way they risk their necks and lives clambering among the pile and what they imagine themselves to be in the way of pirates. Call it "The Second Landing of Van Riesbeck".

He adds, "I shouldn't worry about the public if I were you, I should try to please myself which is a much more difficult job."[26]

Here might have been *Table Talk below the Mountain* to rival *Plain Tales from the Hills*. But, even so, the range is very narrow – as his journeys around Cape Town were narrow – 5 miles from the centre to Newlands, 16 miles to Muizenberg, 26 miles to Simonstown. It is only Lahore writ large, not India. He would hardly wish to return to his earliest days of writing, to "The City of Dreadful Night", even if he were able. Instead he had his English dreams, his children to play with, Carrie happy and contented, and, after Rhodes's death, hours spent consulting and advising with the architect, Herbert Baker, on his atrocious "imposing" monument to the great man. What a waste it seems.

So much for the Horatian private man, but he was also the man at the public centre of things. There is here a touch of his parents' pleasure at having the Dufferins' friendship, in his relations with the great public men of South Africa. But, of course, it was more than that. Had not Rhodes himself said, "Kipling has done more than any other since Disraeli to show the world that the British race is sound at core and that rust or dry rot are strangers to it"?[27] He was the great Laureate of the Empire and he had chosen to make Cape Town his seat for more than a quarter of every year. No wonder that Rhodes sent a carriage to meet the Kiplings when they came out to their first tenancy of The Woolsack in December 1900. And Kipling had the close friendship of the Governor of Cape Colony also, Alfred Milner.

Indeed, he and Carrie and their new friend, who shared their enthusiasm, the intelligent Lady Edward Cecil (née Maxse), were united in the important political task of bringing Rhodes and Milner into better rapport.

Then in 1901 Milner was recalled to London, and in spring 1902 came the sudden death of Rhodes. It was a grievous blow, for Rhodes' strange personality and his wild visions gave an almost fictional dimension to the South African Anglo-Saxon dream. Kipling would never find this again in the closest of his Imperialist friends – neither in the supreme proconsul Milner, who had returned with a band of brilliant young men, as the war was ending, to the task of welding the beaten Dutch Republics into the British scheme, nor in Dr Jameson, Rhodes' adjutant, who took over the Cape mantle as Prime Minister and tenant of Groote Schuur. They, like other politicians, were governed by some degree of political practicality, some sense of the immediate and possible, however much Jameson's notoriously disastrous raid into the Transvaal Republic in 1895 may have led posterity to think him a reckless adventurer. True neither Milner nor Jameson trusted the Boer leaders any more than Kipling, but they recognised far more than he ever could the necessity of attempting agreements and compromises; they had to deal with practical measures. Kipling was completely at one with Milner's hopes for a strong white South Africa, with an honourable paternal treatment of the blacks (one of their dislikes of Boer social vision was its narrow, harsh attitude to the natives), and, above all, a constant influx of the best English immigrants. It was in both cases a dream that was not realised, but there is a difference in the disappointment of Milner the politician (however aloof and high-minded) and that of the apostle.

As Kipling saw his hopes fade over the years, his position changed. From honoured poet of the court, walking across to Jameson at Groote Schuur to hear the latest measures to be taken in the Cape, or entertaining Amery or Lionel Curtis or some other of Milner's young men come to report the splendid progress of the Anglo-Saxon dream in the Transvaal, he became the recipient of continuing news of disaster, the court poet of a dynasty that was at its end. Increasingly in his correspondence, even from 1903 onwards, there comes a kind of shrill, hysterical, gossipy note whenever South African politics are being discussed, a note of the supporter in the grandstand who sees his team steadily losing and yet cannot admit to himself that they were playing a losing game from the start – it is a reflection in little of the world view that he was proclaiming back home in England.

Just as in the Boer War and in the years after it, he was to feel that the

Conservative Balfour government's dead cultured aristocratic hand barred the way to a wider, less class-ridden British Empire, so it is the burden of his complaint against his British upper-class opponents in South Africa. None more than Sir Walter Hely-Hutchinson, of the family of the Earls of Donoughmore, who had come from Natal to replace Milner as the Governor of Cape Colony. He, it was, that Kipling saw as the chief aid to the Boers in subverting Milner's scheme to maintain a British-dominated South Africa.

In 1903, Joseph Chamberlain, the Imperialist hope in the Tory cabinet, came out on a visit to the Cape. Kipling had already been among those who had warned Chamberlain of Boer intransigence: "It is difficult to believe that Hofmeyer was sincere in his recent promise, and impossible to believe that even he could dam up or divert the waters of strife that he has led in channels of his own crooked digging since 1881. After all, we are only the children of our own works."[28] For Kipling, it was hard to believe that any Boer politician, Hofmeyer or any other, could truly have had a change of heart, or even of mind. But in February 1903 Kipling has to write to Milner, then in England, that Chamberlain had been taken in by the Boers: "he has come; he has seen; he has been spoofed; and Hely-Hutchinson who we only deemed a fool has done it."[29] Kipling himself, he says, first cottoned on when Hely-Hutchinson's sixteen-year-old son parrotted his family's view that "Merriman [the Cape Dutch leader] is intellectually the greatest man in South Africa". All the same, he adds, he has written a poem in praise of Chamberlain's work, for he is their only hope and may yet act when he finds that the Boers have lied.

By April, he is reporting to Milner that his friend Gwynne is leaving South Africa for good, in despair at Hely-Hutchinson's attitude up-country where Hutchinson claimed to be only carrying out Chamberlain's wishes. Sir Walter had told Gwynne, "The Dutch are the natural aristocrats of the land," and Lady Hutchinson had declared, "The Progressives [Jameson's British Settlers' party] will not win as they are no class. It is better to get the loyalty of the aristocracy of the land [the Boers] than the traders [the British]."[30] It was all that Kipling hated most in the voice of the cultured British Tories.

And it was not only in *public* life. A story is told of how he and Carrie advised a visiting English lady that larders in South Africa should be on the south side because they were south of the Equator. "Then with the British sniff that abolishes the absurd, the lady replied, 'Hm! I shan't allow that to make any difference to *me*.'" How could such people cooperate with the tough, hard-working British settlers, the ex-tommies whom Kipling was urging to return to the land they had conquered?

226

And, in fact, public affairs went from bad to worse. By September 1903, their one hope, Joe Chamberlain, left the Conservative Party and Balfour's cabinet. In 1905, the Transvaal was granted a constitution of its own and by the end of the year had come the Liberal landslide at Westminster. Milner, already lost to South Africa, was brought before the House of Commons and reprimanded. By the end of 1906, the Transvaal and the Orange Free State were granted self-government. In 1908 the last blow fell when Jameson lost the election in the Cape. By February 1909 the Union of South Africa, following the South Africa Act of 1908, had been formed, with Afrikaner-dominated governments in all the former colonies save Natal. But, by that time, Kipling had severed his connection with South Africa forever, though he continued to think of The Woolsack as his privileged home for two decades to come.

To an American friend, Duckworth Ford, he wrote in September 1907, "I will go to the Cape in December to see the burial, but I must then hunt for another country to love." [31] The Kiplings did indeed leave South Africa for the last time in April 1908. And, in a few years' time, the strange shaping of European events was to find him a new country to love for the rest of his life – France, which, at the time of the Fashoda incident in 1896, had seemed to be our greatest enemy. From South Africa in later years he never hoped much. As he wrote to Milner of the Botha Government, it had one policy: "The Englishman an Uitlander and the Dutch a Child of God." [32]

In his fight against the Balfour set in England, Kipling wrote a fascinating political fable, "Below the Mill Dam". But all his "political time" in South Africa produced nothing of the kind. I think it is that, in England, there was a genuine tension in Kipling between the traditional, historical land he loved and the new, efficient England his right-wing radical views demanded, just as in India there had been an even deeper tension between both the old caste India of the Hindus and the remains of the military world of their Moghul conquerors and the efficient India that the British sacrifice was making. In South Africa there was no such conflict. The old Dutch East Indian Cape meant nothing to him; the Boers, even the cultivated Cape ones, were to him merely narrow-minded, ignorant farmers and the Africans were servants to be cared for and used. He praised and recommended Olive Schreiner's *Story of an African Farm*. But however strong her later sympathies with the Boer cause, the appeal of her novel is in its story of adolescence and its visual sense of the veldt, not in any racial of political tension.

Ironically, he never visited Natal, the only place where he would have found his beloved Indians, and where, as I know from my mother's family's love of Kipling (they are a Durban family), he would have been greeted by an Englishness and an anti-Boer sentiment that would have warmed his heart.

There was no argument within himself, only a clear-cut policy that Tory snobbery and Boer political deviousness and Liberal bloody-mindedness refused to see. Without such inner tension, Kipling's creative imagination could not work even in the making of purely political fables.

This is not the place to argue the merits of the wild Imperial dreams of Rhodes or the academically planned paternalism of Milner and his young men, but, in both cases, their aim was to remake South Africa in a *new* shape. Kipling, in going along with such complete change, inevitably lost the power to create out of the land as it was. He simply did not see the Africans, the people of the country, let alone wonder about them. In this, Kipling was in no way different from most other whites of those days, but for the creative imagination, such blinkers are death.

True, in India, when Westminster appeared particularly obtuse, Kipling had had his dreams of a white settlers' land based on Kashmir. It made for odd polemic articles, but it never informed his writing. From the start, in South Africa, the blacks are "hubshis". When Punch (Kipling) had found a Negro, or someone quite as dark at the Southsea school in "Baa, Baa, Black Sheep", he had said, "That's a hubshi. Even Meeta used to laugh at a hubshi. I don't think this is a proper place." But South Africa was inhabited by hubshis.

The Sikh narrator of "A Sahib's War" may protest in the name of Kipling's beloved India, "I have a pass to go to Stellenbosch where the horses are. Do not let him herd me with these black Kaffirs!" But Kipling must speak for himself and, in his South African work, the black people of the land are scarcely there at all even as the most taken-for-granted part of the scenery. Liberal apologies, that Kipling had the measure of the Afrikaners' racialism and that this was one of his objections to what he feared would be their narrow rule, have a certain truth, but it cannot hide the aesthetic nullity that he made of South Africa over nine winters. Racial objections are not even necessary. It was his imagination that died, or, rather, that, luckily for us and him, was absent from that idyllic scene, far away on the Roman frontiers of Northumbria and on the marshes of Pevensey.

Yet the Southern African natural scene *did* leave its small but splendid mark on two of the best of *The Just So Stories* – the fourth story, "How the Leopard Got Its Spots" and the fifth, "The Elephant's Child". The first is a tribute to the veldt land and the rain forests; the second is a tribute to the African jungle and the Limpopo River.

The first seven of *The Just So Stories* are without doubt the cream of the collection. They are all united by the same little joke. It is typical of their excellence that this should be an entirely adult joke, for the special merit of the best of these stories is that they are written to be read aloud by adults to children.

Kipling, like anyone who cares for playing with children, knew that to identify with children does not mean losing your adult identity. For what children enjoy is not only the sense of participation in shared games, but the sense that some part of their enjoyment is mysterious to the adults, and equally some part of the adult enjoyment is mysterious to them. Much of the delight for the adult and for the child in story-telling as in any game lies in this interplay; it is a continuous flirtation between the two worlds. Every adult knows the pleasure of suddenly seeing what a child is putting into the game or the reading; equally, I am sure, children find much of their enjoyment in revelations of the jokes and absurdities that adults add to the stories or games for their own delight. And, of course, as with every recreation or art, some part of our and their pleasure comes from what neither we nor they can guess, but only vaguely apprehend. It is probable that the pleasing little Darwinian send-up that unites these first seven and best stories was lost altogether on Kipling's and other children. The whale's throat, the camel's hump, the rhinoceros's skin, the leopard's spots, the elephant's trunk, the kangaroo's physique, the armadillo altogether, are all jokes about evolutionary adaptation. And, as such, they are closely related to the natural scene, the surroundings – Kipling's forte – and they are most fully realised in the two stories with South African settings.

When the stories of private man's advancement begin, we are in the land of Tegumai and Taffy, of Kipling and his own children, and sentimental whimsicality takes over; while the last stories are again too marred by humans, cosy (the Cat that Walked By Himself), or mock-oriental (the Butterfly that Stamped).

What is the key to the magic of those first seven stories? First, of course, they are meant primarily to be read aloud to very young children who either do not yet read, or read with difficulty. And not just read aloud, but recited and acted – above all, chanted. Not of course in the way that people would recite and act them who have been told that is what they should do; but in the way that people recite and act them who as much enjoy games and reading with children for their own sakes as for the children's, because adults and children in such games are both happy exhibitionists. For that reason every individual word in *The Just So Stories* counts as much as it would in one of Kipling's ballads. Kipling in *The Just So Stories* is extremely self-conscious and yet also more free to play and display himself than in any other of his work. They must have been a joy to him and he communicates his joy.

Yet – and this is less usually recognised – there are important differences between these seven stories, the kinds of play indulged are quite distinguishable.

In the camel and rhinoceros stories, we get a special emphasis on funny adult words and expressions which have clearly appealed to his children, by their difficulty of pronunciation, or, perhaps, and this one can only guess, because they were favourite words of grown-ups. "When the world was so new – and all ... He lived in the middle of a Howling Desert ... most 'scrutiatingly idle ... that's made a' ·purpose", in "How the Camel". A little more ingenious and playful in "How the Rhinoceros", "more than oriental splendour ... it was all done brown and smelt most sentimental ... two piggy eyes and few manners". Language has changed greatly since then, but the phrases, the very sounds of the words, and the cliché pomposity in some of them still appeal, I think, to children.

The leopard and the elephant stories keep up these mocked phrases and word plays – "He would indeed! ... They didn't indeed! (Leopard) ... full of 'satiable curiosity ... do you happen to have seen a crocodile in these promiscuous parts?" (Elephant). Or, in the Leopard story, when the Ethiopian has turned black to fit in with the forest scene on the wise Baboon Baviaan's advice, the Leopard asks, "But what about me?" ... "You take Baviaan's advice too. He told you to go into spots" ... "So I did" (said the Leopard). "I went into this spot with you, and a lot of good it has done me."

But beyond this verbal play, these two stories are filled with colour – "forest full of tree trunks all 'sclusively speckled and sprotted and spottled, dotted and splashed and slashed and hatched and cross-hatched with shadows" (Leopard); or the famous "great grey-green greasy Limpopo River, all set about with fever trees" (Elephant).

In the Kangaroo story the mood changes completely. It is almost a chant – "Not always was the Kangaroo as now we do behold him," it begins, and then for many pages it is carefully orchestrated.

"Still ran Dingo – Yellow Dog Dingo – always hungry, grinning like a rat-trap, never getting nearer, never getting farther – ran after Kangaroo.
He had to!

    Still ran Kangaroo – Old Man Kangaroo. He ran through the ti-
trees; he ran through the mulga [etc., etc.,]
    He had to!"

It also contains in Kangaroo's frivolous impudence a kind of gaiety
unusual in Kipling – "Make me different from all other animals; make
me, also, wonderfully popular by five this afternoon!"
    As for the Armadillo story, it is full of more obvious, but perhaps
slightly more grown-up tongue-twisting fun as the Tortoise and the
Hedgehog evade the young Jaguar's hunger by confusing him. " 'Are
you sure of what your Mummy told you,' said slow and solid
Tortoise, 'Are you quite sure? Perhaps she said that when you water a
Hedgehog you must drop him into your paw, and when you meet a
Tortoise you must shell him until he uncoils.' "
    But each of the seven is a triumph in the special art of communicat-
ing with young children. Kipling had glimpsed the Camel's Arabian
desert and the Rhinoceros's Arabian sea shore from a ship; he had
touched upon the Kangaroo's Australia; he had sailed in the Whale's
ocean; he had "never sailed the Amazon . . . never reached Brazil . . ."
"Oh, I'd love to roll to Rio. Some day before I'm old," he was sixty-
one when he eventually got there in 1927; but the South African veldt,
and rain forest, and the Limpopo he had seen and felt. This is why
the Leopard and the Elephant are the most visual of all *The Just
So Stories*. It was an artistic gain from the South African years, if a
small one.

5 FOLLY AND MISRULE: ENGLAND 1902-1914

In March 1905 Kipling wrote to Mrs Hill from "The Woolsack" about his book that had appeared the previous year.[1] This was *Traffics and Discoveries* which contained his South African stories. He told her that it had really been put together for the purpose of carrying one political pamphlet, "The Army of a Dream", and that, in that respect, it had failed. It is hard to know whether he emphasises this in order to play down the literary failure of the others. Certainly the South African stories, as I have already suggested, are insignificant. The naval stories also are inconsiderable. But the collection is better than that. Two stories point to directions in which he will later excel: "Wireless", and "They".

And there is one excellent story in this volume, which has been neglected by later readers, although it was the subject of much discussion in right radical political circles when it first appeared in the *Monthly Review* in September 1902, two months after the cultured *fainéant* Arthur Balfour had succeeded the aged Lord Salisbury as Conservative Prime Minister of England. This story, "Below the Mill Dam", is a political fable expressing Kipling's alarm and dismay at England's apparent inability to address herself socially, imperially, culturally and technologically to the future. It embodies his antipathy to the traditional élitist, conservative but, at the same time, *laissez-faire* cultural and political outlook of Balfour's country-house world.

Then came the Liberal landslide of 1906. Kipling, like many Tories, saw it as a "political avalanche [which] overwhelmed a bewildered, a not in the least intending it, England" – a judgement which, like all sweeping dismissals of sweeping democratic votes, tells us more of the speaker's very limited social and geographical knowledge (confined so much to the south) of his country than of his political acumen. This new radical menace from the left he came to see as a combination of demagogy, incipient anarchy, and pure corruption, to be labelled for convenience with the portmanteau word "socialism", or sometimes under stress, "howling syndicalism". This menace, as he saw it, from the left, Kipling satirised in "The Mother Hive" (1908) as he had attacked the Balfourites in "Below the Mill Dam".

That neither of these two fables has commanded much attention among later Kipling readers is perhaps not surprising, for the particularity of political satire and fable seldom allows it to be much read by later generations – Swift's terrible imaginings have been handed over to children in order to remove their sting (something to which Kipling drew attention), Dryden's and Byron's satirical poems are more honoured than read; I suspect that *Animal Farm* will suffer both these fates when time has wholly reshaped the dreadful outlines of Stalinist conformity.

Neither of Kipling's two fables quite rivals Orwell, let alone Swift, although some of his invective and denunciation in verse has a fierceness that recalls his great poetic forebears. But he was seen as their Laureate by those who read the social and political auguries of the time in the same apocalyptic terms. It seems, therefore, appropriate to accompany a short account of his public life and statements in the years up to the outbreak of the Great War with some discussion of these two satirical fables, and of his positive fictional vision of how England's society could be transformed – "The Army of a Dream", as well as the political satirical poems which begin in 1902 with the championship of the rights of the tommies returned from South Africa to a new, vigorous and less class-bound society, and end in 1912 with "The Benefactors", a poem prophesying an alternative to coal to free us from the tyranny of the miners' union. Even the best of this work, among which I include the two political fables, seems, in the last resort, to be impaired by the muddle of his social ideas, and, more importantly, by the deep contradiction between the political theories he formulated and the nature of his romantic artistic powers. Yet, some are works of force, and none are without interest as the productions under stress of a clever, imaginative and driven man.

At first, the aim is to persuade the returning tommies (and himself?) that all is well with England beneath the ugly surface. Simple faith must be maintained as in "The Return":

> Peace is declared, an' I return
> To 'Ackneystadt, but not the same;
> Things 'ave transpired which made me learn

233

> The size and meanin' of the game.
> I did no more than others did,
> I don't know where the change began.
> I started as an average kid,
> I finished as a thinkin' man.
>
> If England was what England seems,
> An' not the England of our dreams,
> But only putty, brass an' paint,
> 'Ow quick we'd drop 'er! But she ain't.

The juxtaposition is strange and typical of Kipling. I was a boy, I have grown up, therefore things must not be what they appear to be, but what I have always wanted them to be. It is a persistent illogical romantic illusion from which he, as persistently, woke up to nightmare reality. It made nonsense of his political ideas and activities, although his political dreams were far from ignoble and his political nightmares often infinitely more prophetic, more persistently far-seeing than those of most of his more level-headed contemporaries. It made his contact with the outer world often, I am sure, painful – alternating from moods of manic Stalkyish hilarity to moods of savage, suspicious gloom and despair, as events, on rare occasions, fitted into the jigsaw which he had invented and which could never be composed, or, more often, obstinately refused all his cunning and his force to make them fit. It led to a determined, sometimes exhausting division of the private compartment of his life from the public one. It led to a limiting departmentalising of his very many and very various friendships. But, on the positive side, it threw up a lively firework show of poems and fables and dark stories and farces (some of his best farces are the result of his political frustrations of these years). It's a show well worth looking at today even when the setpiece Great Message that he intended all his many rockets and catherine wheels and squibs to announce has fizzed away into nothing.

Only the heady impact of victory in war could allow Kipling to believe that England was really the England of our dreams. If he could sustain the illusion, there were thousands of returned tommies who could not. To them Kipling offered the Empire, emigration, colonisation, the old hope of renewal in Australia that Dickens had given to Mr Micawber and poor fallen little Emily in 1848, but with an added realism that the tommies knew and had tested the promised land, South Africa.

Me that 'ave followed my trade
In the place where the Lightnin's are made;
Twixt the Rain and the Sun and the Moon –
Me that lay down an' got up
Three years with the sky for my roof ...
For I know of a sun an' a wind
An' some plains an' a mountain be'ind ...
An' a Dutchman I've fought 'oo might give
Me a job were I ever inclined
To look in an' off-saddle an' live
Where there's neither a road nor a tree –
But only my Maker an' me
But think it will kill me or cure
So I think I will go there and see! Me! [2]

The gipsy trail with a Dutchman for a boss! It must be a terrible alternate England that could lead Kipling to offer such advice.

What was it, this England, that the returning tommy so longed to escape, the England so much *not* of his dreams? We can see in the returned tommy's complaint of "Chant Pagan":

'Ow can I ever take on
With awful old England again,
An' 'ouses both sides of the street,
An' 'edges two sides of the lane,
An' the parson an' gentry between,
An' touchin' my 'at when we meet –
Me that 'ave been what I've been?
Me that 'ave watched 'arf a world ...
An' I'm rollin' 'is lawns for the Squire, Me!

Me that 'ave rode through the dark
Forty mile, often, on end ...
I am takin' some letters almost
As much as a mile to the post,
An' mind you come back with the change! Me! ...
I am doin' my Sunday-School best,
By the 'elp of the Squire an' 'is wife
(Not to mention the 'ousemaid an' cook) ...
My livin' in that state of life
To which it shall please God to call
  Me! [3]

Rudyard Kipling, with genius and drive and his wife's economic sense, had won for himself a freer, more rewarding, more liberating calling. But I do not doubt that he was irked by Sunday-school England as much as his imaginary tommy. This may seem strange to those who picture him as first, the second squire of Rottingdean (second to his cousin Stanley Baldwin's brother-in-law, Ridsdale) and later the master of Bateman's, the squire of Burwash, the comprehending master of Hobden, that prototype farm labourer of England.

There are great contradictions and evasions here as in all else he said and did.

There was much in the squire's role, especially the technically progressive squire's, that married with his political hopes for England; there was more in the agricultural life that offered to his desperately doubting spirit the assuagement of the recurring seasons and the recurring cycles of social history. But, in fact, the most part of Kipling's squiredom was the poetic dimension that the English countryside, visual and sensual, gave to his imagination and his work increasingly from his visits to Tisbury in the nineties onwards, a dimension that finally came to coincide with a small area of East Sussex. He had many good friends and varied among the wealthier residents of the county, some, though not all, of old Sussex families, but, for the English country hierarchical life and, even more, for the world of the village, I think he had as little taste as he had for any settled group, whether London sophisticates, or Vermont small-towners, or cultured Cape burghers, whom he found it hard to bear. The village is hardly pleasantly painted in "They" or "The Wish House" or "My Son's Wife" – and there are more satirical overtones to the Sunday at church in "An Habitation Enforced" than is usually allowed. Unlike the returned tommy, who must emigrate or stifle, Kipling had until 1908 The Woolsack to winter in, and after that, Engelberg or St Moritz and skating, or after the War, the pleasure cruise, the motoring holiday, the Riviera. That his escapes were increasingly a rich man's (and a sick man's) escapes does not make them any the less vital comings up for air for a man who regularly found the English settled world turning into a stifling grave. His sincerity, his empathy, then, with the man who is doing his Sunday-school best, who cries, "Oh! it's 'ard to be'ave as they wish," who will "arise and get 'ence – trek South and make sure if it's only my fancy or not that the sunshine of England is pale, and the breezes of England are stale, an' there's somethin' gone small with the lot,"[4] is, I am sure, complete, and was with him all his life.

236

For the moment, with the Victorious War behind him and hopes of a new society before him, he could only urge emigration to the south to those who couldn't bear England, and, luckier himself in his two homes, compensate by trying to make England a better place for the talented, the ambitious, and the young. It meant a fairly full-scale attack on all the entrenched Establishment and this he made in three or four or five poems and in "Below the Mill Dam".

Some of these poems, notably "Rimmon" (1903) and "The Song of the Old Guard", directly relate to the necessity of purging the army of the old officer class who, in his opinion, had so nearly lost us the war before Roberts and Kitchener came on the scene. The military case may not be quite so simple as he suggests, but that does not affect the fierceness of the poems.

Perhaps the most striking is the satire upon the Old Guard's self-satisfied resumption of power:

> Know this, my brethren, Heaven is clear
> And all the clouds are gone –
> The Proper Sort shall flourish now,
> Good times are coming on . . .
> A common people strove in vain
> To shame us unto toil
> But they are spent and we remain,
> And we shall share the spoil
> According to our several needs
> As Beauty shall decree,
> As Age ordain or Birth concedes
> And, Hey then up go we!

until at last:

> Then come, my brethren, and prepare
> The candlesticks and bells,
> The scarlet, brass and badger's hair
> Wherein our Honour dwells,
> And strictly fence and strictly keep
> The Ark's integrity
> Till Armageddon break our sleep . . .
> And, Hey then up go we!

The scarlet and brass and badger's hair may point at the officers alone, but the Beauty and Age and Birth extend the attack to the

237

cultured class from which they come. And, as if to underline that the old guard is but part of all the old order, we get "The Old Men" of 1903:

> Because we know we have breath in our mouth
>   and think we have thoughts in our head,
> We shall assume that we are alive, whereas
>   we are really dead . . .
> The Lamp of our Youth will be utterly out, but
>   we shall subsist on the smell of it;
> And whatever we do, we shall fold our hands
>   and suck our gums and think well of it.
> Yes, we shall be perfectly pleased with our work,
>   and that is the Perfectest Hell of it!

The fierceness of this Angry Young Man's attack (Kipling, like many another angry young man, was nearly forty) is apparent, but, perhaps, rather general.

In the most famous of these poems, however, "The Islanders", it is not so vague. It attacks all classes and all aspects of English life, but its strongest play is against the upper and upper-middle classes, the complacent supporters as he saw it of a Tory government that, in its cultured aristocratic indifference, was too idle to listen to its great man, Joseph Chamberlain, in his warning of the German menace and his plea for Imperial unity.

In his scornful attack on the nation's determined blindness to its dangers, only a glancing blow is made at his later enemies – the trade unions, the Socialists, or the worshippers of democracy:

> [When the enemy invades]
> Will ye pray them or preach them, or print
>   them, or ballot them back from your shore?
> Will your workmen issue a mandate to bid them
>   strike no more?
> Will ye rise and dethrone your rulers (because
>   you were idle both)?

or at the commercial classes:

> Ye say it will 'minish trade.

But it is the field sports of the upper and upper-middle classes and the

238

oncerns of scholars and gentlemanly men of letters that come in for
he greatest lashing as unworthy trivialities standing in the way of the
ational realism and preparedness:

> Because of your witless learning and your
>   beasts of warren and chase
> Ye grudged your sons to their service and your
>   fields for their camping-place.

The famous:

> With flannelled fools at the wicket or the
>   muddied oafs at the goals.

And most splendid of all:

> Will ye pitch some white pavilion, and lustily
>   even the odds,
> With nets and hoops and mallets, with rackets
>   and bats and rods?
> Will the rabbit war with your foemen – the red
>   deer horn them for hire?
> Your kept cock-pheasant keep you? He is master
>   of many a shire . . .

And then surely lest Balfour himself should seem to be forgotten:

> Arid, aloof, incurious, unthinking, unthanking, gelt,
> Will ye loose your schools to flout them till
>   their brow-beat columns melt?

It is the castigation of "Recessional", but without the pseudo-
religious note that would allow the castigated to assume a pious
reverential look and forget it. He takes each sacred cow of the clubs
and senior common rooms and slaughters it messily before its worshippers' eyes. But then the right sort of people had known that he
was a bit of a bounder from Simla days. But the bounder was also
now a respected member of the Athenaeum and an honorary doctor of
the great Universities, whose pulpit by right of conquest was *The
Times*.

This poetry of invective has still, I believe, power to affect, for,
apart from its telling hits at contemporary fetishes, it expresses a

mood of anger at complacent conservatism and contented obsole scence which is general and recurrent.

But, of all the planks on which the platform of the Imperialis Radicals of the Right, of whom Kipling was the Laureate, was built the weakest was their home social policy. In origin, this should no have been so. Radical Imperialism descended from notable socia reformers – Sir Charles Dilke and Ruskin back in the seventies. Thei dream of the Anglo-Saxon Empire as the basis of civilisation had bee closely bound with social change and the reinvigoration of Englan itself. Incidentally, it is this that ties the radical Charles Dickens, th advocate of emigration to the colonies as a panacea, the co-supporte with Ruskin and Tennyson of violent suppression of the black rebel lion in Jamaica, to Kipling. This link, which united their commor fears of social disorder, has always intrigued me as an admirer of th art of two such different men.

Yet, to straddle all the concerns of the serious, radical Imperialists – knowledge of the colonies; of the fiscal, economic and immigration policies that would serve best to tie colonial prosperity to the mother-land; understanding of the naval and military needs that would bind them together and protect them from the Imperialist desires of other less fitted races (German, French, Russian); and a detailed, felt know-ledge of England itself in all its regions and classes, so that its social structure might be re-shaped to make it the strong mother-centre that the great Anglo-Saxon Empire could depend on – was probably be-yond the range of any man or group of men, however able.

Joseph Chamberlain came nearest to it, and was certainly the only man among them who possessed a knowledge of England itself that went meaningfully beyond the home counties and the governing classes. Beside him, Milner and his kindergarten – Leo Amery, Geoffrey Robinson, Lionel Curtis – brilliant intellectually though they were – indeed the whole radical right – the Maxses in the *National Review*, St Loe Strachey in the *Spectator* – seem remote and academic as soon as they begin to speak about the condition of England, and the social changes they envisage. Even their opponent, the very Liberal opponent C. F. G. Masterman, though an "intellectual" seems to have had a close and felt understanding of English life beside these men of the radical right.

Milner spoke with conviction of "another socialism which is born of a generous sympathy and a lofty and wise conception of what is meant by national life ... not merely so many millions of individuals each struggling for himself ... but ... the people of this island as a great family bound by indissoluble ties to kindred families in other parts of the world and striving after all that makes for productive power and social harmony".[5] But some earnest work in the East End of London as a young man under the influence of Toynbee and a knowledge of the Inland Revenue were surely not sufficient to give him understanding of the country that was at the centre of his vision. The rest of his experience had been Egypt and South Africa. The brilliant young men around him had gone straight from Oxford to organise war-shattered South Africa. This colonial experience, of course, was essential to their schemes, but it was only a part of the equipment. An equipment that, after Chamberlain's stroke in 1908 removed him from their midst, is surely fatally lacking. That their hopes should have centred round Bonar Law, a Canadian, is an ironic comment.

The whole concept of racialist Anglo-Saxon superiority which these clever men truly believed seems now as absurd as it is repugnant. But its practical weakness lay surely in the demands of experience it asked for, experience and knowledge of real life and not of theory in its supporters. When it came to important social aspects of English life they seem curiously deficient. And Kipling, their literary spokesman, was no exception.

We can see this most clearly in his political prose pieces of the pre-1914 period. In them he offers his positive alternatives to the suicidal, trivial, self-regarding English society that he attacks in the poems I have quoted. These prose pieces fail, though in different degrees; but their failure is instructive both about Kipling and about the incompatibility of creative, living art and collectivist political ideals, however benevolent their intention.

The discussion of Kipling's positive political ideas in those years has been a great deal befogged by an unwillingness to associate a man of high ideals, a generous benevolent man, and a considerable artist, with corporate social ideas at all, because, in their later European forms, they accrued enormities so detestable to our generations. There can be no doubt whatsoever of how much Kipling would have abhorred the form right-wing corporativism took under Hitler in Germany. Apart from his continuing apprehension, as expressed in poems and speeches of his last years, of the resurgence of the German absolutism he had spent most of his life in fighting, again and again in his work he expresses his respect for the Jewish contribution to Western civilisation. It is notable that in his most direct statement about his ideal of a reformed English society finding its corporate expression in national military service, "The Army of a Dream", he goes out of his way to make the Jewish school contingents the victors in the day's military exercises. That this respect for Jews is often mixed up with a sort of

241

slang, common to the whole Victorian and Edwardian age, that we have come to associate with anti-semitism – "To your tents, O Israel. The Hebrew schools stop the mounted troops . . . Pig, were you scuppered by Jew-boys?" – should not for a moment allow us to confuse Kipling with the world of Belloc. If I seem to labour this it is because even excellent and enlightened critics like Lord Annan refer loosely to "Kipling's anti-semitism".

By contrast, we must, I fear, convict Shaw, the Fabian, of an acceptance of the brutalities carried out in the Stalinist name of collectivist efficiency. But then, as has often been pointed out, there is nothing in Shaw's work, even at its best, to lead us to expect him to have any proper realisation of the meaning of individual suffering. Kipling is an artist at almost the opposite extreme from Shaw in this, a man hypersensitive to human feelings. He often wilfully accepted cruelty as a means of punishing or suppressing evil, and he did so sometimes with an unattractive relish. But he is quite incapable of confusing it with the ordering of human happiness or of reducing men to figures as Shaw could. His artistic heart is not in his collectivist dreams.

"The Army of a Dream", a long, two-part account of a dream in which Kipling spends an afternoon with, in turn, the recruiting section and the citizen army on manoeuvres of an ideal England which has accepted military service as an integral part of national life, can hardly be read save as a curiosity. Yet there can be little doubt about the trouble he took in making as attractive as he possibly could this propaganda, which was published in four days' issues of the right-wing *Morning Post* in June 1904. He is deeply concerned to remove all suspicion that his utopia is an imposition of the present social structure by compulsion. Compulsion there is in the ideal state, in so far as military drill is taught at schools from the earliest years, and in that a man who does not volunteer for some branch of the services does not exercise a vote. But, these foundations once swallowed, everything is done to make this society under arms as attractive as can be – the victory of the Jewish Voluntary Schools over the private day schools in manoeuvres is only one small example of his conscious shaping of things to avoid the charge of disguised class propaganda and prejudice.

As a result, most of it reads like a modern recruiting pamphlet, with its constant stress on training for trades, foreign travel experience, increased widespread education and so on. It shows army organisation deliberately used to alter the social structure by encouragement of the efficient and the officer type, but there is no class suggestion in the definition of that type. The excellent restaurants of the citizen army

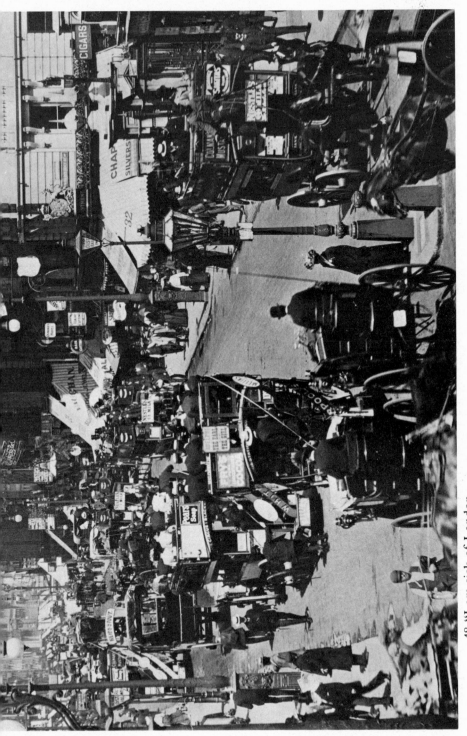

48 "I am sick of London
   From Shepherd's Bush to Bow"
A view of the Strand from the Golden Cross Hotel, Charing Cross, in the 1890s. (*Popperfoto*)

MISS NELLIE FARREN,

IN "RUY BLAS."

Stereoscopic Co⁷

49 "His love of the Cockney music hall, of Nellie Farren and Fred Leslie, his solace at this lonely and perplexed time", page 147. (*Raymond Mander and Joe Mitchenson Theatre Collection*)

50 Portrait of Rudyard Kipling by Lady Granby, afterwards Duchess of
Rutland: Kipling bowdlerized or made beautiful by the Souls with whom
he felt so uncomfortable. (*Bateman's*)

51 An early Cook's poster advertising the "excursionism" that Kipling so despised. (*Thomas Cook*)

52 "Norwegian cock-fighting" on the *Norman Castle* outward bound for the Cape in 1894. (*Stone Collection, Birmingham Reference Library*)

53 Rudyard Kipling telling one of the Just So Stories aboard ship in 1902 on one of his trips to Cape Town. (*Bateman's*)

54 Flying fish wings taken by Rudyard Kipling coming from Australia, 1891. (*Grenville Taylor Collection*)

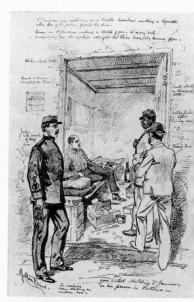

55 Cecil Rhodes leaving Cape Town. (*Illustrated London News*)

56 Drawing of Melton Prior sketching Dr Jameson in the prison at Pretoria. (*Illustrated London News*)

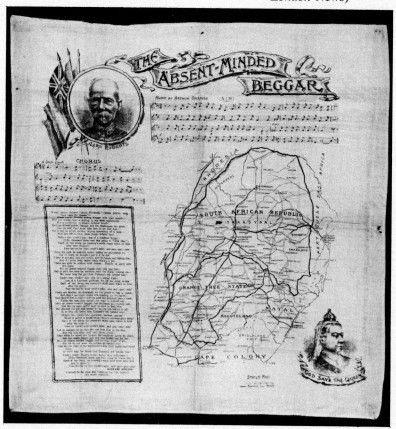

57 "The Absent-Minded Beggar." (*Grenville Taylor Collection*)

8 The CIVs in the Guildhall on their return from South Africa, 1900. (*Guildhall
rt Gallery*)

59 The Woolsack: the house given to the Kiplings by Cecil Rhodes for
their winter residence at the Cape. (*Cape Argus*)

60 Eventide, Driefontein, South Africa.

61 War correspondents at Glovers Island: Kipling *right foreground* with
Julian Ralph, US correspondent (?); Perceval Landon, *Times* correspondent, later a tenant at Bateman's; Gwynne, one of Milner's young
men and later editor of the *Morning Post*. (*Radio Times Hulton Picture
Library*)

bring together not only all ranks but also their womenfolk, quite a revolutionary proposal for 1902. The whole "all classes pull together" dream has the air of a boy-scout jamboree. Indeed its spirit is most closely echoed in Kipling's later association with Baden-Powell's Boy Scouts and the book of stories he put together called *Land and Sea Tales for Scouts and Guides* (1923). In that book we have the public schoolboy Jones who says, "This would make a thundering good golf links . . ." To which the reply is, "Yes, wouldn't it? It would be even prettier as a croquet lawn or basket-ball pitch. Just the place for a picnic too. Unluckily it's a rifle range"; and here too we have William Glasse Sawyer of "His Gift", who proves that the unathletic boy of uneducated background can serve the nation better than many others, for he turns out to be a skilled cook.[6]

As a tale for adult conversion, "The Army of a Dream", for all its talk of social change, is both absurd and remote from the facts of English life. The miners have been lured out of their harmful strike by a compulsory cruise as stokers on naval manoeuvres between Land's End and Gibraltar. "They'd had a free fight at Gib with the Port's battalion there; they cleared out the town of Lagos; and they'd fought a pitched battle with the dockyard-mateys at Devonport. They'd done 'emselves well, but they didn't want any more military life for a bit." Even here, however, it is the pit-owners who are more furious than the reformed miners, for they think that this salutary lesson to their workers has done no more than prolong the strike. And the landed gentry, too, have lost "the top end of Scotland where a lot of those silly deer-forests used to be". It has now become a manoeuvres area. Nothing has done more, it fatuously records, to reconcile the ordinary city-dwellers to the new national life than the privilege of military funerals for all and the free spectacle of seeing so many cortèges pass in the streets. In short its absurdity is as wide as its intended appeal. It suggests that to Kipling's question, "What shall they know of England who only England know?" the simple answer was "More than those who know nothing about England at all." Nor is the fact that it is told in officers' mess slang a help.

Negligible though "The Army of a Dream" may be as serious propaganda, more relevant to us now is its significant decline in artistic balance. The adventures of Mulvaney and Co. had been shared by a Kipling who was an onlooker but who yet felt with them, both in their barrack life and in their private joys and sorrows. There is a serious decline with Pyecroft and the naval stories, but yet there is still some shared fun in the motoring farces and some shared excitement in the naval action stories, however overlaid with technical talk. Now, in this dream of a nation united in common service, a chief plank of appeal in which is the fact that men's private lives are enhanced by their periodic corporate status and not diminished as the lives of Mulvaney and Ortheris and Learoy had been by the old regular service system, we have absolutely no sense of individual private existence at all. And Kipling, who had formerly participated emotionally, is there only as a dream V.I.P. visitor expressly to provide the astonished exclamations of delight and admiration which belong to those who find to their surprise that washing powders wash whiter.

The fable against the Tory old guard, "Below the Mill Dam", is a more serious work and, therefore, a more telling artistic failure. We enter the Mill Dam with the sound of the nine-hundred-year-old song of Domesday Book that is made by the wheel in which lives the Spirit of the Mill – "Nun-nunquam geldavit. Here Reinbert has one villein and four cottars with one plough" etc. And it is the Black Rat (the old English Black Rat), parasitically resident in the Mill, who "luxuriously trimming his whiskers, says, 'I confess I am not above appreciating my position and all it means.' " The Grey Cat, a more sophisticated parasite upon the old system, demurs, " 'Appreciation is the surest sign of inadequacy.' " But then she adds, " 'But I know what you mean. To sit by right at the heart of things, eh?' " Then follow some very good pages of mockery of cultured upper-class complacency: " 'To possess – er – all this environment as an integral part of one's daily life must insensibly of course . . . the ineradicable offensiveness of youth is partially compensated for by its eternal hopefulness . . . isn't it almost time that the person who is paid to understand these things shuts off those vehement drippings with that Screw-thing on the top of that box thing?' . . . They were such beautiful little plants too. Maiden's tongue, hart's hair fern, trellising all over the wall, just as they do on the sides of churches in the Downs. Think what a joy the sight of them must be to our sturdy peasants pulling the hay . . . the so-called 'little but vital graces that make up life' [Rat] . . . 'Yes, life, with its dim delicious half tones and veiled indeterminate distances.' [Cat]"

So, the Rat and the Cat in defence of their comfortable places beside the obsolescent wheel. And all the time – an excellent comic note – the senile wheel itself is pouring out its rambling anti-ruling-class historical liturgy: "Book, book, book, book. Domesday Book . . . the Abbot of Wilton kept the best pack in the county. He enclosed all the Harrington Woods to Shut Common. Aluric, a freeman, was dispossessed of his holding. They tried the case at Lewes . . . William de Warenne on the Bench. William de Warenne fined Aluric eight and fourpence for the arson, and the Abbot of Wilton excommunicated him for blasphemy. Aluric was no sportsman. Then the Abbot's brother married ... I've forgotten her name, but she was a charmin' little woman. The Lady Philippa was her daughter. That was after the barony was conferred. She rode devilish straight to hounds. They were a bit throatier than we breed now, but a good pack, one of the best. The Abbot kep 'em in splendid shape. Now who was the woman the Abbot kept?"

The whole interchange of cat and rat and the background chorus of the wheel is at once both beautifully exact and zany. It makes one regret that Kipling so seldom adventured into mockery and satire. And it builds up, as Kipling always does at his best, an absolute sense of this small dark, decaying, ferny, damp corner in which the mill wheel is running down and the farm cat and the black rat live in slothful ease.

But, against this, the new forces are lifeless, unfelt. The glee of the water stream as it feels the propulsion of the newly constructed dam, the power of the newly installed dynamo are not communicated; all that we feel is the overturning of the life of the rat and the cat; and because the rat and the cat are alive to us, it is felt as an offence of privacy, not a triumph of technological progress. Machines are made for men. Kipling himself had said so. But the voices of the up-to-date farmer and his engineer adviser appear as brutal intrusions on this dark little corner we have come to know by the power of Kipling's evocation. They may kick the cat into the stream and stuff the rat but it is all brute force, however much it may be in the cause of a cleaner, more efficient, more up-to-date England. In the last resort, artistic creation is too individual, too personal an activity to work on behalf of an abstractly conceived social progress. Kipling, in particular, is too dependent upon tensions of despair and delight, of anxiety gnawing at hope, above all too embedded in the particular place and the particular human condition, to use his gifts in celebration of mere efficiency. In "The Bridge Builders", the engineer, Findlayson, wins through, but only after agonies, and, in any case, we are aware that Findlayson's bridge is a particular bridge and the mud flat where he suffers his drugged dream of the Gods is a particular mud flat; and that both will pass in time as do all mud flats and bridges. The rat and the cat are individual humanised animals but the new mill dam and the electric dynamo that sweep away their little dark corner of lazy comfort are simply words on the page.

To a great extent this is true of his later political fable, "The Mother Hive" (1908). Here the menace to the British Imperial civilisation is not so much Tory old guardism as it had been when Balfour ruled in

1902. The new enemies were progressivism, liberal individualism, pacifism, cosmopolitanism, egalitarianism, little Englandism, class division – all the elements in the Liberal Government's rule that worked against a cohesive, well-armed Empire ready both physically and psychologically to resist the growing German menace to the English world-civilising mission.

This corrupting enemy is represented in the fable by the Wax Moth, a deadly progressive female who enters the beehive, and, laying her eggs, sets up an internal rot. It is notable that this destructive stranger "dodged into a brood frame, where youngsters who had not seen the winds blow or the flowers nod, discussed life. Here she was safe, for young bees will tolerate any sort of stranger." It is the susceptibility of the young to new ideas that allows the progressivist Wax Moth to spread her deadly eggs.

The language of the wax moth is less subtly caught than the dialogue of the cat and the rat, there is a touch of *Punch* or of Peter Simple in the take-off of progressive language. Nevertheless, it is accurate enough to be funny, and, once again, to invest the Wax Moth with the only real individuality among the inhabitants of the hive. It is, perhaps, less accurate because a part of Kipling was busy finding Sussex and the English countryside and was acquiring strong sympathies with the tastes of the black rat's squirearchy, while no part of Kipling had ever sought to enter the rootless, cosmopolitan London intelligentsia world of the Wax Moth. But, if there is more exaggeration in the mockery of the irritating progressive Wax Moth than in that of the old English black rat, there are many palpable hits.

Of course, the final answer for Melissa (the heroine young bee) and her proper hive-minded bee associates is to leave the decaying hive and form a colony swarm elsewhere. If Liberal-ruled England is doomed, then Australia or Canada will save civilisation. It was not really what Kipling believed or felt about the White Dominions, but, as an admonitory ending addressed to the heedless, Bandarlog English electorate, it is adequate. What is not adequate artistically is the balance of forces, for once again the Wax Moth, detest and despise her though Kipling may, is real, and her destructive effect upon the hive is an example of Kipling's narration of disaster at its best. But the "good" bees with the true hive-instinct remain, as they must, a collective negative, imaginatively unrealised. As for the Bee Master and his son, the depersonalised voices equivalent to the up-to-date farmer and the engineer who transform the mill, they are no more than awesome voices, as they disinfect and destroy the rotted hive. They represent, no doubt, the forces of Darwinian selective necessity which lay so strongly behind the racial supremacy theory on which the radical Imperialism that Kipling espoused was based. But they would be more effective if they represented the Jehovah of his ancestors purifying Sodom and Gomorrah with fire and brimstone.

The flaw in the fable goes deep. The worst disorder that the Wax Moth's corruption brings about is the multiplication of misfits and oddities. Kipling was quite sincere in his contempt for the Wax Moth when she enthuses about them as "all so delightfully clever and unusual and interesting". We know what he thought about the Bandarlog. Yet, only a year later, he was to begin with "The House Surgeon" and a few years later, "In the Same Boat", a series of stories, uneven but containing some very good work, that were to continue for the rest of his life, stories working through compassion not contempt and studying in depth exactly these misfits and casualties of society that he so brusquely dismisses to the Bee Master's flames.

In truth, his collectivist solutions, and corporate analyses – however much they may interest many modern critics and sociologists because they appear to defy the English nineteenth-century historicist sociological tradition and offer a comparison to the continental theories of Durkheim or Pareto – belong only to the political surface of him, not to his true creative art. As indeed, I think, do the racial theories that attach to them, as his empathy with his Indian characters shows.

His imaginative excellence is always with diversity, and a diversity which includes more of those who are lost and twisted and anxious and, above all, alone, than it does of the self-sufficient, the gregarious, or the conformist. It is exactly, of course, because he is aware of these potentially tragic depths in himself and in others that he is so apprehensive of anarchy and destruction. And exactly because he is so apprehensive that he espouses the ideas of a civilising mission and the White Man's Burden. But in his best fiction where this idea is pursued, notably in *Kim*, the rulers carry out their lonely arduous task in order that the *diversity* of the Great Trunk Road shall flourish. We may suspect the factual truth of this picture of British India, but we must surely honour its artistic embodiment. And we can have no doubt of Kipling's belief in it. But the diversity of the Great Trunk Road, the Indian society worth preserving at such cost of administrative toil, of Mulvaney's bitterness and Orde's thankless death and Findlayson's nightmare, is the complete opposite of the dehumanised dynamo and the swarm hive society he puts forward in these fables of the first decade of this century. But there was always some confusion in Kipling's mind between the vague progressive individuality of cranks like the Wax Moth and collectivist socialism, simply because, for different reasons, he feared both. As late as April 1919, he writes to Doubleday that "The Mother Hive" gives all the history and "development of socialism that emerges in Bolshevism".[7] The hive is surely on the other foot.

How little his creative side responded to the paternalistic, technological utopia which his hysteric side, never so publicly apparent as in the Liberal Government years from 1906 to 1914, demanded for protection, may be seen in one of his very best short stories, surely one of the best science-fiction stories of all time, "As Easy as A.B.C." This was written probably in 1907 (a year before "The Mother Hive") but not published until 1912.

Here we have a picture of the world in 2065, when under the benevolent technological rule of the Aerial Board of Control, a small group of experts from many countries (including Japan) – no Anglo-Saxon, or racial, or even colour purity in *this* ideal society – an era of world contentment and prosperity has been established in which wars have been eliminated, and longevity and physical health generally established in great degree by scientific control of the birth rate as well as of all other aspects of life.

Democracy, the last of history's tyrannies, has been eliminated. As McDonough's Song, the accompanying poem, says:

> Holy State or Holy King –
> Or Holy People's Will –
> Have no truck with the senseless thing.
> Order the guns and kill.

Because democracy has meant the rule of the crowd and the end of privileged individualism, it has been outlawed by a world that has suffered too much from its tyranny. Nowhere is this anti-democratic privacy more cherished than in the remote little town of Chicago where is kept a veiled statue, "The Nigger in Flames", that is the very symbol of the old terrible crowd power, a portrayal of the lynching of a negro. Yet from this very private corner comes news of an outbreak of democratic madness by a small group and the consequent threat of violence, when the rest of the population, especially the women, is held back with difficulty by the mayor from physical revenge upon the would-be democrats.

The members of the Aerial Board of Control are brought in to help authority and are only able to restore order by using the dread ray that brings human activity to a stop. As for the recidivist democrats, they find their place carrying out their antics of voting and speech-making on the London music-halls.

It is hard to convey, in summary, the power and tension of the story's dramatic events, which are, of course, heightened by Kipling's own pessimistic view of humanity that lies behind it. But the real subtlety of the story comes not from the narrative alone but from two other aspects.

In the first place, the very story itself contradicts the proposition of the technological paradise it purports to portray. For it is only in this moment of breakdown, in this unexpected visit of the pestilence of disagreement and conflict in this perfect world that Kipling's creative imagination can work upon it. It may be said that this is an objection to the technological paradise, the world of human will subjected voluntarily to expertise, which, though it may be implicit in the story, is not in Kipling's consciousness. But this is not so. For Kipling puts into the mouths of his benevolent world rulers strangely ambiguous remarks which suggest most clearly that they and he are sadly disillusioned with the vacuous, "perfect" creature world they rule. Dragomiroff, the Russian, says: " 'We have cut the birth rate out – right out! . . . Oh! that is quite well! I am rich – you are rich – we are all rich and happy because we are so few and live so long. Only *I* think Almighty God He will remember what the Planet was like in the times of the Crowds and the Plagues. Perhaps He will send us heroes. Eh, Pirolo?' " And the Italian answers: " 'Perhaps He has sent them already.' "

And later when the ray is first used (benevolently, of course, bringing only a very temporary deafness and blindness to the raging crowd) we are given a hint of something missing, when Dragomiroff, the very wise old man, cries out in fear: " 'Pardon,' he moaned, 'I have never seen Death.' "

And then again the mayor of Chicago tells of the delight with which he first heard the recidivist democrats make their complaints: " 'What did they talk about?' said Takahira [the Japanese member of the Board of Control]. 'First how badly things were managed in the city. That pleased us . . . we hoped to catch one or two good men for city work. You know how rare executive capacity is. Even if we didn't, it's refreshing to find anyone interested . . . You don't know what it means to work, year in, year out, without a spark of difference with a living soul . . . I assure you, we . . . have done things that would have discredited Nero . . . but . . . there isn't a Kick or a Kicker left on the Planet.' "

In his fear of the anarchy of crowd tyranny, of the breakdown of order, never so intense as in these Lloyd George years of growing social welfarism, Kipling invents a future utopia in which pain and conflict and diversity have been abolished, but he records his recognition of his sense of inestimable loss, for without them, as he knows, his fiction is unimaginable.

There is need only for a brief survey in this primarily literary study of the actual political tensions of Kipling's life in these pre-war years which led him to the impasse of the fables and the disillusionment of "As Easy as A.B.C.". He shared the general aim of the right-wing radical Imperialists – a world federation of Anglo-Saxon countries emerging from the British Empire and based upon full ties of economy and defence, but, above all, upon the possession of a common social culture. Yet there is little evidence of his being steeped in reading of the Victorian pioneers of Imperial theory, save Ruskin, whom, in any case, he came to through Uncle Ned and the pre-Raphaelites. It is notable that, in 1904 when the Secretary of the Empire League asked for reading lists for schools, whereas Joseph Chamberlain put forward the bible of the Imperialists, Seeley's *Expansion of England* of 1883, Kipling's list is entirely made up of Hakluyt, Mungo Park and other explorers' tales as well as adventure stories by Americans like Herman Melville and Dana. The romance of Imperialism for him was felt through individual exploit rather than through historical or social theory.

It is hard to say how much of the Imperialists' racial mystique he really felt deeply. My impression is that it was always undercut by his imaginative particularity, and, also, by his early unconscious absorption of India which weakened not only his racial but his colour exclusiveness. There is seldom in what he says that alarming quality of religion of race that can suddenly startle one as it does in the casual utterances of Rhodes, or, even more extraordinarily, of the superficially unemotional Milner. Yet broadly he accepted it, as his constant hope that the United States might turn aside from her increasingly mongrel path and return to the road of Anglo-Saxon purity suggests.

Where he differed from many of his colleagues, from Rhodes's inclusion of German Rhodes Scholars in his Oxford bequest, from the practical politician Chamberlain or from Milner with his boyhood residence in Germany, was in his implacability towards Germany. On the other hand, if he could never assimilate the Teuton into the Anglo-Saxon dream, his admiration for France, beginning perhaps as a recognition of a necessary ally against Germany, had by the outbreak of the First World War grown to an acceptance of French culture as almost the loved equal of English.

But, however inconsistent his Anglo-Saxon mystique, he was committed to all the aims of the Imperialists. First to the strengthening of common defence. This meant the espousal in England of the policy of National Service. If his general conscription aims were less naive than "The Army of a Dream" would suggest, they were hardly less hopeless. When, in 1906, General Roberts was persuaded into forming the National Defence League to advocate national military service, Kipling was a vociferous adjutant of his old friend. The same year, of course, saw the advent of the Liberal Government with a huge majority and made any likelihood of success for the scheme highly improbable. But government apart, the nation was, in general, when not absolutely antipathetic, at least apathetic to the whole idea. Nor were most of the military chiefs, with their exclusive training, very favourable. And Roberts, who had been old when he was the hero of the Boer War, was now venerated rather than listened to. In fact, of course, it took two terrible years of war to reconcile the English to so uncongenial a measure. And Kipling found himself in 1914 and 1915 making recruiting speeches, when he openly declared the volunteer system to be wrong. In this, as in their social reform ideas, the right-wing radicals were out of touch with the nation – Indian-born Kipling, German-born Milner.

The white colonies, too, whose rallying to the flag of Anglo-Saxon civilisation against the menace of the backwood, peasant-cultured Boers had been so promising, waxed hot and cold over common Imperial defence as they did over Tariff Reform to strengthen Imperial economic links and over encouraging British immigrants, whose increase was so required to offset the alien elements like the Boers or the French Canadians. The democratic system in Australia or Canada was almost as inimical to the true interests of the British Empire, as the Imperialists saw them, as in South Africa or in Britain itself, bringing to power Labour-dominated governments in Australia or French-Canadian-influenced governments like those of Laurier in Canada. The periodic Colonial Conferences of these years and elections in the dominions threw Kipling into wild elation or despair, at least until the question of Ulster swallowed up everything else. Yet, I suspect that Kipling's reactions were mixed with a profound irritation and boredom as much with the colonial enthusiasts as with the affairs of the colonies themselves. It is notable that he wrote two good farcical stories during this time in which colonial dignitaries are the principal butts. And farce was always Kipling's method of paying off scores.

"The Puzzler", published in 1906, has as its central figure,

Penfentenyou, "his colony's Premier in all but name . . . Politically, his creed was his growing country; and he came over to England to develop a Great Idea in her behalf." He is probably meant for Canadian, for he had been in "De Thouar's First Administration". The character is from the start satirically as well as sympathetically seen. But what he learns from England, he learns from a farcical incident in which various distinguished Englishmen indulge in a schoolboyish joke with an organ-grinder's monkey up a monkey-puzzle tree. The narrative is in the middle rank of Kipling's humorous tales. But its moral is without any ambiguity. Distinguished Englishmen, caught in illegal trespass as a result of their absurd joke, act together. Penfentenyou learns an important lesson from this, as the story's end declares, "Now and again, from afar off, between the slam and bump of his shifting scenery, the glare of his manipulated limelight, and the controlled rolling of his thunder drums, I catch his voice, lifted in encouragement and advice to his fellow-countrymen. He is quite sound on Ties of Sentiment, and alone of Colonial Statesmen ventures to talk of the Ties of Common Funk." The explicit lesson is simple. Whatever else, the Imperial countries must stand together for the practical reason of defence against common enemies. An additional point is that (Balfour and the Tory old guard notwith-standing) the colonials have much to learn from the English Establishment. But the most important thing they have to learn is that of humour, of the serious value of play, of coming off their earnest high horses. I think Kipling must have suffered a good deal of bore-dom at the junketings attendant upon the Colonial Conferences.

A very good farcical story, "The Vortex" (published, ironically, in August 1914), confirms this view. For here the butt of the story is Mr Lingnam, "a Voice of Imperial declaration" from Penfentenyou's Dominion. There is no doubt of his deadly power to bore. "We dined at eight. At nine Mr Lingnam was only drawing abreast of things Imperial. At ten the Agent-General, who earns his salary, was shamelessly dozing on the sofa . . . At midnight Mr Lingnam brought down his big-bellied despatch box with the newspaper clippings and set to federating the Empire in earnest . . . 'Reciprocally coordinated Senatorial Hegemony' . . . elaborated for three quarters of an hour. At half past one he urged me to have faith and to remember that nothing mattered except the Idea." When we remember that Kipling and his fellow Imperialists were dedicated to exactly such federation, we can get something of the boredom he had suffered from colonial visitors to Bateman's. But revenge comes the next day, when a still talking Mr Lingnam finds himself in the centre of a vast bee swarm in an English village. Like many of Kipling's best farces it involves a whole village cast and is reached by that vehicle of lawlessness and release from conventional restraint, the motor car.

Perhaps his relations with Canada in these years suggests best this gap between the surface, public political frenzy and the inner, private dislike. Canada was the white dominion that Kipling had known longest; it had been twice his relief from what he was not enjoying in the United States; he had designed it as his bolt-hole in the event of Anglo-American war over Venezuela. Despite so many disappointing backslidings on the tie with Britain, during Sir Wilfred Laurier's long premiership, it had been the first colony to give some chance to Joseph Chamberlain's Tariff Reform policy when, as early as 1897, it granted preferential tariffs for English goods. Kipling celebrated this by a poem in *The Times*, "Our Lady of the Snows". Canada, in the poem, ends with a call to the other white colonies to follow her suit:

> They that are wise may follow
> Ere the world's war-trumpet blows,
> But I – I am first in the battle,
> Said Our Lady of the Snows.

It was to Canada, late in 1907, that Kipling and his wife went on what must be seen as his only official tour of a dominion, in these years when he was the most famous spokesman for British Imperialism in the world. His first purpose was to receive a doctorate from McGill University at Montreal, but they made a triumphal journey from coast to coast (to Vancouver beloved by them as by all the British as home from home) by a special private car of the Canadian Pacific Railroad, like royalty.

An article by J. Castell Hopkins in the *Canadian Annual Review of Public Affairs* for 1907 allows one to see a Canadian view of the visit. It must, however, be said that some part of its note may have been due to Kipling's always uncomfortable relationship with his old profession – journalism. Hopkins writes: "A brief but interesting incident of the year was Mr Rudyard Kipling's visit to Canada. He was known to the cultivated by his work, to the mass as the poet of the Empire, but his personality was for Canadians entirely a matter of newspaper impression." Then he goes on to say "Our Lady of the Snows" had not been popular among a people unduly sensitive to the injury which American misrepresentation of English ignorance of their climate had done to the country.[8] Poor Kipling! One is bound to sympathise with his improbable gaffe, but it shows the dangers an artist runs when he uses his gift for words in a politically fraught context. Kipling had been so instantly converted to the beauty of snow that first day at Brattleboro, how was he to guess the complicated overtones the word implied for the Canadians? Yet in his good intention he had hit upon a phrase that could be used by the Americans to insist to Canada upon British ignorance of their country – the one thing of all he wished to avoid; and he had unwittingly increased the inclement image of Canada that deterred so many British immigrants! How unfair, too, to his beloved Vancouver the snowless! And he must have taken such trouble to please the Catholic French Canadians with "Our Lady". It is a farcical incident, but instructive. Mr Hopkins goes on to say that "for reasons, however, not known to the public, Kipling did not meet the people at all; he addressed the Canadian Club at Toronto, Montreal, Ottowa, Winnipeg, Vancouver and Victoria; his views were clearly enunciated, and far flung over the stretches of half a continent; but his personality did not touch the masses, who would much have liked to hear and see him." [9]

It was hard for the famous Kipling and his wife not to have acquired a V.I.P. regality and, in different ways, they surely loved it; but they had not the royal power of appearing "to meet the people". In truth it was the last thing that either of them would have wanted to do. The V.I.P. echo comes in Hopkins's account of a Vancouver occasion: "At the Canadian Club luncheon in Vancouver, on October 6th, Mr Kipling received an ovation from a gathering representative of all that was best in the financial, social and political life of the city." [10] His main concern was to urge more immigration of British working families – "England has five millions of people to spare." [11]

In his account of his visit, "Letters to the Family", published soon after, Kipling accounts for Canadian resistance to British immigration as one result of the blight that the Liberal Government had brought upon England, making the working classes, to Canadian views, "rotten with socialism". But in Mr Hopkins's account we see the problem in a somewhat different light. Canadian labour opposition, particularly in Vancouver, was to coloured immigrants – Chinese and Indians, British though they might be. To Kipling, these fears seemed absurd when they were letting in Eastern European and Central European immigrants, "races to whom you are strangers, whose speech you do not understand, and from whose instincts you are separated by thousands of years". These were the aliens, inimical to British interests, not the coloured Asian British, above all, the Indians. "I do not understand how the Dominion proposes to control an enormous Oriental trade, and, at the same time, hold herself aloof from the

Asiatic influx which is the natural concomitant of that trade." At last he is driven in defence of the Indians he knew so well to say only that, "Hindus who came to Canada did not come to stay and were not therefore to be feared as settlers." [12]

To Canadian emotion about coloured invasion he replies with simple material fact; yet, basically, what disappointed him was how materialistic was the Canadian approach to what was, to him, a life-and-death struggle for the preservation of English civilisation. One of the paradoxes about Kipling is that for a man who disliked public appearances and speaking, he put some of his most deeply personal and revealing statements into his speeches. As a result, *A Book of Words*, that incorporates them, makes splendid reading. His speech to McGill University is no exception. It is his most direct and fierce attack upon materialism, a clear warning that the sterling quality of the students will be worth nothing if their sense of their duties is swallowed up by material prosperity.

There is, therefore, some disingenuousness in his praise of Canadian pioneer virtues. [The Canadians say]: "Shall we make a city where no city is? ... They do it, too, while across the water, gentlemen, never forced to suffer one day's physical discomfort in their lives, pipe up and say, 'How grossly materialistic!' " [13] Yet to Lord Milner, who proposed a visit to Canada, he wrote in 1908, "You will have to face the impact of young, callow, curious and godlessly egotistical crowds who will take everything from you and put nothing back. Their redeeming point is a certain crude material faith in the Empire." [14] The Canadians, he tells him, want slabs of praise. Perhaps it is not disingenuous, but simply that Kipling disliked in mass what he could admire in individuals. But the whole Canadian experience, I think, suggests his incompatibility with the colonial world his theory exalted.

As soon as he is distanced from it, of course, his lyricism returns. His Canadian enthusiasm was strongly reinforced by his friendship with Max Aitken, later Lord Beaverbrook, whom he met in 1910 and whom he actively helped to win his first election at Ashton-under-Lyne in that year. The families soon became very close and Beaverbrook's second son was named Peter Rudyard. It may have been the fact that he was staying with Aitken at Cherkeley Court when the news of the 1911 victory of the Imperialist party in Canada over Laurier came in, but his letter to Milner reaches the height of his lyrical excitement about Imperial events from afar off: "It's some few years – 7 or 8 I think – since I have been happy . . . Seriously don't you think it's the best thing that's happened to us in ten years." [15]

Aitken's materialism and power-seeking were evident, but they could be seen, as Kipling had always seen Rhodes' money sense, as subordinate to his prophetic faith in Empire. In addition he was a lively, Stalkyish personality. It was not until after the war, that Kipling decided that main chance ruled Beaverbrook's prophetically proclaimed principles and, almost uniquely in his life, erased for ever a close friendship. But in the years leading up to the War, Aitken and his friend Bonar Law, as the hopes of Unionist salvation from Balfour-like decay, kept Canada green in Kipling's mind.

Yet the elation about the 1911 Canadian election is a rare sunshine in the grim weather of Kipling's political experience of those years, especially from 1910 onwards. Any pleasure at the reduced Liberal majority of that year – "There's a feeling in the air, that we can hold them with a little bit in hand" – was accompanied by doubts about the House of Lords: "I have a horrible fear among many fears that the Lords will now compromise – like 'gentlemen', out of some vague idea of saving the country, playing the game, pleasing the King or some other Devil's excuse for selling the pass." [16]

But the horrors of England – the Egyptian scribe Bal-Phour as he calls him in a skit, the detestable Churchill and "Squiff" Asquith and Lloyd George, and the insufficient Haldane, trade union revolutionaries, weak Lords, suffragettes – all were soon to pale beside the Ulster Question. Nevertheless, the almost paranoid nightmare that Kipling (and many right-wing people) made out what they saw as a radical conspiracy in these years produced from Kipling's pen an excellent farce. "The Village That Voted the Earth Was Flat" was not published until 1917 in the book of stories, *A Diversity of Creatures* – it is dated as 1913; but Carrington says that Mrs Kipling's diary dates its writing to the summer of 1914. If the latter is true, it is a frolicsome lead up to the War. It has not, I think, received its due because *A Diversity of Creatures* contains one or two of Kipling's finest serious stories, beside which it pales.

The farce, as so often, depends on the motor car. And in this case the pirate-hero motorists are Kipling, an eminent journalist, a brilliant young ex-Oxonian and a Tory M.P. They are charged with speeding in a village. Brought before the local Justice of the Peace, they are, in their opinion, monstrously and very pompously convicted. Charged and convicted shortly after them is the famous music hall impresario, "Bat" Masquerier. The J.P., it emerges, is the local landowner and a Radical M.P. Something of the air of conspiratorial myth that entered Kipling's views in those years may be gauged from this description of the village, "They are all Rads who are mixed up in this from the Chief Constable down," or again (apparently a hit at Bunyan whom

Kipling greatly admired as a writer), "That comes of stuffing the bench with Radical tinkers." On this radical village the combined powers of parliament, press and music-hall have their Stalky revenge in a well-sustained, quick moving narrative with lots of variations of people and scene, and, above all, a dominant comic idea that is very original. It is worth noting that one of the sins of the Radical J.P., Sir Thomas Ingersoll, is his addressing Masquerier in the dock in antisemitic tones.

This story was the last comic fling before Armageddon broke out, it is also a piece of violent farce at a time when Kipling's political speeches and intentions had, like those of most of his associates, reached a point of hysteria which threatened violence. The promise of Home Rule for Ireland, made by the Liberal leaders to the Southern Irish politicians, on whom, after 1910, their parliamentary majority depended, brought the Right Wing to a point of frenzy. They believed that the Government proposed to coerce Ulster by force into acceptance of identification with the rest of Ireland in Home Rule; whatever their justification, there is no doubt that, in cooperation with many high-ranking serving officers, including Sir Henry Wilson, who gave information of Government plans from the War Office, they were prepared, as they thought justifiably, to organise military resistance in Ulster.

Kipling, of course, had always strong and equivocal feelings about Ireland, perhaps because of his mother's Irish ancestry. But the Macdonalds were Scots Wesleyan immigrants and his natural sympathies, apart from his strong Imperial feelings against any weakening of the Irish tie with England, were with the Ulstermen. He had known and liked Carson, the Ulster leader in the Commons, from early in the century when they were neighbours at Rottingdean. In September 1912, Carson launched the Irish covenant which considered "using all means which may be found necessary to defeat the present conspiracy to set up a Home Rule Parliament". By January 1914, Milner had come back into politics with the more overtly rebellious scheme of the British Covenant – he envisaged "action over here [i.e. in England] . . . falling short of violence or active rebellion, or at least not beginning with it".[17] On 3 March 1914 a letter appeared in all newspapers announcing the formation of the British Covenant and calling for signatures. "The time is fast approaching when the evident intention of the Government to pass the Home Rule Bill into law without giving the nation, by General Election or Referendum, an opportunity of passing judgement on it, will plunge the country into civil turmoil. The resistance . . . will be a well-justified resistance. We appeal to all our fellow countrymen to join in a solemn protest, etc." And the protest to be signed reads, "I . . . . solemnly do declare that, if the Bill is so passed, I shall hold myself justified in taking and supporting any action which may be effective to prevent its being put into operation, and more particularly to prevent the armed forces of the Crown being used [etc.]"

Among the twenty signatories, including Milner and Roberts, was Kipling. The only other artist was Sir Edward Elgar. Kipling contributed to the paper, the *Covenanter*. And, along with Lord Astor, he headed the fund contributions with a sum of £30,000 – an enormous amount of money for that time.

In March, the Government's plans to reinforce troops in Ulster were halted by a near-mutiny of senior British officers at the Curragh barracks in Southern Ireland. But preparations still went on. In April, 30,000 rifles purchased in Hamburg reached Ulster. And Southern Ireland was not long in getting help from the same source. In fact, only the outbreak of the Great War brought the explosive situation to an end in a far greater European explosion.

Kipling might write jauntily:

> But Bobs arranged a miracle
> (He does it now and then)
> For he'll be Duke of Orange sure,
> And we'll be Orange men.

but his political speech of May 1914 at Tunbridge Wells was more seriously violent. He accused the Liberal Cabinet of acting as they did for monetary gain, and of bribing the Members of Parliament by giving them a salary of £400 a year. He also aired the fierce Marconi scandal of 1912, in which cabinet ministers were suspected of financial interests in the wireless telegraphy company to which they had granted government contracts. Officers had honourably sacrificed their own careers rather than use arms to compel Ulster. But, "do not be deceived . . . if the Cabinet thinks that murder will serve the Cabinet's turn again, they [the officers] will attempt it [resistance] again. And they will go further . . . Civil war is inevitable unless our rulers can be brought to realise that, even now, they must submit these grave matters to the judgement of a free people." [18] The Stalkyish motor offence of "The Village That Voted the Earth Was Flat", seems indeed farcical beside the unlawfulness the Imperialists felt they might have to engage in against the Government if Home Rule really threatened the Empire.

And yet, at the very same period, in December 1913, Kipling's sense of the immediacy of German invasion was so strong that he wrote "The Edge of the Evening", a story in which some right-minded Americans staying at an English country house assist their hosts in killing two German spies, advance guard of invasion, who have landed in the grounds in a biplane. And, in a National Service League speech at Burwash in September 1913, he said, "The nearest a man can come in imagination to his own death is the idea of lying in a coffin with his eyes shut, listening to the pleasant things he thinks his neighbours are saying about him; the nearest that a people who have never known invasion can come to the idea of conquest and invasion is a hazy notion of going about their usual work and paying their taxes to tax collectors who will perhaps talk with a slightly foreign accent." Even attempted invasion, he went on, didn't mean that: "It meant riot and arson and disorder and bloodshed."[19] He had predicted it so long that he was not surprised when Armageddon broke out and, more than most, he had some idea in advance of what it might be like.

Carefully kept apart, there were always incompatible needs within Kipling, to avoid collective life in which his shaky sense of identity might be lost, and to seek group association that would assuage his anxious search for himself. They only met in collision under too great pressure, as in London in 1890, or in America in 1895; but the explosion that was marked by the greatest shattering was in his public life during the immediate pre-war years, for then his burning feelings were stoked by the infective hysteria of the group he had joined.

6 HEALING, HOME AND HISTORY

In September 1902, the Kiplings left Rottingdean, almost midway on
the coastline of Sussex, for Bateman's, a remote house near the small
village of Burwash in the inland heart of East Sussex. It was a remove
from increasing involvement with the masses to near-isolation, for
even in the five years of their stay at Rottingdean, changes in social
habit had brought ever more horse-bus loads of holidaymakers from
Brighton two and a half miles away to what had so little time before
been a quiet village green. More and more people were taking holidays
and asking more from them. Kipling was now a very famous man and
it was a natural part of some Brighton holidays to go out and see
where he lived. This prying and peeping led to much disagreeableness
– Naulakha with trippers rather than reporters – and anyway, the
house was right beside the green and the high walls did not preserve
the family privacy.

The removal to Bateman's was a departure, too, from family
intimacy and memory to an area, in the main, of strangers. Kipling's
first visit to Rottingdean had been to stay with the Aunt and the Uncle
at their cottage, North End, then only two years in their possession, in
his last summer before leaving for India. Its very name, North End,
had been given to it to connect it with their London home in North
End Road, Fulham, the centre of Kipling's happiest English childhood holidays. The green, during the Kipling's five-year residence, was
quite a family estate, for three of the larger houses on it, known as the
Green houses, were connected by kinship. As well as North End and
the Kiplings' Elms, there was The Dene which had belonged to
the Ridsdales since the late seventies, and Cissie (Lucy) Ridsdale had
married Kipling's cousin, Stanley Baldwin, in 1892. It was a world of
Macdonald cousins.

In moving from Rottingdean, Kipling was leaving behind that mixture of sparkle and despond which characterised so many of the Macdonalds and over which, I think, he kept such a tight rein in himself. He was also leaving behind unbearably happy and unhappy memories, for, at The Elms, Josephine, his eldest, had given him some of her closest companionship. She was five when they moved there, a time of mental and physical growth in children that gives promise, not only of the delight that he had known with the small child at Naulakha, but of a much more active partnership in walks and games of invention. These he clearly shared with Josephine. The autobiography of his niece the novelist Angela Thirkell, the Burne-Jones's granddaughter, *Looking Back*, gives a pleasing account of the games of Roundheads and Cavaliers, in which she and Josephine were the King's men and Kipling Oliver Cromwell's man (an agreeable role to him, for he was always anti-Charles I – "Holy People or Holy King . . . Have no truck with the senseless thing.")

From Angela's account, Josephine, who now had her own governess, was a forward child, writing about her father, the Roundhead, "He is a horrible man, let us do all the mischief we can to him"[1] – a nice turn of seventeenth-century phrase for a child of six. Kipling must also have seen her changing from a small American into a quickly growing English girl, although Angela Thirkell tells us the Kipling children had the American habit of breaking their boiled eggs into a glass and stirring with a passion. From 1899 until 1902 he had to bear the unhappiness of Rottingdean without her.

Many, including Lockwood, attest how unbearable The Elms became to Rudyard and, indeed, to Carrie, after Josephine's death. His niece, Angela, over thirty years later, says, "I feel that I have never seen him as a real person since that year,"[2] and his daughter, Elsie, wrote, "She belonged to his early happy days, and his life was never the same after her death; a light had gone out that could never be re-kindled."[3]

The other great change from Rottingdean to Burwash was scenic. The greatest delight of travel in England is the rapid change of soil and dominating climate and, therefore, of vegetation, over very short distances – far more striking than in other small countries like Holland or Denmark or Ireland. The change from The Elms to Bateman's was from the rolling chalk South Downs close-cropped by grazing sheep to the Weald land of woods and brooks and cattle. I think that there is little doubt that this change of scenery from harsh, sea-gale-swept open land to lush, fertile covert scenery had great significance for Kipling. Scene and place are the basis of his imaginative world, but the Sussex distinction I have described is the subject of some of his best writing in the stories of these pre-war years. In the stone-age story of the Puck cycle, "The Knife and the Naked Chalk", Una and Dan, the two children, are on a visit to the Downland seaside from the Weald (as, indeed, Elsie and John Kipling may often have visited their great-aunt, Georgie) and they get into conversation with a local shepherd, who urges the virtues of the chalkland over the "messy trees of the Weald . . . they draw the lightning and . . . so, like as not you'll lose half a score of ewes struck dead in one storm . . . Now press your face down and smell the turf. That's Southdown thyme." But Una says of the Downland, "It's just like the sea, you see where you're going, and – you go there, and there's nothing between." And Dan concurs, "When we get home I shall sit in the woods all day."

This is an amusing example of how Kipling disliked a rebuff. In this story the shepherd says, "You come to talk to me the same as your father did," and the whole passage implies a former regular relationship between the father and the shepherd. Yet in fact, old Steve Barrow, the well-known local shepherd, refused to let Kipling hear the old Sussex ballads he knew, saying, "That Rudyard Kipling would send 'em to Lunnon and make a mort of money out of 'em." [4] Perhaps not an unfair judgement of the Kiplings' strong commercial sense.

Despite the accompanying poem in praise of the Downs, I think that, at that time at any rate, Kipling's longing was for the Weald and the lushness and privacy. I was raised in the South Downs and spent much of my adolescence there; but also I stayed much in the Weald as a youth. I can testify to the polarisation that the scenery has in memory between the open and agoraphobic and the enclosed and claustrophobic. Because the novelist, of all artists, pivots most between the public world he feeds upon and the private world in which he creates, such an antithesis is very powerful. I have no doubt that in finding Bateman's, Kipling found once again the privacy that had been despoiled in Vermont. And that it gave him the impetus to create a whole new world out of the Sussex countryside, which, if it does not rival his "India", is still a composite imaginative creation of haunting power.

Rottingdean had seen the end of the past – the Stalky stories were brought together and completed there; *Kim* was, at last, made whole; the *Just So Stories* completed. A wonderfully productive time, but the last of his boyhood and of India and the jungle world. The summer and autumn months at Rottingdean in those years were not empty times either. Here he made his practical contribution to "The Army of a Dream" by his organisation of the Rifle Club, which, no doubt, he hoped would be the start of a whole chain of such groups linking the men of England in fitness, defence and fellowship. The flavour of it can be found in his story, "The Parable of Boy Jones".

At Rottingdean he made a very close friendship with his cousin, Stanley Baldwin, which was to endure even the political divergences of his last years. Baldwin would seem to have been in private as well as in public life a peacemaker – something badly needed in the Macdonald world. Kipling's affection for his aunts and cousins was as great as Baldwin's, but he had surely neither the same patience nor the same tact. And these were badly needed with Phil Burne-Jones who, with worldly failure, had grown a strangely moody man, now gloomy, now witty. Rudyard's enormous success could hardly have helped. And the temperamental effects were far too near home.

Then there were political differences, that at a time when Kipling was becoming increasingly obsessed with politics, must have been difficult. His beloved cousin, Margaret Burne-Jones, Angela's mother, had married a radical academic, Mackail. Even Baldwin's in-laws, the Ridsdales, in some degree squires of the village, were not wholly untouched by the Liberal virus of the time. Aurelian, the second son, was to be Liberal Member of Parliament for Brighton in the wicked government of 1906; but this was after Kipling had left. As for Aunt Georgie, she was too beloved of her nephew, especially after the Uncle's death, for politics to divide them. Her Morrisite and Ruskinian preachings in the village would be no more to her nephew than an indulged, occasionally tiresome folly. The often repeated story of the incident of the peace celebrations of 1902 in Rottingdean is so pleasing because it shows Kipling in an unusually conciliatory light (something apparent to any readers of his letters but characteristically never publicised). Yet it must have been a vexation because it involved him in a public scene, something he detested.

Lady Burne-Jones (Aunt Georgie), with characteristic courage, met the Treaty of Vereeniging which ended the Boer War with the display from North End House of a large black banner, bearing the words, "we have killed and also taken possession". A crowd gathered during the evening to demonstrate against this show of "pro-Boerism", and their attempts to pull down the banner might have led to some show of violence against the house. Kipling and Aurelian Ridsdale needed a good deal of tact and persuasion to disperse the objectors. Among them surely must have been a number of Kipling's rifle club members whose patriotism he was so ardent to stir. The move to Bateman's was planned before this incident, but it must have helped to make the parting sweeter.

And for Carrie, surely, the move from Rottingdean must have been something like Rudyard's escape from the Balestiers in Brattleboro save that then they were pushed, and now they went of their own accord.

The new artistic inspiration that came to Kipling with this last move in his life was compounded of three elements, which curiously intertwine in many of the stories – psychological illness, psychic phenomena and the Sussex countryside.

The earliest story that announces this new world of Kipling's is, "They", published in August 1904, nearly two years after the move. When one says that this story reveals much of Kipling's desperate mourning for his dead Josephine; and that it expresses to the full his almost mystical love of children; and that it does both in the form of an enigmatic account of the psychical phenomenon of dead children returned to a beautiful old house and garden to assuage their parents' grief; and that it was published in the year of the knockout success of *Peter Pan* on the West End of London stage; the reader may expect the worst. Yet "They" has little of the whimsy or of the sentimentalism that might be feared. Of Barrie's particular sort of self-consciously fey writing Kipling was, thank God, quite incapable, as also of any self-consciously childlike humour. In his writing for children, even very small children, as with the *Just So Stories*, he is always assuming that they will enjoy and share his level, never that he should pretend to some general fancy of a child's mind. He could be embarrassingly sentimental about children. He had been so in "Wee Willie Winkie" and in "His Majesty the King" back in 1888, and was to be so again in 1928 in "The Debt" at the time of George V's grave illness. But in both cases, he is writing of little white sahibs in India founded upon his treasured memory of his own tyrannical little self in the Bombay household of the eighteen-sixties. When one thinks of what sentimental horror Dickens would have made of a story of dead children returning to comfort us, one can for once be thankful for Kipling's sometimes crippling conscious self-restraint. The defect of "They" is less grave: in the last resort, it has a small touch of that paraded mystery which makes all but a very few "psychic" stories irritating, but a very small touch.

It is almost a direct fantasy of Kipling's longing to see and touch his daughter again. A man, motoring westward across Sussex from the Weald in the east, from Bateman's in fact, comes, by chance, in the centre of the county, by a rough track, on to the lawn of a great Elizabethan country house, hedged with yews clipped to the shapes of great peacocks and horsemen and maids of honour. Here he sees children peeping at his intrusion from upper windows and playing and giggling by the fountain. The blind lady who owns the house accepts casually his talk of the children, to whom she devotes her life, but whom she cannot see. The narrator's conversation with the blind woman is well organised to suggest to the reader what the children are without the narrator knowing it.

A few months later, the narrator returns and, this time, his conversation with the blind woman is interrupted by the drama of an illegitimate village child ill with meningitis. (Only just in time for the reader, in fact, for the conversation about the nature of the dreams of blind people, interesting enough in itself, is just about to run into Kipling's increasing weakness – pretentious specialised knowledge – with Freemason's talk of The Egg.) Only the narrator's modern means of transport can bring a doctor and a nun nurse to the dying child, after a well-described motor dash about the Sussex countryside.

Months later, in a cold autumn, the motorist returns again. This time he learns from the village shop that the bastard child has died and that the mother, Jenny, is "walking in the wood". He still does not realise that it is to this house and its woods and gardens that bereaved parents go for comfort. And here Kipling earns high marks, for so often, when a narrator is behind the reader in comprehension, irritation grows with his slowness to understand. But in "They" one is convinced that the narrator is an intelligent man who can only learn gradually what sort of place he has found and why he is drawn there. At last, on this cold day, in the great hall of the house, beside a great fire, while the mistress discusses estate affairs with a cheating tenant farmer, the narrator, sitting idly by, comes to know by the feel of a child's fingers and its kiss on the palm of his hand what these children are that he has glimpsed and heard for so long – for the kiss is the "half-reproachful signal of a waiting child not used to neglect even when grown-ups were busiest – a fragment of the mute code devised very long ago . . . Then I knew." The kiss is a dangerously conventional token that Kipling risks. But, as often, where emotion is very deep, the risk is safely taken. Only the end of the story seems unsatisfactory. The narrator announces that he will return no more. "'You think it is wrong, then?' she [the blind woman] cried . . . 'Not for you' [He replied] A thousand times no. For you it is right . . . For me it would be wrong.' . . . 'Why?' she said . . . 'Oh! I see,' she went on, simply as a child, 'For you it *would* be wrong.'"

She may see; but we do not. Or rather, there are many reasons why the narrator might not wish to indulge the possibility of contacting the dead child again. It may be that he thinks that indulgence in the occult will become a drug and destroy his active life. It may be that he

265

believes that psychic gifts may be indulged by women but not by men. It may be that he is Kipling and *his* life is to create art. It may be that he needs to face his own grief without such occult aid. And many other reasons. The devotees of late Kipling love to be teased by such alternatives. They seem, at times, to suggest that such mystification is an element of fine art, a sign of Kipling's greater maturity and delicacy in these years. I have no doubt that it is an artistic defect, that he fudges the excellent story a little because none of the answers satisfies him and he hopes to get away with leaving a mystery. There may be, there must be a mystery in any psychic experiences for those who are convinced by them. That is legitimate. But there must be a reason why this particular narrator, invented by Kipling, refuses to repeat the experience; and, about that, Kipling, whose invention it is and who alone knows why he wrote it, prefers to remain gnomic. It is a weakness, not a strength.

Why does he so fudge what might have been one of his good stories and is still a delight to read? This, I think, lies deep in the conflicts of his later years. In his early Indian stories, he had used the supernatural brilliantly – but it is plainly used as a device and in the tradition of Poe and the Gothic. Then, first with "The Finest Story in the World" (1891) and later in "Wireless" (1902) the idea of reincarnation is played about with to explain something much closer to him – the source of imaginative writing. Now, in 1904, psychic communication is used in "They" in a matter extraordinarily personal to him, to assuage his deep grief.

Of course, increasingly as conventional religion had broken down in the mid and late nineteenth century, people had been turning to the occult. But the younger Kipling's scepticism about this, associated in India with Madame Blavatsky's frauds, is clearly expressed in the comic story, "The Sending of Dana Da" (a story probably of the eighties) where an occultist is farcically visited by a plague of kittens.

However, his mother claimed to be "psychic". And what his mother claimed Kipling would hardly have allowed himself openly to mock. Now, by 1904, his sister Trix had given herself up to the pursuit of psychic experience. But, with her, this spiritualistic concern was clearly associated with a breakdown of personality. From his letters to the writer Rider Haggard, it is clear that Kipling himself experienced what seemed transcendental experiences, for he and Haggard agreed that such intense, mystic moments cannot be prolonged. Like many Celtic families, many of the Macdonalds experienced what they believed to be second sight, Rudyard among them. But he carefully avoided using his gifts or, at any rate, making them public. Indeed, his words to Haggard suggest that he does not believe such powers are in the control of those who are visited by them. This was the chief reason, surely, why he did not believe in organized attempts to make contact with psychic powers.

The pressure upon him, both from within himself and from friends and acquaintances, above all from Trix, to resort to mediums after his son was killed in action in 1915, must have been considerable, as it was upon many bereaved people in the Great War. His answer was firmly given in the poem, "En-Dor":

> Oh the road to En-Dor is the oldest road
> And the craziest road of all!
> Straight it runs to the Witch's abode,
> As it did in the days of Saul,
> And nothing has changed of the sorrow in store
> For such as go down on the road to En-Dor.

No doubt he had his beloved sister's tragic mental distress in mind when he wrote this. Perhaps there were many reasons for not resorting to En-Dor.

It was often the conventional middle-class man's attitude in the first decades of this century, especially where their wives or mothers or sisters had taken up mediums, ouija boards and "psychic intuitions". I remember, as a small boy in the twenties, overhearing many conversations between my father and his club friends (retired majors, naval commanders, tea planters) about the dangers of spiritualism – "Much better not play around with it" – "Leave it to the women folk" – "Old as the hills and as dangerous." Then, there would be the usual round of unexplained mysteries experienced in India or elsewhere in the East, or in my father's case, the innate psychic nature of the Scotch; and at last they would end with the hackneyed, "There's more things in Heaven and Earth, Horatio . . ."

Kipling was much more intelligent than this, however he might often want to hide it. If he had really had intimations of survival after death, he would, of course, have given himself up to them, even if he believed that they were not under the control of those who received them. Who would not, unless they had God's express word that it was wrong to do so? Especially after his daughter had died, or later after his son was killed, or, as with declining health, the prospect of death increasingly pressed upon him. He did not have any simple Christian faith that forbade such communication with the dead; much though one side of him increasingly sought for some answer in Christianity.

The narrator of "They" leaves the spirit children's world behind because mysteriously it is wrong for him. Kipling, I think, left it behind because he had no intimation of it, could find no assurance that his mystic experiences or his daemon gave any indication of life after death. It is not a masterful power to renounce that he felt, but a touching unwillingness to admit to ignorance. That is why the ending rings so untrue, so fakedly gnomic.

And all this, seen purely artistically, is sadly unnecessary, for, in truth, the strength of the story lies in the evocation of the Sussex countryside, not in its psychic mystery. The opening passage where, "I let the country flow under my wheels. The orchid-studded flats of the East gave way to the thyme, ilex and grey grass of the Downs, these again to the rich cornland and fig-trees of the lower coast . . ." is the beginning of a whole life of the Sussex countryside, which, if it never equals his Indian evocation (the place is so much smaller, the body of the stories describing it so much less), is the real healing of the wounds that Kipling felt, the real recapture of his famous daemon. And the human inhabitants, the peasantry, greedy, lusty, suspicious, are also there, although in two of his later and best stories he was to find a brutal heroism in the Sussex country folk he does not yet detect.

The best of these stories is "The House Surgeon", the story of the discovery of the psychological source of the haunting of a house and hence its exorcism. Here the theme is a deliberate device. The story is consciously his Sherlock Holmes piece. Conan Doyle was a neighbour in Sussex and an old friend with whom, as he told Rider Haggard, he later found increasingly little in common. There is an odd irony in this imitation of Sherlock Holmes in psychic form, for years after this story was written, Doyle was completely to capitulate to spiritualism. The intention to imitate is obvious, the haunted house is called Homescroft, and the narrator-investigator says, "I am less calculated to make a Sherlock Holmes than any man I know." Nevertheless, his investigation makes one of Kipling's most enjoyable and professional stories. Not the least, because the central characters are as unexpected as is Kipling's sympathy with them – a Scottish Jewish furrier and his Greek wife with their vulgar, nouveau-rich suburban home. But this unexpectedness is increasingly to be an exciting feature of his later stories, and one which often atones for their artistic failure. Yet, finally, the story succeeds because here the psychic is a device with no very deep roots and worked out in a well-known convention.

He uses it again in two very interesting stories of psychological healing, "In the Same Boat" (1911) and "The Dog Hervey" (1914). But, in both cases, the psychic element is so irrelevant or so metamorphosed into an appearance of medical psychiatry that its use as a solution or a means of identification of the source of the ill obscures and weakens otherwise interesting situations. Both stories have the excellent late Kipling quality of introducing unexpected characters, little known in most serious fiction. In the first, one of the two lost young drug addicts is a very down-to-earth, beautiful, intelligent, uncultured daughter of a rich north-country businessman. In the second the victims of despair are a well-to-do plain, tasteless daughter of a doctor who dishonestly insured his doomed alcoholic patients, and one of his few would-be victims to survive, a breezy, wealthy, lost yachtsman. I know of no other English fiction of value where I could find such people so well understood. But the cause of the drug problem in the first story is the old recurrent nightmare we first met in "The Brushwood Boy" and its solution is the unlikely one that both drug addicts had mothers who had seen the nightmare scenes in reality, when they were pregnant. As to the confused and elliptic "The Dog Hervey", which might have proved to be a good, longish novel (and might not), the psychic is used only as second-sight mechanism to bring the two lovers together as a cure (we are back in the world of Balzac at his most absurd).

There are three elements about these stories which are revealing. In the first place, the best things in both tales are the really frightening and graphic descriptions of oncoming black despair. In the second place, once the two men and the two young women have discovered the semi-psychic causes of their ills, they emerge as wholly sane, healthy people. And this is because, in the third place, it is always a mechanism from outside them that is the cause – what their mothers saw when they were carrying them is a very good example. There is no inner conflict in mental illness: it is all external chance.

I do not, for a moment, doubt Kipling's deep concern and real compassion for those he saw as the sick casualties of a sick society; and, even more, later, for the mental casualties of shell-shock of whom he wrote some goodish stories after the Great War, but he is never willing to probe deeply into their nature, although he registers the horror of their malady so well. I feel convinced that he shared their despairs, as we know many of his mother's family did. I also think that he, too, clung to the idea of some outside force that would save him from them, because he shrank so sharply from the idea of any deep self-inquiry. It is, perhaps, why he chose to see his creative power as a daemon that descended upon him unsummoned, rather than some amalgam of his own experiences, thoughts and emotions. Was it that an *inner* view of despair, or joy, or imagination came too close to the old puritan introspection which his families had inherited and left behind? Or was it, quite conversely, that this *external* view of imagination and despair fitted the old Calvinist concept of grace or damnation arbitrarily visiting us from above, which he otherwise so fiercely condemned all his life? I cannot answer those questions. I can only say that all his accounts of the suffering of the mentally sick are horribly convincing, yet all his solutions, psychic, medical, or, in later stories, some suggestion of Christian healing, are so confused and ambiguous that they obfuscate rather than clarify his art. It is this obfuscation unfortunately that many of the admirers of his late work have taken for gnomic wisdom and deep compassion, whereas they only shake his usually perfect control of narrative and render his syntax sometimes almost unintelligible.

The real balm to him in these years of private grief and black despairs and of political alarmism lay in the Sussex countryside he discovered, travelling in his beloved motor car, and, at last, that small piece of it, Bateman's, lying in a lush well-watered valley not far from the Sussex border with Kent. His daughter, in her afterword to Professor Carrington's biography, notes the sad light that filtered into the house and the uncomfortable seventeenth-century furniture that matched its age. But she also notes that her parents never seemed to notice. I am not convinced, therefore, by Mr Amis's theory that Bateman's is the original of the desolate haunted house in "The House Surgeon", despite the almost psychic discomforts that Mr Amis and his camera crew seem to have experienced there. I think it is more likely that Kipling drew that house, as he himself said, from the rented Torquay house they so disliked. But if Bateman's interior may not be to our taste, and was surely not comfortable, I think we must remember that comfort was not a quality which either Rudyard or Carrie placed high in their stoic-puritan scale of values. Outside, both in setting and in garden, it is, like their earlier houses, very beautiful and quite remarkably peaceful in its pastoral mood.

Elsie Bambridge makes clear the strain that her mother's tense nature imposed upon the household. And, though his absorbing love of children and particularly his own must have always made Rudyard the pacifier of their mother's mood, no creative artist fails to impart tension to a household; and Kipling, despite his innate gentleness, had melancholy to match his high spirits. For all that, this was a happy family time compared to the years after their son John's death in action or the loneliness after his daughter, Elsie, married in 1924. Any house that is intended to run like clockwork must be painful to those who are intended to work like wheels or cogs, yet there are records of servants long in service and others who returned on regular visits. Governesses, secretaries, farm managers, all had difficult lives but, surely unusually interesting work and contacts. This is very frequently the case with those who work for the very eminent. They also all had flats or cottages provided for them which relieved both them and the family.

Miss Ponton's fascinating narrative of working for the Kiplings at different times both as governess and secretary has a few concealed barbs, especially about Carrie's bossiness, but she never gives the feeling that her overworked life was anything but varied and rewarding.

With the village and, indeed, with the farmworkers, their contact was limited and uneasy. For all the very real sense of farming life that he conveys in his Sussex stories, neither Kipling nor Carrie were cut out to deal with tenant farmers who knew more than they. They appear to have been happier after they had found a good farm manager. Kipling's view of the farm labourers appears to have been paternalistic: to Miss Ponton, who had to deal with them on one occasion in the absence of the Kiplings, he said, "You'll get on with the farm hands all right if you treat them as boys of 14 and the women as younger in intellect."[5] Yet in his splendid story, "The Friendly Brook", and in his treatment of Hobden in the Puck stories, his empathy with them is complete.

So much has been written or implied about Carrie by critics and reviewers in recent years, that perhaps this is the place to set out the opinion of her I have formed after reading a large number of Kipling's letters and some few of her own, and Charles Carrington's notes of the contents of her diaries, and after talking with a number of people who knew her, mostly, of course, when they were children. I am especially indebted to Helen, Lady Hardinge, who knew the Kiplings well, first as a child and then later as a young married woman. But, of course, the short sketch here is my own deduction.

As I have thought about what I have read and what I have been told, I am led to believe that their daughter Elsie Bambridge's account of life at Bateman's and of her mother in her excellently graphic appendix to Carrington's biography, is a just and living picture, always remembering that she wrote as a dutiful and loving daughter.

Novelists' wives are a butt for all critics and biographers. I wonder if it is not in part jealousy, for biographers and critics grow very proprietary about their favoured subjects. And these women, whom the great men married, knew so much and, in the estimation of the critic and biographer, could appreciate so little.

It is true that a good number of novelists' wives have not comprehended very closely the depths of their husbands' work. Carrie Kipling, Lady Hardinge tells me, seemed to dwell on the surface details of her husband's stories – how will they get the bucket up out of the sea? she asked many times of one story he was writing. But, in a sense, this must have pleased Kipling, for these are just the sort of practical details that he fusses with and wishes his readers to respond to, just the sort of details he liked to discuss with the many technicians and professional men whose company he cultivated. The deeper meaning of his work he hugged close to himself (so close that too often in later years he rendered it unintelligible). Her diaries are entirely mundane in their concerns – financial transactions, a bare list of visits made and visitors received, increasingly, after 1918, servant troubles. The occasional heightening of tension, during Rudyard's serious illnesses and in the two years after her son John had been reported missing in 1915, are only the more striking because of the usual flat chronicle they interrupt. The limits of her comprehension are perhaps marked by the rather touching story that Carrie was overheard, looking at a volume of his work, and saying to herself, "I do think some of it will live." Her simple view of art's power over the emotions is illustrated by her remark as she left with tears in her eyes at the end of a performance of Barrie's *Dear Brutus*: "He's no business to do it." Perhaps a different more emotionally free wife would have loosened this side of his art to its improvement. I do not easily see him married to such a woman.

As far as his art goes, I believe that he may have suffered much more from his long reliance (until after the turn of the century with the writing of *Kim*) upon the views and advice of his parents, highly praised though this relationship has always been. Certainly Carrie must have felt great inferiority here. Of her interference in his work – a far more serious matter – I have no evidence. According to Rider Haggard it was she who persuaded Kipling not to publish "On the Gate", which was copyrighted as "The Department of Death" in 1916, until 1926. But, since this story of the reception of the dead at the judgement gates in the crowded year of the war casualties, 1916, was written only a year after her beloved son was killed, I am not really surprised at her reaction. Mr S. W. Alexander, in a letter, tells me that when Kipling wrote an eye-witness account of the landing of the Canadian troops in Flanders at Beaverbrook's request, he, as Beaverbrook's chief aide, came on many occasions to Brown's Hotel to receive Kipling's dictation. When Carrie was present, he writes, she "sat beside him and a number of times she said, 'Now, Rud, don't you think so and so might be a better word?' " But he adds, "sometimes he agreed".[6] In any case, though it might have been irritating, this was not interference with his imaginative work. She certainly never sat beside him while he worked on his books and poems, and she also saw that nobody else did (though amusingly enough, Kipling seems to have enjoyed telling visitors that they were the *only* people he could tolerate in the room – he said it to Haggard, and to General Taufflieb, and, I think, to others). This, of course, was one of her two functions in relation to his work: to act as a watchdog and to listen to his reading of what he had written at the end of the day. Like everything else she did, she seems to have carried it out with complete efficiency, but perhaps a little too evidently.

By 1919, when Dorothy Ponton, formerly the children's governess, returned to them for a few years as private secretary, Carrie's domain in Rudyard's daily routine was firm and extensive. She opened all the mail and, after consulting with him, dictated all the replies. Also, following the discovery that autograph hunters had been after small cheques signed by the great writer, she alone signed cheques. Carrie's other job was, with his agents and publishers, all friends of hers and his, to manage the finances of his work, and, on her own largely, to manage their general finances. Those who want to see how good she was in business affairs should read her letters to Bok (the editor of the *Ladies' Home Journal*), firm and business-like but full of unexpected compliments about the typist and the office boy at the *Journal*'s premises. She it was who made the Kiplings rich, and we know from the history of their honeymoon that she had good reason to think that, if she did not, they would be poor.

If, as I suggest, his nervous stability was always shaky, this financial security may have saved him from many desperations. But it had its price. In the first place, most of his stories were sold to both American and English magazines and some of the better ones suffer from it by a magazine stamp and occasionally by a touch of writing for two sets of readers. As he became so very eminent, magazines bowed to him – the muddled, hardly intelligible "The Dog Hervey" appeared as "the different kind of story that you will find in *Nash*'s". More serious, I think, is that considerable riches isolated him more and more in his later life; although it also made him a rare and sympathetic portrayer in fiction of the self-made man, and, despite his many county and aristocratic friends, saved him from simple social snobbery. Riches never brought him to idleness, the neurotic need to work and the work ethic together prevented that; but they did palliate the effects of over-work. On Carrie, the effect of success was, perhaps, less happy. Her

273

French ancestry seems to me to predominate here. She was essentially the French bourgeoise housewife – fussy and suspicious in her household management, method and competence being her gods. I am told that, to the end of her life, she checked the household laundry for herself. It is not surprising that when Kipling was asked why they did not have a house in London after the war, instead of always staying at Brown's Hotel, he answered, "Mother couldn't run two houses." Many are witness to the fact that her conversation could be amusing and trenchant, but her experience in America, and, above all, in New York during Rudyard's illness, had made her as suspicious of strangers as it had him. To this their wealth added, for she suspected people of being after their money. She had the American work ethic and belief in the privileges of success, but she had not got the warmth to strangers that usually accompanies it. Here, too, I think her conventional coldness to the stranger is much more French. As a result, there were many who took offence, especially other women, and particularly on their many sea voyages where social life is very confined.

Yet here it is necessary again to remember the extraordinary position as celebrities that the Kiplings occupied. Kipling, though no doubt he loved his fame, hated its public effects. Carrie had suffered its worst excesses in New York in 1899; now she was determined to use all the powers that money provided them to hold the inquisitive and the impertinent at bay. Kipling maintained an extraordinary politeness in his rebuffs but, with her help and after her initial perusal of the day's mail, rebuff he did, sometimes with a humour that must have given them great pleasure. As when, later, in 1925, he wrote to a lady in Leamington: "Dear Madam, I have to thank you for your letter of June 10th. I don't remember ever having been in Leamington except once when I only passed through in a motor. I would, therefore, have been quite unable to have had the pleasure of meeting you; and the rumour that a poem was written by me with you as its subject, is quite unfounded, with all good wishes, yours sincerely." [7]

Most of the curious or the impertinent could be held at bay by letter. Carrie was not prepared to be more solicitous with those (like fellow passengers on deck) who sought to break the barrier in person. Many well-intentioned people must have been hurt in the process. And, probably, Rudyard missed getting to know some rewarding people as a result. But it was more important that Carrie fully understood his need suddenly to fade out on social occasions as his creative imagination took him away from the scene. Other, less understanding, wives would have been embarrassed at their husbands remaining seated but obviously completely abstracted on such occasions. Carrie,

62 Photograph used for the frontispiece of the printed version of Kipling's speech at Middlesex Hospital, 1908. (*Grenville Taylor Collection*)

A SPIT FROM THE PANTILES.

63 Cartoon of Rudyard Kipling from the *Saturday Westminster Gazette* of 23 May 1914, after he had made a speech in Tunbridge Wells attacking the Liberal Government, his last political outburst before the War. (*By kind permission of the Kipling Society*)

64 Ulster Day, September 1912. Lord Charles Beresford, F. E. Smith, Sir Edward Carson and other leaders arriving at City Hall for the signing of the Covenant. (*Radio Times Hulton Picture Library*)

In 1898 the boys of Horsmonden School, ...ent, asked Rudyard Kipling for a contri...ution to their magazine, *The Budget*. He ...nt from South Africa "Some Hints on ...choolboy Etiquette" recalling his life at ...estward Ho twenty years earlier. The boys ...en asked Max Beerbohm for a comment ...nd he sent this drawing. (*British Library*)

AU REVOIR, KIPLING!

Rudyard—After the warmth I have experienced, I take it all back about the "snows!"

66 Cartoon in the *Canadian Courier*, 26 October 1907: Kipling's tribute to Canada, "Our Lady of the Snows", had caused great resentment there, for its emphasis on inclement winter weather kept away immigrants and visitors. (*By kind permission of the Kipling Society*)

67 Rudyard Kipling in his first motorcar, a Locomobile "Steamer", in *The Autocar*, 31 May 1902. Later in 1902 he changed to a Lanchester. (*International Printing Corporation*)

68 Following up the first breakthrough achieved by the newly developed tank, cavalry of 9th Hobson's Horse attack under fire near Cambrai, November 1917. (*Imperial War Museum*)

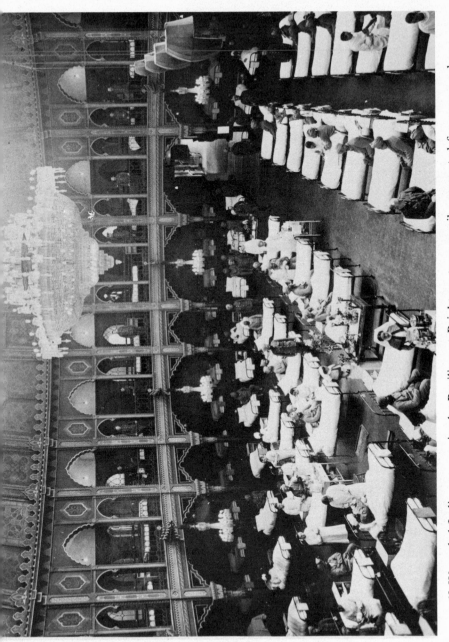

69 Wounded Indian troops in the Pavilion at Brighton, temporarily converted for use as a hospital: some bureaucrat may have reasoned that Indian wounded would feel at home in these bizarre surroundings. (*India Office Library and Records*)

70 John Kipling in the Irish Guards: he was killed in 1915. (*Bateman's*)

71 Kipling with American officers during World War I. (*Library of Congress*)

"Despatches – Is He Mentioned?" by
Edgar Bundy.

"The Avenger" by Frank Dicksee

Since it is rather too late for the Knife
All we can do is to mark the pain

from "A Death Bed", 1918, the culmination of Kipling's long held loathing of
the Kaiser.

74 "He had predicted it so long that he was not surprised when Armageddon broke out", see page 259. Cartoon in the *Graphic*, 17 August 1912. (*By kind permission of the Kipling Society*)

see page 259

75 Vlamertinghe Military Cemetery, 1918. (*By kind permission of the Kipling Society*)

it seems, knew that this was no selfish foible, but a necessity of creation. She filled in for him as well as she could and, for the rest, saw
that nobody broke his reverie.

The criticism of her isolating him from others is made widely, and
not only by those who suffered. Their daughter mentions it in her
afterword. An old friend, Julia Catlin (later Taufflieb), who expressed
a particular affection for Carrie, supports the charge in her unpublished memoir. The "Missus", as Rudyard called her, "was a masterful
woman and built up a Maginot line around Rud, which, of course,
kept out all intruders; but sometimes this lost for Rud the opportunity
of knowing rather charming people. I always felt this isolation a mistake." [8] However, it is often necessary in a mature, busy life to miss
meeting some charming people.

It must be remembered, surely, that Carrie had seen something of
what an overcharged and overworked life could do to Rud's nerves.
His utterances of this pre-Great War period show what a tense state
he was in, and much of her over-protection may have come from her
sense of his strain. This guarding was to grow in the war years and
after, but once again with some good reason, for, from 1915, he began
to suffer agonising bouts of undiagnosed gastritis and greatly needed
to be protected from the very sociable side of his nature; and later,
she, too, became quite an invalid. Sometimes I cannot but think it was
by their mutual agreement that she protected him, as when Nancy
Astor, in the twenties, complained that, at Cliveden, he sat on a sofa
and applied for Carrie's opinion before answering questions, so that,
try as she might, she could not get him alone, although she was the
hostess. [9] I suspect that this reflects, too, his determination that no one
should treat his wife as the appendage of a celebrity. She was, after all,
a foreigner in a world either of his family or of his admirers and old
friends. In a letter to Dr Conland in December 1900, Kipling shows
himself very aware of this. They had been, he says, to stay with
Carrie's relations from the Southern States who lived in the Midlands,
in a big house with a butler and valets. "It did me good because Carrie
was the guest of honour and I was only the man who had married
her." [10] Nevertheless, she seemed to many a dragon on guard. And
this was made all the more difficult probably by Rudyard's remarkable quality of creating a cord of sympathy between himself and
others. It is so unexpected in all we read of his brusquerie and his stiff-
upper-lip philosophy. But some portraits and photographs of him
reveal how it could have happened, through the gaiety and life that
they reveal in his eyes, and I understood it entirely when I saw a short
home-made film of him talking and playing with his friends and his

children in the garden of Bateman's. Also, I think that everyone sensed or even knew that he would not use them either in fiction or in life. His poem, "The Comforters", assures us of this:

> Or, if impelled to interfere,
> Exhort, uplift, advise,
> Lend not a base, betraying ear
> To all the victim's cries . . .'

I am sure from all that I have been told that it was so.

The sense of confidence he inspired was extraordinary. A woman friend, who was staying with them, found herself naturally telling him of an anxiety that usually she would have confided only to another woman, if at all. It was only when he had said, why don't you talk with the Missus about it, that she confided in Carrie, who was sensible, helpful and kind. It must sometimes have been difficult to be the partner of a man with that quality even if one were not so very reserved by nature as was Carrie.

That she had begun to overplay her guardianship even before the war, we can see in Lady Mary Maxse's letter to her mother of 1913, when Kipling came to visit Brigadier Ivor Maxse at Farnborough, near Aldershot: "We had the Rudyard Kiplings for Sunday – he was delightful and she was nice too, but a little aggressive, as is the case with wives of great men. He went out on Brigade training with Ivor and it was interesting to watch his intense delight in the field days. He teemed with inspiration and vision the whole time. Mrs Kipling now hardly ever allows him to leave his own fireside, and telegraphed him to return on Tuesday evening, and this is, of course, very destructive of new ideas." [11]

That Lady Mary reported this means that it must have been current gossip in the Radical Right world in which Kipling moved, and yet it seems inflated, for, in 1913, he lived a very full social and political life. One wonders, perhaps, whether a truth did not become greatly magnified because, as he moved in many sets and kept each set apart from the other, each set had to find a scapegoat for not owning him and all blamed Carrie.

Of course, he had married a master of his finances, of his household and of himself. But then, she had married a mother's boy and more still a father's boy – not that this was his fault or his parents' intention. He had not lived easily in 1890 without any master. He brought out the master in her, as she, perhaps, satisfied some desire for dependence in him. But he was clearly aware of criticism of her, and

276

naturally tried to guard her against it. Of their mutual devotion there can be no doubt at all. They shared a deep but harsh humour. In social and political matters, they thought alike, and their philosophy of life, I suspect, was the same bleakly stoic one. It suited her temperament, however, more than his, or at any rate she had buried her softer side deeper than he had. The children surely suffered more from her, for she was a stern disciplinarian, and he was not.

There is a relevant story related with delight by young Oscar Frewen, son of Kipling's improvident neighbour on an old Sussex estate. He tells how, at a luncheon in 1914, Carrie engaged in argument with a shocked American woman, in defence of spanking boys at school. She said it was the only thing that separated "us" from the lower classes.[12] I am sure that this was the kind of exaggeration of her real views that she delighted to use in upsetting her fellow Americans. The social attitude would have upset Kipling himself less than the attitude to children.

Yet her relation with John, their son, was very close. Kipling had always preached that a mother was a man's centre of existence and so it was in his family. Only John, I am told, could relax his mother when she became obsessed by failures of punctuality or service, or overcome by daily detail.

But the bond between Rudyard and Carrie was surely forged so close as it was by her courage at vital moments in their lives together and by her resourcefulness – they are the virtues he admired most in his good scout heroines like William the Conqueror who, I think, were his preferred women. The privacy that the Kiplings mounted against the fame they achieved was a formidable barrier, and its success had inevitably made their lives a source of rumour among the curious to whom they denied entrance. No one has suffered so much from that rumour as Carrie. But what do her detractors think might have been Kipling's alternative? I do not accept the idea of a never-forgotten love for Flo Garrard, which is sometimes hinted at. The old Goethean romantic idea of a life-dominating love appears from time to time in his stories, but I am not convinced that it comes from his own personal experience more than the hundred other themes that he repeats in his work. The fallacy arises from a misjudgement of the novelist's essential capacity for empathy, especially strong in Kipling.

That he married Carrie primarily because she was the dead Wolcott's sister does not seem supported by the chronology of events; and, even if it had been so, they clearly soon formed a marriage relationship that quite outgrew, in its complexity, their mutual devotion to a dead man. I think it likely that Kipling was much in love with

Wolcott. Worry about the nature of his own feelings may have played some part among all the other anxieties crowded in on him in those brief London years. Yet I believe it to be more probable that he did not allow himself to glimpse anything that was unorthodox in his feelings for his friend. To suppose that Kipling's life would have been different had Wolcott lived, as is often said to me, is greatly to misunderstand both Wolcott and Kipling, and more still such men in the age in which they lived, In any case, excellent friend and useful literary collaborator though Wolcott was, his attitude to the marketing of Kipling's work was much the same as his sister inherited. Should Kipling have remained free of all attachments? Given his reliant temperament, the question is academic, but his years on his own do not suggest that he was well calculated to withstand either solitude or emotional venturing. Their marriage, like most marriages, had the defects of its virtues, but it had for him the greatest virtue – of giving him, despite all domestic tensions, the security that he desperately sought. As for her, she had happiness out of a life that was not always easy and played with dignity, if not always with wisdom, the difficult role that is seldom perfectly played – the celebrity's helpmate.

Finally, on this constantly reiterated point of her restricting his social life, one may firmly say that, as far as his art was concerned, it is a total misunderstanding of his creative development. Kipling's later work has as its chief excellence variety and surprise of subject. It is notable that his volume of stories published in the Great War (1917), which contains many of the stories written in the 1910–1914 period, was called *A Diversity of Creatures*. It bears on the title page the quotation from the *Arabian Nights* – "Praised be Allah for the diversity of his creatures." What it lacks is cohesion. Alone, in the years after India, the Sussex stories give that homogeneity, that sense of a unified created world which is the spell cast by most great writers over their readers. But the Sussex stories are few. To have changed this imbalance he should have lived more fully in one area, Carrie should have confined him more, not less. But if that had happened, Kipling would have been forced to look more deeply into himself and that he could never quite do. His is the failure, as with most writers – not some outside force, like Carrie. To put the blame on her is too like the comforting half-truths of external psychic forces and influences during pregnancy and daemons that he liked to tell himself. Of course, an artist has visitations; but what he makes of them comes from himself.

As a matter of fact, his social contacts during these pre-war years with neighbours, with visitors to Bateman's, by visits to London, and to the Universities, were exceptionally widespread. Politicians, administrators, foreign visitors, old Sussex families, eminent retired Sussex residents, young people and children of all kinds, service officers, engineers, dons, surgeons and physicians (he became in his last thirty years especially interested in his boyhood love – medicine). He was always sociable and reserved. And even after the Cape failed them, there were holidays in Switzerland and the Pyrenees and Egypt.

The company lacked writers, especially serious writers. James was visited out of deep affection; Conrad, though well within motor range, was not often seen; even Doyle had lost his savour. He could get very close to a more popular writer like Rider Haggard, though I am inclined to think that their friendship has been seen as unique in Kipling's life because the correspondence with Haggard is the only one ever published. In Egypt in 1913 he thoroughly enjoyed the company of A. E. W. Mason. He could spend infinite pains on a young popular writer like the forgotten novelist, Guy Boothby. His relations with the old-fashioned literary hierarchy were more remote than in the nineties. Edmund Gosse in his Librarian to the House of Lords grandeur – and, I suspect, his interest in avant-garde writers like Gide – had become unattractive to him.

He still met many eminent authors at the Athenaeum Club, but his relations with new writers, let alone the avant-garde of the time, were almost non-existent. He was never publicly critical; and, even in private, he tried to be as tactful as possible where his brother authors were concerned. Coulson Kernahan reports that at the house of Kipling's neighbour Feilden, someone reported how Israel Zangwill at the Society of Authors called Kipling "A wild ass of a man." Kipling at once turned the conversation with a compliment to Zangwill's wit and said, "Where's John? I'd like him to see Kernahan's photographs." [13] In great degree this alienation from contemporary writers was part and parcel of his hysteric state about politics, for few others were not at least "liberal" in his eyes, but perhaps his too easy assumption that all "intellectuals" were Bandar-log relates, too, to his Victorian dislike for the growing "looseness of talk" in mixed company. It is a serious limitation to his intellectual growth, but it is less important for his creative work. It is not the kind of people that a writer knows, it is what he makes of them. The more serious charge is that he made so little of all his wide circle of friends – but then such use was repugnant to him. For this reason, to detail or discuss his wide circle of friends, interesting though many of them are, is not in place in this book.

The hunting gentry of one or two of his stories are no more than adequate stereotypes; the doctors of some of his later stories quite interchangeable; there seem to be portraits of friends in "The Dog Hervey", but the whole story is so confused; the only clear picture is that of Feilden's Southern States wife in "The Edge of the Evening". But the most important influence, even though he does not appear in person, is Feilden himself.

Henry Wemyss Feilden, in his forties, had been a famous explorer especially of the Arctic and I am convinced that in his talk, which must indeed have been fascinating, Kipling found the most satisfactory parallel to his own creative process about which he was so unwilling to speak directly. For this reason Kipling's address to The Royal Geographical Society – "Some Aspects of Travel" – given in February 1914, characteristically contains more revealing insights into his approach to his art than any of his conversational remarks overtly about writing. For example he discusses the power of smell – how "for me, as for others, a fried fish shop can speak multitudinously for all of the East from Cairo to Singapore – but it does not cover the South Seas for there they use cocoanut oil".[14] He lists all the parts of the world that he knows by their pervading smells. Then again he talks of the image pictures made by men walking under strain, so that the leader of an expedition may carry with him a haunting triangle

$$\begin{array}{c} \text{mileage} \\ \triangle \\ \text{sickness} \quad \text{supplies} \end{array}$$

And he tells how, from the earliest years, he has seen all events and people as they relate to places, carrying in his mind's eye a little atlas that he had pored over as a boy. I believe that these remarks ostensibly about travellers – and there are many more – come very close to explaining how his own vision worked under creative stress and illuminate the sense of place and particularity that are his most powerful artistic strengths.

Kipling was constantly trying, as he thought, to strengthen his work with realistic detail, technical exactitude. It was not his inborn inaccuracy in relation to detail alone, I think, that made him so often inexact. It was that he was not a realist at all. His forte was the creation of his own world out of his impressions of the real world. The facts – accurate or inaccurate of the real world – are only important in so far as they impress the reader with the truth of his created world. But this created world has always its own powerful and exact geography of place and colour and smell and touch. He carried the map of Kim's journeys in his mind exactly as he carried his map of Mowgli's jungle. In this he was in his good work like William Golding at his best, say in *The Inheritors*.

280

These strengths were to the fore in the two Sussex tales of these years in which he directly put forward relationship to the country, relationship to inherited roots of habitation, as the balm to cure the terrible tensions of the age. Unfortunately both the stories, "An Habitation Enforced" (1905) and "My Son's Wife" (1913) are impaired by the impact of his own irrelevant anxieties, but each is well worth reading. In each, the farm and the woods, the flooding brooks and mill streams are absolutely evoked; and in the second story, in particular, Kipling's special vision of the Sussex labourers, small farmers and villagers has begun to take sufficient shape to give a sense of Kipling's own invented world to the Sussex scene. It was this vision that makes two later Sussex stories, "The Friendly Brook" (1914) and "The Wish House" (1926) arguably the best individual stories of his later years.

"An Habitation Enforced" has a typical Kipling central figure, a young New York millionaire tycoon, so wedded to the work ethic that he suffers a serious nervous breakdown. This, as usual, is graphically and horribly and very briefly described. On doctor's orders he goes with his young wife on an indefinite tour of Europe, to little avail, until, by chance, they are recommended by an acquaintance in a London hotel to stay at a Sussex farm. Here he begins to get well and here they both become fascinated by a derelict eighteenth-century house. He buys the house and all its large estate, and settles to farm management with the same totality with which he has governed his great tycoon's empire, but without the neuroses of the city. And his wife bears him an heir. It is only then that they learn why both the county (rather improbably said to "speak at luncheon in low-voiced eddies" – "low-voiced", the county!) and the peasantry have received them so warmly, when Sussex generally is so exclusive: it is because Sophie, the wife, is descended from a former owner who had emigrated to the States. There are key sentences that suggest the country's special healing powers: "It's the proportions [of the house] . . . people don't seem to matter in this country compared to the place they live in . . . the foreknowledge of deliciously empty hours to follow . . . climate, all climate." (This last is a peculiarly insincere attribution, for the Kiplings were to escape English winters all their lives, save for the years of the war.)

Alas, with all its excellencies of scene and background characters, "An Habitation Enforced" doesn't convince. The healing of Mr and Mrs Chapin seems improbable, their discontented return to Brown's Hotel after a few days, much more likely. It is an improbable scheme, but Kipling has made a hundred far more improbable situations convincing. I think it is the pressure of outside urgencies that mars the story. A weary Londoner, yes, but Americans are not needed to make the point. I suspect that the story is addressed to his wife, is a fantasy that welcomes her to the English land he had brought her to live in and tells her that she is its true spiritual heir. If so it is a touching mark of his love for her and his realisation of her isolation, but it is also an inartistic sentimentalism.

"My Son's Wife" is spoiled not by the intrusion of personal pressures but by the overweight of moral and social theory under which it sways ominously near to collapse. Yet, finally, it is the better story of the two.

A young man, Frankwell Midmore (a curiously un-English, American name) suffers "from the disease of the century". His neurosis, however, is not the blank depressions which Kipling so well describes but involvement in London's intellectual bohemia. Kipling's description of the way that the London avant-garde Bandar Log intelligentsia lives is violently hostile, but not as wholly off target as one might expect. "It demanded Work in the shape of many taxi-rides daily; hours of brilliant talk with brilliant talkers; some sparkling correspondence; a few silences (but on the understanding that their own turn should come soon) while the other people expounded philosophies, and a fair number of picture galleries, tea fights, concerts, theatres, music halls and cinema shows; the whole trimmed with love-making to women whose hair smelled of cigarette smoke . . . he and his friends had helped the World a step nearer the Truth, the Dawn, and the New Order."

Perhaps the first question is, well and why not? – it is not *such* a bad life. The second is to remember the sour grapes of the ageing. Nevertheless, there is a charge of triviality and silliness made. And the picture, exaggerated and without any sympathy, is not too far away from the world of Orage and Middleton Murry as seen in Katherine Mansfield's journals. As so often, Kipling is stating the same case as Lawrence, but Lawrence, of course, knew intimately the world he attacked. Kipling, it must be said, knows it well enough to write a letter for Frankwell Midmore in his unregenerate days that is a passable imitation of a minor Bloomsbury "witty" letter. But he goes too far all the time, especially after he has shown that Midmore had got involved with "the Immoderate Left". We stray too often into *Punch*.

His other point has some validity, but once again he thumps it into the story until he almost breaks the fabric. It is this: a good deal of the high-minded talk and cultural concern and social reform of the London intelligentsia turns out to be simply a life of promiscuous sexual affairs covered in romantic talk. He gets in some good hits at chatter about souls and self-expression – "these are things that each lonely soul must adjust for itself" – which still survived on from the nineties. It is the plain man's case against Bloomsbury (as also the cause of the plain man's intense interest in the group today).

And Kipling counters it in a plain man's way that recalls to me at once the talk of my father's club friends in Sussex in my boyhood. If these London decadents really want promiscuity and illegitimacy and easy morality let them go into any Sussex village and find out who's really related to whom. But here they will find it woven into the hard, stoic peasant's existence, not paraded as a new way of life, and part of the Beautiful New Order. The point is neither so relevant nor so telling as Kipling (or my father's friends) thought. But the picture of Sussex village people, notably here a greedy, libidinous, cheerful old farmer, is excellent, and its natural setting superbly done.

Midmore's salvation through Surtees and the hunting set is less satisfactory. Once again Surtees is produced too much as propaganda – "not a highbrow writer but containing more truths than you'll ever find in your etc., etc." The hunting set are too perfunctorily portrayed and too uniformly "nice". But it must be said that this conventional side of Kipling by no means always fails. In the end, after a well-sustained account of a flood in the village, Midmore proposes to the hunting daughter of the local solicitor, who has shown herself, William the Conqueror-wise, a true Kipling heroine by her off-hand courage and initiative in the crisis. The dialogue of their love-making is, in its studiedly off-hand chap-to-chap manner, as remote from our day as the dialogue of Jane Austen's lovers or mid-Victorian sentiment, but, if it is read as a period piece, it is effective and touching.

Yet, Kipling's real success with Sussex (apart from the high triumph of the Puck stories) came in 1914 with "The Friendly Brook", a story of Sussex farm life that has no external irrelevancies, no political or ethical axe to grind, and no contrasted London or insufficient gentry to spoil his creation. The story has a well-constructed, interesting and credible melodramatic theme. Its opening of two men hedging has the only symbolic overtones, where the uncared-for hedge has grown "all manner of trees" that suggests, but lightly, the anarchy he perpetually dreads.

With great peasant caution, and suspicion, and secrecy, the two men Jesse and Jabez (clearly lifetime companions) probe into the reason why the farmer Jim seems willing to sacrifice one of his fields to the brook's flooding. This framing of the main story is, as not always, a powerful assistance to its realism, because it is the essence of Kipling's Sussex villagers that they live a life of intense privacy, in a relationship of jungle suspicion. Kipling has prepared us for that by his opening dialogue and, if he were then to communicate Jim's secret story to us directly, we should not believe that anyone outside the village (and even then only one or two intimates) could know it. As it is, we are told it by Jesse in a Sussex voice to his workmate Jabez, and, even then, only after considerable havering.

The story itself touches upon the world outside just enough to set the village in 1914 England, but no more. Jim, a farmer, living with his possessive old mother, adopts a baby girl. And we have off-stage noises of the Barnardo's people and their letters – "these Lunnon childern Societies". Mary, the girl, as she grows up, gives us a touch of the changing village, for she is studying to be a school-teacher. Out of the blue appears her drunken father, with the law on his side (for the Lunnon Childern Society has muddled the papers and Jim and his mother have gone on compounding the muddle out of avarice by accepting five shillings a week they do not need). He settles down to regular visits and regular blackmail, with the threat of removing the daughter Jim loves. The whole scene is made more *guignol* (but not crudely) by the old mother's being now paralysed and communicating by slate. I think that this is cribbed from Zola's "Thérèse Raquin". But at last the villain falls drunkenly into the flooding brook, and his body is carried miles downstream, passing Jim the farmer, at work with Jabez, on its way. In gratitude or perhaps out of sheer superstition, Jim sacrifices his meadow to the stream in payment.

The story has the rare advantage in a Kipling story of bearing only a coincidental moral – "He [the drunkard] had the business right enough, and he had the law with him – no gettin' over that. But he had the drink with him, too, an' that was where he failed, like." Weakness will suffer, hard work triumph. But it is a jungle law. More important is the jungle itself – the villagers might be from Zola's *La Terre*, but Kipling has none of Zola's savagely comic horror of them. On the contrary, if they are secretive ("naturally they weren't goin' to let me see where they kep' their monies") this, in Kipling's view, is the nature of sensible men. Again they are avaricious but their life is very hard. Everything they do and say is a necessity, not a pretence or a luxury. In his letters and in his autobiography, Kipling speaks with conventional dislike for this peasant society; and, when he dealt with them at Burwash, he wisely saw them as they were. No doubt, he and Carrie delighted in being peasants themselves in their local business affairs. But in the stories, he expresses sympathy with this stoic life, and sees in it that group life which he advocated as anarchy's greatest enemy.

He also allows himself to accept manners, ethics that he will not face in his own world – the loves in the village world are often intense but they are enjoyed precariously and unorthodoxly, sexual morality is not mixed up with niceness, mothers are possessive, grim and to be thwarted, and so on. Their world is a pagan one cut off from society above. With all that, there is a compensating bond of craft and place between these people that removes them from Zola's hideous (and comic) bestial countryside. I think, perhaps, that Kipling has found some equivalent of the Indian peasants who formed so vital a background to his early stories, with the additional advantage that he is nearer in sympathy and understanding to the Sussex peasantry. If only he could have treated the gentry as fiercely and as tenderly as he treated the white sahibs of India, he might have made a Sussex world akin to the world he created out of India.

But, if we know now that his Punjab was a threatened world, bound to disappear, its guise for him in the eighties was that of an advanced outpost, not a disappearing relict. His Sussex was so evidently disappearing rapidly under his eyes with the invasion of commuterdom and growing towns. It simply could not function even in his imagination as a world on its own.

> Farewell to the Downs and the Marshes
> And the Weald and the forest known
> Before there were Very Many People
> And the Old Gods had gone!

It is this that renders his whole new ideal of the land and its traditional craftsmen, as epitomised by his hero "Hobden", the labourer, a romantic conservatism as foolish as the Merry England socialism of Uncle Topsy Morris that he had laughed at as a young man. "The Friendly Brook" in *A Diversity of Creatures* is followed by his famous poem, "The Land", which traces the history of the archetypal labourer, Hobden, down from Roman times to his own day:

> Hev it just as you've a mind, to *but* – and here
> he takes command
> For whoever pays the taxes, old Mus' Hobden
> owns the land.

But, of course, it's not true. The historical approach that Kipling adopts stops at his own day, or soon after. "So they drove it long and crossways in the lavish Roman style," and so on through the ages of changed farming when, despite each change, Hobden the craftsman's wisdom still applies. This is dubious in the modern farm world, as Kipling could see if he came today to East Anglia. The very machine technology that he lauded, and that he championed to the countryside in "Below the Mill Dam", has changed farming, not in the old way of changes from medieval open field to Turnip Townshend's era, but in a more fundamental way that puts a more powerful question mark over all the traditional lore and folk wisdom of old Hobden, even over his job as a farm labourer.

The second story of village life, "The Wish House", was published in 1924, in a world of charabancs and council-provided football grounds. Nor does it lean so heavily on farming lore, for its central figure is an old woman. It is probably Kipling's most successful single story; certainly his best story in the psychological fashion that so many recent critics, mistakenly in my opinion, take for the necessary sign of maturity in fiction.

Two old women are talking – Mrs Ashcroft and her seldom seen friend from girlhood, Mrs Fettley from thirty miles away, for we have come a long way in ten years from the world of "The Friendly Brook", where the hill folk and the valley folk, with only a few miles between them, looked at each other as distant strangers. Mrs Fettley has been shaken by the bus: "'Most folk got out at Bush Tye for the match there, so there weren't no one for me to cushion agin', the last five mile.' ... the tile-sided cottage trembled at the passage of two specially chartered forty-seater charabancs on their way to the Bush Tye match; a regular Saturday 'shopping' bus, for the county's capital, fumed behind them; while, from one of the crowded inns, a fourth car backed out to join the procession, and held up the stream of through pleasure-traffic." And changes are closer to them than that: "'On'y last week ... me daughter ordered a quarter pound of suet at the butcher's; and she sent it back to 'im to be chopped. She said she couldn't bother with choppin' it.' ... 'I lay he charged her then?' 'I lay he did. She told them there was a whisk-drive that afternoon at the Institute, an' she couldn't bother to do the choppin'.'"

To an extent, we measure Grace Ashcroft and Liz Fettley by the strangeness to them of the changed world around them. It is important, too, as the basis of Kipling's own empathy with them, on which there is never a word of comment from him. Any story, in which the author takes his readers into a life likely to be unknown to them should, I think, be much judged by the tact with which he discloses it. Apart, perhaps, from a certain detailing of the food which the old ladies bolt down for their high tea, there is not a moment in "The Wish House" in which we are conscious of Kipling telling us of a narrower, more ignorant world of different manners from his and our own. Everything emerges from the talk of the old women themselves.

They sense from the start that this may be a last meeting, for Mrs Fettley is going blind and thirty miles, even in the 1924 world of local buses, is a long way for her to come. Before the story ends they *know* it *is* the last, for Mrs Ashcroft reveals that her cancerous leg grows worse not better. And we realise, too, that their intimate talk is a measure of this finality, for they have only laid aside for an hour their usual peasant distrust of intimacy. Each tells the other of the central loves of her life, which is, in neither case, her husband.

It is promiscuous Grace Ashcroft's story that is central, and central to it is the cancer, which she believes that she has taken upon herself so that Harry Mockler, the man she loves, shall suffer no ills or pains. Not that she had known Harry's love for very long – only one harvesting and then, through one winter, when she had prolonged the happiness by securing him a job at a livery stables near the house in Kensington where she was a kitchen maid. It had been clear to her even during harvesting that he wouldn't keep his love for her for long – for he'd burned the rubbish from the field early – " 'The sooner that old stuff's off an' done with,' 'e says, 'the better.' 'Is face was 'arder 'n rock when he spoke. Then it comes over me I'd found me master, which I 'adn't ever before. I'd allus owned 'em like."

And, in the end, by paying the price of cancer's terrible pain, she owns Harry, not as her lover, but as a man who, unknown to himself, stays healthy only because she has taken upon herself his mortal malady. The supernatural means by which she secures her wish is neat and frightening and all that a psychic story requires; and since we are only asked to believe that she believes in it, we are easily able to accept. By a stroke of genius, too, Kipling lays the Wish House, where the token dwells that gives Grace Ashcroft her desire at such a cost, in "a basement-kitchen 'ouse, in a row of twenty-thirty such, an' tiddy strips a' walled garden in front" in a broken-down Kensington street. Here it is "in Lunnon ... the streets stinkin' o' dried 'orse-dung blowin' from side to side lyin' level with the kerb" that this village girl makes (or believes that she makes) her superstitious tryst. Ancient village lore found living in a sleazy London street – the effect is subtle and very convincing; and cleverly combines Kipling's present world in Sussex with his old boyhood wandering of the streets of Earls Court in 1882.

There is happy invention on almost every page of this story. Grace is told of the Wish House by a small girl who has learned it as a childish game. As she preserves Harry Mockler alive, Grace knows that if she has not his body no one else has, for his grim, possessive old mother will see to that . . . "I knowed she do watch-dog for me, 'thout askin' for bones." At the last, Grace's story finishes. As she shows her sore to her old friend in proof, the district nurse comes in, bright and patronising and uncomprehending, and the old women turn back into nice old ladies having a natter. Only one urgent whisper from Grace to her friend as she bends to kiss her goodbye recalls the fierce drama – "It *do* count, don't it – de pain?" – for Grace believes that her pain will be accepted as a price to ensure that Harry *will* never marry. It is a story of fierce, insane possessive love and Kipling conveys his terrible anti-heroine with all the love that he clearly feels for those whose will to endure is as strong as their desire.

Incidentally it contains in the very well-observed relations between the little girl and Grace, a picture of that strong sexual need for physical love that some children feel with adults portrayed as I have never seen it in other fiction. And its portrayal, if discreet, is also completely explicit in the man-loving Grace's dislike for it.

The superstitious terror of cancer that is conveyed in the story has been rightly, I think, associated with Kipling's own dread of the disease, which he thought a family malady, especially, no doubt, in those first years of his agonies of gastritis, which even a complicated operation of 1922 had not cured. But as it is the dread illness of the West in this century, its place in the story does not suggest any ir-relevant personal concern. Indeed the story avoids all Kipling's many hazards.

With the new century, first in *Traffics and Discoveries* (1904), Kipling normally prefaced or followed (sometimes both) his stories when they were collected, with poems, often written quite separately and often themselves in Kipling's later years more or less painfully obscure. Sometimes this is a happy conjunction, giving extra meaning or clarity to story and poem, sometimes it makes for a crossword-puzzle obscurity, more flattering to the ingenuity of the reader than really enriching of the works; sometimes it produces difficulty which unsophisticated Kipling devotees love to ponder, but which is surely due to lack of any worthwhile relationship. Occasionally the jux-taposition throws light upon the author as much as upon his work. This is so, I think, with the poem "Rahere" that follows "The Wish House". Here, "King Henry's jester, feared by all the Norman Lords" is seized with a black melancholy, "Hence the dulled eye's deep self-loathing." And as the Court physician says, "For it comes – it comes, said Gilbert, as it passes – to return." In his torment, Rahere walks through the streets, and passing the gallows, he sees:

Beneath the wry-necked dead
Sat a leper and his woman, very merry, breaking
    bread . . .
And she waited on him crooning, and Rahere
    beheld the twain,
Each delighting in the other, and he checked
    and groaned again.

For he sees that passion can endure. As the physician comments,

> For it comes – it comes, said Gilbert, and thou
>   seest it does not die!

Any physical pain or malady, Kipling counts as bliss beside the agonies of despair.

It is, I think, this that he reiterates in his "Hymn to Physical Pain" placed before his story, "The Tender Achilles" of 1929:

> Wherefore we praise Thee [physical pain] in the deep,
> And in our beds we pray
> For Thy return that Thou mayest keep
> The Pains of Hell at Bay!

Physical pain, at the last, can be seen as coming from without, perhaps from our physical heredity. But despair, even if inherited, or, in our day, metabolic, seems to demand inward inquiry. If Samuel Johnson's work had not delighted Kipling, as it did, he would surely anyway have loved this man, so rational and urbane, who yet suffered such terrible pains of hell in his agonising despairs.

Johnson's insularity, too, no doubt, pleased him in some of his moods (though hardly in his devotion to London surely) if only for its truculence. Yet his own love of England was always tinctured by the fear of confinement there:

> England is a cosy little country,
> Excepting for the draughts along the floor
> And that is why you are told,
> When the passages are cold:
> "Darling, you've forgot to shut The Door!" . . .
> Shut, shut, shut the Door, my darling!
> Always shut the Door behind you, but
> You can go when you are old

Where there isn't any cold . . .
The deep verandah shows it –
The pale magnolia knows it –
And the bold, white Trumpet-flower blows it –
There isn't any Door that need be shut![15]

And again:

Father, Mother and Me,
Sister and Auntie say
All the People like us are We,
And everyone else is They.
And They live over the sea,
While we live over the way,
But – would you believe it? They look upon We
As only a sort of They![16]

His angry irritation at insularity is only thinly disguised by the playfulness of either poem. But still in those first years at Bateman's he had found foundation enough to speak with revulsion of the life of an expatriate whom he met in Egypt on his visit there in the spring of 1913: " 'Yes,' said the Face, 'I have been here all the time. But I have made money and when I die I am going home to be buried.' – 'Why not go home before you are buried, O Face?' – 'Because I have lived here so long.' . . . Think of it! To live icily in a perpetual cinematograph show of excited, uneasy travellers . . . unknowing and unsought by a single soul abroad; to talk five or six tongues indifferently, but to have no country – no interest in any earth except one reservation in a continental country." [17]

Years before, Lockwood had written from Florence to Rudyard in Brattleboro making similar complaint of the English colony there, yet son and father (and mother) alike never shed the retired Anglo-Indian's sense of exile in England. Perhaps Kipling's greater power to do so at last was strengthened after his parents' death, the cutting of that powerful link with his past. He had been an assiduous son to the last. He had talked over the historical foundation of the Puck stories with Lockwood and had received the usual fatherly cautions about craft and care and assiduity; but Lockwood's serious influence probably ended with *Kim* whose wonder lies in so little evidence of such admonitions.

Alice's last days would seem to have been a little sad. Tisbury – and their desolate windswept home – could hardly be Lahore again, even though Bikaner Lodge may have had a desert-like garden through their fear of unhygienic shrubs; "Clouds" must have demanded an altogether more sophisticated culture than the Viceregal Lodge. Her health in the last years was poor and she lived up a steep hill away from the village. Her grandchildren, I have been told, found her shrill and scolding. After all, though Rudyard had visited her often, his marriage to Carrie had cut her off from her brilliant son. And her brilliant, beautiful daughter had been left to her, a desperate nervous wrecked woman. One of the saddest things I have read in the collections of letters are Trix Fleming's letters to her publishers in 1902 and again in 1905. Trix had suffered periodic nervous breakdowns from the late nineties that had brought her away from India and her husband, usually to find refuge with her parents; particularly did she grow close to Alice. They both claimed psychic visitations, although Alice must have watched with alarm as Trix accumulated clairvoyant, time-travelling, telekinetic and exorcistic powers that went far beyond the Celtic second sight which Alice perhaps shared with her son.

Trix, too, felt cut off from her brother by his marriage. Forty years later one can feel her hostility to Carrie in her letter to Sir Ian Hamilton. She remarks, "His two literary agents – his wife, the first and keenest – a true business Yankee." [18] And again in September 1945, after visiting Bateman's, in her letter of thanks to Mr Parish, the tenant, she makes her feelings about her dead sister-in-law very clear: "Though Carrie Kipling died there I was not at all conscious of her except for a moment in the dining room when I looked at your wife's sweet face in Carrie's chair. Strangely enough, during my visit to Bateman's after his death, I could not feel him at all. I felt lost and lonely; now you have, as it were, given him back to me and I am unspeakably grateful!" [19]

After all, mother and sister had been equal partners with the famous man in *Quartette* in 1885. Now in 1902 she and her mother put together a volume of their poems and Trix secured its publication anonymously, but not before she had encouraged the publishers by revealing her mother's and her own identity. It is touching to see her suggestion that their relationship to Ruddy might become an open secret but the Kipling name must not appear. They responded by asking for designs by Lockwood, and even these were secured anonymously also. Trix recovered enough to return to India. The volume appeared. But in 1905 when her ill-health brought her back to England, she has to write to say that after two and a half years she has received no statement of royalties. [20]

For Trix, there was in her old age to be recovery and a happy time talking on radio about her dead brother, helping Edward Shanks with his biography. But for Alice there was no such time. She declined and died of heart failure at the end of 1910, with Lockwood, Rudyard and a distraught Trix at her bedside. She outlived her gaiety, her talent and the loose but strong silver rein with which she had only half intentionally bound her son. Lockwood died in early January 1911 of a heart attack, at "Clouds". Kipling wrote to Mrs Hill: "Dear as my mother was, my father was more to me than most men are to their sons."[21] To Miss Plowden at the funeral, he said, "I feel the loneliest creature on God's earth today."[22]

But I think the most revealing of all the stories about Kipling's devotion to his father is contained in a letter of the American, William Dean Howells, to his daughter Amelia after Rudyard was thought to be dying in New York in 1899. He tells how he had dined with Kipling only ten days before, and when Kipling saw him "in a plump, elderly man's difficulties with a new pair of rubbers, he got down and put them on for me. He said he always did it for his father."[23] He was then thirty-four.

With their death went the escape from England of talking over old Indian memories, and now, with most others, he was to be almost confined to England's shores for four terrible years.

It was well that he had come to know and love one, Sussex, corner of them so well, before this terrible trial began. But I have yet to talk about that connected body of writing in which during those pre-war years he most satisfactorily expressed, through English history, his sense of civilisation's constant renewal, and, in description, the English, especially the Sussex countryside, as the one constant.

The cyclical view of history which marks *Puck of Pook's Hill* (1906) and *Rewards and Fairies* (1910) was a well-established theory of the nineteenth century, deriving, as Kipling derives his, from the decline of the Roman Empire. During the late nineteenth century, men, who had lost faith in a benevolent ordering of the universe and could see nothing but chance where once had been the Divine plan, felt that their pessimism could be limited, at any rate in the short run, by a picture of historical civilisations rising and falling and being replaced by others. For Imperialists, perhaps, to make such a comparison between Britain and Rome gave a comforting sense of accepting one's worst fears (the end of the British Imperial system) and yet having faith that the torch of law and order and decency and culture would not be forever extinguished. As has often been pointed out, Kipling's arrangement of the collection *Puck of Pook's Hill* is very significant. The first story, "Weland's Sword" tells of the old heathen god's adaptation to a

Christian world, and the next three stories show the return of law to the land after the Norman conquest; only then does he go back to the fading-out of law and order with the Roman legions on the Wall in the fifth century. Thus renewal is asserted from the start.

I have no doubt that this was the overall philosophy and even perhaps plan of these two volumes of stories as Kipling originally worked them out while Josephine and her cousin played at Cavaliers and Roundheads in the Rottingdean garden, or as John and Elsie romped with the lion cub in the grounds of "The Woolsack" or sailed the pond at Bateman's, but it does not dominate the final arrangement of the stories. This, I think, is largely random. The cohesion arises far more out of the conception of the past as containing many secret moments which, when illuminated, tell us by what tricks and strains and endurances and renunciations and sudden visions men have stretched the fabric of civilised knowledge and behaviour without rending it. These stories contain more than any other of Kipling's stories the idea of intuitive flashes or insight – as when Pertinax, Parnesius' fellow captain on the Roman Wall, in his cynical, adaptable power of leadership one of Kipling's most interesting characters, guesses from the wording of Emperor Maximius's optimistic, cheery letter that the Emperor's cause is lost; or, as when the Red Indian Chief passing a Philadelphia window, where Talleyrand, the destitute French exile, sits playing dice with himself, guesses that there is a bad man and a great chief. In no group of his stories does Kipling bear such effective witness to his sense of coincidence in human life or of the purely marvellous.

It is said that children are put off the stories today by their appearance of being merely a dressed-up pageant. This may be a little to do with the pictures that still accompany the stories where the nineteen-hundreds costume of the children, Dan and Una, only adds unreality to the rather dressed-up look of the Romans and medieval and Elizabethan and French Revolutionary characters they are talking with. Kipling's illustrators were often far from a happy choice. The illustrations to the Puck stories should go.

Of course, the talk of governesses and nursery tea and Latin lessons and so on in the framework of the stories does mask their fine quality for adult readers. Not more so for me, I must say, than the constant reappearance of old Hobden, poaching or hedging, which for many serious critics is the central theme of the collection, the assertion of England's common man weathering every historical change. Yet, on occasion, the *comments* of the children are a splendid dramatic device heightening the effect of the stories, as when, in the last story of

Harold's survival into Henry I's reign as a lost, half-witted old man protected by Rahere, the jester, Dan comments, at the most subtly moving moment, "I think this tale is getting like the woods, darker and twistier every minute." [24] But there is no doubt that "The Eye of Allah", Kipling's finest story of historical conjecture, which was not published until 1926, gains by not being set like the two collections in the Dan-Una-Puck framework.

Yet the stories are so excellent that they can well support their "told to the children" setting. And there are advantages. One of these is that, when Puck takes the children back into the past, the narration is always made by some figure from that time – three stories, for example, by Parnesius, the Roman legionary officer; three by Sir Richard Dalyngridge, a Norman knight; two superbly narrated by Pharaoh, the Anglo-French smuggler turned successful Pennsylvania tobacco merchant in the seventeen-nineties; one by Culpepper telling of the Plague in a seventeenth-century village, and one by St Wilfrid – and so on through a wonderful array of voices. Of course, they are Edwardian in their note even when, as with Culpepper, the seventeenth-century note is well preserved, but they are beautiful self-revelations of the men who tell as well as of the stories they are telling – Browning's *Men and Women* without Browning's self-conscious quirks.

Only the stories told by highborn women fail: "Gloriana", where Queen Elizabeth narrates, and "The Marklake Witches", told by a Regency county girl, have all the unreality of Mrs Burton or Trix in a Simla historical pageant.

Many of Kipling's most cherished themes are embodied in these stories – the desolate obligation of obedience in the Roman Wall stories – the only ones where didacticism overcomes the evocation; the political wisdom of mercy in "Old Men at Pevensey"; the special civilising contribution of the Jews to society in "The Treasure and The Law"; the terrible price to be paid by the individual for society's advances in "The Knife and the Naked Chalk"; the whole debate about the gipsy trail in life in "Brother Square Toes" and "A Priest in Spite of Himself", where the super-gipsies Talleyrand and Napoleon are given life in a small-time smuggler's tales; the tragic quality of loyalty in "The Tree of Justice".

These stories alone make the two volumes an enlightenment, for Kipling's sense of delight in man's diversity has full sway. The best of all, I think, is a story of sheer wonder, "The Knights of the Joyous Venture", where Kipling's fancy knows no bridle, adding Norman knights to a Viking trading ship with, among the crew, a Chinese found half dead on the icy shores of Muscovy, and taking the whole wondrous band to fight a battle for gold on the West African coast against gorillas. It is Kipling on his top form.

The two volumes also contain some of his best accompanying verse: the much-loved lyric poem, "The Way Through the Woods"; the strange hymn to Calvary, "Cold Iron"; the Roman legion's marching song, "Rimini"; "A Smuggler's Song" in which the little girl is told: "Them that asks no questions isn't told a lie; Watch the wall, my darling, while the Gentlemen go by!", and best of all, I think, the sinister prophecy of eventual disaster sung at Napoleon's cradle, "A St Helena Lullaby". Here Kipling's pessimistic determinism has seldom been more telling:

> How far is St Helena from a little child
>   at play?
> What makes you want to wander there with
>   all the world between?
> Oh! Mother, call your son again or else
>   he'll run away,
> (No one thinks of winter when the grass
>   is green).

The dark and cautious pessimism of this poem, set against the gay delight in adventure for itself that marks Sir Richard Dalyngridge's fabulous exploit against the gorillas, may be said to straddle the whole contradiction in Kipling's character. We cannot possibly hold those politically strident years from 1900 to 1910 wasted that produced such magnificent stories and poems.

7 ARMAGEDDON AND AFTER

The Great War

As one would expect, the wartime activities of Rudyard Kipling play very little part in the three war stories that he produced. For this reason, I shall only outline his life in those years to suggest the particular quality of his attitude to the War.

The death of his son, John, at the battle of Loos in October 1915, put an effectual end to his imaginative use of war. In 1916 he wrote "On the Gate", a story of the overworked task of St Peter and his assistants in that year of the terrible casualty lists. Its surface is mockery of bureaucracy, very effective. Its deeper demand is that call for mercy for all sinners that was to press upon him increasingly after the war, with the attendant dismissal of all creeds and divisions – Bradlaugh, Calvin, Ignatius Loyola all work together to receive souls with compassion. The story was not published until after the war, no doubt, as Haggard says, at Carrie's request: perhaps she found the subject unbearable treated in Kipling's determined humorous surface tone. Perhaps Kipling himself felt the underlying mood of mercy, even though it is not explicitly extended to the German enemy, who are never mentioned, to be inappropriate while the war lasted. Anyway, save for some of "The Epitaphs of War", Kipling's poems for the rest of the war continued to be fierce and hating condemnations of the enemy and all who aided him. In one single poem he seems to allow himself public lamentation "My Boy Jack":

> Have you news of my boy Jack?
> *Not this tide . . .*

But the answer is stoic:

296

Oh dear, what comfort can I find?
None this tide, nor any tide
Except he did not shame his kind . . .

His fictional creativity came to an end until the hostilities ceased. But, before John's death in 1915 had hit him so cruelly, he did write three excellent war stories in which ruthlessness, not mercy, is the mood. "Swept and Garnished", "Mary Postgate", and "Sea Constables" were all, in fact, published in magazines (in that order) between January and September 1915, before his personal tragedy.

His unwritten epitaphs to John are to be seen in the two grinding public tasks he undertook after his son's death – the long, arduous and searing preparation (written with agony and bloody sweat, Miss Ponton tells us) of *The Irish Guards in Wartime*, which was not finished until 1923, and the inspection of war graves, first in Flanders, and then as far afield as Gallipoli, Palestine and Mesopotamia, that he undertook as a Commissioner of War Graves in the years after the war. By using his impressions of the Flanders cemeteries in the celebrated story "The Gardener" (1926), he was able to come closer to his feelings for his dead son than in any other fiction.

But, in the years after the short and powerful trio of 1915 stories, the most marked effect of the War on his imagination was in his continued concern for the rest of his life with the mental and nervous effects left by their war experiences upon ex-soldiers and ex-officers. Eight of the stories in the last two collections of his life – *Debits and Credits* (1926) and *Limits and Renewals* (1932) – are directly concerned with this subject. The last of these stories, "The Miracle of Saint Jubanus", was first published as late as 1930.

But, testimony though they are to the degree to which he saw the post-war world not as a new beginning but as a tragic aftermath, they also directly look back to his pre-war dwelling upon despair, its sources, and the hopes for its cure. Indeed his most terrible general evocation of madness, "The Mother's Son", is used as a preface to one of the least successful of these stories – "Fairy Kist", written first in 1924.

These and other post-war stories have been acclaimed by recent critics as his stories of compassion, and so, of course, they are; but not, I think, as the critics intend to suggest, a new and final compassionate phase in his old age. It seems to me, as I have suggested, that compassion is the mark of much of his best work from Indian days continuously onwards. It may be, as Mr Alan Sandison has ably argued, that, apart from *Kim*, the great lack in Kipling's work is love.

297

Yet I am not convinced of this. Surely the love of human beings that pervades *Kim* is not so easily distinguishable from the love that informs his compassion for Holden and Ameera in "Without Benefit of Clergy", or Findlayson, the engineer in "The Bridge Builders", or for the Soldiers Three, or, at moments when she seems most alone, for Mrs Hauksbee, or for Badalia Herodsfoot and Grace Ashcroft, or for many of the characters of the Puck stories. What distinguishes them from *Kim*, of course, is that in the stories in which they appear alongside the compassion-near-to-love goes much hatred – something that is almost entirely absent from his wonderful novel. And interspersed in all the pre-war collections are many stories of almost pure hatred and revenge, although sometimes that hatred is masked in hilarious farce. The compassionate post-war stories of healing (contemporary and historical) have very little hatred mixed in with their sorrow; and there are few stories beside them expressing pure hatred.

More important, one of the best of the post-war stories, "Day-Spring Mishandled", and one of the most surprising, because it stands all alone in his work in its subject matter, is a direct account of the crippling effects upon a man of talent and good nature that cherished hatred brings. Even so, as I shall suggest, this theme is to be found in an early Indian story. It may be, then, that the Kipling critics of the academic revival in the years since his death, have labelled the late stories they so much admire "compassionate", not because of this quality which they share with all his work, but because of the near absence of indulged hatred in which they are certainly different from his earlier work. No doubt his son's death, in its hideous setting, as he constantly points out, of the deaths of millions of others, set Kipling's mind in his last years much upon the theme of all-embracing mercy; but, as importantly, I believe, another reason for this change was also that he had come close to exhausting his strongly-felt emotion of hatred by what he had written during the war.

Almost all of the early war stories and poems express direct hatred. Their compassion is given, as in "Mary Postgate", not for the hated, but for those who hate. Kipling was intensely moved by the stories of the sufferings of the Belgian refugees who flocked into the ports near to his home, and by the previously unimaginable horrors of trench life. What he saw of trench life in his official tours of inspection horrified him. He was to learn much more of its horrors than most civilians when he gathered first-hand accounts for his Irish Guards history. But he used all his bottled-up horror and all his bottled-up grief in the early war years to stoke his hatred – first, against the enemy, then, against neutrals who refused to assist in saving the civilisation they claimed to belong to. His poems and stories were public vehicles that affected the determination of the British, or the conscience of the Americans, and he wrote, I am sure, with this in mind.

The purpose he intended was the winning of a war that he believed to be not only just, but necessary, in order to save the world from a brutal tyranny; and one of the greatest elements in winning the war he conceived to be a determination which must be fed by detestation of the enemy. To this extent, some of the stories and the poems which are among his most powerful work are war propaganda. I do not believe we can get away from that; to read them only in the many other ways in which they can be read, for he is subtle, is to mistake what he meant. It is for this reason, I believe, that he never mentions the undoubted sense of sympathy that was often latent between fighting men on both sides – and not only in the dramatic expression of the famous 1914 Christmas truce in the trenches. He must have heard something of it, I suspect, certainly in the later war years from the many officers and non-commissioned officers he interviewed for his history – in this respect, he was far less protected from the unvarnished truth of the trenches than most Great War civilians. But he would never have repeated the story lest it weaken our war effort.

Here is the evidence of the culmination of his violent anti-Germanism (growing since the early nineties). In the Indian stories, the enemy command respect. Fuzzy Wuzzy is a damned good enemy. Adam Strickland in "A Deal in Cotton" (1904), in administering a district of Sudan, feels a greater link with the Arab slave dealer than with his Sudanese he saves from being sold into slavery. It is the chivalric notion of "East is East" – "when two strong men stand face to face". There is no element of this in anything that Kipling has to say of the German enemy. Already, in his science-fiction fantasy, "With the Night Mail" (1905), that includes brilliant parodies of the newspaper advertisements of the year 2000, the world is ruled by an Aerial Board of Control that includes all races and both sexes, war has been abolished in 1967, everything is international; yet the Danes are still admonished for using German equipment. His speeches and articles of the Great War, even given his natural violence of expression, have to be seen as purposely exaggerated to stimulate hatred of the enemy. Yet, we feed upon what we write and say, and I think, that starting from sincere motives, Kipling's anti-Germanism over the years does verge on racist obsession. In the *Daily Express*, for example, in May 1916, he writes, "One thing we must get into our thick heads is that whenever the German man or woman gets a suitable culture to thrive in he or she means death and loss to civilised people, precisely as germs of any disease . . . mean death or loss to mankind. There is no question of hate or anger or excitement in the matter, any more than there is in flushing out sinks . . . as far as we are concerned the German is typhoid or plague – *Pestio Teutonicus* if you like." [1] The supposed rational note of "there is no question of hate" is a typical mark of a violently irrational argument.

In the twenties, when the reaction to the Great War was at its height, such utterances (and Kipling made many) were dismissed as bad faith. I do not believe Kipling can be charged with Bottomley-like bad faith; but I think that he can be charged with an excited sincerity that is near to the point of no return. As such, it is often repulsive. And it continued after the war and towards all kinds of Germans. In 1917, in Bordeaux: "I do not believe the Germans can be converted. The activities of the German socialists, especially the Liebknecht clan, are designed to deceive us." But this was the year when peace plans from every side – Tory elder statesman Lansdowne, the Pope, the Labour Congress at Stockholm – threatened that total and crushing defeat of Germany which he alone thought safe. And, after the war, he could see Germany's dreadful years only as "the manoeuvres to abolish her internal debt cost Germany no more than a few thousand old unusable people wiped out, perhaps, by starvation". [2]

His last letter to his friend, Jim Barrie, in Canada, states the position calmly, and the last page of it was not written until 4 January 1936, thirteen days before his death. Germany, he wrote prophetically, "is a well-equipped gunman in the middle of the traffic; the traffic is apt to be a shade 'jerky'. She has been explaining what she is arming for for five or six years – as she did for six or seven before the War. In these matters I have noticed she keeps her word!" [3]

His anti-Germanism was far too fanatical to examine the social and economic effects which the *à l'outrance* policy of his friend Clemenceau in the early post-war years might be having. This side of the rise of Hitler to power was invisible to him. But the march of time came to vindicate him, for in his deep distrust of Germany, his constant demand for vigilant armament, his despair at American isolationism (or return to the hated American neutrality of the early war years), he was to prove right. In 1939, we knew that we should have so armed, we knew that we needed American support as soon as we could get it. The poem, "The Storm Cone" (1932) and his speech to the Society of St George in 1935 are often cited as evidences of his awareness of the Nazi menace. And rightly. After all, he banished his cherished Indian "ganesh" sign from his publications when the similar swastika became associated with the Nazis. Had he lived, he would have loathed Hitler's wickedness, but to a great extent he would have seen it as the racial continuation of vileness like the Belgian atrocities, every report of which he believed.

In this, he was the spokesman of very, very many middle-class homes (as I can vouch for from my own memory of my family home when I was four and five years old, where anti-Germanism was an hysteria, where my mother ordered my twice-wounded brother out of the house because he expressed doubts about German barbarity; and my father told me at five how the splendid Aussies had not taken prisoners but crucified the Germans they captured, because of German wickedness to the Belgian women). It was for such violent British feeling that he spoke when he wrote:

> It was not suddenly bred,
> It will not swiftly abate,
> Through the chill years ahead,
> When Time shall count from the date
> That the English began to hate.[4]

And he also spoke for himself.

One of the most dreadful of all Kipling's expressions of hate is his poem of 1918 written on a rumour that the Kaiser was dying of cancer of the throat – of which his father the Emperor Frederick had died. The poem has extra overtones of horror, when we remember that it was exactly this disease that Kipling had feared so much as the family malady. The poem "A Death-Bed" (1918) juxtaposes the Kaiser's monomaniac utterances with the doctor's supposed comments:

> "This is the State above the Law.
> The State exists for the State alone"
> (This is a gland at the back of the jaw,
> and an answering lump by the collar-bone.)
> Some die shouting in gas or fire;
> Some die silent, by shell or shot.
> Some die desperate, caught on the wire;
> Some die suddenly. This will not . . .
> "There is neither Evil nor Good in life
> Except as the needs of the State ordain."
> (Since it is rather too late for the knife
> All we can do is to mask the pain.)

And so on in many verses more revolting to me than anything Kipling ever wrote. Yet if such a poem had been written about Hitler, especially when the facts about the concentration camps became known to us, I do not know how many of my generation would not have found ourselves responding to "its sense of justice".

For this reason I must reject the well-intentioned attempts by recent critics to try to remove the element of propaganda, of brutal anti-Germanism, in a story like "Mary Postgate". It is a fine story, it contains a whole and perfect study of the hysterical breakout of a suppressed spinster. I have come to admire it, although for years its brutality made me refuse to recognise its merits. But its compassion, vaunted by post-1945 Kipling critics, is entirely for Mary Postgate, never for a moment for the dying, suffering German airman. Indeed, it is bad faith towards Kipling's intention to try to disguise this. The story was published in *Nash's Magazine* and *The Century Magazine* in May 1915, at a desperate time for the allied forces. It was advertised in the *Daily Express*. Would Sir Max Aitken (as he then was) and the magazine editors have carried anything, however subtle its art, that threw a bad light on hatred of the enemy? I think it is also quite to mistake Kipling in a way that would have put him in a rage to think that his concern for British morale and American sympathy was less than theirs. What we have to revise is not our view of the degree of violence that the War finally released in Kipling's spirit, and perhaps also the degree of violence, of hatred, inseparable from waging an all-out war; but, perhaps, most unacceptably to the critic, the possibility that a fine and subtle work of art can also be propaganda written in a spirit that we find repulsive.

What were the public activities of Kipling behind which these violent feelings festered? In the first months of the war, the Kiplings, near as they were to the Channel, were actively concerned with the Belgian refugees. They undoubtedly heard many first-hand accounts (and possibly second- and third-hand versions) of German enormities in Belgium. He writes, in September, to his old American friend and publisher, Doubleday, in desperation, telling him of the Germans' cutting off a Belgian surgeon's hands so that he could not operate. This story, he notes, comes to him from an American woman friend in France. (No doubt the Kiplings' long-time friend, Julia, who was shortly to have to flee from her house in Compiègne, where the Kiplings had stayed happily a number of times since she settled there in 1907.) Belgian women and girls are publicly raped by German officers' orders, he says. "And so this hell dance goes on and the U.S. makes no sign . . . Be as neutral as you like but do not pass these brutalities over in silence." [5]

It is perhaps because of his vague reports of such terrible stories that his friend Theodore Roosevelt wrote to him in November to say that above all *authentic* accounts of Belgian atrocities were needed in the States.[6]

But by 1916 his remonstrances to the neutrals, particularly the United States, ceased to be in private letters and became public in "The Question" (1916):

> If it be found when the battle clears,
> Their death has set me free,
> Then how shall I live with myself through
>   the years
> Which they have bought for me?

The Belgian sufferings were to make the first of the trio of war stories, "Swept and Garnished". The equivocal role of America made half of the "Sea Constables". The naval narrative of this was to come from his journeys with the Harwich flotilla in September 1915, which he undertook for the Admiralty to give the public some account of naval activity. He sailed in the ship of Admiral Bullard, in control of the East Coast, whom he had first met in the nineties on one of his Channel manoeuvres expeditions. Bullard's reminiscences show that once again the Silent Service tradition foiled Kipling's wish to associate with the whole ship's company. Kipling would have liked to talk to the men; Bullard agreed but had to point out that they would be reserved with the Admiral's guest. Kipling saw the point and remained aft. Not the way he had reported in the days of *Soldiers Three*. Nevertheless, "Sea Constables" has one of the clearest and most effective narratives of all his naval stories.

Before this he had seen something of the Flanders trenches for himself and had reported for Beaverbrook on the landing of the Canadian troops on the French shores. His knowledge of trench warfare, of course, was to be made solid by all he learned in writing his Irish Guards' history. Nevertheless, the extraordinarily powerful map sense of trench life that he conveys in a story of the war written later in the post-war years, "The Madonna of the Trenches", comes, I suspect, from this early first-hand experience that his sketch-making mind fixed into firm shape. Almost as soon as he returned from the naval trip, he was seized with the first of his agonising attacks of gastritis, herald of the physical pain that was to return again and again. From this were to spring the series of post-war stories of illness and medical surmise that promise so much more than they ever fulfil.

And then, in October, John Kipling was reported missing. As

Kipling was to say many times to would-be comforters, theirs was only the case of thousands. But it was none the less an agony for them both. For Carrie, because John had been so much *her* son, so much the one person that softened her. For Rudyard, because since a son is a mother's knight, his own grief must be hidden in order to comfort her. It must, indeed, have been a terrible time for their daughter, Elsie (then nearly twenty years of age) who had to comfort them both. Missing, of course, meant hope; and Carrie went on hoping for long after her husband had put all hope out of his mind. But for her, as Miss Ponton tells us, there was the extra agony that she feared that if her boy were a prisoner, the Germans would especially ill-treat him because he was Kipling's son. They pulled all their strings with our embassies in the neutral countries, and with the despised neutrals themselves, through the American Embassy and the Swedish (Kipling was particularly honoured as a Nobel Prize winner), to get news direct from Germany. It was a routine they had been through many times before on behalf of friends, when for example two of John's friends had been killed – George Cecil and Oscar Hornung. It brought Carrie Kipling even closer to her neighbour, Lady Edward Cecil, George Cecil's mother, whom she had known since the Boer War days at Groote Schuur, and made them a close friend of Mrs Cuthbert (later Lady Rayleigh) whose husband had been reported missing in company with John.

Regimental friends of John's came to talk of him and some we shall hear of again in their post-war life. But nothing, of course, could really help. Kipling only occasionally burst out. To their old friend Julia, who visited them at Brown's Hotel, he made no mention of John until he was seeing her into her car on her leaving, when he pressed her hand so that it almost hurt and said, "Down on your knees, Julia, and thank God you haven't a son." [7] Already by January 1916, he wrote to his friend the American, Forbes, "John was wounded as well as missing. We have no word of him and I fear that there is but little to hope." [8] Carrie went on hoping for many, many months. They learned of John's being wounded through Rider Haggard's indefatigable efforts in tracing a Guardsman, Michael Bowes, who had last seen John alive. The man told Haggard that he last saw John crying with pain from a mouth wound, but he hadn't liked to help him from fear of humiliating him. Haggard did not pass this painful circumstance on to the Kiplings. It is grimly ironic to place this against one of Kipling's "Epitaphs of The War" – "A Son".

My son was killed while laughing at some jest.
    I would I knew
What it was, and it might serve me in a time
    when jests are few.

John Kipling's death is perhaps particularly poignant, for he was so ordinary a typical public schoolboy officer of those years. Not a handsome Rupert Brooke or Julian Grenfell. A tall, gangling youth with glasses. The well-known picture of him standing with his myopic father at the rifle range has a cruel absurdity. His short sight prevented him from going into the Navy as he wished. Whatever we hear of him seems to fit this conventional picture – dressed up as a suffragette in family charades, we may imagine the pantomime dame that this would be in the Kipling household; playing with a tame lion cub at The Woolsack; taking over the doting Great-Aunt Georgie's house at Rottingdean on half-holidays from his nearby preparatory school; delighted to be going to Wellington because he wouldn't have to hear any more about the wretched "Recessional" his father had written; telling Rudyard that the talk he had given to his house at Wellington had "not been badly received"; having to be coached on their Swiss skiing holiday in 1913 because he had done badly at school exams. Kipling, after all, had written to Haggard that his children showed no signs of imagination and that he was thankful for it.[9]

That flesh we had nursed from the first in all cleanness was
    given. . .
To be blanched or gay-painted by fumes, to
    be cindered by fires
To be senselessly tossed and re-tossed in
    stale mutilation
From crater to crater. For this we shall
    take expiation.
But who shall return us our children?[10]

The rest of the war was marking time. In 1916 Kipling accepted a commission to go to Italy to report on the Italian front. "War in the Mountains", the resulting publication of 1917, was made in the form of an interview with Roderick Jones, a journalist friend from Cape Town days, who from 1915 was the head of Reuter's, and from 1916 in charge of the wireless and cable propaganda in the Ministry of Information. Some adverse comment on the number of elegant aristocratic shirkers in Rome was cut at the request of the Government.

Rome and the Vatican impressed Kipling in a very historical-novelish kind of way – "the absolutism and arrogance of the impenitent ages ... hang ... in the still, suave air".[11]

But his attitude to the Roman Catholic Church, once so favourable, had become more hostile since the support of the hierarchy for the Southern Irish in the years before the War. It was to grow more so still when the Pope put forward his peace plan in 1917, and by 1918 evoked his poem "A Song at the Cock-Crow":

> The last time that Peter denied his Lord,
> The Father took from him the Keys and the Sword,
> And the Mother and Babe brake his Kingdom in two,
> When the cock crew – when the cock crew –
> (Because of his wickedness) when the cock crew!

We have gone a long way here from the praise for the Roman Catholic priest over the Anglican in his East End social work in "Badalia Herodsfoot" in the early nineties; or the obvious superiority of the Catholic padre, Father Victor, to the Church of England, Reverend Bennett, in *Kim*. It illustrates, however, I think, the degree to which Kipling had no continuing concern with Christian theology. The Catholic Church had been the preferred Christian body in his earliest days because he thought its priests less narrow-minded, more practical, tougher, and more fitted to their social task because of their celibate life, not because of their doctrinal beliefs. Now, on political grounds, he reverses his attitude. He told Rider Haggard at this time that he believed that the Pope was attempting to regain power and would bring back the Inquisition. He tells Theodore Roosevelt in 1918 that the enemy to civilisation is the Papacy, not Roman Catholicism, and its menace has been shown in Australia and Canada, and, above all, Ireland.[12] In short, the Pope is seen to undermine British Imperial unity.

But his mind, I think, under the misery of John's death and Carrie's desperate unhappiness, was full of pessimistic fancies. In 1918 when Haggard came over from his new winter home at St Leonard's on the Sussex coast to Bateman's, he found both the Kiplings very aged and ill-looking. When he asked Rudyard if he thought that the earth was one of the hells (for he believed in reincarnation), Rudyard replied that he didn't *think*, he was certain of it.

Only one thing during the War's horrible years roused any sense of hope in Kipling. It is a curious, touching, almost comic note. The bravery and success of the Indian troops serving in France gave him a

76 Kipling signing autographs after his installation as Rector of St Andrew's University. (*Library of Congress*)

77 Mr and Mrs Rudyard Kipling at the wedding of their daughter Elsie to Captain G. Bainbridge at St Margaret's, Westminster, 22 October 1924. (*National Portrait Gallery*)

78 Rudyard Kipling in Jamaica in 1930, published in the *New York Times*, 6 April 1936. (*Library of Congress*)

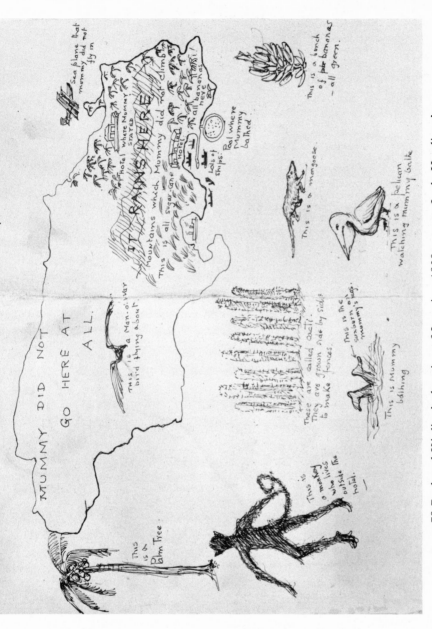

79 Rudyard Kipling's drawing of Jamaica, 1930, sent to Lady Hardinge's children. Lady Hardinge accompanied Kipling and Carrie on this trip. (*By kind permission of Lady Hardinge of Penshurst*)

80 "Even before the First War during his visits to Vernet-les Bains, France was becoming Rudyard Kipling's second home", page 334. Vernet-les Bains, 1911, *left to right* Lord Roberts, the Bishop of Perpignan, Kipling, Lady Edwina Roberts. (*Radio Times Hulton Picture Library*)

81 Fairlawne, Tonbridge, 1928, *left to right* Victor Cazalet, Hugh Walpole, Elizabeth Russell (author of *Elizabeth and her German Garden*), Kipling, Mrs Cazalet. (*From* Hugh Walpole *by Rupert Hart-Davies, Macmillan, 1952; by permission of Mrs Thelma Cazalet-Keir*)

82 Kipling at a garden party at Bateman's in 1926. (*Frames from a film, reproduced by kind permission of Mrs Lancelot Hard*)

83 From 1897 until 1902 the Kiplings lived at The Elms, Rottingdean, whence they were driven by increasing invasions of trippers from Brighton. In September 1902 they moved to Bateman's (above). (*Photo Eileen Tweedy*)

84 The desk in Kipling's study at Bateman's. (*Photo Eileen Tweedy*)

85 Mr and Mrs Rudyard Kipling at Nice. (*Associated Press*)

great sense of pride. He visited the Indian soldiers' hospital set up in the Brighton Royal Pavilion. No doubt they had been housed there in some simple hope that Nash's fantastic dome would make them feel at home.

Kipling published a small collection of imaginary letters of these Indian soldiers under the title of *The Eyes of Asia* (1917). The scribes are, expectedly, all Punjabi Moslems, Afghans or Sikhs (a fair enough coverage of the Indians serving with the Allied forces, but also a selection to Kipling's liking). And, because he is speaking in their words. We get, little of the commendation of Indian bravery that he expressed and felt privately. We have instead Kipling's idea of the Indians' first views of England and France. What is surprising is the contrast with the Indian picture of England in the eighteen-nineties, "One View of the Question", when everything in London was seen as corrupt, decadent, and potentially anarchic. Now everything that the Indian troops see in England and in France calls for admiration and exhortation to copy. Only once, in praising France, does an Afghan find some similarity to his primitive tribal code. He notes with delight the French refusal ever to forgive the enemy. For the rest, it is what could generally be called Western progress that the Indians commend – vaccination, water sterilisation, care for dogs, post-mortems that eliminate murder by poison, the refusal of French priests to attempt conversion (!), education. Above all, Kipling's imaginary correspondents again and again stress the value of education for women, and Girton College, Cambridge comes in for special commendation for producing women able to serve society. It is curious to come on this residue of liberal imperialism, of the old Macaulayish civilising mission view of Empire, which, though strong at times, had never been more than a small part of Kipling's view of British India when he was there.

In part, it is a simple expression of his admiration for women's war work. In part, it shows, I suspect, that he thought of Indians with affection still, but no longer felt that powerful attraction towards their way of life that gives such force to his Indian work. He remembered only the other aspect of his Indian days – his love and admiration for the District Commissioners, the dedicated Englishmen who served the Indians for their good. Perhaps it should be seen as another reminder of the unexpectedness of Kipling, his capacity for difference in what seems so monolithic a construction of prejudice and dogma.

But, then, unexpectedness had increasingly become the expected mark of Kipling's fiction – a truly extraordinary achievement, for however much we prepare ourselves to be indifferent to the surprises of approach, or subject, he never fails to catch us off our guard.

307

One of the striking features of the 1915 trio of powerful stories is not only that they are so horrible, but also that they approach war's bestiality from such unusual and different angles; and yet they are deeply united by a strange vision.

"Swept and Garnished" is the story of Frau Ebermann's visitation in her comfortable Berlin flat by the spectres of five little Belgian children. It is the least horrible of the trio. It appeared early in 1915, hot-foot upon the terrible stories of the atrocities in Belgium, and is the most superficially propagandist. Yet it is a well-organised short tale and, as so often happens when Kipling is hating, exudes an odd extra sense of the author's loving, detailed care. For someone who had put away from himself all things German for two decades, Kipling never-theless conveys a vivid sense of the comfort of this Berlin bourgeois life and surroundings – "the yellow cut-glass handles of the chest of drawers, the stamped bronze hook to hold back the heavy puce cur-tains, the mauve enamel, New Art finger plates on the doors", the bronze-painted steam pipes, the imitation marble top of the radiator; Anna, the maid, ready to carry out her mistress's every request, to see that every object is exactly in its place; Frau Ebermann's expectation of talking over the strange events that disorder the apartment's perfect pattern with friends at coffee the next day.

The threat to this orderly, cosseted existence is developed in fine crescendo. First, the elderly lady has symptoms of influenza, and then the influenza produces the hallucination of small, but significant disor-ders in the household scene: "an imitation lace cover which should have lain mathematically square with the imitation marble top of the radiator . . . had slipped." From then on, despite all the medicaments and inhalants, "as she wriggled her toes luxuriously on the hot-water bottle," everything goes awry, despite Anna's announcement, on her return from the chemist's, of "Another Victory. Many more prisoners and guns." First, one little girl of ten appears and stares at her, and, later, the same girl returns with three much younger children, one a boy. Frau Ebermann's remonstrances at their invasion of her flat, their reiterated account – shadowy in detail, but powerful in effect – of the destruction of their village and their certainty of their instructions to go to Berlin and await the arrival of their own people – all these menacing horrors come as naturally as some sweet, sentimental con-versation in a story of a kind lady's welcome of poor orphan children to her home. It is the Victorian children's story in reverse, "They" turned upside down.

At last, when she can evade no more, the comfortable lady, who wants life to be comfortable during this distant war the Germans are winning so splendidly, admits that her son has written from Belgium that *some* children have been killed crossing the village street in front of the German horses and guns. She explains it, as people do to little children who can't easily understand – "Yes, yes; believe me, *that* is how the accidents to the children happen ... One runs out to look, but one is little and cannot see well. So one pops between the man's legs, and then – you know how close those big horses and guns turn the corners ..." It has happened perhaps not twenty times, she says. But the boy monstrously reports, "Thousands." And then, as a final horror, something that may not come over to the modern reader, but reminds me of how I was told again and again as a small child, that the Germans had cut off the little Belgian boys' right arms so that they could never serve their country. In the story it is implied very quietly. The sister plucks at the little boy's sleeve to take him away, and he cries out in pain. " 'What is that for?' said Frau Ebermann, 'To cry in a room where a poor lady is sick is very inconsiderate.' 'Oh, but, look, lady!' said the elder girl. Frau Ebermann looked and saw." Au revoir, cry the children and are gone. And Anna comes in to find her mistress on her knees assiduously cleaning everything in the room. "It was all spotted with the blood of five children – she was perfectly certain there could be no more than five in the whole world – who had gone away for the moment, but were now waiting round the corner, and Anna was to find them and give them cakes to stop the bleeding, while her mistress swept and garnished that our dear Lord, when He came, should find everything as it should be."

In 1915 this story must have been very satisfying or disgusting, according to one's attitude to war propaganda. Now I think it is a masterly parable of cosiness brutally dispersed.

"Mary Postgate" has been much more noticed. It is deeply shocking, and I reject all suggestions that its brutality can be explained away. It is true that the overall psychological tragedy of the story, unlike "Swept and Garnished", transcends its propaganda. In the last resort, Kipling is aware with deep pity of the waste of a human life that can only be brought to some sense of exhilaration by a cruel act of vengeance. And he prepares this sense of the waste of Mary Postgate's life most carefully. She is that extinct creature, whom I remember well from my mother's bridge parties in my childhood, a genteel middle-aged spinster without money reduced to being a paid lady-companion to a wealthy old woman. A camel-like creature whose deadness to life, whose existence solely as a machine, are pointed out by the old lady she works for. Miss Fowler, the employer, is a lively, humorous Victorian relict, kind enough but patronising, and unfeeling enough to comment on her companion's nullity. Not that it hurts Mary Postgate. To Miss Fowler's question, "Mary, aren't you *anything* except a companion? Would you *ever* have been anything except a companion?" she replies, "No. I don't imagine I ever should. But I've no imagination, I'm afraid." Yet she has a power of loving slavishly, which is given to Miss Fowler's nephew, Wynn, who grows up heavily teasing her, expecting constant service of her, and echoing his Auntie's unconsidered comments – "You haven't the mental capacity of a white mouse," he cries. When the nephew is killed, training for the Flying Corps, the Aunt says, "I never expected anything else, but I'm sorry it happened before he'd done anything." But Mary, perhaps because of her lack of imagination, translates this directly, "Yes. It's a great pity he didn't die in action after he had killed somebody."

She takes on, in her lifeless, phlegmatic way, the task of burning in the garden incinerator all the dead young man's childhood toys and boyhood sports things. Going to fetch petrol from the village, in order to light the fire, she arrives when the pub-keeper's little girl is killed by a stray German bomb. She returns to her job, to find in the Portuguese laurels the young German airman, who has fallen from his plane, and is dying in great agony. He begs in broken English and French for a doctor. But she says, "Nein. Ich habe der todt Kinder gesehn."

Wynn, the nephew, she reflects, "was a gentleman who, for no consideration on earth, would have torn little Edna into those vividly coloured strips and strings". So, methodically she burns the toys, and, at last, the memorial pyre is spent, and the young German gives forth the rattle she has heard at so many family death beds. Satisfied, she goes in to have a luxurious hot bath. At tea time, she looks, "as Miss Fowler said when she saw her lying all relaxed on the other sofa, 'quite handsome'".

It is not easy to respond wholly to such a story. And few have done so. I remember that, when I put it forward as an example of Evil in English literature in the Northcliffe lectures, the late Bonamy Dobrée rightly sprang to Kipling's defence, but wrongly insisted, I am sure, that the story was to be seen entirely as an understanding portrait of the pathological behaviour of a repressed woman under the impact of war's horrors. It is the line taken by all who want to defend the story. It *is* that, of course; and an excellently told account of such a woman it is, restrained and exact. But it is *not* only that.

Kipling is not, it is true, saying this is how we all act in war-time. But he *is* saying that the unimaginative and desperate logic of this woman has its own fitness, is right for the times, given the wickedness of the enemy. This defence is put into Mary's thoughts: "she had never believed in all those advanced views ... of woman's work in the world; but now she saw there was much to be said for them. This for instance was *her* work – work which no man least of all Dr Hennis [the village doctor] would ever have done. A man at such a crisis would be what Wynn called a 'sportsman' ... Now a woman's business was to make a happy home for – for a husband and children – Failing these – it was not a thing one should allow one's mind to dwell upon – but 'Nein, I tell you! Ich habe der todt Kinder gesehn' ... *But* it was a fact. A woman who had missed these things could still be useful ...''

Kipling is aware that it is inhumanity, a nature unfulfilled that is required for such an act. He suggests, maybe, that he and the reader could not meet the requirement, would feel pity or softness. But, I feel sure, in its context, that the story tells us that Mary's terrible ruthlessness is the fitting response to German "awfulness" (as I remember it used to be called). Whether he believed with Mary that our airmen would not drop stray bombs, I doubt, though he may have thought that they had stricter orders against such unloading than the Germans. He is not emphasising, I think, that only "awfulness" on our side will check the German "awfulness", though he may have thought that too. He sees Mary's act as a satisfaction to her, and, I think, he believes that only a nation that can demand such satisfaction can hope to wage sufficiently fierce a war upon evil people who maim or kill children. And we must notice how, in both these stories, the victims are *children*, for it is that which in Kipling's code (held all through his life) puts the Germans out of consideration as human beings. In short, there is a savage and horrible satisfaction for Kipling in writing the story, although it has other and more bearable layers on top of that. But its narration, the use of every word so tellingly, is something that must make us read with equal satisfaction, though not with the same satisfaction as the author's. Any rejection of it, such as I made for years, or any attempt, as by so many critics, to read it more pleasantly, is, I believe, a refusal to face the difficult truth that aesthetic satisfaction is not one with ethical satisfaction, although the critic has every right to distinguish the moral impulse which disgusts him from the story which is such a wonder to read.

There is an underlying connection between these two stories, not just that they tell of two elderly women and the home front in Germany and England, but that they suggest, more than almost anything that Kipling wrote, the animal quality of human life. Frau Ebermann in her overheated flat is like some comfortable animal in a den it supposes to be a safe refuge from the jungle outside; Mary Postgate, with her narrow range, from house to village, and from house to garden, moves like a creature marking out its bounds of territoriality, and, in the end, whatever the cause, she watches the death of another creature that has fallen out of the sky into her territory with the satisfaction of a jackal that sees a vulture fall and die before it. We expect almost that she will eat the man. It is this animal quality underlying the war stories that gives them a special horror, for war is the open admission, however noble its justification, that men and women are beasts of the jungle.

At first sight, "Sea Constables" has none of this cramped, claustrophobic quality of the animal's den. To begin with it has a lively frame for its telling. Four naval officers, three of them war-time officers who have been rich city men, assemble for luncheon at a very smart West End of London restaurant. They are in civilian clothes, and, as they eat and drink with rare satisfaction through a gourmet meal, they are watched with disgust by a foreign millionaire and a foreign actress – " 'The latest thing in imported patriotic piece-goods. She sings, 'Sons of the Empire, Go Forward!' at the Palemseum. 'It makes the aunties weep,' " says one of the officers. "Now what's the matter with those four dubs yonder joining the British Army or *doing* something?" asks the actress of the millionaire she is lunching with.

It is obvious that these rich foreigners, who so easily comment on apparent British shirking, are American neutrals. And, when the four men begin to exchange accounts of the various dangerous activities they have been carrying out in terrible conditions, defending England's shores, it is, at last, to a story of the pursuit and defeat of a neutral ship, carrying oil for the enemy, that we settle. This neutral, or "Newt", too, is a millionaire; and, I think, an American though this is made less obvious in his speech, and implied only in his talking about "the uplift of democracy". When at last, after a long chase and many adventures in the fog-bound, gale-swept seas, the neutral is forced to give up and land his cargo at a small Irish port, he has caught pneumonia. He begs of Portson, the stockbroker naval officer, who has run him to ground, to take him to England and the doctors. "I said, of course, that that was out of the question, *Hilarity* being a man-of-war in commission. He couldn't see it. He asked what that had to do with it. He thought this war was some sort of joke, and I had to repeat it all over again. He seemed rather afraid of dying . . . and he hoisted himself up on one elbow and began calling me a murderer. I explained to him – perfectly politely – that I wasn't in this job for fun. It was business." And, a few hours later, the blockade-running American dies.

We are less likely to reject this story, for although Portson's action is coldly brutal and his tone of talking to the dying man more so, this is active warfare and the neutral is supplying a barbarous enemy with its vital war supplies for money. The weakness is structural rather than ethical; it is hard to believe that the dying man could, in any case, have been got to England in time, or that a country Irish doctor would not have been a wiser choice. But apart from that, the story works most efficiently. The framework – as by no means always the case with Kipling – is relevant and well realised, the sea chase moves quickly and, almost uniquely in his naval work, is not rendered unintelligible by technicality. The moral is unpleasant, yet it is the real meaning of the Stalky ethics so much admired by many who reject this war story. When Portson says, "I wasn't in this job for fun. It was business," he echoes exactly the creed of *Stalky & Co.*, a creed which is designed to teach the young what is business in life and what is fun – not at all the same distinction as that made by conventional moralists. I find the Stalky code repulsive, but, if it is not acceptable in the situation of war-time and "Sea Constables", it is hard to see when it ever could be. Finally, the ships chasing the neutral through the minefields of the North Sea, and through the cold, white fogs of the Irish Channel, recall, like Frau Ebermann's cosy flat and Mary Postgate's narrow garden, the jungle where the pack join together to run an intruder to death; and death, when at last it comes, kills like a beast – the "Newt" dies in a stinking hole, an oil-fumed cabin like an animal run to ground.

After the loss of John, there are no more such stories, although the condemnation of Kaiser and neutrals alike in poems is as terrible and, I fear, as personally satisfying to Kipling, as the 1915 trio. The mercy for all sinners (Germans and neutrals not mentioned) asked for in the delayed "On the Gate", written the year after John's death, has a muddled generality bordering on sentimentality which is, I think, one of the faults that deny many of his ambitious late stories success. Of the many tales of the healing of war's mental wounds, most of them diffuse and over-elaborate, the most simply satisfactory is probably "The Woman in His Life". In this story, a typical Kipling hero, a young veteran of the battle of Messines who, through engineering, builds up a thriving post-war industry, collapses from overwork and singleness of satisfaction. The wily cockney valet (once his batman) of his Jeeves–Wooster West End luxury flat existence saves his master from complete breakdown by persuading him to keep an Aberdeen terrier bitch. At this point all who are allergic to dog worship will leave. I like dogs well enough, but I am not a devotee; however, I love cats enough to understand what Kipling is saying. There is no doubt that, in his last rather wan years, Kipling's emptiness was in part filled by studying (and loving) the Aberdeen terriers he kept at Bateman's. He attempted, alas, to write a whole book out of this – *Thy Servant a Dog*. It is a worthy attempt to speak through a dog's senses of feel and smell and sight, but it is marred by the sentimentality with which Kipling covers his real egoistic conviction, which is that the magnificence of dogs lies in their complete subservience to their masters. There is something of this ultimately sugary possessiveness in "The Woman in His Life", yet the exact observation of the habits, movements and needs of a domestic dog and the gradual absorption in them to his own mental relief of the neurotic master is very convincing. The climax of the story in which the hero overcomes all his half-remembered fears of the trenches by descending into a badger set to rescue his dog is very effective. It is hard to take as a whole; but it is an interesting example of how Kipling's skill can reconcile an open-minded reader to the most unpromising themes.

"A Madonna of the Trenches" is one of a number of stories he wrote after the war, imagining that the ritual and fellowship of Freemasonry might be the proper means to cure the war's mental and nervous casualties. They are all, including "The Madonna of the Trenches", which is the best, far too overcrowded.

It is most interesting that when he wanted, in his last years, to bring a variety of men together, to emphasise the underlying fellowship of humanity, to give men some bond of play and ritual that could relieve them from the necessary but confining disciplines of caste and rank and class and race which keep anarchy at bay, he should have turned again to the Freemasonry which had been one of his principal releases from the sharp division of British India. Freemasonry had been a solvent of the fiercely disciplined and caste-bound life of the British Army in India from the late eighteenth century. Kipling was inducted into the Lodge of Hope and Perseverance in Lahore in 1885, when he was eight months short of the statutory twenty-one years. He became secretary of the Lodge (one of five in Lahore), and, in *Something of Myself*, he tells how he was "entered by a member of the Brahmin Somaj [a Hindu], passed by a Mohammedan, and raised by an Englishman. Our tyler was an Indian Jew."[13] That this multi-racial aspect of the Lodge was what he sought is confirmed by the fact that, when he moved to Allahabad, he chose to enter the only Lodge that had many non-Europeans among its members. In these post-war Freemasonry stories, the emphasis is strongly upon the mixture of classes and trades. Here his fellowship with doctors is expressed as strongly as in the other group of purely medical "healing" stories. But there is also a very lively and sympathetic concern with tradesmen – grocers, tobacconists, apothecaries, and hairdressers – an affectionate and admiring feeling for the petit-bourgeois world that is as effective in its way as that of Bennett or Wells. The other feature of the stories is a pleasing delight in the ritual and furnishing (particularly eighteenth-century furnishing) of the Lodges.

Alas, the stories themselves are so overlaid with muddled themes, obscure literary and biblical references, and started hares, that, for once, Kipling's extraordinarily economic craftsmanship is lost in prolixity.

"The Madonna of the Trenches" is the best of these stories because in its recall of trench warfare he brings to this central horror of the war his map-like vision and his impressionistic power of detail; but all this is lost in his attempt to fuse two of his most cherished hopes – survival after death and elective affinities, life-long enduring passions.

A young private, Strangwick, insists at the front that his nervous collapse is due to the creaking of the dead soldiers beneath the duckboards in the trenches. His Medical Officer, Keede, doubts this from the beginning. Some years after the war is over, the young man breaks down at a Masonic ceremony, and Keede, who is present, is able to elicit the full cause from him. He had witnessed in a supernatural vision at the trenches the passionate reunion of his dead aunt's apparition with his Sergeant, who then commits suicide to join her in the after-life. On the Sergeant's lips had been St Paul's saying (to be used by Kipling often in the stories of this period) – "If, after the manner of men, I have fought with beasts at Ephesus, what advantageth it me, if the dead rise not?" To equate the enduring through a lifetime of an undeclared passion with St Paul's suffering for Christ, however creditable to Kipling's compassion for human suffering, is a damaging confusion: the one is a staple of high romantic literature, the other is at the centre of Christian belief. One does not have to be a Christian to feel the difference in quality between these two experiences. One may reasonably ask what is the meaning of this passionate love sustained into eternity (are the middle-aged lovers destined for the flames like Paolo and Francesca?), and how long will the overturning of young Strangwick's view of life last? At the heart of this vividly told story, as with so many of the stories in which he uses Christianity as a symbolic device for the demand for compassion, there is plain sentimentality clothed in a metaphysical authority which it does not possess.

Kipling's other story of the war is for many of his admirers his finest work. "The Gardener" is brilliantly carried out, full of subtle, ambiguous, yet meaningful, nuances. It is also his saddest story because it is the one in which he allows his deepest sympathy most open range and ends on pity without any active solution. And it is without violence. All this probably makes it his most agreeable story; yet I believe that it is finally flawed by one of his annoying, puzzling endings which have so captivated those who want to range him on the side of the "clever", and, in particular, because this "puzzling" ending is encased in cliché. The main body of the story certainly demands the highest praise.

Helen Turrell, a young woman of means and family, goes from her village to the South of France for her health. While there, she learns that her brother, George, "an Inspector of the Indian Police, had entangled himself with the daughter of a retired non-commissioned officer, and had died of a fall from his horse a few weeks after his child was born". This nephew Helen adopts – "luckily it seemed that the people of that class [the boy's mother's family] would do almost anything for money". Aunt and nephew, loving and loved, are a popular feature of the village. When Michael, the nephew, wishes to call her "Mummy" like the other boys at school, she explains that she is only his aunt, but that he may call her "Mummy" at bed-time. When he learns that she has told the whole village of his parents' illicit love, he upbraids her – " '*Why* did you tell?' – 'Because it's always better to tell the truth,' Helen answered ... 'When the troof's ugly I don't think it's nice.' " Yet later, at ten, rather improbably precocious, he accepts his bastardy with, "Don't you bother, Auntie. I've found out all about my sort in English History and the Shakespeare bits. There was William the Conqueror to begin with, and – oh, heaps more, and they all got on first-rate."

These changes in his attitude to his supposed bastard birth work admirably against our knowledge of his real bastard birth by Helen herself (which, of course, Kipling never states). Just before Michael goes to Oxford, the war breaks out. Luck seems always to be on his side, until "a shell-splinter dropping out of a wet dawn killed him at once. The next shell uprooted and laid down over the body what had been the foundation of a barn wall, so neatly that none but an expert would have guessed that anything unpleasant had happened." This parallel to Helen's burial of her relationship to him is Kipling at his best.

Then follow some fine pages describing her return from grief to a deadened "normality". (Is it Carrie's progress he describes?) At last Helen goes off on a visit to Flanders to see Michael's grave. Here, amid a number of interesting encounters, is one especially well conveyed with a Mrs Scarsworth, who chatters on about her many visits on behalf of bereaved relations, only at last to break down with the revelation that it is her illicit lover she has come there to honour. At the end, Helen herself goes to the great graveyard and, despite all her documentation, is lost before the endless rows of crosses. A man, planting there, asks her " 'Who are you looking for?' – 'Lieutenant Michael Turrell – my nephew' said Helen . . . as she had many thousands of times in her life . . . 'Come with me and I will show you where your son lies.' " Then the story ends: "When Helen left the cemetery, she turned for a last look. In the distance she saw the man bending over his young plants; and she went away, supposing him to be the gardener."

Many interpretations have been put on this – that it was Michael himself; Alexander Woollcott, the American theatre critic, had a friend to whom Kipling confided that the gardener was Helen's brother and Michael's father; and so on. I find all this bewildering. The last words, with their echo of the Bible account of Mary Magdalene at Jesus's grave, are surely clear enough. It is a not unusual Kipling use of the Holy Writ. And, as if to point it, he follows the story with a poem – "The Burden":

> To lie from morn till e'en –
> To know my lies are vain –
> Ah, Mary Magdalene,
> Where can be greater pain?

The fact seems clear enough. All that annoys me is the pointing up of so fine a story by such a cliché. Not because it is a Christian one that Kipling chooses, but because he doesn't need to define his ending at all. We need neither Christ himself nor anyone returned from the dead; a gardener, perspicacious enough to see the truth, after all the hundreds of visitors who have come to the graveyard, would have been enough.

In *Anna Karenina*, Levin says, "Christ would never have said those words if he had known how they would be abused. Of all the Gospel those are the only ones remembered." "Supposing him to be the gardener" is, as with "The Madonna of the Trenches", although less seriously, a misjudgement of taste – it both reduces the story which has worked perfectly on its straight human level, and treats the Christian quotation as a ready-made text.

This defect in an outstanding story is perhaps to be seen as part of that need to express the inexpressible which dogs so many writers in the half-century after Darwin. It can be parallelled in Conrad's "The Horror! the horror!" in *The Heart of Darkness*, where the author is searching after some idea of evil that transcends the rational, that goes beyond words.

But, at the last, it is the artistic victories of the story that remain with the reader, not its concluding mistake. Helen Turrell has denied her life's meaning out of convention, has condemned herself to a life of tacit deception. All this is shattered by the momentary intense action of a shell-splinter. This whole theme is expressed symbolically in Helen's thoughts when she is being shuttled from one Government authority to another after Michael is missing: "Once, on one of Michael's leaves, he had taken her over a munition factory, where she saw the progress of a shell from blank-iron to the all but finished article. It struck her at the time that the wretched thing was never left alone for a second; and, 'I'm being manufactured into a bereaved next-of-kin,' she told herself, as she prepared her documents." Such is the extra meaning of "killed in action".

The Post-War Years

The impact of Kipling's life after 1918 upon his work is small. In a sense, the War had been the cumulation of all his anxieties of nearly thirty years: the Allied victory, the realisation of his hopes of the same period. Of course, those hopes were in no way fulfilled and he could see that they would not be. The Imperial unity evidenced in the war effort had soon been dissipated. As in the Boer War, the military successes of the Dominions had inclined them to independent actions rather than concerted ones.

Imperialism was increasingly becoming a combination of rhetoric supported by little more than pious platitudes and the pursuit of common economic interests. I went, as a schoolboy, to the British Empire Exhibitions held at Wembley in 1924 and 1925. And I remember how the deeply held, stiff-upper-lipped, unvocal Imperial sentiment of my head-master-brother and the loudly jingoistic, near-to-tears, euphoric Imperialism of my South African mother were alike nonplussed by what they found there – a combination of a mammoth trade show and a large-scale fun fair. This commercial spree had little to do with the swords and assegais and the pictures of Lord Kitchener that decorated the walls of our home, or the battle sword above his wife's photograph that adorned my brother's study. It had even less surely to do with Anglo-Saxon world civilisation and lives of sacrifice to stave off anarchy that underlay the Imperial visions of Milner and Kipling. So much for the white Dominions.

From 1930 onwards, Kipling found himself increasingly at odds with his beloved cousin, Stanley Baldwin, over the trend of events – the Simon Commission, the Round Table Conferences – that ended in the Government of India Act of 1935. That was the culmination of a new India that loomed ahead through all the post-war years; it was inevitably one in which the Westernised Indian élite would dominate. It could only mean the end of the India that had held Kipling's imagination throughout his life – the India of the peasants and fighting men on the one hand, dark, mysterious, beautiful, childlike, violent, and, on the other hand, the India of the Englishman's sacrifice, of devotion, duty, grim jest, febrile gaiety, the liberating joke. It was this polarity that made *Plain Tales* and *Soldiers Three* and *Kim*. And if he found himself at odds with his cousin Stanley, the man who most loudly agreed with him was the unspeakable Winston Churchill, architect of most of the Liberal enormities of 1906 to 1913 and the wicked man behind the shameful rebuking of Milner before the House of Commons.

It is a measure of Kipling's post-war avoidance of active political involvement, that he made only one visit to a white Dominion in all these post-war years – this an enforced stop in Canada when he brought Carrie home after a serious illness while they were holidaying in Jamaica in 1930. And this stay in Canada was only to avoid setting foot on the United States with their memories of that earlier terrible illness and death in 1899.

As to India, he was a Vice-President of the India Defence League, with, among others, his old unbendable right-wing friend, Carson. But, when he wrote a short introduction to Lady Atholl's 1934 Report against the proposed measure of independent government, his words (perhaps out of affection for his Prime Minister cousin) were very restrained: "It is not easy to give a notion of the complexity of India to people unacquainted with the administrative fabric of even British India. But this pamphlet overcomes the difficulty with success, and is, to my mind, a temperate exposition of some of the graver perils inherent in the proposed scheme for the political reconstruction of the sub-continent." [14] It is hard to recognise the violent political Kipling of 1895, let alone of 1912, in this distanced writing. He saw little hope of communicating with this new world, and had little inclination to find a way of doing so.

The war did, at last (though all too late to satisfy Kipling's longing) bring together England and her great Anglo-Saxon cousin, the United States, against the Teutonic threat. Then, two months after the Armistice, Teddy Roosevelt, the man with whom throughout the War he had corresponded in a communion of hopes for a strong Anglo-American future, died. A man who, after Kipling's heart, had written to him of the League of Nations as "a product of men who wanted everyone to float to heaven on a sloppy sea of universal mush".[15] Yet even "Greatheart", as Kipling called him, had also written to his friend in the month of the Armistice, November 1918, to defend those bêtes noires of Kipling's, the American Irish and the American Germans, reminding him that some of both were among his Gloucester, Mass., fishermen in *Captains Courageous*. Roosevelt goes on in this letter to doubt whether there is such a thing as an Anglo-Saxon American, he knows that he is certainly not one. As to the Southerners, who talked in so pro-English a way, they had not been foremost to get America into the war (shades of the Feildens, Kipling's loved Sussex neighbours, such loyal Confederates, such patriotic Britons). If Roosevelt could tread so hard on Kipling's corns, what could Kipling hope for from the other American leaders, even when Woodrow Wilson with his dangerous cosmopolitan ideas was out of the way? And, indeed, for the rest of his life Kipling was thoroughly out of sympathy with American action whether on the demanding of payment of War Debt or of increasing isolation in the face of growing European dangers. Once or twice, in the early years, he burst out into bitter public denunciation of American faithlessness, but, on the whole, he kept his invective for private ears.

It is this that made the sculptress and journalist Clare Sheridan's publication of his anti-American views in the *New York World* in 1933 so abominable to him. If – and he later denied it publicly – he did, in fact, say many of the things she reported, he acted with uncharacteristic lack of caution, for although she was a daughter of his old friends and neighbours, the Frewens, visiting them from the States, she was also declaredly on the first lap of a European tour commissioned by the well-known American newspaper. According to her, she was charmingly received at Bateman's and Kipling was soon deep in conversation with her two small children at the edge of the fish-pond. She joined them, and, so she tells us, held this adult conversation about his views on the world and the United States' selfishness in the intervals of his story-telling to her children. If this was indeed so, it would have represented to the Kiplings (and Carrie had to deal with the resulting American fury, for Kipling himself was suffering his worst bout of gastritis) not only a new and horrible affray with the invasive press, but an absolute defiance of their basic code that divided the public from the private, and, worst of all, a blasphemy to Kipling, the use of children and his devotion to them as a means towards a shabby, prying indiscretion.

But of Kipling's growing and continuing disgust with America in his last years there can be no doubt, although there is only one story which gives a clue to his feelings. It is a not unentertaining satirical piece about Prohibition, called "The Prophet and the Country" (1924). With his increasing addiction to indirect presentation, Kipling sets his mockery of America in the mouth of a disappointed ex-realtor of Omaha, Nebraska, who has made a satirical film about the disastrous effects of Prohibition in America but cannot get it shown because of his countrymen's hostility. "I" (Kipling) meets the American and hears his story when stranded at night on the Great North Road. The concept of the man's movie attack on his own people is amusingly told. One sentence about ageing American womanhood is of a virulence that stays in the mind – "the trained sweetness and unction in the otherwise hardish, ignorant eyes; the slightly open, slightly flaccid mouth; the immense unconscious arrogance, the immovable certitude of mind, and the other warning signs in the poise of the broad-cheeked head." But, finally, as so often in the stories of his last decades, the most powerful effect comes from incidentals – a superb evocation of the moon coming up over the Great North Road, the convincing account of the cutting and juxtaposition of the photography in the projected movie. Its force is considerable but constantly deflected. Incidentally it reveals Kipling's rather complacent knowledge of the narrow limitations of his England – "North of London stretches a country called 'The Midlands', filled with brick cities, all absolutely alike, but populated by natives who, through heredity, have learned not only to distinguish between them but even between the different houses." The facetious tone would hardly mollify a Midlander.

Europe, save for France, was hardly more satisfactory than the United States, Kipling was closely associated with Rider Haggard in the short-lived Liberty League of 1920, intended to alert England to the dangers of Bolshevism. According to Haggard, when Kipling spoke for the League in April 1920, he was well-informed but had learned the speech by heart, so that it smelled of the lamp and had no hold over the audience. Perhaps here, too, for all the apparent strength of his feelings, he was not really involved as he had been in the pre-war days. The episode is chiefly memorable for the humorous verse in the *Daily Herald* in March 1920:

> Every Bolsh is a blackguard
> Said Kipling to Haggard
> That's just what I say

> Said the author of "They"
> I agree, I agree
> Said the author of "She".

But I have no doubt that the menace of Soviet Russia was much in Kipling's mind all through these last years. It is surely part of the danger against which he counselled in his famous 1935 speech to the Society of St George, which is usually held to be a warning entirely devoted to Germany and Hitler.

Nevertheless it *was* his old German enemy whose resurrection after the war so alarmed him as I have already said. He never relented in this. But there is no doubt that the rise of Hitler put him on immediate alert. The "Storm Cone" – "This is the Tempest long foretold" – appeared in 1932. On Armistice Day 1933 he took occasion to write to the *Morning Post*, warning of our military unpreparedness. Then in the same paper on 13 November 1933 came his poem, "The Bonfires", with its warning of what he believed to be all the delusive panaceas based on the easy ways out:

> We know the Father to the Thought
> Which argues Babe and Cockatrice
> Would play together, were they taught.
> We know *that* Bonfire on the Ice.

And, at the last, his 1935 speech.

Conversely, it may be said that his affection for France grew into a love affair; for the most part of his private life to which we shall come. But in his small book of collected speeches made in France, *Souvenirs of France*, published in 1933, he spoke publicly, as he perhaps never would have done of England, about himself in relation to France, recalling his boyhood visit with his father to the Paris Exhibition, his subsequent discovery of France by motor car, his early discovery of French literature and its influence, even referring to the Boer War time of his unpopularity with the French and of French written attacks upon him. Such a public exposure of his private affairs is almost unknown in Kipling's life, and shows, I think, how he came to trust French reticence, French pride, and French courtesy, not to say French thrift – "call it sou-mindedness if you will. Myself I respect it." [16] But, perhaps, his chief bond with Frenchmen of public position – his old friend Clemenceau, Foch, Joffre, Poincaré even – was their common anti-Boche sentiment, the hard French policy that led up to the occupation of the Ruhr. And on his 1921 visit to Algeria, he was delighted by the incorporation of the Algerians both by French education and by French suffrage into *la civilisation française*. It was an assimilation he would have opposed in India in his youth, but by now he, no doubt, speculated on whether Anglo-Saxon civilisation could afford to be so tolerant of diversity in its Empire as he had once believed.

At home, his political influence might have been considerable, when at last decent conservatives ceased to associate with the blackguardly Lloyd George and the Coalition came to an end in 1922. He was a close friend of Bonar Law, was indeed the one who alerted Beaverbrook to Law's serious ill-health when the Laws and the Kiplings were on holiday together at Aix-les-Bains in 1923. His friendship with Beaverbrook was close. His beloved cousin Stanley was Chancellor of the Exchequer in Bonar Law's government that succeeded the Coalition in 1922. Later, the cousins were to disagree politically, but in these years they often found delight in agreement for there was a deep ethical inheritance that they shared. Baldwin recognised this when he once wrote, "I had breakfast with Kipling at Brown's Hotel, and two hours' talk ... I was highly pleased to find that he had come to the same conclusion about the Government that I had, and by the same road, after almost as long and anxious a cogitation. We have common puritan blood and he said a thing I have often acted on. When you have two courses open to you and you thoroughly dislike one of them, that is the one you must choose, for it is sure to be the right one." [17] It is surely a clue to the ambiguity seen in both men: for to puritans they seemed to be direct, but to non-puritans their actions were often so seemingly perverse as to appear cunning. Kipling's very close friend, Milner, although he refused office under Bonar Law, too, might in the ordinary course of things have been expected to play a part in Conservative affairs from now.

Such was the position that faced Kipling in 1923, offering him at last a role not just of political notoriety as in 1913 but of real political influence. For many reasons it was not to be so. By 1925 that hope had gone. In May 1923, Bonar Law had resigned and in five months he was dead. Milner went to South Africa for a holiday, a healthy man, late in 1924, contracted encephalitis and died in May 1925. By 1925, Beaverbrook had become increasingly concerned in building up his newspaper empire. The rift between him and Kipling remains obscure but it was very soon complete. Kipling was in disagreement with Beaverbrook over India and Ireland, but so he was with his cousin Stanley. But, increasingly, Beaverbrook attacked the Governor of the Bank of England, Montagu Norman, and through him,

Baldwin. Kipling, it seems likely, came to think that these violent attacks, objectionable to him anyway on family grounds, were not due to principle but were part of a campaign for the strengthening of personal power and the increasing of the *Daily Express*'s circulation in its rivalry with the *Daily Mail*. It is not known whether a direct quarrel took place, more likely Kipling simply ceased to see his former intimate. Such a change of heart was rare in his life, for he did not admit to intimacy easily; but when it came it was complete. There may have been harsh words, however, for it is thought that Beaverbrook's fury over Baldwin's attack in 1931 – "What the proprietorship of these papers [those of Northcliffe and of Beaverbrook] is aiming at is power without responsibility, the prerogative of the harlot throughout the ages," was intensified because he recognised them as Kipling's words lent to his cousin for public use. Only his cousin Stanley remained to Kipling in the Conservative inner circle in his last years, and *their* paths increasingly diverged. It would certainly have seemed to Kipling monstrous publicly to oppose his cousin, except under great pressure of conscientious disagreement, and, in bad taste, to advertise himself as the Prime Minister's cousin by making public his support where he agreed.

Yet I think it is likely that the most important cause of Kipling's dissociation from active politics came from his increasing ill-health and, with ill-health, an ever-growing introspective, meditative frame of mind. In the summer of 1922, he suffered from a cruel return of the mysterious gastritis which had visited him shortly before John's death in 1915, and had troubled him from time to time since then. The pains, however, were now far more intense and his whole physical condition sadly in decline. No doubt these agonies were the more dreadful because of his belief in a family inheritance of cancer. An operation towards the end of the year by his close friend, the famous surgeon Sir John Bland Sutton, must have reassured him on his cancer fears, but his recovery was slow and not lasting. A medical adviser or a surgeon who is a close friend is probably not always the best attendant, however brilliant. His daughter, Elsie Bambridge, in her memoir of her father tells us that it was not until he suffered a particularly violent attack in Paris in 1933 that French doctors diagnosed, correctly, duodenal ulcer, a condition that modern medicine associates closely with nervous anxiety and depression. It was then too late for more than alleviating diet and medicines. How gallant he was in time of extreme pain appears from the unpublished memoirs of his friend Julia Catlin Taufflieb, who writes how, on this occasion in Paris, doubled up with pain, Kipling clenched a cushion to himself and said,

"I think this time that I'm going to have twins."[18] In relation to his dissociation from political activity, it is worth noting, too, that the first year of Stanley Baldwin's premiership, 1922–3, coincides with Kipling's absence from the scene through illness and subsequent convalescence in Cannes. Again he was too ill to make any public pronouncements at the time of the General Strike in 1926.

His private life was inevitably more reclusive than before the war. During the war the Kiplings had lived primarily at Brown's Hotel, now they were principally at Bateman's. His daughter Elsie Bambridge in her vivid memoir of her father at the end of Carrington's book has painted a sombre picture of the loneliness and tension of life there. Rudyard's illness had given a new rationale for Carrie's obsession with protecting him from strangers; her own rheumatism, which had taken them each war year to Bath for the waters, grew increasingly painful and she suffered, it appears, from diabetes. The sense of loss and of time closing in upon these two invalid people must have been immense and the more so because of a stoicism that forbade any utterance or complaint.

Their daughter says little of her own burden in such a household; but there is little doubt that for many years Carrie's suspicion of strangers' possible fortune-hunting motivations kept many admirers away from her daughter. Lady Hardinge recalls, too, how, when once she spoke to Elsie of the many young men who were always at Bateman's, she replied, "Yes, but they come to see my father." These young men, of course, included the large number of former brother officers of John's, who assisted Kipling in his compilation of the wartime history of the Irish Guards. It was one of these, a wealthy young officer attached to the Foreign Office, George Bambridge, who, in 1924, won the Kipling parents' agreement to his marriage to their daughter.

His position inevitably took Elsie out of England to European embassies. The Kipling parents visited her in Brussels and Madrid and Paris. From Madrid comes one of the rare accounts of Kipling speaking of a brother author, for Elsie arranged a meeting between her father and a Polish diplomat with whom he discussed Conrad.

But life at Bateman's was, of course, the more lonely without their daughter, and their reliance on each other the greater. Yet, whatever the strains of this life, there can be no doubt of the devotion on both sides. Carrie had nursed him through so many illnesses, and when she fell ill on board ship on a holiday voyage to Jamaica, Helen Hardinge, who accompanied them, recalls that Kipling would let no one else care for his sick wife, even emptying the slops himself. It is idle really to comment on unions which have become so close as this. Their disad-

325

vantages are always apparent to those outside, even close friends. And it is the disadvantages to Rudyard that have found most comment. The advantages are fully known only to the couple themselves.

Probably Carrie's suspicious nature was most evident in the village; but Kipling himself surely shared much of it. This is the only aspect of his private post-war life that is reflected in his stories. "Beauty Spots" (1932), a Stalky-like farce, is concerned with the turning of the tables against village spreaders of rumours. It is no more than an amusing story, but its social attitude is a good corrective to the false stereotype of Kipling as a snobbish would-be gentleman. Mr Gravell, the hero, is, as so often in Kipling, a self-made man, who retires to the country to investigate manuring for his hobby. From the first, he shows no disposition to be involved in village life. He is a man of single purpose. But this is not what Major Kniveatt believes: he is sure that this nouveau riche has come there to buy his way on to various local councils. He sets about spreading slanders and rumours to destroy Gravell's character. So much for the widely held view that, in Kipling, all regular officers are on the side of the angels. It is notable that one of the rumours the Major spreads is that the self-made hero's son is half-caste because his complexion is so dark (something actually due to war-time poison gas). It is strange to find Kipling putting into print this absurd canard about his own birth that had dogged him for so many decades. Such self-identification of Kipling with self-made men is surely very understandable, for this is exactly what he was. His friends and acquaintances covered a remarkably wide social field, but notable Kipling friends in the post-war years were just two such men – Morris, the motor-car man (later Lord Nuffield) and Sir Percy Bates, the director of the Cunard Shipping Line. Some of the appeal of Rhodes and Harmsworth and Beaverbrook had been exactly this.

But "Beauty Spots" and another farce of the same period, "Aunt Ellen", have another purpose than attacking the village. The true hero of "Beauty Spots" is the self-made man's son, who avenges his father by means of a practical joke involving a pig. When the Major becomes the laughing stock of the village at the end of the story, Kipling writes, "The generation that tolerates but does not pity went away. They did not even turn when they heard that first dry sob of one from whom all hope of office, influence, and authority was stripped for ever – drowned in the laughter in the lane."

This is Kipling's attempt to express his admiration for the post-war generation, by attributing to them Stalky-like exploits that he had invented for his own youth. Yet there is a real difference between 1878 and 1928 as he knows. The poem, "The Expert", that follows, says:

Youth that trafficked long with Death,
And to second life returns,
Squanders little time or breath
On his fellowmen's concerns.

For Kipling, pity had always been strong, tolerance almost unknown. How different from these post-war young men.

There is no doubt of the friendship that the Kiplings formed with the many young men who had been their dead son's regimental comrades. One of them, Rupert Grayson, has given in his book, *Voyage Not Completed*, what I think is the best picture of life at Bateman's I have found. He gives, too, a picture of the close relationship of the Kiplings that puts them in a very different light to the hen-pecked husband of unspoken legend. "Carrie," he writes, "was never far from his side and undoubtedly influenced him in everything he did. He rarely told a story that he did not call on her to finish . . . they had an acute sense of humour, and together at table they passed the conversation from one to the other like a ball in a juggler's act. She invariably interspersed her talk, which never failed to be lively, with a neat little cough followed by a most infectious laugh." [19] I think this account of what was clearly a practised, entertaining double-act that the performers greatly enjoyed, explains much of why children and young people liked being with them more than older strangers did. It is easier for the young to sit back and enjoy the old enjoying themselves, than it is for most middle-aged people, who, unless they are close friends, feel called upon to take part in a performance when they are only really intended to be lookers-on. How disconcerting it could be, is suggested by the anecdote of their neighbour William Ramsay, who lived, during Rudyard's last years, in the cottage that had once been the Kiplings' guest-house. He tells of Kipling showing him the Bateman's sundial with its inscription, "It's later than you think", while Carrie said off-handedly, "Oh, Rud always brings his guests to read that, when he thinks they should be going home." [20]

There is no doubt of their siege attitude towards most strangers. The past carried too many memories of insensitive invasion. The symbol of it is their living into the nineteen-twenties and thirties without a telephone, dependent on telegrams. And it should be noted that it was Rudyard who particularly abominated the telephone. But young strangers always received a welcome from both of them (so long as warning had been given) as so many have witnessed, from Rupert Croft-Cooke, a very young master at a Sussex preparatory school in the twenties, to Arthur Gooden, an American undergraduate at Oxford as late as 1935.

327

But this is merely to speak of strangers. The isolation of the Kiplings is very exaggerated: to innumerable ordinary elderly folk their life would have seemed like living at London Airport. Shared loss in the War brought them very close to Lady Edward Cecil, now the widowed Lady Milner and the lively editor of the *National Review*, a journal much after Kipling's heart. To the Feildens and Maude-Roxbys, close friends and neighbours, had been added the Husseys of Scotney Castle. With Mrs Hussey often came her nephew, Ralph Anstruther. Enid Struben, another old friend, whom Kipling had first known as a young girl in Cape Town, brought her son Somerset de Chair. Lady Rayleigh, whose first husband had been lost with John at Loos, brought her children to Kipling's house. The generations had moved on from the children who were friends of Elsie and John. The Kipling parents had formed as close friendship with the daughter of their old American friend Julia Catlin now married to the French General Taufflieb, as with her mother. When they went to France they stayed as often with her and her English doctor husband as they did with the Tauffliebs. In return, when the Stanleys went on holiday, they sent their two little daughters to stay at Bateman's.

Talking with many of these people, then children, now that they are adults, has given me a close impression of how much Kipling's famed power with children rested upon his absolute interest in them and their activities. Mrs Stanley's daughter, Jane Hard, who stayed there at different ages as a child, has described the delight of the evening session at Bateman's when they told Kipling all that they had been doing and he brought it alive and gave it a new dimension by the questions he asked about even the most apparently insignificant details. He remembered children as individuals when they were absent – to P. G. Maude-Roxby, son of neighbours, he sent a postcard of a very wide gate in Malta, saying it was suitable because he was a fat boy.[21] He thought of what would interest them, but he clearly also thought that they would be interested in what he considered interesting. It is this combination of consciousness of his youthful audience, carried through what was always youthful in himself, to a final fusion of the things that interested both them and him, which lacks any of that self-consciousness of most people who like children and try hard with them.

This surely is why Ralph Anstruther remembers even today Kipling's postcard explaining to him the manner and purpose of a new phenomenon – windscreen wipers on cars. And his information and manner change subtly with a child's growing up. Three letters written to Jane Stanley (now Jane Hard) over the years of her girlhood give this feeling very well, for their manner is not different but their subject matter is. In 1926 when she was a very small girl, he writes from Cap Martin, "To day I saw a man in the street with a little tame fox on a chain like a dog but it did not walk in the middle of the pavement like a dog does. It crept along close to the wall. All the other dogs that saw it were filled with curiosity and wanted to speak to it." Seven years later, he sends her a detailed description, with his characteristic sketches, of the decoration of the lounge of her father, Dr Stanley's, new yacht in which Kipling is sailing and which she has never seen. Here, as with windscreen wipers, he is sure that what is new to him will also fascinate her. There is a log fire, he tells her, faked but ice-cold to the touch. He has never known such a thing before. It is "made for looks". And at last, in 1935, when, as an adolescent, she is to leave France with her sister, not just to stay at Bateman's, but to live at a girls' boarding school, he writes reassuringly, "You'll both find an English school very interesting, and in some ways *very* funny."[22]

Of course, he could and did tell wonderful stories to all these children, the local river Dudwell became the Nile, the whole scene was transformed as Vermont and the Sussex Downs had been for Josephine, and the Sussex Downs and the Weald and the marshes had been for Elsie and for John, but these children of later years, the children of other people, the grandchildren he never had, were as much individuals as his own children, interesting to him for themselves. There was clearly showmanship in his stories told to children as there was, I suggest, in the public act that he and Carrie gave, but all human beings, children as much as any, he valued (or didn't value) for themselves.

Nevertheless, this well-known happiness he felt in the company of young people and children should not conceal the large and extremely varied circle of adult friends and acquaintances apart from those already mentioned, that Kipling saw even in his last years; not only visitors to Bateman's, but the fellow members of his clubs whom he saw on his fairly frequent visits to London and those who came to see the Kiplings at Brown's Hotel. The Kiplings stayed away at weekend house parties and, if these were increasingly staid Tory households like those of the famous puritanical Home Secretary, Joynson-Hicks, or the proprietress of the *Morning Post*, Lady Bathurst, there were houses like the Cazalets' where Kipling met a wider circle of people including writers like Wodehouse and "Elizabeth" (of *Elizabeth and her German Garden*). Those who signed the book for his candidature at the Beefsteak Club in 1924 include, as well as Edward Elgar (a co-signatory of the Ulster declaration), a number of middle-brow to

329

popular writers – Maurice Baring, Ian Hay, A. E. W. Mason, W. B. Maxwell, Owen Seaman, H. A. Vachell, and Hugh Walpole. During the time of his membership, when he lunched often at the members' table and might easily have conversed with any of them, there were, apart from old friends from all the periods of his life – Dunsterville (school), Charles Whibley (the old W. E. Henley days), Landon and Gwynne (South Africa) and Castlerosse (a brother officer of John's) – a number of writers – Duff Cooper (who was influenced by *Rewards and Fairies* to write *Talleyrand*), Dunsany, Philip Guedalla, Barrie, Edward Knoblock, Harold Nicolson, Frederick Lonsdale, E. V. Lucas, A. A. Milne (Kipling much admired *Winnie the Pooh*), Alfred Noyes, R. C. Sherriff (what did Kipling make of *Journey's End*?) and his ardent admirer, P. G. Wodehouse. There were also – sole connection that I know of with Bloomsbury, save that they held their country court on the other side of the county of Sussex – Clive Bell and Desmond McCarthy. Can acquaintance at the club account for the very personally warm tone of Desmond McCarthy's praising assessment of Kipling's work at the time of his death?

It is at the Athenaeum Club that we get a happy and unexpected picture of Kipling in 1926, when Hugh Walpole writes, "A wonderful morning with old Kipling in the Athenaeum. He was sitting surrounded by the reviews of his new book, beaming like a baby."[23] But even with middle-brow and popular writers he seldom formed close friendships. Julia Catlin Taufflieb says that when she visited Cannes with the Kiplings, he did everything he could to avoid "Elizabeth"; and his letter to Baroness Orczy, creator of the Scarlet Pimpernel, though very courteous, offers Carrie's attack of "throat of the Riviera brand" to refuse meetings either in Monte Carlo or Cannes.[24] But these are women writers, of course. Nevertheless he uses the same excuse, "My wife has an attack of the local 'throat'," to excuse them to Somerset Maugham in Monte Carlo ten years earlier.[25]

His friendship with distinguished academics had become much closer since his youthful membership of the Athenaeum in the eighteen-nineties. He had now links with both Oxford and Cambridge, and honorary degrees from other universities as well. In 1923 he was made Rector of St Andrew's University, and delivered an address on thrift in youth as the basis of independence and success which is a beautifully expressed sermon in his Samuel Smiles Self-made Man manner. But the important aspect of his now easy relation with the university world is that he freed himself from one of the many hang-ups that came from his youth – a sense of loss at not having been to a university that was too often compensated for by an abrasive philistinism.

He was never to be an intellectual, but, from the time of his playing about with Horace as a distraction in the darkest war years, a greater note of literary scholarship runs through much of his writing. It is always the old-fashioned Victorian man of letters type. He was probably much influenced by his friendship with George Saintsbury, the literary historian, whom he saw in his retirement at Bath each year of the war when he took Carrie there for spa treatment. But Saintsbury was surely of all that vanishing band of Victorian literati the most humane and the least affected. It was a good schooling.

Apart from Kipling's poems after translations of Horace which have a decided feeling of old-fashioned dons at play, there are a number of aspects of his post-war work that reveal this academic influence. Not least the ambiguous juxtaposition of many of his poems and stories, and the use of literary parody. The two can be found together in three extracts from a pastiche of late Elizabethan–Jacobean drama with which he prefaces three separate stories. These extracts concerning the fortunes of a soldier-courtier called Gow are excellent parodies and always very pertinent to the story they accompany; they also make me hungry to read the whole play from which they purport to come, although, no doubt, it was never written. Here I think literary play does go beyond scholars' fun and dons' delight to add an extra dimension to the work, cutting across time and forcing the reader to merge the language and violence and concerns of the world of Webster and Walter Raleigh with the language and concerns and violence of the Great War and the twenties and the American Prohibition. It shows Kipling happy in the literary age of Joyce and Eliot.

I am not so sure about the much praised "Proofs of Holy Writ", a story written in 1932, after his last collected book. It is a picture of Shakespeare and Ben Jonson discussing the latest proofs of the Authorised Version of the Bible sent down to them from the supposed authors at Hampton Court for their correction. It is the sort of piece of old-fashioned dons' recreation which is usually called "delightful"; and so it is, but no more. On the other hand, his parody of Shakespeare's *Merry Wives of Windsor* with a preface by Samuel Johnson, is excellent. The most important work to be marked by this new ease with scholarship is "Dayspring Mishandled", one of the three really good stories of the last collection, which will be discussed later. But, of course, he had always been an excellent parodist, and his sense of historic language and of historic possibility had been fully shown in *Rewards and Fairies*, receiving, even then, Cambridge acclamation from G. M. Trevelyan, the historian.

Another youthful hang-up which his vast success had allowed him to conquer was the unfulfilled medical ambition of his late schooldays, when he is said to have hung around St Mary's Hospital. He had the friendship of one of the most famous doctors of this century, the Canadian, Sir William Osler, who ended as Regius Professor of Medicine at Oxford. An even closer friend, nearer to his own age, was the surgeon John Bland Sutton, a Middlesex Hospital man. It was, no doubt, through him that Kipling gave an address to the students of Middlesex Hospital in 1908 – "A Doctor's Work", in which he was able to set out his concept of the ethics of a profession that he had once hoped to enter.[26] A gratifying thing to do. Already in *Rewards and Fairies* his imagination is haunted by the history of what might have been in medicine. But his illness brought him, from 1915, increasingly in touch with doctors, especially Bland Sutton. He developed many rather typical layman's theories about the relation of medical science to psychology and mysticism. Out of these views came two much-admired late stories, more strange than successful, I think. No doubt his greatest triumph came when he was able to put such unorthodox views forward to a respectful audience at the Royal College of Surgeons in 1922, the year of his own only partially successful operation.[27] Indeed all this intimacy with the upper echelons of the medical world seems ironic placed beside the too-late diagnosis of his fatal ulcers.

The sick bed and what hovers around it, both of palpable nurses and doctors and shadows of crueller pain and death, are present in his best late story, "Dayspring Mishandled", but only as an incidental. The two "medical" stories are of a different kind. Both are marred a bit, I think, by the presentation of the doctors in them as a sort of *Stalky and Co.*, especially in their off-duty moments. This may be what Sir John Bland Sutton and his friends seemed like to Kipling, but it is not how they seem in Sir John's autobiography. I suspect that it is a mark of tiredness in Kipling that he reverts to this characterisation. Both these stories, like too many of the later ones, are highly elaborate in their telling, far too much so. "Unprofessional" (1930) is the more ambitious, and its failure goes therefore deep. Kipling is anxious to assert what, I think, all but a few scientists will agree: that, in many of the most important scientific discoveries, an intuitive leap often carries the worker forward at a vital moment in an experiment, however much his discovery made from intuition must be checked and rechecked by deductive observed tests before it can be accepted. Kipling was well aware of the necessity of orthodox scientific laboratory procedure. But he wanted – and this is legitimate, I think, at any rate in fiction – to suggest that natural science might be more akin to apparently irrational "sciences" like astrology. He had already brilliantly expounded this in the Puck story where the seventeenth-century Nicholas Culpepper explains his diagnosis of rats as responsible for the spread of the plague by astrological reasoning. Now, in "Unprofessional", he organises most elaborately (more elaborately than a short story can bear) a situation in which four distinguished doctors have both inclination and finances to test the relations of the behaviour of cancer cells to the "influences" of the planets.

That imagination, not thinking, is the basis of scientific advance, and that modern medical science is too usually all technique and no advance, is what the millionaire Herries wishes to demonstrate. Unfortunately, as one might expect, the story does not work – the gap between the well-described laboratory technique and apparatus, on the one hand, and the rationally presented but ultimately mystical astrological waves on the other is never closed. Only by starting from some actual contemporary medical approach and twisting it to involve astrological happenings could Kipling's imaginative purpose have been achieved. Now that science fantasy has been so much developed, I can imagine the story being contrived convincingly. But all Kipling's elaborations are symbolic rather than deceptive – for example, to suggest the element of chance that so often misleads the scientist in an experiment, Kipling makes the cancer patient confuse the doctors because she has on top of her mortal disease an impulse to suicide. It is all too cleverly done. And this confused cleverness is marked by his introducing for readers who might be lost among the medical jargon, this strained analogy with the fine arts – "This was as if Raeburn had volunteered to prime a canvas for Benjamin West."

The range of Rudyard Kipling's life in his last years can, as in the pre-war years, only be fully judged if we take into account his many journeys abroad. Sadly and increasingly a large number of these were undertaken for the sake of either his own or Carrie's health. They were among the few lucky invalids who could "go abroad on doctor's orders", and, in the limited medical knowledge of between the wars, "going abroad" was frequently prescribed by the doctors of the rich. I have no doubt that it was of the greatest help to the Kiplings, whose genuine physical disorders were much exacerbated by the melancholy that their sometimes solitary life at Bateman's aroused, especially, no doubt, in winter.

In the years between 1920 and his death, they went to Mesopotamia and the Holy Land (for the War Graves Commission), to Algeria, to Brazil (where as in Algeria Kipling was cheered by a Latin culture thriving outside Europe), to Jamaica and to Marienbad in Czechoslovakia

333

(for Carrie's health), to Belgium and to Spain (to visit their daughter).

But the main centre of Kipling's extra-English love and hopes was now France, and there they visited often, regularly, and in many areas. Kipling was a widely known and respected writer in France, particularly in *rangé* circles. His friendship with Clémenceau, whom he had met originally through Lady Edward Cecil, was a close one.

Even before the war, France was becoming Kipling's second home. He already spoke French fluently although inaccurately. (Carrie, it seems, spoke little French.) He had come during his first visits to Vernet-les-Bains to love the Pyrenees. Already, in his travels through the Massif Central and the Perigord–Dordogne area, he had tasted the delights of motoring in France before the War.

Now, after the War, Julia Taufflieb settled near Strasbourg and Julia's daughter, married in 1917 to an English doctor, Stanley, was settled near Paris. The Kiplings had now two homes in France to stay at. For a while, too, Elsie and George Bambridge were at the Paris Embassy. 1921 was the apex of Kipling's official honouring in France. He was given a doctorate at the Sorbonne and made there an excellent speech in English, typically finding the fundamental racial differences of France and England, on the one hand, and of Russia and Germany, on the other, in their folklores. The sound, *rentier* tradition of France and England coming from the Prince who gains both the treasure and the princess; the recurrent Evil of Germany and Russia being apparent in the ever-returning myth of the werewolf.

Something of the dull, conformist literary world in which Kipling found himself in France, however, may be seen in the literary guests at the dinner after the Sorbonne ceremony – Hanotaux, André Chevrillon, René Bazin, Henri Bordeaux. From this high occasion in Paris, he went on to Strasbourg. General Taufflieb had been made Commissioner of his native land, Alsace, newly returned to French rule; and Kipling was able to enjoy, both at the University and at the High Commission ceremony, the opportunity to welcome Alsace back from the hands of the Boche.

But the main part of his joy in France lay in motoring. There seem to be few areas he did not visit, although towards the end of his life he and Carrie chose rather to winter at Monte Carlo or Cannes. He was in London on his way to Cannes when he died.

These French visits did produce three stories – "The Bull that Thought" (1924), "The Miracle of St Jubanus" (1930), and "Teem" (1935). The evocation of France is that of a man who loves that country, but perhaps the love is a little self-conscious, a little the stereotype of France made by many Englishmen, especially of the upper middle classes, in the twenties, when many of them decided to settle there. It is a real affection – and, of course, with Kipling, a splendid eye, but it is (and Kipling says so) the France of the *bonne bourgeoisie* and of village life, that they loved. It is, after all, the era of Agatha Christie's Hercule Poirot. How did those middle-class Francophiles feel when the Front Populaire arrived, I wonder? Kipling did not live to see it. How much he loved the countryside may be seen in his letter about Les Baux, quoted in a life of Lord Montagu of Beaulieu,[28] where he speaks of its wild rockiness as more awful than either Chitor or Amber – surely his highest praise. But the evocation of the Camargue and the Crau, in "The Bull that Thought", is spoiled by a lot of embarrassing wine and food talk, and that of the Auvergne village in "The Miracle of St Jubanus" by the cliché quality of the wise country curé and the foolish atheist village schoolmaster.

But the interest of two of these short stories – "The Bull that Thought" and "Teem" – lies outside their disputable artistic merits. Some critics of Kipling, struck by what they feel to be his evasion of the final ethical and metaphysical problems he propounds, have declared that he is really to be seen as an aesthete, an artist for whom the craft in his work is the final value of life. I am not convinced by this case, although I am well aware of what a deeply conscientious craftsman he was, and more than that, how, at certain times his daemon, the source of his creative powers, was as near to a god as he could reach. But, in the first place, I do not believe that he evaded convictions, I think he was always and increasingly a seeker, but that he remained, despite any para-psychological experiences, in doubt, an agnostic. For some reason, however, such a state of doubt does seem to have been one of the many things about which he felt shame or guilt, and, believing as he did in jungle cunning, he covered it up. Hence the appearance of evasion. Yet, even if he had no religious conviction, he was never satisfied with doubt, always seeking. Art and making may have been his highest certainty, but there were other spiritual states in which he wanted to believe that prevented him from being content with the aesthete's creed.

It is possible to read "The Bull that Thought" as the account of a bull with exceptional skill in the bull-ring and "Teem" as a statement by a truffle-finding dog of the skills needed for finding truffles. It is also very reasonable to read both stories as metaphors for the tactics and skills of the artist. Those who think that Kipling's creed was ultimately that of an aesthete tend to place these stories very high in his canon as expositions of his real creed of life. I do not myself find them convincing parables of art's power, for if that is what they seek to describe, they tell only of ploys and tactics and ruses – things that Kipling sometimes used in his stories with telling effect, sometimes with embarrassingly self-conscious cleverness. They are certainly not the key to his artistic magic. I prefer his earlier parables of art, its powers and its glories and sufferings in the story "The Children of the Zodiac" (1891), and the poem "The Last Rhyme of True Thomas" (1893).

That his own fine creative powers were still alive in these last years is proved by two stories, "Dayspring Mishandled" (1928) and "The Church That Was at Antioch" (1929), to which a less good but rewarding story, "The Manner of Men" (1930), may be seen as an appendix.

"Dayspring Mishandled" is the story of a Stalky joke that misfires, a picture of a life wasted in hoarded-up hatred and complicated revenge. It is a new and significant extra twist in Kipling's concern for forgiveness in his last years – or almost new, for, long ago, in an Indian story of 1887, "The Watches of the Night", the practical joke revenge on a self-righteous scandal-mongering colonel's wife goes too far and destroys the wellbeing not only of her but of her amiable husband. In that story we are told that the implacable author of the vengeful practical joke, Mrs Larkyn, "was a frivolous woman in whom none could have suspected deep hate . . . She never forgot." [29] The story, like many of Kipling's slighter Indian stories, is more profound than it seems at first glance.

But Manallace, the practical joker of "Dayspring Mishandled" is altogether a more serious protagonist. A young man of literary genius who, in the nineties, sells his talent for bread by joining the talented team who write pot-boilers for the magazines of a new style entrepreneur of popular reading (some precursor of Harmsworth?) We are in Kipling's early-nineties London. Another member of the team is an altogether less attractive figure, Castorley, a pompous, abrasive, snobbish and uncaring man. He comes into money and devotes himself to gentlemanly scholarship. Chaucer is his chosen field and Kipling wisely shows that, amid all his vulgar pomposity, there is a genuine expertise and care for his subject. He is a true Chaucer expert. But Kipling exposes his vulgarity by his language – "the freshness, the fun, the humanity, the fragrance of it all, cries – no, shouts itself, as Dan's work." He is an awful non-phoney.

In the bohemian world of their youth, Castorley and Manallace had both known a beautiful woman, but she loved another man, and refused alike Castorley's attempts to get her to bed, and Manallace's love. This is a bit *La Bohème*, but we are in the 1890s London of the Café Royal and Romano's. Castorley hates her for it, and, when she

becomes paralysed, refuses to subscribe to a fund for her needed operation. Manallace nurses her until her death in 1915.

One night, when Manallace and Castorley are working together in a
government department in the War, Castorley, in confident mood,
speaks of the dead woman in terms which "I" (Kipling) cannot quote
but which seems to him to justify Manallace's life lived for revenge
against Castorley. Here we are on very difficult ground. There is no
doubt that this fine story is weakened by our not knowing what enormity Castorley said, for we are not allowed to be judge of Manallace's
justification, which is a centre to the story. Yet, if, as I suspect,
Castorley declared that her paralysis was syphilis contracted by whor-
ing, it is hard to see how a man like Kipling could have written it out
even in 1928. Censorship (*pace* Longford and Muggeridge) *does* matter even in good art. Manallace sets himself by attending Castorley's
Chaucerian lectures to learn all about the composition of early print-
ings of Chaucer and then spends a decade or more of his life in
preparing a forgery of a new Chaucer fragment which finally makes
Castorley a world figure in scholarship.

It is Manallace's intention to destroy Castorley mentally by exposing the fraud. But two things intervene: Castorley is attacked by an
incurable cancer, and Manallace learns that if he destroys Castorley
before natural death does, he will merely advance the schemes of
Castorley's adulterous wife (a beautifully drawn greyish, pale evil
woman) to marry again. And she guesses about the forgery. The cycle
is complete. Manallace, a good and loving man, has wasted years of
his life in a vengeful joke against a bad man. Stalkyism, that essential
Kipling weapon of the good against the bad, is shown to rebound
futilely upon its performers. I suspect, too, that there is some degree of
admonition to Manallace, the young man of genius, who has in any
case contented himself with turning out pot-boilers. However that
may be, it is one of Kipling's best and most original stories.

(The objection has been made by some literary critics that the
Chaucerian fragment forged by Manallace but invented by Kipling is
not Chaucerian at all. Probably. It is lucky that too many naval engineers and cancer specialists and Asian zoologists and arbiters of Simla
social precedence have not got going at Kipling's work. In "They" I
am always irked by a mistake about wild flowers in the autumn downland. But that really isn't the point in Kipling.)

One other first-rate story in these later years, "The Eye of Allah", I
have already mentioned along with the Puck stories. The third, "The
Church That Was at Antioch", is a delight to read. The young Roman
patrician, Valens, who is posted to the police service at Antioch, is

presented to us with the same affection as Parnesius on the Roman Wall or District Commissioner Orde on the Frontier; and we are equally prepared to believe that he deserves it. But whereas Parnesius and Orde learn the nature of men and how to govern them in savage outposts, Valens learns in the intrigues and hatreds of a crowded city life. The Jewish Christians and the Gentile Christians (Paul's converts) of Antioch are in dispute over the eating of forbidden foods at the Passover feasts. The orthodox Jews of the city are looking for and seeking to use any disturbances that may come out of the Christian deliberations, as a cause of civil complaint against the Christians to Valens's uncle, Lucius Sergius, head of the Antioch police.

Kipling is at his story-telling best here. There are no frames (either the over-complicated kind of his later work or the brash "I" voice of his early work). Valens has only a few days – a week perhaps – in which to learn how to administer justice decently, for at the very moment when he has proved himself he is killed by an assassin's dagger. The short life is well chosen for the short story. In 25 pages we are convinced both by Valens's political action and by the spiritual growth that accompanies it. And – no easy task – Kipling maintains all the time behind this individual story the sense of the teeming, tense city all the time on the verge of mob rule. But, as if this were not enough, Kipling dares to introduce the figures of St Paul and St Peter, who have come to decide the point at dispute in the Christian quarrel over the feast ritual. His success is complete. Each is an absolutely convincing figure as much in their extraordinary outward appearance, as in their widely different modes of thought and feeling.

There is little comfort in this story for those who would claim Kipling in his later years for orthodox Christianity. As far as the world goes, Valens preaches the gospel of duty to the civil law from everyone and the unconcern of the civil law with a man's religious thoughts and practices where they do not break the law. It is the creed of Gallio when St Paul was brought before him at Achaia in the Acts of the Apostles and it is one of Kipling's favourite texts. As early as "The Judgement of Dungara", the Assistant Collector of the Berbula Hills is called Gallio and says to the Lutheran missionary – "Heigh ho! I have their bodies and the District to see to, but you can try what you can do for their souls. Only don't behave as your predecessor did, or I'm afraid that I cannot guarantee your life." It is Parnesius's declared civil creed on the Roman Wall. The story, "Little Foxes" (1909) of Adam Strickland's administration in East Africa is followed by the poem, "Gallio's Song":

Whether ye rise for the sake of a creed,
Or riot in hope of spoil,
Equally will I punish the deed,
Equally check the broil;
Nowise permitting injustice at all
From whatever doctrine it springs –
But – whether ye follow Priapus or Paul,
I care for none of these things.

It is reiterated by St Paul in the late twin story to "The Church That Was at Antioch", which tells of the lasting psychological (and spiritual) effect of Paul upon the captain of the ship in which he was wrecked on Malta – "The Manner of Men" (1930).

But "The Church That Was at Antioch" does not stop at this simple message, inheritance of the staple of British rule in India, it goes further into the nature of man's spiritual life. Valens is a Mithraist, and he sees in Christianity many of the rituals and symbols that make his private military religion a comforting discipline. Parnesius had come near to making the same identification. I do not think that this approval of some aspects of Christianity via Mithraism suggests any strong religious belief in Kipling. He sees Mithraism as a sort of Freemasonry, a fellowship and ritual bound by a Deistic hope rather than any transcendent certainty. It is the feasting of the Christians in fellowship that awakens Valens's sympathy.

But there is a further dimension which marks Kipling's latest work. When Valens dies from the assassin's dagger, he tells his uncle, the Prefect of Police, "Don't be hard on them [those responsible for his murder] . . . They get worked up . . . They don't know what they are doing . . . Promise!" The uncle answers, "This is not I, child. It is the Law." "No odds . . . Men make laws not Gods." In short, Kipling now asks that mercy should transcend Gallio's administration. And the story now takes us deeper, for St Peter recognises Valens's words as a reflection of Christ's, "Forgive them for they know not what they do." Yet the idea of Christian salvation as such is rejected, for Paul wishes to baptise the dying Valens, but Peter scornfully rejects this – "Think you that one who has spoken these words needs such as *we* are to certify him to any God?" And the following poem specifically rejects any doctrinal claim to supremacy:

He that hath a Gospel
Whereby Heaven is won
(Carpenter or Cameleer,

> Or Maya's dreaming son),
> Many swords shall pierce Him
> Mingling blood with gall;
> But His Own Disciple
> Shall wound him worst of all! [30]

Again and again Kipling uses the Christian texts and doctrines familiar to his readers, deeply imbued with his own family background, but they are seldom employed for purposes that cannot be explained either by humanist ethics or by spiritual search. Only once in the poem, "Cold Iron", that accompanies a story in *Rewards and Fairies*, does he seem to lay emphasis on any basic Christian doctrine – and here I think he uses the Crucifixion as a symbol for sacrifice and atonement, which were already beginning to play an important part in his general ethical creed and were to dominate stories like "The Wish House" ten years later.

But Jesus's plea for forgiveness of his enemies is certainly a central point of his later thinking. His son John's death surely turned him to this, for it first becomes central in "On the Gate", a tale of 1916. But the same allegory of judgement of souls is repeated in "Uncovenanted Mercies" (1932). The earlier story is cast in a witty-serious satire upon bureaucracy; the later one, making the Judgement Seat a railway station, is more a satire upon what we should now call social workers. Neither is unentertaining, although the flow of epigram and paradox has for me something of the irritating effect of that of a famous man of letters of the age who met Kipling only once to shake hands with him at Barrie's funeral – Bernard Shaw. And the plea for compassion is so general that it comes close all the time to sentimentality.

But it is certainly not so in "The Church That Was at Antioch" and Peter's rebuke of the narrowly doctrinal Paul is one of the best moments in Kipling. Yet, in the long run, Paul was very close to Kipling's heart as we may see in the poem that follows the story of Paul's shipwreck, "The Manner of Men". The words of "At His Execution", where St Paul makes his dying plea, have been seen by many critics to be that rare thing in Kipling's work – a revelation of himself:

> I was made all things to all men,
> But now my course is done –
> And now is my reward –
> Ah, Christ, when I stand at Thy Throne
> With those I have drawn to the Lord,
> Restore me to my self again!

In so far as Kipling both longed and feared to be restored to himself, to find himself, I am sure that they are right.

Now, in early January 1936, the month following his seventieth birthday, it was to happen. On his way with Carrie to join the Tauffliebs for their usual winter stay in Cannes, he had a violent haemorrhage at Brown's Hotel and was rushed to the Middlesex Hospital where, with his wife and daughter by his bedside, he died four days later in the early morning of 17 January. In 1899 in New York and in 1923 at Burwash and in London, Carrie had used all her strong powers to protect him from the press and public. Now, at Brown's, where they had passed their honeymoon night, she had no one to protect. Indeed the news of his death was overshadowed by that coming from the bedside of the dying George V. Kipling would not have resented this, for his post-war friendship with the King had been one of his most cherished relationships, although, even from a monarch who was his personal friend, he refused resolutely any state honour as he had from all governments. He was cremated and his ashes were buried in the Poets' Corner at Westminster Abbey, near to Charles Dickens.

There is one sentence in the story "Teem", spoken by the truffle-hunting dog narrator that is a central clue to the way in which Kipling tried to preserve himself as an artist from the rest of himself in water-tight compartments – "Outside of his art, an artist must never dream!" It is hard to know what he thought he meant. Even if we accept his view of artistic creative impulse as a daemon suddenly seizing hold of one like a mystical experience or a state of grace, it does not vanish and leave the mystic untouched. A mystic is a mystic all the time, even when he is catching a train or buying bananas, and so it is with a writer. He dreams because he must. Also like a mystic, a writer or an artist must always be "toward", always ready for the daemon, and this means that he can never live in absolutely separate worlds of "real life" and of "fantasy". I'm sure that Kipling felt and knew this. But what he means by "never dreaming" outside of art, I suspect, is something else: there is to be no introspection, no looking into oneself. You must only weave tapestries when an external observation has set up a shape or a story in your mind, don't let the stories grow out of yourself. This belief led him for so much of his life to an off-putting philistinism, a false dichotomy between action and thought. But it also made him the remarkable writer that he is, for in attempting the impossible, a purely externally orientated art, he produced stories in new areas and exploited themes untouched by other writers. Yet it also stood in the way of his developing into one of the greatest writers, because he feared to follow his doubts and anxieties and haunting sense of guilt deep into himself, where their source surely lay.

That he suffered from this fear of self-knowledge is apparent in all his work, save *Kim*, where he dares to ask, "Who is Kim?" Even if he dare not accept the answer that we all receive, that there is no more than a partial answer. This central omission is a personal suffering that, loving his work and, with all his blemishes, the man himself, a biographer must feel painfully too. Nor is it easy to offer an explanation as so many critics seem to think. The spoiled little sahib of Bombay, the cowering little boy of Southsea, the bullied boy of Westward Ho who learned the thrill of bullying – all these have been put forward, but they don't really carry weight when one gets to know the largeness of Kipling's spirit and the degree to which he held it in an iron corset. His mother (evidenced by the excessive idolatry of mothers in his work), Flo Garrard, Wolcott Balestier, Carrie, none of these simple personal explanations suffice.

Freudianism is too easy. Since I began to prepare this study nearly three years ago, various people have suggested that I should look in the Simla stories, in "Without Benefit of Clergy", in *Kim*, in *Stalky & Co.*, in *Soldiers Three*, in *The Light That Failed* for the sexual explanation of Kipling's nature. As sexual clues all these stories contradict each other, but, apart from that, there is only a surmise for the last, and for the rest no jot of evidence in any letters or papers I have read. Heredity? I believe that it plays some part; and that his fear of inherited cancer overlay a greater fear of mental breakdown. He was a gentle-violent man, a man of depressions and hilarity, holding his despairs in with an almost superhuman stoicism. Manic-depressive does no more than repeat this in big words. I prefer if I must a social-historical description of long generations of Evangelical belief ending in post-Darwinian doubt. But the mystery of human personality defies all explanations. When he bade us "seek not to question" other than the books he left behind, Kipling knew that we should, for books and their authors are deeply connected. But he was right in thinking that we could reach only very partial answers to our questions.

For his own sake, however, for his personal happiness and even more for the fullness of his art, he should have sought to find himself. He must have known that no one ever finds more than a fraction of himself. Perhaps he feared irrationally that he would find nothing. All this a biographer who has come to know him a little must say.

But a critic has to say more. He has to say that this persistent evasion of introspection, of further questioning of the source of the despair and anxiety and guilt that enmesh so many of his best characters

in his best stories, does keep him out of the very first class of
writing and from the ranks of Dostoevsky and Tolstoy and Samuel
Richardson and Charles Dickens and Stendhal and Proust. I name my
favourites only, but there are a score of them. In short-story writing,
notably Chekhov. Although, of course, self-knowledge doesn't make a
great writer, but ... On the other hand, the company of the great is
fairly large; the number of writers who have, like Kipling, gone outside the usual range in a hundred different directions and done so with
rarely combined gifts – delicacy of craft and violence of feeling, exactitude and wild impressionism, subtlety and true innocence – is very
small. *Kim*, I believe, is great in its own right; and, for the rest, he did
so many, many things very well indeed that the greatest novelists never
saw to do. It secures him a sure place in Olympus.

REFERENCES

Unless otherwise stated, all quotations from Rudyard Kipling's work are taken from The Centenary Edition, Macmillan, 1965, and The Definitive Edition of Rudyard Kipling's Verse, Macmillan, 1940.

Abbreviations:

KJ	Kipling Journal
HL	Houghton Library, Harvard University
CCHH	Carpenter Collection, Houghton Library, Harvard University
PML	Pierpont Morgan Library, New York City
DW	*The Day's Work*
JB2	*The Second Jungle Book*
LH	*Life's Handicap*
LR	*Limits and Renewals*
MI	*Many Inventions*
PTH	*Plain Tails from the Hills*
RF	*Rewards and Fairies*
ST	*Soldiers Three*
WWW	*Wee Willie Winkie*

1 PARADISE AND THE FALL

1. "To the City of Bombay" (1894), The Song of the Cities
2. "That Boy Again" – *Pioneer*, 5 December 1885
3. C. E. Norton, biographical note to 1900 edition of *PTH*

References

4. A. W. Baldwin, *The Macdonald Sisters* (Peter Davies, 1960)
5. The same
6. The same
7. F. W. Macdonald, *As A Tale That is Told* (Cassell & Co, 1919)
8. Article by Captain Solomon, Head of Jeejeebhoy School of Art – KJ 45, 1938
9. "Tod's Amendment" – *PTH*
10. "The Return of the Children"
11. *Something of Myself*
12. Letter to Florence Macdonald included in an article in the *Methodist Times*, 23 January 1936
13. "On Greenhow Hill" – *LH*
14. A. W. Baldwin, *The Macdonald Sisters*
15. F. W. Macdonald, *As A Tale That is Told*
16. Angela Thirkell, *Three Houses* (Oxford University Press, 1932)
17. "Her Little Responsibility" – *Abaft the Funnel* (USA, 1909)
18. "For to Admire"
19. Florence Macdonald – KJ 46, 1938
20. A. W. Baldwin, *The Macdonald Sisters*
21. Georgiana Burne-Jones, *Memorials of Edward Burne-Jones* (Macmillan, 1904)
22. A. W. Baldwin, *The Macdonald Sisters*
23. Editha Plowden, unpublished memoirs quoted in above
24. F. W. Macdonald, *As A Tale That is Told*
25. A. W. Baldwin, *The Macdonald Sisters*
26. Mrs A. M. Fleming, memories (*Chambers Journal*, March 1939)
27. The same
28. The same
29. "Baa, Baa, Black Sheep" – *WWW*
30. Editha Plowden, unpublished memoirs quoted in A. W. Baldwin, *The Macdonald Sisters*
31. A. W. Baldwin, *The Macdonald Sisters*
32. The same
33. "Baa, Baa, Black Sheep" – *WWW*
34. *Something of Myself*
35. Georgiana Burne-Jones, *Memorials of Edward Burne-Jones*
36. The same
37. The same
38. "My First Adventure", under pseudonym "Nickson" in family magazine *The Scribbler* 1879
39. *Something of Myself*
40. "The Children of the Zodiac" – *MI*
41. Address to Middlesex Hospital, October 1908 – *Book of Words* 1928
42. A. W. Baldwin, *The Macdonald Sisters*
43. Mrs A. M. Fleming, memories (*Chambers Journal*, March 1939)
44. *Something of Myself*
45. Sotheby's Sale Catalogue December 1964, Cormell Price letters
46. L. C. Dunsterville, *Stalky's Reminiscences* (Jonathan Cape, 1928)
47. "A School Song"
48. Speech on retirement of Cormell Price, 25 July 1894

49. Letter to Dean Farrar, 13 October 1899 – CCHH
50. Article by Kay Robinson in *McClure's Magazine*, July 1896
51. F. H. B. Skrine, *The Life of Sir William Wilson Hunter* (Longmans, 1901)
52. "An English School", in *Youth's Companion* (USA, 1893); republished in *Land and Sea Tales for Scouts and Guides* (Macmillan, 1923)
53. "The Mark of the Beast" – *LH*
54. "Beauty Spots" – *LR*
55. *Stalky & Co.*
56. "Stalky", *Land and Sea Tales for Scouts and Guides*
57. Letter to Horsmonden School Magazine, *The School Budget*, May 1898
58. Charles Carrington, *Rudyard Kipling* (Macmillan, 1955)
59. Sidney Cockerell, letter to *The Times*, 7 March 1938
60. The same
61. Catherine Wright Morris, "How St Nicholas got Rudyard Kipling and What Happened Then" – *Princeton University Library Chronicle*, Spring 1974
62. The same
63. Letter of 15 June 1878 – Sotheby's Sale Catalogue December 1964, Cormell Price letters 1964
64. *Something of Myself*
65. Gilbert Murray, *An Unfinished Autobiography* (Allen and Unwin, 1960)
66. Mrs A. M. Fleming – Talk on the BBC, 19 August 1947
67. Tavenor Perry letters – Huntington Library, California, letter of 25 January 1882
68. The same – letter of 22 May 1882
69. The same – letter of 28 May 1882
70. A. W. Baldwin, *The Macdonald Sisters*
71. The same

2 RETURN ON DUTY TO PARADISE

1. "The City of Dreadful Night" – *LH*
2. "The Gate of a Hundred Sorrows" – *PTH*
3. The same
4. "In the House of Suddhoo" – *PTH*
5. "On the City Wall" – *ST*
6. "To Be Filed for Reference" – *PTH*
7. The same
8. The same
9. The same
10. *Departmental Ditties*
11. R. Thurston Hopkins, *Rudyard Kipling* (Cecil Palmer, 1930)
12. Lucille Carpenter, *Rudyard Kipling: A Friendly Profile* (Arus Books, Chicago, 1942)
13. "Beyond the Pale" – *PTH*
14. "Without Benefit of Clergy" – *LH*
15. "Miss Youghal's Sais" – *PTH*
16. "The Return of Imray" – *LH*
17. The same

346

18. "City of Dreadful Night" – January 1888
19. Walter Roper-Lawrence, *The India We Served* (Cassell & Co., 1928)
20. "A Friend's Friend" – *PTH*
21. "The Return of Imray" – *LH*
22. "The Story of Muhammad Din" – *PTH*
23. "False Dawn" – *PTH*
24. "Wayside Comedy" – *WWW*
25. "Route Marchin'"
26. "His Private Honour" – *MI*
27. R. K. Le Gallienne, *Rudyard Kipling* (John Lane, 1900)
28. Lord Lugard, *The Years of Adventure* (Collins, 1956)
29. "Cholera Camp"
30. "The Courting of Dinah Shadd" – *LH*
31. "In The Matter of a Private" – *ST*
32. "Danny Deever"
33. "With the Main Guard" – *ST*
34. The same
35. "Cells"
36. "On Greenhow Hill" – *LH*
37. "His Private Honour" – *MI*
38. "Love O' Women" – *MI*
39. "Mary, pity women" – *Seven Seas*
40. "The Courting of Dinah Shad" – *LH*
41. "Follow me 'Ome"
42. "That Day"
43. "Army Headquarters"
44. "The Education of Otis Yeere" – *WWW*
45. "At the Pit's Mouth" – *WWW*
46. "The Other Man" – *PTH*
47. Lady Dufferin, *Our Viceregal Life in India* (John Murray, 1890)
48. "The Miracle of Purun Bhagat" – *JB2*
49. "The Bridge Builders" – *DW*
50. Brigadier A. Mason, "Kipling's Association with India", in R. E. Harbord, *The Readers' Guide to Rudyard Kipling's Work*, 1963 (published privately for members of the Kipling Society)
51. "Letting in the Jungle" – *JB2*
52. Letter to James Walker, 15 November 1911 (Sotheby's Sale Catalogue, 24 March 1936)
53. Lockwood Kipling, *Beast and Man in India* (Macmillan, 1891)
54. W. S. Blunt, *Diaries* – 22 August 1908 (Martin Secker, 1921)
55. "My Rival"
56. Jottings from Jeypore, signed "Nick" – *Pioneer*, February 1883
57. "Ballad of the King's Jest"
58. H. R. Goulding, "Old Lahore" – *Civil and Military Gazette*, Lahore, 1924
59. Kipling's Diary, 1 and 2 August 1885 – HL
60. Lady Dufferin, *Our Viceregal Life in India*
61. George Younghusband, *40 Years a Soldier* (Herbert Jenkins, 1923)
62. General Sir Ian Hamilton, *Listening for the Drums* (Faber and Faber, 1944)

63. Dennis Kincaid, *British Social Life in India 1608–1937* (G. Routledge and Sons, 1938)
64. George Seaver, *Francis Younghusband* (John Murray, 1952)
65. W. Roper-Lawrence, *The India We Served*
66. Article in *McClure's Magazine* by Kay Robinson, July 1896
67. "India for the Indians" – *St James's Gazette*, December 1889
68. "The Enlightenment of Pagett, M.P." – *Contemporary Review*, Summer 1890
69. *Letters of Marque*, 1887
70. Letter to Mrs Hill, 4 April 1914, from Hotel Paris – CCHH
71. Jorge Luis Borges, *Dr Brodie's Report* (introduction) (Allen Lane, 1974)
72. Shamsul Islam, *Kipling's "Law"* (Macmillan, 1975)
73. Virginia Woolf, *Mrs Dalloway*

3 VANITY FAIR

1 to 11. Article for *Pioneer*, eventually published in *From Sea to Sea*
12. *From Sea to Sea*
13. "In Partibus", Sussex Edition of the Works, Vol. 35
14. Letter to Mrs Hill, 17 June 1906 – CCHH
15. Lord Birkenhead, address to the Royal Society of Literature, 24 January 1952 (published in *Essays by Divers Hands*, New Series, Vol. XXVII, 1955)
16. *Letters of Travel* (Macmillan, 1920)
17. Justin McCarthy, *Reminiscences*, Vol. 2 (Chatto, 1899)
18. The same
19. The same
20. Lord Birkenhead in his address, as above
21. "In Partibus," Sussex Edition of the Works, Vol. 35
22. "Three Young Men", in *Letters on Leave – The Week's News* of *Pioneer*
23. The Same
24. "On Exhibition", written for The Week's News of *Pioneer*
25. "In Partibus", Sussex Edition of the Works, Vol. 35
26. *Letters on Leave*
27. The same
28. Letters to J. B. Booth, quoted in his *The Days We Knew* (Werner Laurie, 1943)
29. "The Record of Badalia Herodsfoot" – *MI*
30. "A Death in the Camp", in *Abaft the Funnel* (Doubleday, 1909)
31. Unsigned article, "What it Came To: An Unequal Tax" – *St James's Gazette*, January 1890
32. Robert Buchanan, "The Voice of the Hooligan" – *The Contemporary Review*, December 1899
33. Lady Emily Lutyens, *A Blessed Girl* (Hart-Davis, 1953)
34. Mrs A. M. Fleming, her comments on Flo Garrard quoted in Charles Carrington, *Rudyard Kipling*, 1955
35. Sir James Rennell, *Social and Diplomatic Memories* (Arnold, 1923)
36. Margaret Newsom – KJ, March 1976
37. Arthur Waugh, *One Man's Road* (Chapman and Hall, 1931)

38. Henry James, "Wolcott Balestier: a portrait" – *Cosmopolitan Magazine*, May 1892
39. Arthur Waugh, as above
40. Henry James, as above
41. *Princeton University Library Chronicle*, Vol. XXII, No. 3, 1966
42. Letter to Mrs Baldwin – Sotheby's Sale Catalogue, 12 March 1968
43. J. Primrose – KJ, March 1963
44. Janet Dunbar, *J. M. Barrie* (Collins, 1970)
45. *From Sea to Sea – Civil and Military Gazette* and *Pioneer* travel articles, 1887–1889
46. The same
47. The same
48. The same
49. The same
50. The same
51. *Letters of Travel*
52. The same
53. "In Partibus"
54. Julian Ralph, *The Making of a Journalist* (Harper, 1903)
55. Speech to Savings Committee at Folkestone, 1918
56. "Independence", Speech as Rector of St Andrew's University, 1923 – *Book of Words* (Macmillan, 1928)
57. Speech to Savings Committee at Folkestone, 1918
58. Miscellaneous notes by the Carpenters – CCHH
59. "Back to the Army Again"
60. "Shillin' A Day"
61. "The Ladies"
62. Letter to William Heinemann, May 1900 – Princeton University Library
63. Letter to W. E. Henley, October 1892 – PML
64. Letter to W. E. Henley, 18 January 1893 – PML
65. The same
66. Kipling Notebook (New York, 1899)
67. Letter to W. E. Henley, December 1893 – PML
68. J. B. Pond, *Eccentricities of Genius* (Chatto, 1900)
69. *Phoenix*, Brattleboro, 15 May 1896
70. Frederic van de Water, *Rudyard Kipling's Vermont Feud* (Countryman Press, Weston, 1937)
71. Letter to Frank Doubleday, 24 March 1899 – Princeton University Library
72. Letter to Mrs Hill, 31 July 1899 – CCHH

4 UNDER-REHEARSED FOR ARMAGEDDON

1. CCHH
2. Letter to C. E. Norton, October 1896 – HL
3. F. H. B. Skrine, *The Life of Sir William Wilson Hunter*
4. Letter to Henry James, 30 October 1896 – HL
5. Letter to Dr Conland, 25 to 29 March 1897 – HL
6. Letter to Stanley Weyman – quoted in KJ 144, 1962
7. "The White Man's Burden"

8. R. D. Evans, *A Sailor's Log* (Smith Elder & Co., 1901)
9. "Poseidon's Law"
10. "The Spirit of the Navy", Speech to Naval Club, 1908 – *Book of Words*
11. Lockwood Kipling's letter to Mrs Trotter booking rooms at Newlands, Capetown, 16 November 1897 – HL
12. Letter to Dr Conland, 17 December 1897 – CCHH
13. Alfred Milner, a letter to Mrs Gaskell, 2 June 1898 – quoted in Evelyn Wrench, *Alfred Lord Milner* (Eyre and Spottiswoode, 1968)
14. Speech to Anglo-African Writers' Club, May 1898
15. Letter to Mrs Hill, 31 July 1899 – CCHH
16. Letter to Mrs Hill, 27 June 1906 – CCHH
17. L. S. Amery, *My Political Life* (Hutchinson, 1953)
18. Quoted in Julian Ralph, *War's Brighter Side* (Arthur Pearson, 1901)
19. The same
20. The same
21. Julian Ralph, *The Making of a Journalist*
22. Editorial of the *Friend*, Blomfontein, 21 March 1900
23. Julian Ralph, *War's Brighter Side*
24. The same
25. The same
26. Letter to G. W. Black, 10 April 1908 – Princeton University Library
27. J. G. McDonald, *Rhodes: A Life* (Philip Allan & Co., 1927)
28. Julian Amery and others, *Life of Joseph Chamberlain* (Macmillan, 1951)
29. Letter to Milner, 26 February 1903 – Milner Papers, Bodleian Library, Oxford
30. Letter to Milner, 21 March 1903 – as above
31. Letter to Duckworth Ford, 16 September 1907 – HL
32. Letter to Milner, 16 October 1911 – Milner Papers, Bodleian Library

5 FOLLY AND MISRULE

1. Letter to Mrs Hill, March 1905 – CCHH
2. "Chant-Pagan"
3. The same
4. The same
5. John Marlowe, *Milner: Apostle of Empire* (Hamish Hamilton, 1976)
6. "The Parable of the Boy Jones" and "His Gift" – stories in *Land and Sea Tales for Scouts and Guides*
7. Letter to Frank Doubleday, April 1919 – Princeton University Library
8. J. Castell Hopkins – *Canadian Annual Review of Public Affairs*, 1907
9. The same
10. The same
11. "Letters to the Family" – 1908
12. "Values in Life" – Speech to McGill University, 1907 – *Book of Words*
13. *Letters of Travel*
14. Letter to Milner, July 1908 – Milner Papers, Bodleian Library
15. Letter to Milner, 23 September 1911 – as above

16. Letter to Milner, 14 December 1910 – as above
17. John Marlowe, *Milner*
18. Speech at Tunbridge Wells, May 1914 – *Daily Express*
19. Coulson Kernahan, *Nothing Quite Like Kipling has Happened Before* (Epworth Press, 1944)

6 HEALING, HOME AND HISTORY

1. Angela Thirkell, *Three Houses*
2. The same
3. Epilogue by Elsie Bambridge to Charles Carrington, *Rudyard Kipling*
4. Colonel S. M. Moens, *The Story of a Village* (John Beal & Son, 1953)
5. Dorothy Ponton, *Rudyard Kipling at Home and at Work* (Published by the Author at Poole, 1953)
6. Letter from S. W. Alexander to the present author
7. Letter to a lady, 12 June 1925 – HL
8. Julia Catlin Taufflieb, *Disordered Memories* (unpublished)
9. Hesketh Pearson, *The Pilgrim Daughters* (Heinemann, 1961)
10. Letter to Dr Conland, 2 December 1900 – CCHH
11. Letter from Lady Mary Maxse, 1913, quoted in Evelyn Wrench, *Alfred Lord Milner* (Eyre and Spottiswoode, 1968)
12. Quoted in Allen Andrews, *The Splendid Pauper* (Harrap, 1968)
13. Coulson Kernahan – as above
14. "Some Aspects of Travel" – Speech to Royal Geographical Society, February 1914 – *A Book of Words*
15. "The Open Door"
16. "We and They"
17. *Letters of Travel*
18. Letter to Ian Hamilton, 20 August 1942, quoted in *Listening for The Drums*
19. Letters from Mrs A. M. Fleming to Mr C. W. Parish, 17 September 1945 – KJ 77, 1946
20. Letters from Mrs A. M. Fleming to Elkin Matthews, 1902 and 1905 – Berg Collection, New York Public Library
21. Letter to Mrs Hill, 10 February 1911 – CCHH
22. A. W. Baldwin, *The Macdonald Sisters*
23. *Life in Letters of W. D. Howells* (Doubleday, 1928)
24. "The Tree of Justice" – *RF*

7 ARMAGEDDON AND AFTER

1. *Daily Express*, 24 May 1916
2. *Souvenirs of France* (Macmillan, 1933)
3. Letter to W. J. Barrie, 30 December 1935 to 4 January 1936 – Toronto Public Library
4. "The Beginnings"
5. Letter to Frank Doubleday, 11 September 1914 – Princeton University Library

6. Letter from Theodore Roosevelt, 4 November 1914 – Congress Library, Washington
7. Julia Catlin Taufflieb, *Disordered Memories*
8. Letter to Forbes, January 1916 – HL
9. Morton N. Cohen, *Rudyard Kipling to Rider Haggard* (Hutchinson, 1965)
10. "The Children"
11. "The War in the Mountains"
12. Letter to Theodore Roosevelt, 21 April 1918 – Library of Congress, Washington
13. *Something of Myself*
14. Preface to Lady Atholl's *Report on India*, 1934
15. Letter from Theodore Roosevelt, 23 November 1918 – Library of Congress, Washington
16. "Souvenirs of France"
17. A. W. Baldwin, *My Father* (Allen and Unwin, 1955)
18. Julia Catlin Taufflieb, *Disordered Memories*
19. Rupert Grayson, *Voyage Not Completed* (Macmillan, 1969)
20. W. A. Ramsay – *Chambers's Journal*, December 1933
21. P. G. Maude-Roxby, "A Burwash Boy's Reminiscences" – *Sussex County Magazine*, August 1937
22. Quotations from unpublished letters to Jane Stanley (now Mrs Lancelot Hard)
23. Rupert Hart-Davis, *Hugh Walpole* (Macmillan, 1952)
24. Letters to Baroness Orczy, 23 February 1933 and 25 March 1933 – Texas University Library
25. Letter to W. S. Maugham from Hotel Hermitage, Monte Carlo, 26 February 1923 – Sotheby's Sale Catalogue, 5 December 1972
26. "A Doctor's Work" – *A Book of Words*
27. "Surgeons and the Soul" – *A Book of Words*
28. Lady Troubridge and Archibald Marshall, *Life of Lord Montagu of Beaulieu* (Macmillan, 1930)
29. "The Watches of the Night" – *PTH*
30. "The Disciple"

INDEX

Arrangement within entries is alphabetical, except for certain biographical material, in which a chronological order has been adopted where it is felt that it will aid the reader.

Abdullah 6
"Absent Minded Beggar, The" 215 (quoted) 213
Absolute, Anthony 46
Academy, The 201
Ackerley, J. R. 94
Aerial Board of Control 248, 299
Afghanistan 76, 105
  Amir of 104, 105
Agra High School 99
Agrippina, Cornelia 86
'Ahmed Kel 84
Aitken, Max *see* Beaverbrook
Aix-les-Bains 323
Alchemist, The 123
Algeria 322–3, 333
All Souls' Church, Langham Place 170
Allahabad 63, 68, 69, 92, 99, 113, 117, 119
  Club 117
Allen, Sir George 99, 119
Allingham, William 14, 29
Alsace 334
Aluric 244–5
Amaranatha Jha 118
Amber 95
Ameera 64–5, 67, 74, 107, 298
"American, An" (quoted) 191
American Notes (Dickens) 174, 189
American Notes (Kipling) 170
Amery, Leopold Charles 172, 173, 213, 225, 240
Amir Nath's Gulley 64
"Amir's Homily, The" 105
Amis, Kingsley 163, 270
Anglicanism 8, 9, 27, 79, 306
Anglo-African Writers' Club 199, 212
Anglo-Indians 35, 67, 145, 146
  condescension towards Kipling 112

Animal Farm 233
animal quality of human life 311–12
animals and birds 125, 184–5
  adjutant stork 2, 94, 123, 182
  armadillo 229, 231
  baboon 230
  bears 108–9, 125, 126
  beavers 175, 185
  buffaloes 63–4
  bull 335
  bullock 73–4
  butterfly 229
  camel 229, 230, 231
  cats 146, 185, 229, 314
  crocodiles 2, 3, 94, 123, 125, 182
  dingo 230
  dogs 66, 70, 80, 93, 113, 185, 268–9, 273, 280, 313–14, 341
  drongos 76
  elephants 83, 228, 229, 230, 231
  gorillas 295
  hedgehog 231
  horses 184, 185
  jackal 2, 94, 123, 124, 182
  jaguar 231
  kangaroo 229, 230–1
  leopard 125, 126, 228, 229, 230, 231
  mongoose 123, 185
  monkeys 2, 95, 124, 125, 126
  parrots/parakeets 64, 74, 80, 82
  rabbits 185
  rat 125, 146, 244–5
  rhinoceros 5, 229, 230, 231
  snakes 2, 66, 95, 123, 125, 126–7, 185
  tiger 124, 125
  tortoise 231
  vultures 76

Index

animals and birds – *contd.*
  wax moth 125, 246–8
  whale 229, 231
Anna 308
Anna Karenina 317
Annan, Noël Gilroy, Baron 124, 173
Annunzio, Gabriele d' 186
Anstell, Mrs 3
Anstruther, Ralph 328
"Anthony Dawkins" 19
anti-Germanism 250, 298–302, 309, 310, 311
anti-semitism 242
Arabian Nights, The 29, 278
Archer, Chad and Isobel 174
architects 146, 181, 199
Ariel 132
"Army Headquarters" (quoted) 86
army life 77–86
  chaplains 79
  national military service 241–4, 251, 259
  officers 77–80, 86, 219–20, 237–8
  private soldiers 80–5, 119, 141, 147, 213, 219–20, 233, 234, 235, 236
"Army of a Dream, The" 232, 233, 241–4, 251, 262
Arnold, Sir Edwin 44
Arnold, Thomas 48
"Arrest of Lieutenant Golightly, The" 79
Artful Dodger 129
"Artist and the Empire, The" 173
"As Easy as A.B.C." 248, 250
Ashcroft, Grace 2, 286–8, 298
Assommoir, L' 46, 141
Astor, Lord 258
Astor, Nancy, Lady 275
"At His Execution" (quoted) 340
"At the Pit's Mouth" (quoted) 89
Athenaeum 18, 159, 160
Athenaeum Club 201–2, 239, 279, 330
Atholl, Lady 319
Atkins, Tommy 80, 136
Atlantic Monthly 119.
"Aunt Ellen" 326
Austen, Jane 283
Australia 164

"Baa, Baa, Black Sheep" 17, 18, 24, 33, 113, 119, 228
  (quoted) 26
"Back to the Army Again" (quoted) 183
Baden-Powell, Robert Stephenson Smyth, 1st Baron 243
Bagheera 3, 125, 126
Bahadur Khan 66, 71
Baker, Sir Herbert 224
Baldwin, Alfred 23
Baldwin, Mrs A. (Louisa Macdonald) 4, 23, 25, 163
Baldwin, Arthur Windham, 3rd Earl of Bewdley 14, 47
Baldwin, Lucy, Lady 206, 260
Baldwin, Oliver, 2nd Earl of Bewdley 10
Baldwin, Stanley, 1st Earl of Bewdley
  suggestion that Trix be companion to 23
  at Loughton 37
  goes up to Cambridge 46
  visits "The Elms" 206
  marriage 260

close friendship with Kipling 263, 323
Chancellor of the Exchequer 323
Prime Minister 325
at odds with Kipling over India 319
attacks Beaverbrook 324
Baldwin family 27
Balestier, Beatty 163, 178, 180
  bankrupt 193
  quarrel with Kipling 192–3
  trial 193
  intention to sue Kipling 196
Balestier, Mrs Beatty (Mai) 178
Balestier, Caroline Starr *see* Kipling, Mrs Rudyard
Balestier, Mrs Henry (Anna Smith) 163
Balestier, Madame (Caroline Starr Wolcott) 163, 178, 180, 193
Balestier, Wolcott
  Freshwater visit with Kipling and Caroline 18, 163
  collaboration with Kipling on *Naulakha* 94, 162–4
  personal charm of 161
  relationship with Kipling 18, 161–2, 164, 190, 227–8
  death 169
Balestier family 163, 177–8
Balfour, Arthur James, 1st Earl of 159, 226, 227, 232, 239, 245, 256
"Ballad of East and West, The" (quoted) 104–5
"Ballad of Fisher's Boarding House, The" (quoted) 62–3
"Ballad of the King's Jest, The" 105
  (quoted) 105–6
"Ballad of the King's Mercy, The" 105
Balliol College, Oxford 46, 201
Baloo 3, 13, 109, 125, 126
Bal-Phour 256
Balzac, Honoré de 60, 113, 269
Bambridge, George 325, 334
Bambridge, Mrs George (Elsie Kipling)
  born 192
  at The Woolsack 221
  in Sussex 261, 262
  admirers deterred by Carrie 325
  John's death 304
  marriage 270, 325
  visits from parents in Belgium, Spain and France 325, 334
  afterword to Charles Carrington's biography 270, 271, 325
Bandar-log 3, 124, 125, 126, 246, 247, 279, 282
Bardolph 83
Baring, Maurice 330
Barrack Room Ballads, The 82, 120, 122, 143, 145, 147, 190
  (quoted) 183–4
Barrie, Sir James Matthew 6, 12, 165, 264, 272, 330, 340
Barrie, W. J. (Jim) 300
Barrow, Steve 262
Bataille de Tripoli, La 156
Bateman's 45, 149, 186, 201, 260–4, 270–1, 276, 278, 290, 314, 325–9 *passim*
Bates, Miss 72
Bates, Sir Percy 326
Bathurst, Lady 329
Bathurst, Mrs 82, 211, 221–3

Index

Baux, Les 335
Baviaan 230
Bayly, Captain E. H. 207
Bazin, René 334
Beadnell, Maria 154
Beardsley, Aubrey 155
Beast and Man in India 100, 101
"Beauty Spots" 49, 326
Beaverbrook, William Maxwell Aitken, 1st
    Baron 255–6, 272, 302, 303, 323
    rift with Kipling 323–4
Bedford, Herbrand Arthur Russell, 11th Duke
    of 87, 111
"Beechwood" 178, 181
Beefsteak Club 329
Beeker, Colonel (and wife) 84
Beetle 41
    see also Kipling, Rudyard
"Beginning of the Armadilloes, The" 229, 231
"Beginnings, The" (quoted) 301
Belgium 325, 334
Bell, Clive 330
Belloc, Hilaire 242
"Below the Mill Dam" 227, 232, 233, 237, 244–
    5, 286
Benares 75, 92–4
"Benefactors, The" 233
Bennett, Arnold 134, 315
Bennett, Rev. Arthur 79, 132, 306
Beresford, George 41, 45, 53, 58
    see also M'Turk
Besant, Sir Walter 113, 139, 141, 202
Bewdley 4, 34
"Beyond the Mill Dam" 146, 185
"Beyond the Pale" 2
    (quoted) 64
Biddums, Miss 4
Bikaner House 101, 291
birds *see* animals and birds
"Birds of Paradise" 210
Bisesa 63–4
Bismarck, Otto, Prince von 149
Black, G. W. 223
"Black Jack" (quoted) 80
Black Rat 125, 146, 185, 244–5
Black Tyrones 81, 82, 84
Blackmore, Richard Doddridge 113
Bland-Sutton, Sir John 324, 332
Blavatsky, Madame 266
Blitherstone, Master 21
Bloemfontein 214
Bloomsbury circle 282–3
Blunt, Wilfred Scawen (Diaries quoted) 100–1
Boer War 211–12, 214, 216–20 *passim*, 225, 263
Boer War poems 12, 217–18
Boer War stories 217–20
Bohème, La 336
Boileau, "Tick" 77
Boileaugange 111, 112
Bok 273
Bombay 1, 3, 4, 5, 170
Bombay Cathedral 27
"Bonds of Discipline, The" 208
"Bonfires on the Ice" (quoted) 322
Book of the Forty Five Mornings, The 159, 160
Book of Words, A 255
Booth, J. B. 147
Booth, William 164

Boothby, Guy 279
Bordeaux, Henri 334
Borgès, Jorge Luis 121
Bounderby, Major 77
Bourget, Paul 145
Bouveret, Dagnan 54
Bowes, Michael 304
"Boy, The" 78
Boy Scouts 243
Boys' Own Paper 44
Bradlaugh, Charles 296
Brattleboro 177–8, 180–95 *passim*
Brecht, Bertold 149
Breitmann, Hans 44, 149
Bremmil, Tom Cusack (and wife) 88
"Bride's Progress, The" 93
"Bridge Builders, The" 2, 94, 182, 245, 298
Brighton Royal Pavilion 307
British Covenant 257–8
British Empire Exhibitions 318
British Social Life in India 112
Brompton Road 37–8
Brook's Hotel 177, 193
"Brother Square Toes" 9, 186, 294
Browning, Robert 98, 113, 188, 294
Brown's Hotel 199, 200, 272, 274, 281, 304, 323,
    325, 329, 341
"Brugglesmith" 3
"Brushwood Boy, The" 12, 34, 48, 182, 198, 269
Buchanan, Robert 152
Buck, Sir Edward 99, 110, 117
Buddhism 44, 132
Budget 51
"Bull That Thought, The" 334, 335
Bullard, Admiral 303
Bunyan, John 256–7
"Burden, The" (quoted) 317
"Burgher of the Free State" 217
Burleigh, Bennet 216
Burma 120
    people 136–7
Burne-Jones, Sir Edward Coley, Bart. 26, 54,
    123
    death 206
    drawings and paintings 30, 31
    fame 35, 98, 199
    father-figure to Kipling 13, 139
    home (The Grange) 23, 28–31
    house at Rottingdean 202, 205–6, 263
    influence on Kipling 30–1
    pacifism 43
    religious beliefs 27
    romantic nature 155, 156
    school 10, 42
    sense of humour 30
Burne-Jones, Lady (Georgiana Macdonald) 18,
    24, 26, 39, 139, 203, 206
    house at Rottingdean 202, 205–6, 263
    Kipling's affection for 139
    memoir of Christmas 29–30
    political activities 263
    temperament 10, 139
    visits to Southsea 25
Burne-Jones, Margaret *see* Mackail, Mrs J. W.
Burne-Jones, Sir Philip, 2nd Baronet 10, 29, 39,
    139, 155, 263
Burnett, Frances Hodgson 113
Burton, Mrs 12, 111, 112

Index

Butterfield, William 42
"Butterfly that Stamped, The" 229

Cabot, Mary 181, 189, 192, 206
Calcutta 68, 115, 116
Caliban 168
Calvin, John 296
Calvinism 27–8, 270
Campbell, Mrs Patrick 155
Canada 179–80, 253–6, 319
Canadian Annual Review of Public Affairs 253
Canadian Club 254
Canadian Pacific Railway 179, 180, 253
Cannes 334, 341
Canterbury Tales 129
Cape Argus 223
Cape cart 216, 217
Captains Courageous 174, 188, 192, 320
"Captive, The" 220
Carlyle, Thomas 44
Carnac, Rivett 35, 99
Carpenter, Lucille 63
Carrington, Charles 20, 23, 28, 51, 55, 63, 101, 102, 152–3, 160, 163, 192, 199, 256, 270, 271, 325
Carson, Sir Edward 257, 319
Castlerosse, Lord 330
Castorley, Sir Alured 336–7
Castries, Miss 68
"Cat that Walked by Himself, The" 229
Catlin, Julia see Taufflieb, Julia Catlin
Cazalet family 329
Cecil, Lady Edward 225, 328
Cecil, George 304
"Cells" (quoted) 82
censorship 337
Century Magazine 302
Cervantes Saavedra, Miguel de 129
Ceylon 164, 169
Chair, Somerset de 328
Challong 167–8
Chamberlain, Joseph 138, 172, 208, 211, 226, 227, 238, 240, 241, 250, 253
Chambers's Journal 18
"Chant Pagan" (quoted) 235, 236
Chapin, George 281
Chapin, Sophie 281–2
Chaucer, Geoffrey 115, 129, 336, 337
Chaudhuri, Nirad 132
Cheever, Eustace 78, 140–1
Chekhov, Anton 343
Cheltenham College 40, 77, 78
Cherkley Court 255
Cheveley, Mrs 88
Chevrillon, André 334
Chicago 175–6
children
    depiction of 5–6, 264–5, 288, 293–4, 308–12
    imagination of 1–3, 5–6, 229–31
' letters to 328–9
    sexual needs of 288
    use of 320
"Children, The" (quoted) 305
"Children of the Zodiac, The" 8, 9, 125, 336
Chitor 95, 116, 125
Chola 6
"Cholera Camp" (quoted) 79

Chota Lal 129
Christianity 32–3, 153, 267, 270, 306, 315, 316, 317, 338–40
    see also Calvinism; Church of England; Methodism; Moravian Church; Roman Catholicism
Christie, Agatha 335
Chuckerbuti, Mr 115
Church of England 8, 9, 27, 79, 306
"Church That Was at Antioch, The" 337–40
Churchill, Winston 208, 319
Chutter Munzil 92
cinema 222, 223
"City of Dreadful Night" (quoted article) 68
"City of Dreadful Night" (story) 37, 55
    (quoted) 59
Civil and Military Gazette 8, 37, 58, 69, 87, 93, 97, 98, 103, 104, 107, 110, 112, 113, 169
Civil Lines (Allahabad) 69, 92
Civil Lines (Lahore) 63, 68–9, 72, 75
Civil Service, Indian 7
Clandeboys, Lord 110
class 87, 109, 112, 238–9, 244
Clemenceau, Georges Benjamin 300, 322
Cleveland, President 191–2
Clifford, Mrs W. K. 144
"Clouds" 146, 199, 291, 292
clubs 69, 74, 99, 107, 142–3, 144, 199–202 passim, 210, 212, 239, 254, 279, 329–30
Cockerell, Sir Sidney 52
cod-fishing 188
"Cold Iron" 295, 340
Cold Lairs 2, 95, 182
collectivism 242, 247, 248
Colombo 164, 169
Colonial Conferences 251, 252
Colvin, Sir Sidney 202
"Comforters, The" 198
    (quoted) 276
"Comprehension of Private Copper, The" 217, 218–20
Comte, Auguste 8
"Conference of Powers, A" 140
    (quoted) 77–8
Conland, Dr J. 188, 189, 192, 193, 202, 211, 275
Connaught, Arthur William Patrick Albert, Duke of 99, 110
Connecticut Yankee at King Arthur's Court, A 176
Conrad, Joseph 167, 279, 318, 325
Contemporary Review 114, 144
"Conversion of Aurelian McGoggin, The" 7
Cooper, Lady Diana 159
Cooper, Duff 330
Copleigh, Edith 72
Copleigh, Maud 72
Copper, Alfred 218, 219, 220
Copperfield, David 20, 28, 154
Cornell, L. L. 57
Cornell University 163
Corpus Christi College, Oxford 10
Coupeau 46
"Courting of Dinah Shadd, The" 80
Covenanter 258
Craig, James 13, 14, 35
Craik, Misses 55, 56, 144
Crane, Walter 97
Crashaw, Richard 47

Index

Creakle, Dr 20, 28
Creighton, Colonel William 47, 130, 131
Croft-Cooke, Rupert 327
Crofts, William 47
Cruze, Michele d' 67
Cuba 204
Culpeper, Nicholas 294, 333
Cunard 326
Curée, La 141
Curiosities of Literature 47
Curtis, Lionel 225, 240
Curzon of Kedleston, George Nathaniel, 1st
    Marquess 110, 120
Cuthbert, Mrs 304, 328
Czechoslovakia 333–4

Daily Express 299, 302, 303, 324
    (quoted) 299–300
Daily Herald (quoted) 321–2
Daily Mail 213, 324
Daily Tribune 170
Dalhousie 102
Dalyngridge, Sir Richard 294, 295
Dan 3, 7, 31, 90, 92, 105, 262, 293, 294
Dana, Richard Henry 250
"Danny Deever" (quoted) 81
Dartmouth 201
Dass, Sir Purun 90, 123
David Copperfield 20, 28, 154
"Dayspring Mishandled" 33, 298, 331, 332,
    336–7
Dé, Grish Chunder 74–5
De Quincey, Thomas 60
"Deal in Cotton, A" 12, 71, 299
    (quoted) 66
Dean's Hotel 104
Dear Brutus 272
"Death in the Camp, A" 150–1
    (quoted) 151
"Death of Manon Lescaut" 54
"Death-Bed, A" 301–2
    (quoted) 301
Debits and Credits 297
"Debt, The" 264
Delhi Gate 59, 60
"Dene, The" 260
"Department of Death, The" 272
Departmental Ditties 69, 87, 122, 201
    (quoted) 96–7, 102
"Devil and the Deep Blue Sea, The" 187
Dickens, Charles 28, 37, 38, 53, 60, 116, 129,
    154, 165, 174, 189, 196, 221, 234, 240, 264,
    341, 343
Dilke, Sir Charles 240
Dirkovitch 78
"Disciple, The" (quoted) 339–40
Disraeli, Benjamin 43
D'Israeli, Isaac 47
"Disturber of Traffic, The" 166, 167
Diversity of Creatures, A 256, 278, 285
Dobrée, Bonamy 310
"Doctor's Work, A" 332
"Dog Hervey, The" 268–9, 273, 280
Dombey and Son 21, 28
Donne, John 34, 47
Doré, Paul Gustave 59, 60
Dormer, Private 78
Dostoevsky, Feodor 37, 60, 343

Doubleday, Frank 162, 190, 196, 197, 248, 302
Dowse 2, 167–8
Doyle, Sir Arthur Conan 192, 268, 279
Dr Brodie's Report 121
Dragomiroff 249
Dravot 167
"Dream of Duncan Parrenness, The" 168
Dreyfus case 196
Drink 46
"Drums of the Fore and Aft, The" 18, 84–5
    (quoted) 85
Du Maurier, George Louis 157
Dufferin and Ava, Frederick Temple Hamilton-
    Temple-Blackwood, 1st Marquess of
    friendship with Kipling 87, 111, 159
    friendship with Kipling's parents 36, 99, 109,
    111
    hands over Viceroyship to Lord Lansdowne
    119
    meets Amir of Afghanistan 104
Dufferin and Ava, Lady Hariot 90, 109, 111
Dufferin Bridge 93
Dunsany, Lord 330
Dunsterville, Major-General L. C. 39, 40, 41,
    51, 330
    see also Stalky
Durbar Room 110
Durkheim, Emile 172, 247

East India Company 22, 204
Ebermann, Frau 308–9, 311, 313
Echoes 102
"Edge of the Evening, The" 259
Edna 310
"Education of Otis Yeere, The" (quoted) 88
Edwin Drood 221
Egypt, visit to 120
elective affinity, fatality of 222
"Elephant's Child, The" 212, 228, 229, 230,
    231
Elgar, Sir Edward 258, 329
Eliot, George 88–9
"Elizabeth" 329, 330
Elizabeth and Her German Garden 329
Elizabeth I 294
Elliot-Hocker 68
"Elms, The" 206, 260–1
Emerson, Ralph Waldo 44, 179
Emma 72
"Empedocles at Etna" 115
Empire League 250
"En-Dor" (quoted) 267
"End of the Passage, The" 2
engines, railway 186
England 289–90, 307, 321
    society 150–2, 233–52 passim, 282–3
"English Flag, The" 159
    (quoted) 151
"English School, An" 46, 47
"Enlightenment of Pagett, M.P., The" 114, 117,
    159
"Epitaphs of the War, The" 296, 304
    (quoted) 305
Epstein's Dive 10
Eric, or Little by Little 44, 51
Erlynne, Mrs 88
"Error in the Fourth Dimension, An" 194
Eurasians 35, 67–8, 71

Evans, Admiral R. D. 207
evolution 229, 246
Expansion of England, The 138, 250
"Expert, The" 326
  (quoted) 327
"Eye of Allah, The" 294, 337
Eyes of Asia, The 307

Faerie Queene, The 115
"Fairy Kist" 297
Fallen Angel 89
"False Dawn" 2
  (quoted) 72
Falstaff 83
famine 96
farm labourers 45, 271
Farrar, Dean 44
Farren, Nellie 147
"Father and Sons" 5
Faulkner, Charles 29
Feilden, Henry Wemyss 280
Feilden family 320, 328
Fenwick 167
Fettley, Liz 286, 287
field sports 238–9
Finching, Flora 154
Findlayson 2, 94, 182, 245, 247, 298
"Finest Story in the World, The" 106, 166, 168
  (quoted) 150
First World War 120, 152, 171, 216, 233, 250,
  296–318 *passim*
fishing, cod- 188
"Flag of Their Country, The" 50
Flaubert, Gustave 103
Fleet 66
Fleming, John 110
Fleming, Mrs J. (Alice Kipling, "Trix")
  birth 4
  ill-health 10, 23, 102, 110, 266, 267, 291
  at Southsea 17–24 *passim*, 28, 34, 36–7, 57
  affection for Kipling 23, 154, 291
  religion in childhood 24
  holidays at Loughton and Brompton Road
    36–8
  holidays at Skipton and Rottingdean 58
  at Lahore 98, 102, 106, 109–10, 111
  writes *Echoes* with Kipling at Dalhousie 102
  at Simla 102, 109–10
  jealous of mother 102, 109
  witticism (quoted) 109
  admirers 110
  beauty 110
  marriage 110, 153
  amateur theatricals 111
  comments on Flo Garrard 154
  spiritualism 266–7, 291
  hostility to Carrie 291
  poems 291
  memoirs and broadcasts 18, 19, 292
"flumdiddle" 40, 50, 80
Foch, Ferdinand 322
"Follow Me 'Ome" (quoted) 84
"For to Admire" (quoted) 11
Ford, Duckworth 227
Fore and Aft 76
Forest, Lockwood de 195
Fort Amara 61, 62, 81
Fort Jumrood 104

Fortnightly 145
Fortnum and Mason 200
Four Square 101, 168, 170
Fowler, Miss 310–11
Fowler, Wyndham (Wynn) 310, 311
Foxy 50
France 54, 322–3, 334–5
Free State Hotel 215
Freemasonry 265, 314–15
Freshwater 18, 163, 167
Frewen, Oscar 277, 320
Friend of the Free State 214, 215
"Friendly Brook, The" 2, 271, 281, 283–4, 285
"Friend's Friend, A" 69
  (quoted) 69–70
From Sea to Sea 141, 170
  (quoted) 138
Futurists 186–7
Fuzzy Wuzzy 299

Gadsby, Captain Theodore Philip 20, 89, 108
Gallio 338, 339
"Gallio's Song" (quoted) 339
Ganges 75, 93–4
"Gardener, The" 297, 316–18
Garrard, Florence 34, 102, 106, 175
  love-affair with Kipling 57, 153–5, 156, 277
Gaskell, Mrs 211–12
Gate of a Hundred Sorrows, The 60, 62
"Gate of a Hundred Sorrows, The" (film) 63
Gatti's music hall 140
Gautier, Théophile 113
"Gehazi" 33
General Strike 325
George V 264, 341
Germany 250, 259, 298–302, 309, 310, 311, 322
"Germ-Destroyer, The" 111
Gerritt, Edna 310
ghats 59, 71, 80, 93, 94
Gilbert, Sir William Schwenk 113
Gilbert the Physician 288, 289
"Gipsy Vans" (quoted) 158
Girl 8
Girton College, Cambridge 307
Gladstone, William Ewart 43, 99, 151
Globe 193
globe-trotters 93, 173–4, 208
"Gloriana" 294
Glyn, Elinor 222
Golding, William 280
Golightly, Lieutenant 79
Gooden, Arthur 327
Gordon, General Charles George 151
Gosse, Edmund 139, 147, 161, 279
Göttingen University 99
Goulding, H. R. 99, 106
Gow 331
Granby, Lord and Lady 159
Grand Trunk Road 75, 76, 92, 93, 128, 129, 182,
  247
Grange, The 23, 28–31
Gravell, Walter 326
Grayson, Rupert 327
"Great and Only, The" 147
Great Game 6, 47, 90, 91, 123, 130–1
Great War 120, 152, 171, 216, 233, 250, 296–318
  passim
Green, Lancelyn 17

Index

Grenoble Hotel 196
Grey Cat 146, 185, 244–5
Guedalla, Philip 330
Gunga Dass 72
Gwynne, H. T. 215, 226, 330

"Habitation Enforced, An" 236, 281–2
Haggard, Sir Henry Rider 272, 296
  books read by Kipling 113
  friendship with Kipling 203, 268, 273, 279, 304, 306
  letters from Kipling 203, 266, 305
  Liberty League 321
  supernatural and 266–7
Haileybury 40, 42, 77, 78
Hakluyt, Richard 250
Hamilton, Sir Ian 110, 111, 291
Hanotaux, Albert Auguste Gabriel 334
Harappa 71
Hard, Jane (Jane Stanley) 328–9
Hardinge, Helen, Lady 271–2, 325
Hardy, Thomas 140
Harison, Frederic 8
Harmsworth, Alfred Charles William 336
Harold, King 294
Harper (publisher) 162, 174
Harries 333
Harris, Frank 145
Harris, Joel Chandler 44
Harvey, Otis 194
Hatt, Dicky 156
Hauksbee, Mrs Lucy 12, 68, 87–90, 111, 136, 141, 157
Hay, Ian 330
Hay, John 189, 204
"Head of the District, The" 115
  (quoted) 74–5, 105
Heart of Darkness, The 318
Heat and Dust 94
Hedda Gabler 147
Heinemann, William 164, 186
Heldar, Dick 156–8, 160, 163
Hell 27, 28, 32
Hely-Hutchinson, Sir Walter 226
Hely-Hutchinson, Lady 226
Henley, W. E. 143, 157, 165, 188, 189, 190, 330
Henniss, Dr 311
"Her Little Responsibility" 175
"Her Majesty's Servants" 184
heredity 9, 10, 11
Herodsfoot, Badalia 56, 148, 298
Hill, Mrs Edmonia ("Ted") 161, 170, 189
  admired by Kipling 135, 153, 173, 175, 182
  landlady to Kipling in Allahabad 18, 63, 117–19
  letters from Kipling to 120, 153, 197, 212, 213, 232, 292
  living with family in Pennsylvania 138
  voyage to San Francisco 134
Hill, S. Aleck 117–19, 134, 135, 137, 153, 176
Himachal Pradesh 86
Himalayas 85, 90, 91–2, 108, 132
Hindoo Holiday 94
Hinduism 123, 198
"His Chance in Life" (quoted) 67
"His Gift" 243
"His Majesty The King" 3, 24, 264

"His Private Honour" 68
  (quoted) 76, 82
history, cyclical view of 292–3
History of the Muir Central College, 1872–1922 118
Hitler, Adolf 241, 302, 322
Hobden 45, 236, 271, 285, 286, 293
Hofmeyer 226
Holden, John 64–5, 67, 74, 107, 194, 298
Holi-Hukk 65
Holloway, Captain Harry 17, 20–1, 24
  attitude to Kipling 19, 34
  death 19, 34
  social status 25
Holloway, Mrs H. (Auntie Rosa) 17, 23, 24, 25, 26, 31
  treatment of Kipling 19, 26, 28, 32, 34
  religious beliefs 27–8
  social status 25–6
Holloway, Harry 19, 20, 26
Holloway, Sir Thomas 25
Holmes 66
Holmes, Sherlock 268
Holy Land 333
Homes in the Hills 111
Hong Kong 136
"Honours of War, The" (quoted) 46, 68
Hooper 222, 223
Hope Lodge 19–20, 26
Hope of the Katzekopfs, The 27
Hopkins, J. Castell 253
Horace 62, 331
Hornung, Oscar 304
"Horse Marines, The" 210
Horsmonden School 51
"House Surgeon, The" 201, 247, 268, 270
"How the Camel Got his Hump" 229, 230, 231
"How the Leopard Got its Spots" 228, 230, 231
"How the Rhinoceros Got his Skin" 5, 229, 230, 231
"How the Whale Got his Throat" 229, 231
Howells, Amelia 292
Howells, William Dean 292
hubshis 26, 228
Huckleberry Finn 51
Hume, Allan 115
Hunter, Sir William Wilson 46, 201
Hurree Singh 132
Hussey family 328
Hyderabad 116
"Hymn to Physical Pain" (quoted) 289
"Hypatia" 115

"Ibbetson Dunn" 53
Ibsen, Henrik 147
Ideal Husband, An 88
Ignatius Loyola 296
Ilbert Bill 107
Imambara 92
Iman Din 71
immigration 254
"Imperial Rescript, An" 148, 149
  (quoted) 150
imperialism 137–8, 143, 171–2, 202, 204–5, 213, 227, 233–4, 238, 240–1, 247, 250–2, 253, 255, 258, 292, 318
Imray 2, 66, 71, 74
In Black and White 57

"In Floodtime" (quoted) 73
"In Partibus" (quoted) 139, 144, 146, 179
"In the House of Suddhoo" (quoted) 61
"In the Matter of a Private" (quoted) 81
"In the Rukh" 128
"In the Same Boat" 247, 268–9
India
  caste system 116, 199, 227
  Civil Service 7
  Congress Movement 100, 112, 114, 115, 116
  cruelty as characteristic of 100
  economic situation 96–7
  fictional 59–97
  Government of India Act 319
  Kipling's views on 68, 95–7, 114–16, 142, 171
  middle-class ruling class of 87, 109, 112
  politics 76–7, 100, 112, 114–17, 142, 319
  soldiers' hospital at Brighton 307
  soldiers' impressions (imaginary) of England 307
  Southern 95, 164
India Defence League 319
"India for the Indians" (quoted) 114
India We Served, The 69
  (quoted) 112
industrialist, American 188
Infant, The 77–8
Ingersoll, Sir Thomas 257
Inglelow, Jean 55
Inheritors, The 280
Invasion and Defence 149
Ireland, Home Rule for 257–8
Irish Guards in Wartime, The 297
"Islanders, The" 238
Isle of Wight 18, 163, 167
Italy 159
Ivers (publisher) 170

Jabez 283, 284
Jhabvala, Ruth Prawer 94
Jacob, A. M. 90
jaddoos 61
Jake (drummer boy) 84–5
Jamaica 333
James, Henry 121, 161–2, 169, 182, 196, 202, 279
Jameson, L. S. 225, 226, 227
Jamiluddin, K. 132
Janoo 61
Japanese people 137, 179
Jeejeebhoy School of Art 5, 15
Jenkins, Ahasuerus 86
Jenny 265
Jesse 283, 284
Jesus Christ 315, 317, 340
Jewish Voluntary Schools 241, 242
Jews 241–2, 294
Jeypore 103
Jim 284
Jodhpur 94
Joffre, Joseph Jacques Cesaire 322
Johnson, Samuel 289, 331
Jones, Hannah *see* Macdonald, Mrs G. B.
Jones, Roderick 305
Jonson, Ben 123, 331
Jorrocks 34, 52
"Jottings from Jeypore" (quoted) 104
journeys, children's 3

Journey's End 330
Joynson-Hicks, Sir W. 329
"Joyous Venture, The" 3
"Judgement of Dungara, The" 92, 338
Jukes, Morrowbie 2, 71–2
Jungle Book, The 3, 7, 104, 119, 120, 122, 126, 190
  see also Second Jungle Book, The
Just So Stories, The 7, 212, 221, 228–31, 262, 264
  (quoted) 230–1

Kaa 3, 125, 126–7
Kabul, British Legation murdered at 76
Kafiristan 90
Kafka, Franz 121
Kandahar 76
Karee Siding 216, 217
Kashima 72
Kashmir 68
Keede, Robin 315
Kernahan, Coulson 279
Khem Singh 61–2
Khyber Pass 76, 91, 104
"Kidnapped" (quoted) 68
Kim
  (quoted) 129–30
  character of Lispeth in 91
  Christianity in 79, 153, 306
  corruption in 131
  evil lacking in 132
  human urban scene evoked 130
  intended readership of 7
  love of people in 298
  mother's interest in 11
  origin of Lama in 31
  poetry of 51
  quality of 120, 122, 128–33, 161
  sex in 131–2, 342
  social ethic in 130
  tribute to Lockwood in 13
  White Man's Burden 247
Kim (character) 3, 6, 47, 67, 75, 76, 79, 90, 91, 92, 105, 128–33, 342
Kim's School 21
Kincaid, Dennis 112
"King, The" 53
King Edward's School, Birmingham 10, 42
King Lear 115
"King's Ankus, The" 2
  (quoted) 126–7
King's College, London 99
King's School, Canterbury 33
Kingsley, Charles 115
Kingston, Mary 55
Kipling, Alice (Rudyard's mother) *see* Kipling, Mrs Lockwood
Kipling, Alice ("Trix") *see* Fleming, Mrs J.
Kipling, Elsie *see* Bambridge, Mrs George
Kipling, John (Rudyard's brother) 20, 34
Kipling, John (Rudyard's son)
  birth 206
  described 305
  at the Woolsack 221, 305
  relationship with mother 277
  death 272, 296–7, 303–5, 306
Kipling, John Lockwood *see* Kipling, Lockwood

Index

Kipling, Joseph Rudyard *see* Kipling, Rudyard
Kipling, Josephine
  birth 128, 180
  in Vermont 192
  at Torquay 200
  at "The Elms" 261
  illness and death 128, 195–7
Kipling, Lockwood
  education 13
  art training and experience 13–14
  meets Alice 14
  marriage 15
  in Bombay 3–4, 15–16
  decision to send children to Southsea 16, 20–4
  character of 17, 63
  recognition by Indian Government 32, 36, 99–100
  at Lahore 68–9, 76–7, 97–102, 109, 110, 112, 117, 119
  letter to Cormell Price 54
  disapproval of *Mother Maturin* 63, 128
  influence on Rudyard 97, 100, 272, 290
  pastimes 98
  friendships in India 98–100, 109
  criticism of India and Christian West 100
  political views 100–1, 117
  Simla seasons 102, 109
  in London 159
  at Tisbury 146
  death 292
Kipling, Mrs Lockwood (Alice Macdonald)
  birth of Trix 4
  character and temperament of 10, 14, 16, 17
  relationship with Rudyard 11–13
  model for Rudyard's writings 12–13
  marriage 15
  in Bombay 15–16
  trousseau derided 16
  decision to send children to Southsea 16, 20–4
  return to India 25
  religious belief 27
  returns to Southsea 32, 36
  takes children to Loughton 36–7
  at Lahore 35–6, 97–102, 109, 112, 119
  ill with shingles 37
  friends at Warwick Gardens 55
  letter to Miss Plowden 57–8
  influence on Rudyard 97, 100, 342
  pastimes 98
  friendships in India 98–100, 109
  Simla seasons 102, 109
  popularity with young men 102, 109
  fetches Trix back to India 106
  witticisms (quoted) 109
  in London 159
  poems 291
  psychic powers 266, 291
  at Tisbury 47, 128, 146, 290–2
  last years and death 290–2
Kipling, Misses (Lockwood's sisters) 8
Kipling, Rudyard
  aspects of life and work
  academic ability and aspirations 11, 20, 24, 46–7
  academic honours 46, 181, 253, 330, 334
  achievements summarised 343
  acting experience 46, 112
  American girls, views on 175

ancestry 7–11
Anglo-Indians' jealousy of 112
animals as types of humans 125
animals depicted 184–5
autobiography 1, 3, 18, 107, 128, 139, 148, 179–80, 216, 314
Balestier, Wolcott, relationship with 18, 161–2, 164, 190, 277–8
Beaverbrook, rift with 323–4
Beetle, original of 41
cancer phobia 9, 288, 324, 342
Cape Town tales, plans for 223–4
compassion 297–8
critics of 120–1, 124–5, 142, 311, 335, 342–3
death, fear of 34
despair and 269–70, 289
didacticism of 8, 48, 52, 64, 84, 173
England, attitude to 289–90, 307, 321
English society, views on 150–2, 233–52 *passim*, 282–3
eyesight 18, 32, 38, 45, 106, 107, 157
farm labourers, contact with 45, 271
father, devotion to 13, 292
France, love of 54, 322–3, 334–5
Freemasonry 265, 314–15
French, knowledge of 103, 334
Freudianism and 342
friendships forged in South Africa 215–16, 224–5
games ability 38, 45, 106
Germany, views on 250, 259, 298–302, 309, 310, 311, 322
gratitude to James Walker acknowledged 99
hatred expressed in writings 33, 70, 298–302, 308–11
heredity and 342
history, cyclical view of 292–3
humour, sense of 30–1, 327
ill-health 195–7, 211, 275, 288, 303, 320, 324–5, 332, 333, 341
immigration urged by 254
Imperial dream 137–8, 143, 171–2, 202, 204–5, 213, 227, 233–4, 247, 250–2, 253, 307, 318
India, views on 68, 95–7, 114–16, 142, 171
Indian life, awareness of realities of 95–7
influenced by Burne-Jones 30–1
influenced by parents 97, 100, 272, 342
influenced by wife 327, 342
insomnia 37–8
insularity and 289–90
introspection feared 341–3
Jews, respect for 241–2, 294
journalism for *Civil and Military Gazette* 58, 69, 87, 93, 94, 98, 102–4, 106, 107, 108, 110, 112–13
journalism for *Daily Express* 303
journalism for *Friend of the Free State* 214–15
journalism for *Pioneer* 104, 113–17, 119, 135, 144–7 *passim*
journalism for *The Times* 217
journalism on Italian front 305
Law, pervasive idea of 122–6, 128
lawbreaking, attitude to 45
life force, hymns to the 188
materialism attacked 255
medicine, concern with 56, 332–3
menace 70

361

Kipling, Rudyard – *contd.*
  microcosm, use of the 2
  misogyny 148, 156–7, 163
  mother and motherhood, attitude to 11–13,
    342
  motoring and 207, 236, 253, 270, 322, 328,
    334
  music and 56, 201
  music hall influence 56, 145
  national military service ideal 241–4
  Nobel Prize for 304
  parody 331
  personality 4–5, 8, 9, 10–11, 19, 23, 30–1, 49–
    50, 102, 136, 142, 275–6, 341–2
  philistinism of 46, 330, 341
  philosophy of 9, 124–5, 339, 340
  physical description of 113
  physical pursuits 38, 45
  place, sense of 2–4, 51–2, 94, 280–1
  political fables 185, 227, 232, 244–8
  press relations 190, 320
  primitivism viewed by 92
  pseudonym ("Nick") 103
  psychological insight 120–1, 286
  puritanism 124–5, 202, 270, 323
  religion, attitude to 7–9, 152, 203, 204, 267,
    270, 306, 315, 316, 339–40, 342
  Roman Catholicism, attitude to 79, 153, 306
  Russia, views on 321–2
  sadistic tendencies 49–50, 106, 126
  school magazine editor, 45, 52–3
  schools 11, 19–20, 26, 34, 38–54 *passim* (*see
    also* United Services College)
  schools reading list compiled for Empire
    League 250
  science fantasy/fiction 169, 248–9, 299
  sex and 107–8, 342
  social life 276, 278–9
  South African involvement 212ff
  squiredom 236
  storytelling 38, 320, 329
  success, effect of 273–4
  supernatural and 266–70
  sympathetic nature 275–6
  technical appreciation 103, 116, 157, 188
  telephone, dislike of 327
  thrift, thoughts on 180–1
  travel, lecture on 280
  Trix, affection for 23–4
  United States, views on 48, 170–1, 174–6,
    188–93, 320–1
  university education, attitude to 46
  upper classes castigated 238–9, 244
  war, views on 152
  war propaganda 299–302
  Western-educated Indians, dislike of 74–5
  wife, devotion to 277, 325–6, 327
  women, depiction of 31, 148–9, 155, 156, 307

  events
  birth 16
  baptism 27
  childhood at Bombay 3, 4–5, 6
  at Southsea 17–34 *passim*
  sent to Hope Lodge 19–20, 26
  visits to The Grange 28–31
  mother returns to Southsea to collect
    him 32, 36

  holidays at Loughton and Brompton Road
    36–8
  at United Services College (q.v.)
  schoolboy writings 52–4, 57
  school holidays 54–8
  talks with Gilbert Murray 55
  love-affair with Florence Garrard 57, 102,
    106, 153–5, 156
  at Lahore as journalist 97, 98, 102–4, 106,
    107, 108, 110, 113
  family tensions 101–2
  writes *Echoes* at Dalhousie with Trix 102
  at Simla 102, 108, 110–12
  joins 1st Punjab Volunteers 106
  hissed at Lahore Club 107
  at Allahabad 113–19 *passim*
  visits parents in Lahore 119
  voyage to San Francisco 134–7, 170, 173–5
  apprehensions about sea travel 134–5, 137
  in Rangoon, Singapore, Hong Kong and
    Japan 136–7
  naïveté displayed 136
  arrives at San Francisco and travels in United
    States 175–6
  land investment in Vancouver 175
  Chicago stockyards 175–6
  stays in Pennsylvania with Taylors 138
  love-affair with Caroline Taylor 138, 152–3
  in London 139–59 *passim*
  life-style in London 140
  holiday in Paris 159
  nervous breakdown and voyage to Italy 159
  meets Wolcott Balestier and Carrie and
    holidays with them at Freshwater 161–3
  voyages to United States, South Africa, New
    Zealand, Australia, Ceylon and India 164
  visits Ayah at Bombay 170
  marriage to Carrie 170
  honeymoon tour of United States, Canada
    and Japan 176–80
  at Brattleboro 177–8
  in Canada 179–80
  in Japan 179
  builds and inhabits "Naulakha" 181–95 *pas-
    sim*
  Josephine born 128, 180
  thoughts on thrift 180–1
  at Washington after Carrie's scalding 191
  at Tisbury and London 47, 128, 194, 198–9,
    236
  press relations 190, 320
  fact-finding at Gloucester, Mass. and Boston
    188
  Elsie born 192
  quarrel with Beatty Balestier 192–3
  return to England 193, 198
  at Rock House, Torquay 200–1
  at Balliol 201
  election to Athenaeum Club 201–2
  at Rottingdean 202, 205–6, 260–3
  John born 206
  Channel cruise 207–10
  visit to South Africa 195, 211
  political involvement 212ff
  at The Woolsack 220–1
  serious illness in New York 195–7
  Josephine dies 128, 195–7
  at Bateman's 206, 260–2, 264, 270–95 *passim*

Index

political activity 232–59 *passim*
visit to Canada 253–5
doctorate from McGill University 253, 255
honorary Oxford degree 46
parents die 292
visit to Egypt 120
War years 296–7, 302–7
sails with Harwich flotilla 303
John's death 272, 296–7, 303–5, 306
reporting on Italian front 305–6
speech to Savings Committee at Folkestone
  (quoted) 181
at Bateman's after War 325–9
appointed a Commissioner of War Graves
  297, 333
doctorate at Sorbonne 334
Clare Sheridan's visit 320
gastritis operation 324, 332
Rector of St Andrew's University 181, 330
on holiday at Aix-les-Bains 323
Elsie marries 325
overseas visits to Elsie 325, 334
other journeys abroad 333–4
Carrie ill during Jamaican holiday and return
  home via Canada 319
further ill-health for Kipling and diagnosis in
  Paris of duodenal ulcer 324
writes introduction to Atholl Report on India
  319
speech to Society of St George 300
death and cremation 341

works see under specific titles, e.g. *Something
  of Myself*

Kipling, Mrs Rudyard (Caroline Starr Balestier)
  meets Rudyard 163
at Isle of Wight with Wolcott and Rudyard
  18, 163, 167
character 169, 270, 272
marriage 170
honeymoon tour of United States, Canada
  and Japan 176–80
at Brattleboro 177–8
in Canada 179–80
in Japan 179
at "Naulakha" 181–95 *passim*
Josephine born 180
household administration and business
  acumen 180, 181, 206, 273, 274, 291
at Tisbury 47, 128, 194, 198–9
convalescence at Washington 191
Elsie born 192
row with Beatty Balestier 192
return to England 193, 198
at Rock House, Torquay 200–1
at Rottingdean 202, 205–6, 260–3
John born 206
to South Africa 195, 211
at The Woolsack 220–1
courage during Rudyard's illness and
  Josephine's death 128, 195–7
at Bateman's 206, 260–2, 264, 270–95 *passim*
visit to Canada 253–5
guardianship of Rudyard 271–6, 325
influence on his work 272–3
effect of success on 273–4
devotion to Rudyard 277, 325–6, 327
relation with John 277

John's death 304
at Bateman's after War 325–9
ill-health 325, 333, 334
Elsie marries 325
overseas visits to Elsie 325, 334
other journeys abroad 333–4
Kipling, "Trix" *see* Fleming, Mrs J.
Kipling and the Children 17
Kipling in India 57
Kipling Journal 160
Kipling Notebook (quoted) 191
Kipling Society 125
"Kipling that Nobody Read, The" 17
Kitchener, Horatio Herbert, Earl 110, 217, 318
kites 65
"Knife and the Naked Chalk, The" 12, 262, 294
"Knights of the Joyous Venture, The" 294–5
Kniveatt, Major 326
Knoblock, Edward 330
Kohat Pass 76, 84, 104
Krenk, Justus 91–2
Kruger, President Stephanus Johannes Paulus
  212

La Martinière College 92
Labour Congress, Stockholm 300
"Ladies, The" (quoted) 184
Ladies' Home Journal 153, 182, 273
Lady Windermere's Fan 88
Lahore 35–6, 60–1, 68–9, 75, 77, 164
Lahore (fictional) 59–85 *passim*
Lahore Club 69, 74, 99, 107, 157
Lahore Museum 13, 35, 68, 109, 129
Lahore School of Art 35, 109
Lalun 61, 65
Lama, the 13, 31, 79, 91, 93, 123, 129, 130, 131,
  132
Lancing College 42
"Land, The" (quoted) 45, 285
Land and Sea Tales for Scouts and Guides 47,
  243
Landon, Perceval 214, 215–16, 330
Lang, Andrew 139, 141
Lansdowne, Henry Charles Keith Petty-
  Fitzmaurice, 5th Marquess of 119, 300
Larkyn, Mrs 33, 336
"Last of the Stories, The" 113
"Last Rhyme of True Thomas, The" 336
Laurier, Sir Wilfred 253, 255
Law, Andrew Bonar 172, 241, 256, 323
Law, pervasive idea of 122–6, 128
lawbreaking 45
Lawrence, David Herbert 141, 282
Lawrence Gardens 67
Lays of Ancient Rome 116
Le Gallienne, R. K. 77
League of Nations 300
Learoyd, John 9, 80, 81, 82, 83, 153, 210, 213,
  244
Leavis, F. R. 121
Leo 8, 125
Lermontov, Mikhail Yurevich 47
Leslie, Fred 147
"Letters of Marque, The" 94
Letters of Travel (quoted) 140, 290
Letters on Leave 144, 150–1, 166
  (quoted) 145, 146, 147, 150–1
"Letters to the Family" 254

Index

"Letting in the Jungle" 96
Lew (drummer boy) 84–5
Liberalism 232, 246, 248, 251, 254, 256, 258, 263
Liberty League 321
life force, hymns to the 188
"Life in the Corridor" 52
"Life in the Studies" 53
Life's Handicap 142, 164, 166
Light of Asia 44
Light That Failed, The 33, 54, 140, 143, 144, 148, 152, 154, 155–8, 222, 342
  (quoted) 158
  two versions of 160–2
lighthouses 167–8
"Likes of Us, The" 113, 119
"Limitations of Pambé Serang, The" 33, 166
Limits and Renewals 297
Limpopo River 212, 229, 230, 231
Lingnam 252
Lippincott's Monthly Magazine 160
"Lispeth" 91, 122
"Little Foxes" 338
"Little Morality, A" 115
"Little Tobrah" 96
  (quoted) 73–4
Lloyd George of Dwyfor, David, 1st Earl 323
locomotives 186
London 55, 56, 139–59 *passim*, 161, 170, 199
  East End 56, 146, 148–9, 151, 241, 306
  literary scene 140–3, 145, 282–3
"Long Trail, The" 164
Longford, Francis Aungier Pakenham, 7th Earl of 337
Lonsdale, Frederick 330
Looking Back 261
Losson, Private 81
Loti, Pierre 141, 145
Loughton 36–7
"Love O' Women" (quoted) 83, 84
Lovell, J. W. 160, 161, 162
Low, Sidney 139
Lubbock, Percy 121
Lucas, E. V. 330
Lucia de Lamermoor 111
Lucius Sergius 338
Lucknow 92
Lugard, Frederick John Dealtry, 1st Baron 78
Lurgan 90, 129, 131
Lutyens, Lady Emily (quoted) 152
Lytton, Edward Robert Bulwer-Lytton, 1st Earl of 36, 99

"McAndrew's Hymn" 188
McCarthy, Desmond 330
McCarthy, Justin 142
McClure, Sam 190
McClure's Magazine 113
Macaulay, Thomas Babington 116
Macdonald, Agnes *see* Poynter, Lady
Macdonald, Alice *see* Kipling, Mrs Lockwood
Macdonald, Edith 10, 37
Macdonald, Florence 7, 12
Macdonald, Frederic W. 5, 10, 14, 17, 23, 27, 164
Macdonald, Rev. George Browne 4, 8, 14, 23
Macdonald, Mrs G. B. (Hannah Jones) 5, 10, 23, 25, 27
Macdonald, Georgina *see* Burne-Jones, Lady

Macdonald, Harry (Henry) 10, 42, 156, 164
Macdonald, Rev. James 7, 27
Macdonald, Louisa *see* Baldwin, Mrs A.
"McDonough's Song" (quoted) 248
McGill University 253, 255
McGoggin, Aurelian 7, 8, 125, 194
McIntosh, Jellaludin 2, 10, 30, 46, 62, 63, 66, 83, 125
Mackail, J. W. 203, 263
Mackail, Mrs J. W. (Margaret Burne-Jones) 29, 31, 56, 263
Macmillan 160
M'Turk 7, 41
machines 186–8, 209, 245, 286
"Madness of Private Ortheris, The" (quoted) 80
"Madonna of the Trenches, The" 303, 314–15, 317
Madras 95
Madura 134
Maharajah Kunwar 94, 163
Maharajah of Kashmir 108
Mahbub Ali 105, 130, 131
Maisie 157–8, 160
Mallowe, Jack 88
Mallowe, Polly 88, 157
"Man Who Was, The" 78
"Man Who Would Be King, The" 92, 167
Manallace, James Andrew 33, 336–7
"Manner of Men, The" 336, 339, 340
Manon Lescaut 156
"Man's Wife, The" 89
Mansfield, Katherine 282
Many Inventions 166
"Maplewood" 178
Marconi scandal 258
Margaret Ogilvie 12
Marinetti, Filippo Tommaso 186–7
"Mark of Solomon, The" 116
"Mark of the Beast, The" 49, 50
  (quoted) 66, 69
"Marklake Witches, The" 294
Marlborough College 39, 77, 78
Marshall, Henry Rutgers 181
Martin Chuzzlewit 189
Mary 284
"Mary Gloster, The" 43, 188
  (quoted) 44
"Mary, pity women" 148
  (quoted) 83, 149
"Mary Postgate" 156, 297, 298, 302, 309–12, 313
Mason, Brigadier A. 94
Mason, A. E. W. 279, 330
"Masque of Plenty" (quoted) 96–7
Masquerier, "Bat" 256–7
Massif Central 334
Masson, David 99
Masterman, C. F. G. 240
materialism 255
"Matter of Fact, A" 166, 169
"Maud" 151
Maude, F. N. 149
Maude-Roxby family 328
Maugham, William Somerset 63, 87, 167, 330
Maupassant, Guy de 145
Maximus, Emperor 293
Maxse family 172, 173, 240, 276
Maxwell, W. B. 330

Mayo, Richard Southwell Burke, 6th Earl of 16, 35
Mayo School of Industrial Art 35
Meeta 26, 228
"Melancholia" 156–7
Melissa 246
Melville, Herman 250
Men and Women 294
menace 70
Meredith, Owen 36
Merriman, J. X. 226
Merry Wives of Windsor 331
Mesopotamia 333
Mesquita 60
Methodism 7, 8, 9, 13, 27, 153, 159
Mian Mir cantonments 2, 75–6, 80
Micawber, Wilkins 234
microcosm, use of the 2
Middlesex Hospital 56, 332, 341
Midmore, Frankwell 34, 282, 283
Milne, A. A. 6, 330
Milner, Alfred, Viscount
  hero of Kipling 46, 146
  right-wing radicalism 172, 240–1, 250, 318
  dines with Kipling at Athenaeum 202
  German associations 208, 251
  Governor of Cape Colony 211–12, 224
  friendship with Kipling 224
  recalled to London 225
  reprimanded at House of Commons 227, 319
  Canadian visit proposed 255
  British Covenant 257–8
  death 323
Milner Court 33
"Miracle of Saint Jubanus, The" 297, 334, 335
"Miracle of the Purun Bhagat, The" 123, 198
"Miss Youghal's Sais" 66
  (quoted) 65
missionaries 163, 166–7
Mithraism 339
Mockler, Harry 2, 287–8
Molesworth, Mrs 144
Montagu of Beaulieu, Lord 335
Monte Carlo 330, 334
Monthly Review 232
Montgomery Hall 67
Moravian Church 9
Morgan, William de 29, 55
Morning Post 215, 242, 322, 329
Morris, Jenny 29
Morris, May 29, 30
Morris, William 29, 42, 43, 97, 285
Morris, Mrs William 29–30
Morris, William Richard (Lord Nuffield) 326
Morrison, Arthur 148
"Mother Hive, The" 185, 233, 245–8
Mother Maturin 57, 62–3, 128, 161
"Mother O' Mine" 12
  (quoted) 160
"Mother's Son, The" 297
motoring 207, 236, 243, 253, 256, 264, 265, 270, 322, 328, 334
Mount Monadnock 178, 179, 181
Mount Nelson Hotel 213
Mowgli stories 2, 3, 13, 31, 95, 96, 122, 123–8, 283, 285
"Mrs Bathurst" 82, 211, 221–3
Mrs Dalloway 130

"Mrs Hauksbee Sits It Out" 88
mugger 2, 3, 94, 123, 125, 182
Muggeridge, Malcolm 337
Muhammad Din 6, 71, 74, 185
Muir College 117, 118
Mullah 75, 105
Müller, Max 100
Mulvaney, Terence 80, 81, 82, 83, 88, 141, 146, 210, 213, 243, 244, 247
Murdstone, Mr 28
Murray, Gilbert 55
Murry, John Middleton 282
Museum of Art, South Kensington 14
museums 35, 38
music hall 56, 140, 145, 147
"Mutiny of the Mavericks, The" (quoted) 175
"My Boy Jack" (quoted) 296–7
"My First Adventure" 30–1
"My Lord the Elephant" 83
"My Rival" (quoted) 102
"My Son's Wife" 34, 114, 236, 281, 282–3
"My Sunday at Home" 198

"Naboth" (quoted) 70
Naples 159
Napoleon I 294, 295
Nash's Magazine 273, 302
Nassick 4, 21
Natal 219, 227–8
National Defence League 251
National Review 172, 240, 328
National Service League 259
Naulakha, The 94, 120, 162–3, 164
"Naulakha" (house) 181, 183, 184, 185, 190, 194, 206
Naval Club 210
"Naval Mutiny, A" 211
Navy, Royal 207–10 *passim*, 243, 303, 312–13
New Gaiety Theatre 111
New York 128, 164, 176, 195–7
  literary scene criticised 191
New York World 320
New Zealand 164, 165
News from Nowhere 42, 97
Newsom, Margaret 160, 161
Nicholson, Harold 330
"Nick" 103
"Nigger in Flames, The" 248
Nilghai, the 157
Norman, Montagu 323
North End 202, 205–6, 260, 263
North West Frontier 76, 77
North West Indian Command 86
Northcliffe lectures 310
Northcliffe, Alfred Charles William Harmsworth, Viscount 336
Northern Ireland 257–8
Norton, Charles Eliot 4, 189, 201
Norton, Sally 203
Noyes, Alfred 330
Nuffield, William Richard Morris, 1st Viscount 326
Nureed 166
Nym 83

"Oaken Holt" 201
occult 264–70, 291
  see also reincarnation

Index

O'Hara, Kimball 99
Old Guard 237–8, 245
Old Lahore 99, 106
"Old Men, The" (quoted) 238
"Old Men at Pevensey" 294
"On Certain Uncut Pages" 8
"On Exhibition" (quoted) 145–6
"On Greenhow Hill" 159, 223
  (quoted) 80, 82, 153
"On the City Wall" 61
  (quoted) 62
"On the Gate" 272, 296, 313, 340
"On the Strength of a Likeness" 156
"One View of the Question" 144, 145, 307
  (quoted) 150
"One Viceroy Resigns" (quoted) 87
"Only a Subaltern" (quoted) 78
".007" 186, 187
opium 60, 63, 94, 95
Orage 282
Orange Free State 214, 216, 217, 227
Orczy, Baroness 330
Orde, Yardley- 74, 115, 182, 247, 338
Oriel College, Oxford 26, 34
Ortheris, Stanley 80, 82, 83, 210, 213, 244
Orwell, George 233
Osborne House 110
Osler, Sir William 332
"Other Man, The" 156
  (quoted) 89
"Our Lady of the Snows" 253–4
  (quoted) 253
Our Viceregal Life in India (quoted) 90, 109
"Outsider, The" 220
Oxford University 10, 34, 46, 62
  see also names of colleges, e.g. Balliol College

pacifism 9
Pagett, M. P. 114–15
pain, physical 288, 289
Pambé Serang 33, 166
Pansay, Jack 89
"Parable of Boy Jones, The" 263
Pareto, Vilfredo 172, 247
Paris, visits to 325, 334
Paris Exhibition 54, 322
Parish, C. W. 291
Park, Mungo 250
Parnesius stories *see Puck of Pook's Hill*
parody 331
Patan 116
Patna 116
Patsie 24
Peachey 90, 82, 105, 167
Pellitti's café 86, 89, 111
Penfentenyou, The Hon. A. M. 252
Perigord–Dordogne area 334
Perry, John Tavenor 56
Perry, Mrs Tavenor 56–7, 58, 102, 153
Pertinax 293
Peshawar 78, 84, 104, 105
Pestonjee Bomonjee 5
Peter Pan 165, 264
"Peterhof" 86, 89
Peythroppe 68
"Phantom Rickshaw, The" 110, 156
  (quoted) 89
Pharaoh 294

Philippa, Lady 245
photography 118, 125
Pickwick 52, 129
Picture of Dorian Gray, The 160
"Piet" (quoted) 217–18
Pilgrim's Progress 129
Pinder Bournes 13
Pioneer, The 4, 16, 18, 19, 35, 63, 68, 92, 93, 99,
  103, 104, 110, 112–17 *passim*, 119, 135, 139,
  145, 166, 170
Pipchin, Mrs 21
Pistol 83
Plain Tales from the Hills 111, 113, 122, 156,
  219, 224, 319
  (quoted) 91
Plowden, Editha 15, 16, 24, 58, 292
poaching 45
Poe, Edgar Allan 60
Poets' Corner 341
Pogrom, Elijah 189, 190
Poincaré, Raymond 322
Poirot, Hercule 335
political fables 185, 227, 232, 244–8
Pond, Major 192
Ponton, Dorothy 271, 273, 297, 304
Pope, the 300, 306
Portson 312, 313
"Poseidon's Law" 208–9
  (quoted) 209
positivism 8
Postgate, Mary 3, 302, 309–12, 313
Poynter, Ambrose 10, 139, 168, 170
Poynter, Sir Edward 24, 26, 29, 35, 157,
  199
Poynter, Lady (Agnes Macdonald) 24, 25, 56,
  139
press relations 190, 320
Prévost, Antoine François 156
Price, Cormell ("Crom")
  headmaster of United Services College 11
  education and teaching experience 42
  father-figure to Kipling 13
  political views 42–3
  influence on Kipling 44, 52
  his library made available to Kipling 47, 145
  career plans for Kipling 54–5, 58
  visits to "The Elms" 206
  retirement 48
Price, Mabel 154
"Priest in Spite of Himself, A" 294
Primrose, J. 164
Prohibition 321, 331
"Proofs of Holy Writ" 331
Prospero 132, 168
prostitution 61, 131, 136
Proust, Marcel 343
psychic phenomena 264–70, 291
  see also reincarnation
public schools 38, 39, 40, 41, 42, 48
  see also names of particular schools, e.g.
  Haileybury
publishers 140, 160, 161, 162, 164, 174, 190, 196,
  197, 291
  fictional 140, 156
  pirating 161, 170, 196
Puck of Pook's Hill 2, 12, 31, 106, 183, 221,
  292–4, 298, 338

Index

Purun Bhagat 90, 123, 124
Pushkin, Alexander 47
Putnam's (publisher) 196
"Puzzler, The" 251–2
Pyecroft, Emanuel 209–10, 222, 223, 243

Quartette 102, 110, 291
"Question, The" (quoted) 303
Quixote, Don 129

Rabelais, François 113
race and racialism 21, 64, 67–8, 71–5 *passim*,
  228, 240–2 *passim*, 247, 248, 250, 254–5,
  314, 334
radical imperialism *see* imperialism
Rahere 288–9, 294
"Rahere" (quoted) 288–9
railway engines 186
Rajasthan 94–5, 114
Ralph, Julian 214, 215
Ramsay, William 327
Rangoon 136
Rape of the Lock, The 115
Rattigan, Sir Terence 99
Rattigan, William 98–9
Ravi river 2, 80
Rawalpindi 104, 109
Rayleigh, Lady 304, 328
Read, Charles 46
Reading, Rufus Daniel Isaacs, 1st Marquess of
  33
"Recessional" 7, 196, 203–4, 205, 239, 305
"Record of Badalia Herodsfoot, The" 56, 148,
  153, 167, 306
Red Indian Chief 293
"Regulus" 52
Reinbert 244
reincarnation 106, 150, 166, 168, 232, 266, 306
  see also psychic phenomena
religion 7–9, 152, 203, 204, 267, 270, 306, 315,
  316, 339–40, 342
  see also names of specific religions, e.g. Chris-
  tianity
Rennell, Sir James 159
Report on India 319
"Return, The" (quoted) 233–4
"Return of the Children, The" (quoted) 5
"Return of Imray, The" 66
  (quoted) 71
Reuters 215, 305
Rewards and Fairies 31, 106, 221, 292, 331, 332,
  340
Rhatore 94
Rhodes, Cecil John 46, 138, 173, 202, 208, 212,
  220, 224–5, 228, 250, 256
Rhodesia 212
Richardson, Samuel 28, 343
Ridsdale, Aurelian 263
Ridsdale family 260, 263
"Rikki Tikki Tavi" 92, 123, 185
"Rimini" 295
"Rimmon" 237
Ringdove, Mrs 116
Ripon, George Frederick Samuel Robinson, 1st
  Marquess of 74, 99, 107
Rivals, The 46
Roberts, Frederick Sleigh, 1st Earl 61, 76, 84,
  86, 111, 119, 199, 214, 216, 217, 251, 258

Robinson, Geoffrey 240
Robinson, Kay 45, 107, 112–13, 119
Robinson Crusoe 6
Rochester 177
Rock House 201
Roman Catholicism 79, 153, 306
Roosevelt, Theodore 189, 204, 303, 306, 319–20
Roper-Lawrence, Sir Walter 69, 99, 111, 112
Rossetti, Christina 55
Rossetti, Dante Gabriel 42, 98
Rottingdean 45, 48, 58, 202, 205–6, 260–3
Round Table Conferences 319
"Route Marchin' " (quoted) 76
Royal Academy 199, 200
Royal College of Surgeons 332
Royal Geographical Society 280
Rugby football 46
Rugby School 42, 48
Ruskin, John 44, 240, 250
Russell, Herbrand Arthur 87, 111
Russia 43, 76–7, 105–6, 321–2
Rutherford, Andrew 122
Ryerson, Margaret 197

Sahiba 131
"Sahib's War, A" 71, 217, 218, 219, 228
St Andrew's University 181
"St Helena Lullaby, A" (quoted) 295
St James's Gazette 114, 144
  (quoted) 151–2
St James's Hotel 196
St Mary Abbots Church 8
St Mary's Hospital 332
St Nicolas Magazine for Children (quoted poem
  submitted to) 53
St Paul 315, 338, 339
St Peter 338, 339
St Wilfrid 294
St Xavier's 92, 131
Saintsbury, George 331
sais 66
Salisbury, Robert Arthur Talbot Gascoyne-
  Cecil, 3rd Marquis of 232
San Francisco 174–5
Sancho Panza 129
Sandison, Alan 124–5, 173, 297
Sardou, Victorien 112
Sargent, Wilton 194, 195
Sartre, Jean-Paul 73
Saumarez 72
Savile Club 142–3, 144, 157
Savoy, The 148, 155
Savoy Hotel 204
Sawyer, William Glasse 243
Scarron, Paul 156
Scarsworth, Mrs 317
Schofield, Sergeant-Major 50
"Schoolboy Lyrics" 57
schools and colleges *see* Agra High School;
  Cheltenham College; Haileybury; Hope
  Lodge; Horsmonden School; Jeejeebhoy
  School of Art; Jewish Voluntary Schools;
  Kim's School; King Edward's School,
  Birmingham; King's School, Canterbury;
  La Martinière College; Lancing College;
  Marlborough College; Mayo School of
  Industrial Art; Milner Court; Muir
  College; Rugby School; St Xavier's; United

schools and colleges – *contd.*
Services College; Wellington College; Woodhouse Grove School
see also names of specific university colleges, e.g. Corpus Christi College, Oxford
Schreiderling, Mrs 89
Schreiner, Olive 227
science fantasy/fiction 169, 248–9, 299
Scotney Castle 328
Scots Observer 143
Scott, Sir Walter 196
Scrap of Paper, A 111
Scudder 189, 190
sculpture, Buddhist 35–6
"Sea Constables" 297, 303, 312–13
Sea to Sea 135
seal cutter 61
Seaman, Owen 330
Second Jungle Book, The 94, 120, 122, 126–7, 190, 198
"Secret of the Machines, The" (quoted) 187
Secret Service *see* Great Game
Seeley 138, 250
"Sending of Dana Da, The" 266
"Sergeant's Weddin', The" (quoted) 81–2, 184
servant/master relationships 71
servants, child treatment by 3–4, 21
Setton 220
Seven Seas 148
Shadd, Dinah 81, 84
Shakespeare, William 83, 98, 110, 168, 331
Shamsul Islam 125
Shanks, Edward 292
Shannon 159
Shaw, George Bernard 196, 242, 340
Shaw, Richard Norman 42
Shere Khan 3, 124, 125
Sheridan, Clare 320
Sheriff, Kate 162, 163
Sherriff, R. C. 330
"Shillin' a Day" (quoted) 183
"Ship That Found Herself, The" 186, 187
ships 187–8, 208, 210, 303
Simla 69, 85–90, 102, 108, 109, 110, 199
Simmons, Private 81
Simon Commission 319
Simonstown 164, 167, 206, 207
"Sin of Witchcraft, The" 217
Singapore 120, 136
"Sing-Song of Old Man Kangaroo, The" 229, 230–1
Sinnett, A. P. 110
Skipton 8, 9, 58
smells, evocative 280
Smiles, Samuel 330
Smith, Anna *see* Balestier, Mrs Henry
Smith, Judge Peshine 193
Smith Administration, The 93
"Smuggler's Song, A" (quoted) 295
smuggling 45, 295
"Snowdon" 86, 89, 111, 199
social discrimination 21
social work 146, 148–9, 241, 306
socialism 42–3, 233, 238, 240, 248, 285
Society of Authors 279
Society of St George 300, 322

"Soldiers of the Queen" 104
Soldiers Three 2, 9, 50, 76, 142, 167, 319, 342
"Some Aspects of Travel" 280
"Some Hints on Schoolboy Etiquette" 51
Something of Myself 1, 3, 18, 107, 128, 139, 148, 179–80, 216, 314
"Son, A" 304
(quoted) 305
"Son of His Father, The" 21
"Song at the Cock-Crow, A" (quoted) 306
"Song of the Cities" 1
"Song of the Old Guard, The" (quoted) 237
Sophie 281–2
Sorbonne 334
Souls 146, 152, 159, 199, 200, 211
South Africa 195, 211–31 *passim*
South Kensington Museum 38
Southsea 17–34 *passim*
Souvenirs of France 322
Spain
visits to 325, 334
war with United States over Cuba 204
Spectator 172, 240
Spencer, Herbert 7, 8
spiritualism 264–70, 291
see also reincarnation
"Spring Running, The" 128
Sri Lanka 164, 169
Stalky (character) 7, 40, 41, 45, 50, 68
see also Dunsterville, Major-General L. C.
"Stalky" (story) 51
Stalky & Co. 34, 40, 41, 44, 48, 50, 51, 52, 53, 56, 200, 209, 262, 342
artistic success of 51
criticism of 49–50, 52
cruelty in 49–50
ethical code 48–51, 209, 313
patriotism in 50
"Stalkyism" 7, 51, 77, 92, 105, 124, 208, 256, 337
Stanley family 328–9, 334
"Steam Tactics" 210
Stendhal 343
Stephano 132
Stevenson, Robert Louis 113, 165, 180
"Storm Cone, The" 300, 322
Story of an African Farm 227
"Story of Muhammad Din, The" 6
(quoted) 71
Strachey, Evelyn John St Loe 172, 240
"Strange Ride of Morrowbie Jukes, The" 2, 53, 71–2, 79, 102
Strangwick, C. (Clem) 315
Strasbourg 334
Strickland, Adam 5, 12, 21, 65–6, 299, 338
Strickland, Agnes 12, 21, 66
Struben, Enid 328
Suddhoo 2, 61, 65
"Sundry Phansies" 57
supernatural 264–70, 291
see also reincarnation
"Supplementary Chapter, A" 89
Surtees, Robert Smith 283
Sussex 45, 48, 58, 206, 260, 264, 265, 270, 271, 277, 278
countryside 261–2, 268, 292
tales 264–9, 281–8
Sutton, Sir John Bland- 324, 332

"Swept and Garnished" 297, 303, 308–9
Swift, Jonathan 233
Swinburne, Algernon Charles 44, 62, 98, 137
Sykes, Godfrey 14
Symond, Charley 30

Taffimai Metallumai (Taffy) 229
Takahira 249
"Taking of Lungtungpen, The" 84
Tallantire 74–5
Talleyrand 330
Talleyrand de Périgord, Count Charles Maurice 293, 294
Tariff Reform 251, 253
Tarvin, Nick ("Doc") 162, 163
Taufflieb, General 273, 334, 341
Taufflieb, Julia Catlin 190, 275, 302, 304, 324, 328, 330, 334, 341
"Tav" 56
Taxila Gate 61
Taylor, Caroline 138, 152–3
"Teem" 334, 335, 341
Tegumai Bopsulai 229
Telegraph 216
Tempest, The 132, 168
Temple Bar 98
"Tender Achilles, The" 289
Tennyson, Alfred, 1st Baron 151, 196, 240
Terre, La 284
"That Day" (quoted) 85
"Their Lawful Occasions" 209, 210
"They" 182, 232, 236, 264–6, 268, 308
"Thing" 10
Thirkell, Angela 10, 261
Thomson, James 55
"Three Young Men" (quoted) 145
thrift 180–1
"Thrown Away" 2
Thrupp, Jerry 220
Thy Servant – A Dog 185, 314
Tietjens 66
Tighe, Larry 84
Times, The 104, 203, 204, 205, 213, 214, 215, 217, 239
Tisbury 47, 128, 146, 194, 198–9, 236, 290–1
Titanic 135
"To Be Filed for Reference" 2, 30, 46, 57 (quoted) 62
To the City of Bombay (quoted) 1
tobacco 62, 73
Tobrah 73–4, 75
Toby 24
Tod 5
"Tod's Amendment" 95–6
Tolstoy, Leo 196, 343
Tom Brown's Schooldays 51
Tom Sawyer 51
"Tomlinson" 145, 151
Torpenhow, Gilbert Belling 143, 157
Torquay 48, 200–1
Tota 64–5, 67, 74
tourists 93, 173–4, 208
Townshend, Turnip 286
Toynbee Hall 146, 149, 167
Traffics and Discoveries 232, 288
Transvaal 214, 216, 217, 219, 227
"Treasure and the Law, The" 294
Treaty of Vereeniging 263

"Tree of Justice" (quoted) 294
Trejago, Christopher 64
Trevelyan, George Macaulay 331
Trilby 157
Trinculo 132
"Trix" *see* Fleming, Mrs J.
Tropic Sun, The 132
"Truce of the Bear, The" (quoted) 108–9
Tsing-Ling 60
Tughlaquabad 95
Turrell, George 316
Turrell, Helen 316–18
Turrell, Michael 316–18
Twain, Mark 44, 46, 56, 113, 176
Twist, Oliver 129
"Two Lives" 53

Ulster 257–8
Umballa 75
Una 3, 7, 31, 262, 293, 294
Uncle Remus 44, 52
"Uncovenanted Mercies" 181, 340
Under the Deodars 112
"Undertakers, The" 2, 94, 123
Unfinished Autobiography (Gilbert Murray) 55
United Services College 11, 34, 38–54 *passim*, 157
  aims of 40–1
  buildings 41, 42
  bullying 38–9, 50
  compared with other public schools 39–40, 41, 42
  debates at 43, 44
  depicted in Kipling's writings 46, 47, 52
  fagging eschewed 41
  headmaster 42–3, 44, 47, 48, 52, 54
  Kipling's study 43–4
  Kipling's view of 39–40
  magazine 45–6, 52–3
  prefects 41
  smoking at 41–2, 44
  sport 45–6
United States 48, 164, 170–1, 174–6, 188–93, 204, 320–1
universities 46
  see also names of specific universities, e.g. Oxford University
"Unprofessional" 332–3

Vachell, Horace Annesley 330
Valens 337–8, 339
"Vampire, The" 155
Vancouver 175, 179
Vansuythen, Major 72–3
Vansuythen, Mrs 73
Vermont 47, 128, 177–8, 180–95 *passim*
Vernet-les-Bains 334
Vezzis, Miss 67
Vic (fox terrier) 113
Viceregal Lodge 85–6, 89, 111, 120, 291
Vickery, M. ("Click") 221–3
Victor, Fr. 79, 306
Victoria, Queen 202
Victoria and Albert Museum 14
Vie Parisienne, La 145
"Village that Voted the Earth was Flat, The" 3, 70, 256, 258
Villiers St 139, 143, 147, 159, 167

Index

"Voice of the Hooligan, The" 152
Volpone 123
"Vortex, The" 252–3
Voyage Not Completed 327

waitress 197
Wales, Prince of (Edward VII) 120
Walker, James 99, 106, 108, 110
"Walking Delegate, A" 184, 185
Walpole, Hugh 330
War Graves Commission 297, 333
"War in the Mountains" 305–6
  (quoted) 306
Ward, Mrs Humphrey 113, 161
Warenne, William de 244
Warwick Gardens 55–6
Washington 191
"Watches of the Night, The" 33, 336
Watership Down 185
Watt, A. P. 197
Waugh, Alec 169
Waugh, Arthur 161, 162
Wavell, Archibald Percival, 1st Earl of 125
Wax Moth 125, 246–8
"Way that He Took, The" 217
"Way Through the Woods, The" 295
"Wayside Comedy, A" 72–3, 113
  (quoted) 73
Wazir Khan Mosque 59, 60
"We and They" (quoted) 289–90
Webb, Philip 146, 181, 199
Weber, Max 172
Webster, John 34, 47
Wee Willie Winkie 18, 264
Week's News, The 18, 24, 89, 113, 144, 145
Weir of Hermiston 165
"Weland's Sword" 292–3
Weller, Sam 129
Wellington College 42
Wells, Herbert George 315
Wesley, John 7, 8, 9, 14, 27
Wessington, Mrs Keith 89
West Lodge, Havant 25
Westminster Abbey 341
Westward Ho (United Services College) *see*
  United Services College
Westward Ho! 115
Weyman, Stanley J. 202
"What it Came To: An Unequal Tax" (quoted)
  151–2
Wheeler, Stephen 58, 97, 103, 112
Whibley, Charles 330
"White Man's Burden, The" 196, 204–5
  (quoted) 204

"White Seal, The" 184
Whitman, Walt 44
Wick, Bobby 78
"Wick House, The" 156
Wilde, Oscar 88, 160
"William the Conqueror" 95, 153, 182
William II (Kaiser) 33, 148, 149, 196, 301, 313
  (quoted) 150
Wilson, Edmund 17, 32, 130
Wilson, Sir Henry 257
Wilson, Thomas Woodrow 320
Wilson-Hunter, Sir William 46, 201
Wilton, Abbot of 244–5
"Winds of the World" 145
Winnard, Mrs 55, 56
Winnie the Pooh 330
"Wireless" 232, 266
"Wish House, The" 222, 236, 281, 286–8, 340
"With the Main Guard" (quoted) 81
"With the Night Mail" 32, 299
"Without Benefit of Clergy" 2, 107, 141, 298,
  342
  (quoted) 64–5
Wodehouse, Pelham Grenville 329, 330
Wolcott, Caroline Starr *see* Balestier, Madame
"Woman in His Life, The" 313–14
Wontner the Prig 46
Woodhouse Grove School 13
Woodward, Benjamin 42
Woolf, Virginia 130, 207
Woollcott, Alexander 317
Woolsack, The 220–1, 223, 224, 227, 232, 236
work, significance of 74, 75
working class, English 147
World, The 53, 119
"Worm, The" 78–9
Wressley 194
Wright, Catherine Morris 53
Wright, Frank Lloyd 181
Wyndham, Percy 146, 199–200

Yardley-Orde 74, 115, 182, 247, 338
Yates, Edmund 53
Yellow Book 127, 155
Yokahama 179
Younghusband, Sir Francis 112
Youth's Companion 47

Zam-Zammah 6, 67
Zangwill, Israel 279
Zola, Emile 46, 59, 60, 103, 113, 141–2, 145,
  196, 284, 285